21st Century Library Management

Dr. Krutartha Chandra Mishra

Ess Ess Publications

4837/24, Ansari Road, Darya Ganj,
New Delhi-110002
☏ : 23260807
Fax : 23274173
E-mail: info@essessreference.com
url:http://www.essessreference.com

First Published 2004

ISBN: 81-7000-392-X

Rs.425/-

Published by:
Ess Ess Publications
4837/24, Ansari Road, Darya Ganj,
New Delhi-110 002.
Phone: 23260807
Fax: 23274173
E-mail: info@essessreference.com
url: http://www.essessreference.com

Printed in India at:
Printline, New Delhi

Dedicated to my respected teacher

Dr. Somanath Mishra

&

Smt. Sovagini Satpathy

PREFACE

In the age of information technology importance of library can hardly be exaggerate especially in educational institutes. Almost every college has a library of its own and a look at the library gives a mirror image of the size, quality and prestige of the concerned institute. A library even if small but well organised can serve students, teachers and researchers in a better way than an otherwise big disorganised library. Apart from organisation, what is needed is good management practices which involves employees, visitors, students and Officers-in-charge. Needless to mention that librarian occupies a pivotal role in improving the library in every possible way. For that he has to be punctual, hardworking, imaginative and an efficient manager of affairs of library. While the routine affairs of the library relay largely on conventions, there are trying situations on many occasions when he has to innovative keeping the interest of the library at any cost. Handling situations intelligently brings glory not only to himself but to the profession as well. A professional attitude will demand thorough involvement, good understanding of problems and good hold over the ongoing affairs of the library.

I, personally feel that much of the tensions and worries will be greatly reduced if we keep the library orderly arranged and the routine formats to carry out business are kept ready for use any time anywhere in the library. A personal involvement on my part in a determined attempt to give or college library a face-lift bore fruits. And I realised that I should share my ideas, planning and methods with my colleagues spread over the entire country.

I shall be extremely happy if my honest attempt can give a smile of satisfaction on the face of librarians managing medium size libraries which are found in most of the colleges in our country. The contents of this book may prove helpful not only to Government organisations but also to cooperative and privately operated libraries. Since no attempt is total, I welcome suggestions from my colleagues to be thankfully incorporated in later editions of this book.

While presenting this book, it is my pleasure to acknowledge with gratitude the sustained support and encouragement of Dr. A.K. Nanda, Principal, Rajendra College, (Autonomous), Balangir and Dr. B.N. Behera, Prof. in charge of Library, Rajendra College, (Autonomous), Balangir.

My sincere thanks are due to Sri P.P. Guru, Sri K.M. Panda and Sri B.N. Dutta in the Library and Sri Nayan Kumar Mishra, Sri Mukesh Kumar Mishra for typing out the manuscript.

I am very grateful to Sri S.P. Dutta, M/s. Pradeep Book Store, Balangir who helped me to successfully complete this work.

I also put on record the sincere efforts made by M/s Ess Ess Publications, New Delhi in bringing out the book in record time.

I will fail in my duty if I do not thank my wife Jharana who managed the house hold work entirely by herself, despite her ill health and made me free from the routine life so that I could devote my time for preparing this book. I am indebted to her.

Balangir, Orissa **Dr. Krutartha Ch. Mishra**
1st April, 2004

CONTENTS

CHAPTER I ... **1**

1:1 What is a Library
1:2 Books in Life
1:3 Dependence on Library
1:4 Library Building
1:5 Area of Library or
Standards for Library Buildings and
Design as per U.G.C. Scheme
1:6 Functions of Library members
1:7 Library as an Information Centre
1:8 Furniture's
1:9 Library Lighting
1:10 Library accessories
1:11 Acquisition of Books for the Library
1:12 Book Selection Policy
1:13 Theories of book Selection
1:14 Ranganathans Five Laws of Library
1:15 Book Selection for a Public Library
1:16 Book Selection for a Academic Library
1:17 Book Selection for a Special Library
1:18 Book selection sources
1:19 Trade Catalogues
1:20 Books Review
1:21 Book acquisition procedures
1:22 Purchasing of Reading materials
1:23 Routine works of Acquisition

CHAPTER - II ... **31**

2:1 How to handle books in the library.

2:2 Routine work of the Library

2:3 Accessioning of books

2:4 Classification

2:5 Cataloguing

2:6 Preparation of shelf list

2:7 Book card

2:8 Arrangement of books in shelves

2:9 Membership card

2:10 Call Number/Marking or Notation

2:11 Working of Binding section

2:12 Mending of books

2:13 Prevention of Insects

2:14 Open shelf system

2:15 Discarding of books

2:16 Loss of Books

2:17 Reference service

2:18 Reading room

2:19 Journal and periodicals

CHAPTER-III ... **58**

3:1 Library Rules

3:2 Library Committee

3:3 Appointment of Librarians and other staff of Library

3:4 Selection procedure of Library Staff

3:5 Duties of the Librarians

3:6 Conduct of the Librarians

3:7 Finance

3:8 Library fund

3:9 Library automation

3:10 Annual verification

CHAPTER - IV ... **79**

(EXECUTIVE INSTRUCTIONS AND CODAL PROVISION)

4.1 Letter No. 4522 dated 15.2.74 of D.P.I. (H.E.) Orissa on Professional training of Librarians.

4.2 Letter No. 32095/EYS dated 2.12.1974 of the Government of Orissa Education and Youth Services Department on Yardstick for entertainment of class III and class IV staff in Libraries of Government colleges.

4.3 Letter No. 26018 / EYS dated 28.7.1977 of the Government of Orissa Education and Youth Science Department on Professional Training of existing Librarian and fresh appointment of trained candidates as Librarians.

4.4 Govt. of India notification date forfulbright scholarship nominations.

4.5 Executive Instructions No. 45546 dated 18.10.1986 of the Directorate of Higher Education, Orissa on Return of Library book by the Borrowers.

4.6 Copy Letter No. F.I. 96 / 81 (CPP- I) dated 5th May 1987 of the Deputy Secretary, U.G.C. for upgradation in salary scale of Librarians in colleges.

4.7 Letter No. 542 date. 3.1.1998 of Govt. of Orissa Home Department on Fixation of criteria for promotion to the rank of Librarian / Appointment to the post ofAsst. Librarian in the Orissa Secretariat Library.

CHAPTER - V ... **101**

(SPECIMEN OF FORMS AND CORRESPONDENCE)

5:1 Specimen of a Book Selection card.
5:2 Specimen of a Book Selection list.
5:3 Specimen of a Quotation letter.
5:4 Specimen of an allocation Register.
5:5 Specimen of an order letter.
5:6 Specimen of Discrepancies in supply form.
5:7 Specimen of an Accession Register.
5:8 Specimen of an Accession Stamp.
5:9 Specimen of Spine Label.
5:10 Specimen of Date slip
5:11 Specimen of Book Card
5:12 Specimen of Book Card.
5:13 Specimen of Location Marks.
5:14 Specimen of Binding Register / Card.
5:15 Specimen of Accession Register.
5:16 Specimen of Stock Taking Register
5:17 Specimen of Stock Taking sheets
5:18 Specimen of shelf list
5:19 Specimen of stock taking
5:20 Specimen of letter Bills for payment
5:21 Specimen of contingent Bill
5:22 Specimen of Application for a remittance in foreign currency
5:23 Periodical order work
5:24 Periodical register
5:25 periodicals register

5:26 Specimen of ledger for periodicals
5:27 Specimen of card system
5:28 Specimen of verso at the law
5:29 Specimen of register law
5:30 Specimen of classified index
5:31 Specimen of bottom law
5:32 Specimen of the bottom law
5:33 Specimen of the top card
5:34 Specimen of routing slip
5:35 Specimen of group routing slip
5:36 Specimen of membership register
5:37 Specimen of Reservation Slip
5:38 Specimen Letter for procurement of books on interlibrary loan basis
5:39 Specimen Letter intimating the borrower for demand book
5:40 Specimen Letter for inter library loan
5:41 Maintenance of record
5:42 Specimen Letter for clear Library dues
5:43 Specimen Letter for recovery of dues report
5:44 Specimen Letter for report of dues recovery
5:45 Specimen Letter for Loss of Library pass book-cum-identity
5:46 Specimen application for loss of books.
5:47 Specimen Letter for loss of token
5:48 Specimen Letter for withdrawal of lockers
5:49 Specimen Letter to curb library malpractice
5:50 Specimen application for consultation facilities
5:51 Specimen consultation slip
5:52 Specimen an clearance application form

5:53 Specimen an clearance certificate
5:54 Specimen N.D.C.
5:55 Specimen Ledger system
5:56 Specimen day book register
5:57 Specimen ledger system
5:58 Specimen date slip
5:59 Specimen book pocket
5:60 Specimen book send
5:61 Specimen borrower's ticket
5:62 Specimen Date slip
5:63 Specimen book pocket (inner back side)
5:64 Specimen book card containing essential information
5:65 Specimen borrower's card/identity card
5:66 Specimen membership-cum-identity card.
5:67 Borrower's card with metal plate
5:68 Specimen records of books
5:69 Specimen of an allocation register
5:70 Specimen of a Bill register
5:71 Specimen of visitors register
5:72 Specimen of annual report
5:73 Specimen of the statistical table on classification
5:74 Specimen on cataloguing.
5:75 Specimen of accession statistics
5:76 Specimen on statistics of periodically
5:77 Specimen of statistical table
5:78 Specimen of visitors register
5:79 Specimen of daily attendance statistics
5:80 Specimen of issue statistics
5:81 Specimen of issue statistics Language wise

5:82 Specimen of issue statistics registration
5:83 Specimen of classified issue statistics
5:84 Specimen of statistics of books consulted
5:85 Specimen of reference queries
5:86 Specimen of statistics of income and expenditure
5:87 Specimen of staff statistics
5:88 Specimen of classing issue statistics
5:89 Specimen of issue statistics material-wise.

BIBLIOGRAPHY ... 199

CHAPTER -I

1:1 What is a Library
1:2 Books in Life
1:3 Dependence on Library
1:4 Library Building
1:5 Area of Library or
Standards for Library Buildings and
Design as per U.G.C. Scheme
1:6 Functions of Library members
1:7 Library as an Information Centre
1:8 Furniture's
1:9 Library Lighting
1:10 Library accessories

1:1 WHAT IS A LIBRARY

Library is an active agency in the fields of education. Through it self improvement and moral reform is possible. It is the act or process of creating a systematic union of individuals. In a Library the members work together for a common end. Library is the cultural centre for a community. It is known as the heart of an educational institution. Further it can be said that library is an arsenal of our domestic culture. Its organisation is not merely a mechanical arrangement of groups and individuals but it is a highly specialised human mechanisms of coordination of technical efforts of trained Librarians for the welfare of the reading humanity.

1:2 BOOKS IN LIFE

A bookless life is an incomplete life. It is the study of books through which good and great men are created. Books influence the depth and breadth of life. Books enshrine the users thoughts and feelings. It bring dreams and aspirations in them which ennoble life. In the words of Bartholine, "without books, God is silent, justice doormat, natural science at a stand still, philosophy lame, letters dumb and all things involved in darkness.

1:3 DEPENDENCE ON LIBRARY

Books meet the natural craving for freedom, for expression, for creativity and beauty of Life. Learners therefore, must have books and the right type of book for the satisfaction of their need. Readers turn naturally to books because their curiosity concerning all manners of things, their eagerness to share in the experiences of others and their need to escape from their own limited environment leads them to find in books food for the minds and the spirit. Through their reading they find a deeper significance to life as books acquaint them with the life in the world as it was and it is now. They are presented with a diversity of human experiences and come to respect other ways of thought and living. And while establishing their own relationships and responses to life, the readers often find that the characters in their stories are going through similar adjustments, which help to clarify and give significance to their own. Books provide satisfactory material for the readers imagination to grow. Imagination is a valuable quality, a motivating power and stimulates to achievement. While enriching their imagination, the books widen their outlook, develop a fact-finding attitude and train them up to use leisure properly. The social and educational significance of the readers books can hot be over estimated in an academic library.

1:4 LIBRARY BUILDING

The Library building of an educational Institution should meet the following functions.

1. Acquiring of books, cataloguing classifying and shelving of a book collection.
2. Sufficient and rapid production of information and material when demanded.
3. Provision of quiet, comfortable and attractive rooms for reading and studying.
4. The provision of individual studies for the use of students doing special work, for faculty members doing research.
5. Assistance in developing the reading habit thereby acquiring knowledge through the independent use of books.
6. Acquainting of the users with the contents of

the Library thereby arousing in them a desire to read and stimulating them to read for culture and for pleasure.

7. The building should be planned for Library work.
8. Every Library building should be planned especially for the kind of work to be done, and the community to be served.
9. The interior arrangement ought to be planned before the exterior is considered.
10. The convenience of arrangement should not be sacrificed for mere architectural effect.
11. The plan should be adapted to probabilities and possibilities of growth and development.
12. Simplicity of decoration is essential in the working rooms and reading rooms.
13. A library should be planned with a view to economical administration.
14. The rooms for public use should be so arranged as to allow complete supervision with the fewest possible attendants.
15. Modern Library plans should provide administration for readers near the books they want to use, whatever system of shelving is adopted.

1:5 AREA OF LIBRARY OR STANDARDS FOR LIBRARY BUILDINGS AND DESIGN AS PER U.G.C. SCHEMES

1. Location

The library should be centrally located with reference to Buildings of faculties and departments, laboratories and hostels.

Rooms to be provided are as follows:

Sl. No	Rooms Normally Separate	Academic Library UCL*	UDL*
	Stack Room	R	–
	Catalogue room	R	–
	General reading room	R	R
	Periodical reading room	R	–
	Special reading room	R	–
	Research cubicles	R	–
	Group study room	R	–
	Seminar room	R	–
	Conference room	R	–
	Exhibition room	R	–
	Librarians room	R	–
	Deputy librarian's room	R	–
	Technical staff room	R	–
	Administrative staff room	R	–
	Committee room	R	–
	Display room	R	–
	Night watchman's room	R	–
	Microfilm reading room	R	–
	Document reproduction room		–
	Audio-Visual room		–
	Store room	R	R

* *University central Library.*

** *University / college departmental Library .*

Each unit rack 2m long may be assumed to house 700 to750 volumes 1 m2 of stack room area may be assumed to house 150 volumes .

Note :1- The centre to centre distance between

consequitive racks is 1.80 m Con the basis of 0.45m of rack depth plus 1.35 of cross sangway width .

Note:2- The distance form an end wall of the stack Con be basis of 1.325m of the end cross gangway plus 0.225m of half rack depth .

3.0 Stack Room

3.1 Dimensions of Stack Room Should be as follows:

a) Clear Length in meters - 1.80n+3.10 where n is the number of rows of book racks*

b) Clear width

1. 3m Con the basis of one rack 2m long plus one longitudinal gangway of m) close to a longitudinal wall,
2. 5m Con the basis of 2 racks each 2m long plus longitudinal gangway of 1m) close to a longitudinal wall.
3. 8m Con the basis of 3 racks each 2m long plus two longitudinal gangways of 1m each) close to each of the longitudinal walls, and
4. 10m Con the basis of 4 racks each 2m long plus two longitudinal gangways of 1 m each) close to each of the longitudinal walls.

Note : Three meters and five meters width are generally only in case of stack spaces, as the stack room and the reading room may be combined in to a single room, in such cases.

c) Clear Height - Floor to ceiling, 2.40m.

Note:1. The height of the rack is 2.20 m and allowance for bay guides is 0.20m.

Note: 2. The stockroom should be combined with necessary devices for effective ventilation.

3.2 Stack room should be so oriented as to avoid direct sum windows

Stack room-windows in the side walls of the stackroom should be opposite each cross gangway.

4.2 Each window should be provided with glass shutters and protected with wire fabric having its aperture sufficiently small to prevent squirrels, rats, etc. from getting in. In its fully open position the glass shutter should not project into the gangway.

4.3 Other Rooms - All windows and ventilators in the rooms accessible from outside should be provided with wire fabric to prevent books, pamphlets, etc. being passed out through them.

5.0 Sizes of Rooms

5.1 Reading Room - The average area per reader in the reading room should be $2.33m^2$, minimum.

Note : The Size of the reading table is 2.4x0.6m. the centre to centre distance between two consecutive rows of reading room tables is 1.8m with seating arrangement on one side of the table only.

5.2 Sizes of other rooms shall normally be as follows:

	For use of	***Area M2***
(a)	Librarian and Deputy Librarian	30
(b)	Classifier, cataloguer, accession Librarian and maintenance Librarian.	09 Per person
(c)	Secretary to the Librarian	19

(d)	Visitors room	15
(e)	Administrative and professional staff not service points and other than those mentioned in (b)	05 Person
(f)	Group discussion room	02 person
(g)	Conference discussion room	02 Person
(h)	Seminar room	02 Person
(i)	Committee room	02 Person
G)	Cubicles	07 Person

6.0 Libraries of all types are expanding at an enormous rate. Increase in demand for documents, official policy and increase in literary make this process inevitable. Since the development of new libraries takes several years, the stock to be accommodated on the opening day, therefore, will be larger than as estimated when planning started. Therefore, it is absolutely essential to estimate the areas of the library requirement to that date.

7.0 Circulation

7.1 Each floor of the library building shall be at one single level to facilitate the movement of book trolley form one part to another. Threshold shall not be provided anywhere inside the building.

7.1.1. The movement of the book trolley from one tire to another, where there are three or more tiers in the stackroom, should be through electric lifts provided within the stackroom with landing at every tier of the stackroom and at other connected adjacent rooms. In large libraries where quick mechanical carriage of bookstand related materials are required, special arrangements such as pneumatic tubes and belt conveyors may become necessary. This may require to be considered at the initial stage of design of the library and its building.

7.1.2. The rooms shall be arranged in such a way that the staff other than those servicing the reading room shall not have to pass through the reading room disturbing the readers.

8.0 Relative positions of Rooms

8.1. The stackroom should be so placed that it is easily accessible from and proximate to every at the library.

8.2. The catalogue room should be like an anteroom to the stackroom in the way from the general reading room to the stackroom.

8.3. The general reading room should be close to the entrance.

8.4. Periodicals rooms may be further removed form the general reading room. But independent access to it shall be possible when the other rooms in the library are closed.

8.5. Special reading rooms may be still further removed from the general reading room.

8.6. The librarian or the deputy librarian should have his room in close proximity to the general reading room.

8.7. The rooms of the technical and administrative staff should be placed in close proximity to the rooms of the librarian and the Deputy librarian.

8.8. The technical staff shall have independent access to the stack and catalogues area.

8.8. The cubicles, the rooms for group study the committee room, etc. may be in a separate wing or a separate floor.

8.9. The exhibition room may be combined with the entrance lobby or placed as close to it as possible.

9.0. The furniture and fittings for library shall be as per IS : 1829 (part I and II) and IS : Library furniture and fittings: Part I Timber (First revision) and part 11 steel and IS : 3663-1981 dimensions for rigid couplings. Tables and chairs for general office purpose.

10.0. Requirement for fitment for drainage and sanitation for library building shall be as per the table enclosed.

Libraries Based on IS 1972-1983 Indian standard code of Basic requirements for Water Supply, Drainage and Sanitation.

1:6 FUNCTIONS OF LIBRARY MEMBERS

In any Library we find two functionaries. They are line and staff agencies. This line and staff agencies furnishes the best solution for the large Library's problem. In an organised library like School, College or University there are several service points. They are acquisition, classification, cataloguing, reference, administrative and maintenance of Building etc. To run these service units smoothly and efficiently delegation of duties amongst the staff members is highly essential. The line and staff method of organization is a recognized one in public administration and management of any organization. It is a suitable approach for the coordination of Library work. It is subject to modification and adjustment according to the needs and requirements of an individual library. To ensure efficiency in libraries the points suggested by Clara W. Herbert may be taken into consideration.

The organization should be as simple as possible.

(Third Revision)

ART GALLARIES & MUSEUMES

Sl.No.	Fitments	For male public	For female public	For male staff	For female staff
(i)	Water closest	A per100 persons upto400 persons and for over 400 persons, add at the rate of 1 per 250 persons or part there of	1 per 100 persons up to 200 persons and for over 200 persons, add at the rate at 1 per 150 persons or part there of	1 for1 to 15 persons 2 for 16 to 25 persons	1 for1 to 12 persons 2 for 13 to 25 persons
(ii)	Ablution taps	1in each water closet	1 in each water closet. 1 water tap with draining arrangements shall be provided for every 50 persons or part thereof in the vicinity of water closets and urinals	1 in each water closet	1 in each water closets

(iii)	Urinals	1 per 50 persons		Nil upto 6 persons 1 for 7 to 20 persons 2 for 21 to 45 persons	
(iv)	Wash Basins	1 for every 200 persons or part there of and for over 400 persons and add at the rate at 1 per 250 persons or part there at	1 for every 200 persons or part there of 3 and for over 200 persons add at the rate of 1 per 150 persons or part there of	1 for1 to 15 persons 2 for 15 to 35 persons	1 for1 to 12 persons 2 for 13 to 25 persons
(V)	Cleaners sinks		1 per floor, min		
(vi)	Drinking water fountain		1 per 100 persons or part there of		

It should not be over organised with unnecessary over head or under organised so that too many conflicting duties are placed on too few others."

2. Authority must always go with responsibility; and these lines should be so clear as to be readily end generally understood.
3. Executives are of two types; those that like responsibility for the execution of work and those that like planning. While the two qualities have to be combined to a certain extent in each executive, a large Library needs to provide for both types with corresponding separation of duties.
4. The organization should be built upon the basis of community needs and be sufficiently flexible to adopt itself to changing demands and conditions.
5. Personnel should be appointed to fit the known requirements of the organization rather than that the organization should fit itself to individuals. This is one of the difficulties of reorganization since libraries must naturally make the most of the capacities of present members of the staff. Yet too great consideration of these personal factors makes for an unbalanced development of the service as a whole. The best organization is the one that gives the largest number of its members individual responsibility and opportunity for creative work and professional growth.

1:7 LIBRARY AS AN INFORMATION CENTRE

Library is one of the important part of a school, college or University. It works as an information centre. It is the channel through which communications move among students and staff at the educational institution.

It provides the necessary information and knowledge for coordination. It works as a link between students and teaching staff. Their inquiries, requirements of study materials, complaints are taken care of by the Library through direct personal contact. Library creates a proper type of image for the organization in the minds of the users of the ;ibrary. It is responsible for building up a healthy social image. There are several functions which a school, college and university Library performs. Among them Library receives and collects information. The information may be from internal sources or from the external sources.

In an educational institution we find there are so many teaching units of different subject. In each subject study some teachers are there. Library collect information from them about study materials, availability and source to get it.

Externally information is also received and collected from outside sources by the library. The information may be received or collected from different firms, governmental departments, research institutions, universities and the general public. Even information is gathered from telephone, news papers, various journals, television, radios and government circulars.

The principal and other teaching officers of an educational institution also gather various types of information when they attend conventions, seminars and pass away the information to the library for reference. The information received and collected is given a suitable space. This is done by converting the information into the written record. The form and size of the written record would depend upon numerous factors like importance of information ,the nature of information and the used to which the information can be put. The information received can not be used by the Library in the form in which it has been received. It has to be processed. Processing involves the preparation of summaries, rates, reports, statistical data relating to various kinds of information. While information is being processed, it would be essential to keep in mind the nature and importance of a particular information. All accumulated and processed information is useless unless it is put to further use. The use of information is only possible through communication. The library furnishes the two way channel for information. It receives information and then it transmits the same to the users of the Library for their use. Library provides past information or the future information according to the need of the users. It is essential to communicate the information promptly, other wise the information gathered and processed at great cost would prove useless.

Academic library like school, college and University can not hope to work smoothly unless the administrative management functions are performed. The library keeps in safe custody the books, periodicals, journals, magazines etc. Besides, it is also responsible for their upkeep and safety. Assets are of different kinds. They may be fixed assets like buildings, machines, library equipments, furniture and lighting systems. Fixed assets are to be maintained and kept in good condition. The assets are protected against hazards of fire and theft.

Various processes of management account for the efficient functioning of a library. There processes are Planning, Organizing, Staffing, Directing, Communicating, Controlling, Co-ordinating and Motivating- library work has to be planned and then organised and executed according to the plan.

Library also prepare records which is an important function at the Library. Library forms are used extensively for the purpose of preparing records. The forms serve as a store house of information. To derive the maximum benefit from the use of forms, it would be necessary that they are properly designed on the basis of needs of the Library.

The college Library does not get enough funds for stationary. In to-days Library, stationary is a costly consumable material. For government institutions, the Government does not provide funds for stationary materials of the School and College Libraries. It is purchased out of the funds collected from the students which is not adequate. Therefore utmost care would have to be taken in the purchase, storage and issue of stationary and supplies. The stationary should be brought at economic prices and reasonable levels of their stocks so that the stocks must be available at all times.

The present day Libraries require for its functioning proper types of machines, equipment and furniture. Library machines may be as simple as small stamping machines or as complicated as modern computers. Whatever be the machine, it would be essential to follow certain principles in their selection. A machine must be utilized to the full. It should be suitable for the purpose for which it has been brought.

1:8 FURNITURE

Furniture promotes efficiency and adds to the look of the Library. The furniture should be scaled in size of the students and staff for physical comfort and economy so that they feel comfortable, self reliant and do more and better work. The following is the list of essential furniture and fittings for a college / University.

Library.

Reading tables for students and staff

Chairs for students and staff

Librarian's table

Circulation or changing Desk and Chairs

Librarian's shelf-list tray

Catalogue charging trays

Card catalogue cabinet

Unit book cases

Bulletin Board

Notice Board

Book Support

'New Arrivals' display case with sliding glass doors.

Dictionary stand

Periodical Desk

Storage Cabinet

Almirah for v.'ork room

Vertical cabinet

Filing Cabinet

Atlas Stand

Pamphlet Boxes

Wall clock.

22. Map stand

Tables and chairs for use of the students should be at sturdy construction and should be at a similar to the height of the reader. The tables may either be rectangular round or square design. The reading room should be provided with two bulletin boards to be used for reading promotion and guidance by display of news-items, pictures, postures, clipped from news papers and magazines. One bulletin board should be large enough to provide effective display and the other board should be of smaller size of about 3x3 feet to provide for notice.

As to shelving it is desirable to have open shelves of steel around all walls space, but floor stacks may also be provided to house the remaining books in the Library. The book shelves should not be higher than the users reach. Shelves should be made adjustable by use of metal strips and buckets to the uprights. Unit book cases at standard dimensions are now replacing wooden shelves even if they are costly. For shelving a magazine separate shelves may be provided in the reading room. A sliding glass-door display case may be provided for exhibition of New Arrivals in the Library. This case needs locking.

The Librarians work room may be well designed and equipped for preparing books for shelves. It may be provided with cupboards or almirahs for storing new books received for accessioning, accessories, stationary supplies and back issue of periodicals. There should be ample space for work table. A lavatory with running water may also be provided.

1:9 LIBRARY LIGHTING

The Library room should get sufficient natural light for comfortable seeing and reading. But it should be also provided with artificial light for which fluorescents lighting is recommended. The Library room should be treated acoustically and the walls and ceilings furnished with light and pleasing colour of high reflective values. A dull furnish of Library fittings is preferred with a view to reduce glare. Incase wood work looks best in light, teak wooden should have hanging curtains which can be pulled well clear at the windows. A noiseless floor covering is essential for freedom at movement and reasonable quiet are requisites to satisfaction in library work. A few flower vases, pictures of authors and sculptures of great men may be provided to decorate the room to bring study atmosphere in the Library.

1:10 LIBRARY ACCESSORIES

The Library require the following accessories.

Accession register (leather bound)

Binding register

Issue registers for staff and students

Attendance Register

Diary Register for receiving letters

Despatch Register

Index register for Journals

Leave Register

Work assignment Register

Visitors Book

Book Cards

Book labels

Book Order Cards

Book packets

Check card for periodicals

Due date slips

Bay Guide or Class guide

Shelf guide or topic guide

Gum paste

Paper cutter

Periodical register

Poster Holders

Printed Shelf Labels

Register Card
Rubber Stamp showing the name of the Library
Stamp pad and ink
Transitional plastic Magazine holders
Alpine/stapler/stapler pins and tags
Withdraw register
Complete Damaged books Register
Guard files
Files
Writing Papers
Typing Papers
Carbon Paper
Page Numbering Machine
Date Stamp
Calculator
Type machine
Binding accessories
Computers
Book trolley
Book press machine
Label printing machine
Audio Visual System
Micro filming
Dust Cleaning Machine
Punched card machine
Over head projector
Display board

1:11 ACQUISITION OF BOOKS FOR THE LIBRARY

Acquisition of books or the reading materials for

a Library is one of the most important step in any Library. This work is taken up with utmost care. We may divide it is some steps. They are

1. Formulating a Book Selection Policy.
2. Selecting Reading materials or books.
3. Placing orders for the supply of books to be purchased.
4. Arranging for exchange of books.
5. Receiving the books in the library.
6. Accessioning the books.
7. Passing Bills for payment.

1:12 BOOK SELECTION POLICY

Each Library formulates a policy for selecting reading materials. This is a guide to the Librarian of the Library. This policy is known as the Book Selection Policy. Book Selection Policy is adopted according to the needs of clientele and the size of the Library and availability of funds.

1:13 THEORIES OF BOOK SELECTION

Book Selection policies are based on 1. Melvil Dewey's Motto 2. McColvin's demand Theory 3. Drury's Principle.

Melvil Dewey's Motto - This theory speaks that "The best reading for the largest number at the least cost". It is one of the guiding principle in selecting books. It reflects the economic principle of "maximum benefit with the minimum effort". This principle is adopted in a developing country like India.

McColvin's Demand Theory - This theory states that demand for books should be differentiated according to its value, variety and volume. This is based on the economic principle of "Demand and

Supply". The demand for good quality books, the demand for a variety of reading materials - variety in subject and in form and demand for large number of volumes should be taken into consideration against the supply position.

Drury's Principle - The purpose of book selection it to procure books and provide the same to the right reader at the right time. It is the Librarian who should provide the user what he wants when he wants. By "right reader" it is meant the reader who is in need of a particular reading material for a particular purpose.

1:14 RANGANATHANS FIVE LAWS OF LIBRARY SCIENCE

Dr. S.R. Ranganathan was the pioneer of five laws of Library Science. These laws are 1. Books are for use 2. Every reader his book 3. Every book its reader 4. Save the time of the reader 5. Library is a growing organism. According to Ranganathan these laws are the fundamental laws of Library Science. These form the normative principles which contain in a latent form all the library practices current at any time and to be evolved at a later time. The implication of the first law 'Books are for use' is that the Librarian should select books that are useful to the readers. He should have assessed the information needs of the readers and select books that will satisfy this need. Every reader should get the book he wants as per the second law. 'Every reader his/her book. The third law Every Book its reader implies that each and every book selected should find its reader. Then only the selection of book shall be justified. The Librarian can 'Save the time of the Reader' only if he makes his selection in anticipation of a demand. 'Library is a growing organism'. The Librarian should see to that this growth is well channeled resulting into a balanced book collection quantitatively and qualitatively.

1:15 BOOK SELECTION FOR A PUBLIC LIBRARY

A public Library is meant to serve a diversified group of users ranging from children to old people, consisting of professional, businessmen, labourers, agriculturists, housewives, students etc. The Librarian should select books to satisfy the needs of these heterogeneous reader groups. The objectives of the public library is to provide information, education and recreation. Accordingly the Librarian should select books for a broad based well balanced collection.

1:16 BOOK SELECTION FOR AN ACADEMIC LIBRARY

The Clientele of an academic library, whether it is a college library or a university library, consists of students and teachers. First and foremost thing is to provide for a curricular needs of the students and teachers. This would mean multiple copies of text books, important reference books like encyclopedias, dictionaries, year books etc., general and subject periodicals should be provided. In University Libraries the requirement of teachers and research scholars engaged in research activities should be taken care of. It is important that learned periodicals appropriate to the needs of the research scholars should be subscribed for. The Book Selection Policy for an academic library should take into consideration :

1. The quality and quantity of the existing collection.
2. The number of students enrolled.
3. The number of teachers engaged.
4. The nature of Curriculum.

5. The nature of the teaching method.
6. The availability of funds.

1:17 BOOK SELECTION FOR A SPECIAL LIBRARY

The user group in a Special Library consists of scientists, industrial workers, researchers, executives etc. The selection of reading materials has to be made on the basis of their special needs. The reading materials is usually in one subject area supplemented by related subjects. The Librarian should select a variety of reading materials such as periodicals, technical reports, government documents, patents, standards, dissertations etc. To quote Ranganathan the Librarian should "select books of needed standards in the numbral subjects of specialisation and in the related penumbral subjects."

1:18 BOOK SELECTION SOURCES

The Librarian cannot be expected to keep track of all the books published in the various subject field. He has to depend on a number of book selection sources. These sources can be categorised broadly into the Human Sources and Documentary Sources which may be further classified into various units as stated on next page.

Human Sources

This will include the Librarian himself, the library staff, the members of the library committee, and other subject experts, the heads of the departments, research scholars, students and other library users. The human sources is "live source" and should be taken to be a valuable feedback from the users of the library and therefore more useful than selecting from documentary sources. Here it may be mentioned that the Librarian

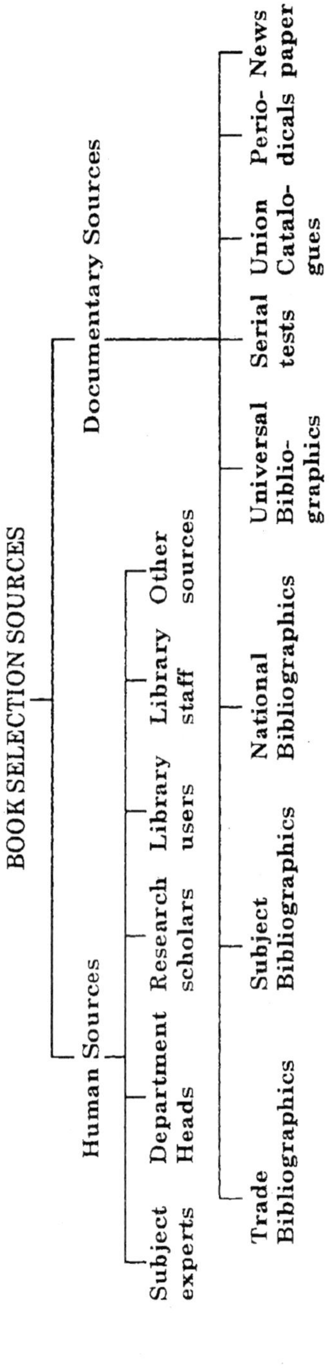
BOOK SELECTION SOURCES
Human Sources
Documentary Sources
Subject experts
Department Heads
Research scholars
Library users
Library staff
Other sources
Trade Bibliographics
Subject Bibliographics
National Bibliographics
Universal Biblio-graphics
Serial tests
Union Catalo-gues
Perio-dicals
News paper

should consider the various book exhibitions, book fairs, seminars, conference etc. as a valuable source for book selection. He himself should arrange for such book exhibitions and fairs which will help him and other members of the book selection committee in selecting books.

Documentary Sources

In the above diagram it is shown that these sources can be categorised into various types of Bibliographics, Catalogues and Reviews. Bibliographics are the basic tools for book selection.

1:19 TRADE CATALOGUES

From time to time the publishers and book sellers bring out catalogues of books published and stocked by them for sale. These catalogues are advertising materials which is mailed to the libraries by these dealers. This is to acquaint the libraries with all the bibliographical data alongwith the prices.

1:20 BOOK REVIEWS

Another valuable and reliable sources are book reviews published regularly in journals. These reviews are critical evaluation made by scholars in the field and therefore more authentic than trade catalogues. There are a few reviewing periodicals exclusively for this purpose.

1:21 BOOK ACQUISITION PROCEDURES

Certain procedure is adopted in the Libraries for book acquisition. A library may add to its collection through purchases, Gifts and Exchanges.

1:22 PURCHASING OF READING MATERIALS

Reading materials may be purchased by a library directly from the publishers. The library may place orders directly with the publishers. In case of foreign publishers the library may experience problems in making payments as foreign exchange permit has to be obtained from the Reserve Bank of India and it involves a lot of correspondence. This method is suitable for Indian publications only.

Reading materials may be purchased by a library through the Publishers Agents and Book Sellers. Purchase through the Publisher's agents and Book sellers is the common practice in India. Foreign books may be purchased in India through these agents and payment may be made in Indian currency. This methods relieves the library from the burden of obtaining permits from Reserve Bank and thereby red tapism can be avoided.

The Library may follow approval method for purchase of books. Libraries may request the book dealers or publishers to send the books on a specified subject area to the library on approval basis. The Librarian and other subject experts may pursue the books and select them on the spot. The books therefore selected and approved are purchased. The books not approved are taken back by the dealers. This method gives the opportunity for the librarians and the subject experts to select the right books after going through table of content and other preliminary pages.

Also reading materials may be purchased through Standing Vendors. Some libraries prefer to appoint one Book Seller, on a contract basis, usually for a year or so, subject to certain conditions. These dealers are termed as Standing Vendors. The libraries should place orders for all the books with these standing vendors. This method may be economical as the standing vendors are selected on the basis of highest rate of discount they offer. Dealing with one Book seller will lesson the burden of correspondence work and other administrative routines.

Many non-commercial Institution offer their publications as gifts to the Libraries. Some Government publication can be obtained free of cost. British Council, United States Information Service and other foreign embassies send books published in their countries free of cost. Some times a philanthropically minded individual may come forward to donate his collection of books to a library of his choice. The Librarian should be on the lookout for such offers, or even solicit such offers and add the books to his collection. But he should not accept unwanted books not relevant to the needs of his clientele or trashes offered for propaganda purposes.

Another way of expanding the collection is to launch an exchange programme through which the Librarian can exchange his spare or duplicate books with another Library participating in this programme by mutual agreement. The Library or its parent institutions may send its publications to other similar institutions and obtain their publications in exchange.

1:23 ROUTINE WORKS OF ACQUISITION

The routine works connected with the acquisition of books may be grouped on four headings. They are 1. Books Selection Routine 2. Book ordering routine 3. Book Accessioning Routine 4. Bill passing routine.

(a) Acquiring the book selection tools/sources and arranging them in a helpful order for quick consultation is the first step. The latest sources should be retained and other out-of date tools should be removed.

(b) Book selection cards for all the books selected should be prepared. All the bibliographical details should be entered in the Book Selection Card. These cards may be kept arranged is a helpful order, subject wise or department wise.

(c) These Book Selection Cards may be periodically forwarded to the subject specialist or the Heads of the departments for their recommendation.

(d) As soon as these cards are received back a list for books recommended is prepared. This may be termed as the Indent for Books. The cards for the books not recommended are separately arranged and be kept.

(e) The indent should be checked with the catalogue to see whether these books are already in the Library. Such items should be deleted from the indent.

(f) After this the indent should be forwarded to the concerned sanctioning authority, with the note indicating the total cost of indent and balance available under the head.

(g) As soon as the necessary sanction is obtained for the indent the orders are placed with the approved vendor. At this stage the Book Selection Card is treated as the Book Order Cards.

(h) On the receipt of books they are checked for the correctness of the title, price etc. against the bill.

(i) At this stage the title of books should be entered in the Accession Register. Here such books get a serial number. This serial number is called the Accession Number of the book. The number is also needed to entered on the backside of the title page and on another page in the book to be determined by the Library.

(j) The Accession Number of the books are also entered in the appropriate place in the Book Order Cards which becomes the Accession Cards now.

(k) The accession numbers are also entered in all the copies of the bill concerned and the bill is certified and signed by the Librarian. Then the Bills passed for payment to the concerned authorities.

(l) The total amount of each bill with the number and the date are entered under the relevant head in the Finance Register and the balance under each head is noted.

At this stage the books accessioned are forwarded to the Processing or Technical Section with the Accession cards for classifying and cataloguing.

CHAPTER - II

2:1 How to handle books in the library.
2:2 Routine work of the Library
2:3 Accessioning of books
2:4 Classification
2:5 Cataloguing
2:6 Preparation of shelf list
2:7 Book card
2:8 Arrangement of books in shelves
2:9 Membership card
2:10 Call Number/Marking or Notation
2:11 Working of Binding section
2:12 Mending of books
2:13 Prevention of Insects
2:14 Open shelf system
2:15 Discarding of books
2:16 Loss of Books
2:17 Reference service
2:18 Reading room
2:19 Journal and periodicals

2:1 HOW TO HANDLE BOOKS IN THE LIBRARY

Care and preservation of books in the library are necessary with a view to prolong their life for use by the readers. The librarian must guard them against decay and deterioration and take protective and preventive measures.

The books deserve care and respect. They should be properly handled so that they could serve many readers. Careful treatment will make these last longer so that the library will have more money for other books. Thoughtless readers, who make pencil or pen-marks in books, turn down the leaves or damage the books by tearing out the pictures, lessen the pleasure of future readers and cause the books to be discarded sooner. Through carelessness, readers sometimes spoil books by exposing them to rain or storm, by letting them become soiled, and especially by straining the stitching in the back. The backs get damaged if pads of paper, notebooks, pencils, or any thick leaves are placed in books. The back of a book where the leaves are fastened together, has a coating of glue. Sometimes the back of a new book is broken by forcing it open when this glue makes it seem stiff, and then the leaves near the broken part soon become loose. The students should be imparted instructions on the care and handling of books in the library and a sense of responsibility and respect for the rights and property of others should be inculcated in them. Students should be made to feel that the library is the common properly of all and the books should not be defaced or mutilated. They must be made to realise the fragile nature of the book, to learn the correct practice in opening and handling books and to practice good citizenship regarding books and their use. The books tend to sag if they stand closely packed upon the stacks and some times the spine and top edges are damaged while pulling them out. Book supports should be used to keep books upright on the shelves. The reference books such as dictionaries, encyclopaedias, directories and picture books are costly and heavy. They should be handled with care so as to prolong their life and utility. The students should be taught the proper method of handling such books. It should be seen that they do not fall into the unscrupulous and bad habit of mutilating papers or tearing away articles or pictures from costly books.

2:2 ROUTINE WORK OF THE LIBRARY

When the library acquire books they require to be processed. The books are prepared, accessioned, classified, catalogued, shelved and charged in accordance with modern methods of library practice.

After a book is received in the library a book-plate should be pasted on the inside front cover, showing work of ownership of the book. A book pocket should be pasted on the inside of the back cover and a due-date slip should also be pasted on the flyleaf opposite the book pocket. A book card on which has been written on the top line the author's last name and on the second line the brief title of the book should be placed in the book pocket at this time. This work of stamping and labeling is done by the Library Attendants under supervision of the Librarians.

2:3 ACCESSIONING

Every book to be included in the stock of the library must receive a serial number called the accession number and be entered in the Accession Book or Accession Register, which is an essential record in the library. The book in and added to the library are entered in the Accession Register in the order in which they are received and the amount paid for them. Every volume or copy is entered on a separate line and given a different number. The number assigned in the Accession Register should be given on the first right hand page after the title page and also on a selected page or pages for identification in case of suspected theft. This number should be written in theupper right hand corner of the book-card and on the flap of the book pocket. Accession Book or register specially designed for the purpose is available from firms dealing in library supplies and equipment. Alternatively a strong bound register of ledger size may be used ruled in vertical columns across both pages to record.

1. Date of acquisition.
2. Accession number
3. Author
4. Title
5. Publisher's name and place of publication
6. Year
7. Pages
8. Binding
9. Source of Supply
10. Price
11. Volumes
12. Class number
13. Bill No. & Date
14. Total number of books in the bill
15. Description of bill amount.
16. Signature of the Library in charge.
17. Remark (Lost. Discarded. Cost written off with date in each case)

If the Register is in several volumes, a separate line and accession number must be assigned to each volume of the set. If the book is lost or discarded, and another copy bought to replace it, the new copy must be given its own accession number and not that of the book it replaces. A book purchased for the library must be entered in the Accession Register and its accession number should be written on the stamp affixed on the title page and also noted on the bill of the supplier, before payment order is passed by the Principal. If a Book is an absolutely necessary record of stock and is also checked by the Auditor when auditing the accounts of the college. It is also a valuable document for the purpose of compiling a report on the working of the Library.

2:4 CLASSIFICATION

The classification of books is the process of grouping them in logical order according to subject and giving to each book a class mark which will indicate the particular group to which it belongs. The Dewey Decimal Classification Scheme published in book form is the one commonly used. It is the most practical as it is easily understood and may be expanded at any tine to cater to the needs of growing library. The Dewey Decimal System divides the whole field of knowledge into ten main classes and assigns to each class one hundred numbers as follows ;

000	099	General Works (Includes encyclopaedias, periodicals etc.)
100	199	Philosophy (Includes work on psychology, ethics etc.
200	299	Religion (Includes my theology)
300	399	The social sciences (Includes economics, government, law etc.)

400	499	Language (Includes dictionaries and grammers)
500	599	Pure Science (Includes mathematics, chemistry, physics, etc.)
600	699	Applied Science (Includes agriculture, engineering etc.)
700	799	Arts and Recreation (includes painting, music etc.)
800	899	Literature (Includes poetry plays) etc.
900	999	History (Includes geography travel, and biography).

For outline of the Division of subjects of the Dewey Decimal classification scheme the following is adapted from the book Dewey Decimal classification and Relative Index written by Melvil Dewey, Eighteenth Edition, 1971, Lake placid club, New York, USA.

The divisions are divided into sections and each section is further separated into small sections as that book on a special phase may stand together on the shelves. Each book in the library is classified according to the group in which it falls. Therefore a book 954, viz: class 9 (History), Division 5 (Asia) section 4 (India).

The number 920 is generally used for all collective biography, that is the lives of several persons in one volume. The books are then arranged alphabetically by the authors under that class. Individual biography is often marked simply with the letter B for a class number, the book number being derived from the name of the biography and followed by the initial of the author. By this means all the lives of one person will be together in alphabetical order according to their authors.

Books or fiction are not assigned classification numbers but that are marked 'F' with the first letter of the author's surname under the letter, or they may be marked only with the surname initial. In either case the Books are shelved alphabetically according to the names of the authors. Several books by one author are arranged alphabetically by title. For reference Books letter 'R' is written before the classification.

* Division of subjects in the Dewey Desimal classification Scheme.

000	General works
010	Bibliography
020	Library Science Cyclopedias
040	General Collected Essays
050	General Periodicals
060	General Societies, Museums
070	Journalism
080	Collected works
090	Book Rarities
100	PHILOSOPHY
110/120	Metaphysics
130/150	Psychology, Physical Phenomena
160	Logic
170	Ethics
180.4	Ancient Philosophy
199.54	Modern Indian Philosophy
200	RELIGION
210	Natural Religion
220/280	Christianity
230	Doctrinal Theory
240	Devotional Theology

250	Pastoral Theology
260	Ecclesiastical Theology
270	Christian Church History
280	Christian Churches and Sects
294	Brahmanism
294.3	Buddhism
294.4	Jainism
294.5	Hinduism
294.5(1)	Sikhism
297	Islam
300	SOCIAL SCIENCES
310	Statistics
320	Political Science
330	Economics
335(1)	Sarvodaya
340	Law
350	Public administration
360	Social Welfare
370	Education
371.4(1)	Basic Education
380	Commerce
390	Social Customs, Folk lore
400	LANGUAGES
410	Comparative Linguistics
420	English Language
430	German Language
440	French Language
450	Indian Language
460	Spanish Language

470	Latin Language
480	Greek Language
491.2	Sanskrit Language
491.42	Punjabi Language
491.43	Hindi Language
U 491.44	Bengli Language
A 491.44	Assamese Language
491.45	Oriya Language
491.46	Marathi Language
491.47	Gujrati Language
494.811	Tamil Language
494.812	Malayalam Language
494.813	Telugu Language
494.814	Karnatak Language
500	PURE SCIENCE
510	Mathematics
520	Astronomy
530	Physics
540	Chemistry
550	Geology (Earth Science)
560	Paleontology (Prehistoric Plants and animals)
570	Biological Science
580	Botany (Plant Life)
590	Zoology (Animal Life)
600	APPLIED SCIENCES
610	Medicine
620	Engineering
630	Agriculture
640	Domestic Economy

650	Business Methods
650/680	Manufactures
690	Building Construction
700	FINE ARTS.
710	Landscape Architecture
720	Architecture
730	Sculpture
740	Decorative Arts.
750	Painting
760	Prints and print marking
770	Photography
780	Music
790	Recreation, Sport, Entertainment
800	LITERATURE
810	America Literature
820	English Literature
830	German Literature
840	French Literature
850	Italian Literature
860	Spanish Literature
870	Latin Literature
880	Greek Literature
890	
891.2	Sanskrit Literature
891.42	Punjabi Literature
891.43	Hindi Literature
U 891.44	Urdu Literature
A 891.44	Bengali Literature
891.44	Assamese Literature

891.45	Oriya Literature
891.46	Marathi Literature
891.47	Gujrati Literature
891.811	Tamil Literature
894.812	Malayalam Literature
894.813	Telugu Literature
894.814	Karnada Literature
900	HISTORY
910	Geography
915.4	Geography of India
920	Biography
930	Ancient World History
940	European History
950	History of Asia
954	History of India
960	African History
970	North American History
980	South American History
990	History of Oceania

CATALOGUING

Cataloguing is one of the mechanical time-saving operation for the discovery of knowledge in libraries. It is the art of making records in such a manner that they may be readily identified, located and examined. Through the proper cataloguing system volumes may be located and used for reference and circulation. Therefore it is one of the most important reference tool in the Library. Cataloguing like the science of chemistry is essentially a laboratory art. Each art is not nearly a practice; it is a valuable discipline also. Cataloguing is first and foremost a discipline in accuracy.

Without accuracy, cataloguing is a snare and an offence. To maintain accuracy and uniformity librarians workout various catalogues codes.

Sl.No.	Author	Title of the code	Year of Ist Publication

Now a days modern Libraries are using card catalogue. The record of most practical use in the card catalogue, which is the key to the resources of the Library. It is a record on cards of all the books in the Library, and from them one can quickly find out what books the Library has on a particular subject or by a particular author. The making of a card catalogue is a technical process best performed by a trained Librarian and therefore it should not ordinarily be undertaken by an untrained hand. A sample of card catalogue is given below.

		Deathof asalesmen, certain private conservation in two self as in miller, author collects plays with a n introduction Bombay
		○

2:6 PREPARATION OF SHELF LIST

The shelf list is a card record showing the Books in class or numerical order as they stand on the shelves, and alphabetized in each class by the author's surname. It is useful for maintaining uniformity in classification and prevents duplication of book numbers when they are used. It is an aid to buying, as it shows what works the Library has in each class; and it may be used in taking an inventory or for annual stock taking.

Sl.No.	Class No.	Authors Surname First	Name of the Book

2:7 BOOK CARD

When a book is on the shelf, a book card is in the pocket. When a reader wishes to borrow the book, the book card is remarked and the borrower's name is written on it, together with his class and roll number. The date on which the book is due is stamped with a rubber dated on both the book card and the date slip. The cards for all books circulated directly the day are kept together in the front of the charging tray untill the close of the college day. They are then counted and a record made of the number of books circulated. The books cards are then arranged alphabetically by the name of the author, and then by title under the author, and filed in the charging tray under due d-gte. When a book is returned, the due date stamped on the date slip should be referred to and the book card looked up under the same date in the charging tray. Before the book card should be compared with that at the top of the flat of the book pocket in order to make sure that the right card is put into the pocket. The book is then ready to be returned to the shelves. Most books are issued for two weeks. Once a week, charging tray should be looked over for over dues on which a fine should be charged as per the Library rules of the institution.

2:8 ARRANGEMENT OF BOOK IN SHELVES

The books in the Library are arranged on the shelves according to their class number, beginning with the smallest 000's and ending with the largest, with the exception of fiction. As each number means a definite subject all books on any subject will stand together. Therefore 5/2 Algebra precedes 5/3 Geometry and follows 5/1 Arithmetic. When two or more books have the same class number i.e. dialing with the same subject, arrange them alphabetically by author. Fiction should be arranged alphabetically by the names of the author; in case of several titles by the same author, arrange alphabetically by title. As no class number is used as a rule for books of fiction, they are grouped together in one part of the Library and are arranged on the shelves alphabetically or by author's name. It is useful to write on the back or spine of the book the first letter at the author's name. To sum up, the books (except fiction) are arranged, first by the class number, beginning with the lowest and ending with the largest; and then under each class or subject alphabetically, by author. Books are placed on the shelves from the left to right across shelf, then down to the next shelf and across from left to right and so on down to the bottom of that section of shelves and then up to the top of next section and so on. A wooden cardboard dummy to show location of the book act in its regular place on the shelf is a useful device. No Library is considered complete in its organization without proper shelf labels or class guides, which assist both the reader and the Librarian in finding the books readily. It is quite as important that a Library should be well marked with shelf labels as it is for a city to be well provided with street signs. It is easier for the searcher to read signs than to ask questions.

2:9 MEMBERSHIP CARD

Each borrower of the Library is given a Library for membership card, which entitles him or her to borrow books from the Library for home reading.

While issuing books the issuing authority record the name of the borrower, class, Roll No. Accession No. Catalogue No, Name of the book, date of issue and the date of return of the book in the issue register and get signature of the borrower in it. If the borrower does not return the book within the scheduled date fine is levied as per Library Rules. A format of the Membership card is given below for example.

MEMBERSHIP CARD

Seal of the
Institution

Name...............Class........... Rol No..........

Sl. No.	Accession No.	Catalogue No.	Name of the book	Date of issue	Date of Return	Signature of the issuing Authority

2:10CALL NUMBER / MARKING OR NOTATION

Each book in the Library bears a number which distinguishes it from every other book . This number is written on the back of the title page in the bookplate, on the date slip, book card and label in the accession book, and the shelf- list card and all catalogue cards made for the book. This number is called the call number, and it consists of class number, author or book number and where necessary volume number. The class number is different for each class, but the same for all books in the same class. The author or book number distinguishes different books in the same class from one another. The volume numbers distinguishes different volumes of the same work, while copy numbers distinguish identical or practically identical books from one another. On the book label, the call number is written in two or three lines; the class number on the first line, the author or book number on the second, and the volume number if required on the third.

2:11 WORKING OF BINDING SECTION

The sheets of a book are protected either by binding or by casing. The publishers issue their books to the public either in bound form or in casing. In binding, the boards are attached to the sewn sheets before the covering material which is either of leather or cloth is added. In casing the cover or case (the boards and covering material) is manufactured separately and glued to the book after the sewing operation. Library books, however, require special style of binding called Library style Binding which can stand 25 to 30 issues against 4 to 5 without binding. In this style of binding there is leather at back and corners and cloth at the sides, the tapes stuck directly to the spine of the book. In this binding and papers are make with a linen joint and are sewn in, while tapes are used and are laid between split boards, or between a thick and thin mull-board glued together. Buckram is cheaper than leather and would last long , as well, except in the case of very heavily used books such as large dictionaries. Pamphlets can be bound separatly, if necessary, ¼ cloth binding with boards covered with stout paper and cut flush with leaves. While binding books, copper sulphate should be mixed up in gum and glue,"

2:12MENDING OF BOOKS

Before deciding whether a book requires mending or rebinding, the book should be carefully examined to determine whether the sewing or stitching is still firm, whether the paper is of sufficiently good quality to warrant mending or bending, and what the probable future demand for the book will be. Before rebinding a well-thumbed book care should be taken to see whether rt is cheaper to rebind it or to buy a fresh copy. If the thread with which the book is sewed has loosened or broken, one signature after another will loosen and only rebinding can restore the book to sound condition. If the paper is of good quality and the inner margins wide enough to permit rebinding, only the simplest kind of mending in a limited amount should be attempted. Even in as simple an operation as mending a tear in a page there is a right and a wrong way. Tears in the margins of pages which do not extend into the print may be mended with a strip of paper, about the thickness of the page covered with paste and laid carefully over the tear after its edges have been brought evenly together. The paper strip should be long enough to extend over the ends of the tear and wide enough to extend beyond its edges. The overhand beyond the edge of the book permits of a neat trimming with a pair of scissors. Tears reaching into the print may sometimes be mended by moistening the edges slightly with paste and bringing them neatly together. To strengthen this further, a piece of soft mending tissue should be gently rubbed over the tear to make the tissue adhere to the torn edges. While drying, the book should be put under a weight or into a press. When dry the superfluous tissue may be removed, taking care always to pull toward the tear from both sides. The fibers of the tissue act as a binder and help to make the mended tear almost invisible. At other times it may be necessary to paste a strip of thin, tough, transparent tissue over the tear after carefully matching the edges.

2.13 PREVENTION OF INSECTS

Dirt and dust invite bookworms, Vermin and insects. There should be regular dusting and cleaning of the books and the bookshelves by the library attendant.

The books should also be exposed to adequate air and sunlight for a short time in case the library room does not get sufficient sunlight and is in a damp place. Crude creosote diluted with kerosene oil should be sprinkled on the shelves and naphthalene balls should be spread on the sides of the books, Dry "neem" leaves, margosa leaves or tobacco leaves, copper sulphate etc, should be placed in the folds of the book pages. Books and wooden material in the library may also be treated with some insecticide in case there is danger of attack of white ants, silverfish, bookworms or termites. Spraying with flit and D.D.T.or gammaxene powder in the building gives satisfactory result to drive out these pests in the library. It should, however, be ensured that the fluid does not stain the materials. The use of nylon threads, synthetic adhesives and book cloths made of synthetic materials. Or plastic treated fabrics may be used for protection of books against insects especially in tropical climates. As repellents a mixture of methylated spirit, mercuric chloride and beechwood creosote brushed on the book and its case and copper sulphate added to the water used in conjunction with paste and glue. If the above stated protective and preventive measures are taken the condition of the books and other reading material is sure to be maintained and their maximum longevity is promoted for the benefit of the users of the library.

2:14OPEN SHELF SYSTEM

The books under this system will have to be kept on open shelves which means that book-racks will not be provided with doors, locks and keys and the students will be permitted to walk amidst the book-racks and allowed to handle any books they like and to take them to the reading desk without any let or hindrance. This enables a student to have free access to books; to learn to handle them and to browse at his leisure. In open access there is no need to have the help of a Library Assistant for taking out and bringing the books needed by readers. The old leisurely way of issuing books is dispensed with. The reader is no longer called upon to apply for books with the aid of catalogue and the librarian is no longer required to waste his time in writing entries of books issued in the Register and to cancel the same during most of the day. A new method has been evolved by the library profession to save the time of the reader as well as the librarian, which can be described as 'Reader's Ticket-cum-Book Card" or "Reader's Card-Cum-Book Card" method. This method is quite simple and at the same time secures lighting speed and foolproof accuracy. The reader takes the book out himself from the shelf and brings the same at the counter for being entered on the book-card and his own card before issue by the librarian or the counter assistant .The essence of open-access lies in:

(i) Putting the books in open shelves, free from doors and locks;

(ii) Admitting the reader inside the stack-room;

(iii) Freedom for readers to walk amidst the books in the open shelves;

(iv) Browsing by readers without let or hindrance :

(v) Guidance to readers by the librarian, both in anticipation and on demand, and

(vi) Right of readers to take away any book to the reading room for study or to the counter for getting it issued for study at home

This system no doubt carries with it a certain risk of loss which can be minimized by making suitable arrangements in the library for the entrance and exit of readers before introducing it. In this system it should not be possible for anyone to enter the library or to leave it except by one prescribed door. The library should be so arranged that all readers enter and leave by the same door. Strict vigilance is essential and every one should be checked out by the library attendant. Some students are by nature mischievous and some are also book thieves. They deliberately cause destruction of books by tearing off pages or taking them away stealthily. A competent attendant should be placed at that door or the prescribed door should be controlled by the librarian with the aid of a mechanical device. All the other doors and windows are to be made book proof by use of mesh shutters. Too minimize the damage due to loss, rare and costly books, pamphlets and small sized books should not be given an open access. They should be kept locked in closed shelves and issued only against formal application. During examination season, certain general books such as fiction and storybooks may be denied an open access as a temporary measure. One or two glass-paned cases may be provided for special or valuable books.

Another precaution that should be taken is that no reader should be allowed to replace on the shelves the books taken out of the shelves. Otherwise, books will be misplaced. A book misplaced is virtually a book lost. The students should be trained to leave the books, after reading them, either on the reading tables or at the issue counter. The racks should be so arranged that the width of the cross-gangways between rows of book-racks should be atleast four and a half feet in width so that crowds of children can frequently walk and stay between the book-racks browsing and handling books.

The college should also provide a property counter or desks with lockers in which the students may keep their own books and other material when they go to the library. The student should be trained in the habit of keeping their books etc. in the property counter or desk-lockers before entering the library.

No library should introduce open access system without providing first such safe guards, as it would be putting too great stream on human nature to keep the books unlocked under the conditions that obtain at present in many Libraries of different Colleges and Universities.

2:15 DISCARDING OF BOOKS

Systematic weeding out of books for rejection from the library is most important. It will most conveniently be done as a matter of routine at stock-taking or whenever new books in any number are added to the library. It should be done at the discretion of the librarian, although where the specialists are concerned the librarian will find it convenient to consult the subject teachers, most nearly concerned. Before all things, congestion should be avoided on shelves;

a book which will not be read and which is allowed to remain on the shelves for decorative purposes increases the difficulty of finding 'live' books.

It is standard library practice that at least once every year the librarian should examine every book on the shelves and note its condition, its up-to-date ness or its out-of-date ness and has it been borrowed during the past year, and then decide whether it should be discarded and in its place a newer and better book on the subject be acquired. It is also worthy of note here, what McColvin says in regard to libraries; "Books which are shabby, dirty, no longer in use, no longer of appeal, are a liability when retained on the open shelves. They create an impression of out-of- date ness, repel readers, and involve unnecessary labour in keeping them in order".

According to Ranganathan, on an average the book looses its value considerably in about five years, but classics are an exception to this rule. As such, book books whose thought-content is outmoded either in its facts or in its appeal should be weeded out . Earnest Grimshaw prescribes that the following types of books are to be discarded:

(i) Books which are badly written ;

(ii) Books with fine print

(iii) Badly produced or unattractive books ;

(iv) Out of date books;

(v) Books which are too old or too young in their treatment of a subject;

(vi) Text-books which are obviously text books;

2:16LOSS OF BOOK

The advisory Committee for libraries appointed by the Government of India recommended that practices of holding the librarian responsible for paying the cost of books lost during the time he was in charge of the library should be put to an end and that no State Government should require a librarian to iurnish security or to pay for any loss of books, unless gross negligence or dishonesty is proved against him. The Education Department is, therefore, well advised to issue departmental instructions to all heads of recognized Schools, Colleges in the State and also to amend the Education Code in terms of the recommendation of the aforesaid committee. The authority should also ensure that there are regular checks for missing books. A seminar of librarians of Rajasthan held at the University of Rajasthan, Jaipur in 1970, recommended as under:

"The loss of books in any library is inevitable and stock taking should, therefore, be a means not only to ascertain the books but also to evaluate and assess the quality, Strength and usability of the book collection. " Mr S.C. Verma, UGC Fellow, Book Writing Project, Department of Library Science and Documentation, university of Rajasthan, Jaipur, who conducted time and Cost Analysis of stock taking in school library, College library, and University library, came to the following conclusion.

"Loss of books from a service library is a must and inevitable. The authorities have accepted it. Cost and time analysis has proved its futility. However, loss of books from a library is a social is a social problem, which has to be fought out at the social plane. Instead of punishing the librarian, the authorities must look to this aspect of the problem Punishing of a librarian for a wrong done by some others, who are burglariously inclined, is neither just nor legal. Hence, unless there are sound and sufficient reasons to believe that the librarian and his staff have been negligent in their duties and that the management, too has not lacked in providing sufficient staff and other physical facilities, the government and authorities responsible for the management of libraries must be prepared to write off such lost books.

When books are stolen from the library for being sold out in the open market or in the black-market, as well as to some other libraries, the loss many be treated "positive loss". To restrict such loss, security measures should be tightened and assistance of police may even be called for to trace the culprit. The following preventive measures should also can taken in the matter:

No library bookseller, Scholar or student should ever purchase any reading material belonging to any library from any person, whatsoever may be its price and persons found selling such books should immediately be handed over to police. Library authorities of such books if traceable from the rubber stamp or with the help of any other mark on the book may also be informed immediately after finding such books so that roper action may be taken in the matter by all concerned. No one should encourage the practice of taking out books illegally libraries.

2:17REFERENCE SERVICE

States should take the responsibility of production of sufficient amount of reference books in various regional languages. The organization and success of reference service predetermines the systematic acquisition and scientific arrangement of reference material. The authorities concerned with the College should provide sufficient finance for the purchase of reference material and for the establishment and development of a separate reference wing in the College library. The various College/University in the region should also cooperate for the inter-library loan of reference material and to satisfy the inquires of each other. This will help in the increase of overall standard of reference service to the College students in the region. Additional grants should be provided by the state government to fulfil their gaps in the reference collection and for the appointment of component staff in various schools libraries. The number and nature of student population in a school/college should be given consideration for the planning of reference section and annual expenditure on it.

Proper initiation and instruction in the use of material and provision of proper guidance and reference service at School/College level will be helpful for the Students to become the better adult-users of public libraries and academic libraries of higher level at a later stage.

2:18 READING ROOM.

The reading room is an important and essential adjunct to the school and College library. The reading room must be made the most attractive place in the school/college so that students will be naturally drawn to it. It should be housed in a spacious well-lit hall with the walls suitable coloured and decorated with flowers and artistically framed pictures of great men so as also to serve as an Art Gallery or the College. Walls should be distempered in a soothing colour such as green. The floor must be smooth and without holes which accumulate dust. There should be space for flower vases and provision should also be made for hangings life curtains. In short, the reading -room should be beautiful and everything possible should be done to produce an atmosphere of composure bad love lines. A sufficient volume of light must be cast on walls and tables to make reading pleasant, and careful attention must be given to fixtures from the point of view of appearance. Where electricity is available fully indirect light is desirable and fluorescent lights are favoured in place of ordinary ones. Windows should be provided with curtains or drapes so as to add a touch or grace and welcome colour. The furniture, that is, tables, chair and reading desks, should be carefully designed from the point of view of both artistic effect and function efficiency. In decorating the room, full cooperation of the students should be obtained in order to give them the feeling that it is their own reading-room.

2:19 JOURNALS AND PERIODICALS

A good college Library should also provide will-selected periodicals and newspapers for recreational reading and for information purposes. Some college no doubt subscribe to a few news papers, journals and magazines but they do not generally make them properly available to the students for information and research. The literature on serial publications has grown rapidly in extent and importance. Magazines and journals are an assets to the college libraries if they are selected with a n eye to the needs of the students. One or two daily news papers are also necessary for having current information and also for clip ping local history items for the information file. For example ,there should be periodicals on hobbies and recreation ,games and sports, travel and geography etc. Some educational journals may also be subscribed to for use of the teachers. Magazine titles should be evaluated every year and new titles subscribed to and old titles dropped if found unsuitable or less valuable . Some contain articles, stories, poems by the best writers, some contain mainly trash and many are a mixture of good writing and trash. The librarian should choose carefully out of the magazine available in the library those that are too be read regularly, and put aside those that are least valuable to the students.

Magazines appear at regular intervals ranging from once a week to once in three months. Several issues of a magazine ,such as all those published from January to December, make what is called a volume. Magazine holders or protectors should be employed when the periodicals are displayed in the reading room for use of the readers. The magazine parts making a volume should be well bound into a book, usually with a title page and often with an index and preserved in the library. For audit band check purposed a separate register should be maintained which should contain information regarding Periodical Publications subscribed to by the college library

CHAPTER-III

3:1 Library Rules
3:2 Library Committee
3:3 Appointment of Librarians and other staff of Library
3:4 Selection procedure of Library Staff
3:5 Duties of the Librarians
3:6 Conduct of the Librarians
3:7 Finance
3:8 Library fund
3:9 Library automation
3:10 Annual verification

3:1 LIBRARY RULES

Each and every library needs rules. Rules should be few but plainly set out and their observance enforced. For example the following Library rules adopted by one of the college of the Orissa named the Rajendra College (Autonomous), Balangir is given below.

GENERAL RULES :-

1. The teaching and noon-teaching staff and the students of the College only shall use library. No books will be issued to outsiders without special permission of the Principal.
2. Library will remain open from 10.30A.M. to 4.30 P.M. everyday except Sundays and other holidays and between 9.00 A.M. and 1.00 during vacation.
3. The last hour of every working day is 2-00 P.M. after which no books will be issued or returned.
4. No books shall be taken out of the Library without the knowledge of the Librarian and until it is properly entered in the Loan register and the receipt acknowledge by the borrower.
5. Each borrower must examine the condition of the book at the time of issue. The responsibility will be fixed on the borrower incase of any damage or mutilation of the pages.
6. No remarks, notes, underlining or any sort of disfigurement in the books is allowed. Otherwise they will have to replace the book.
7. The Librarian will report to the Principal the name of the person responsible for improper use of the Library books.
8. IN CASE A BOOK BORROWED IS LOST, TEN TIMES OF THE PRICE OF THE BOOK WILL BE REALIZED FROM HIM/HER UNLESS HE/SHE REPLACES THE

BOOK WITHIN ONE MONTH. IF THE LOST BOOK IS A PART OF A SET TEN TIMES OF THE COST OF THE SET WILL BE REALIZED.

9. All students and the staff must return the books at the end of session for annual verification..

10. Books of the general section will be issued only to members of staff on requisition.

READING ROOM

11. The reference books, question papers, syllabus and journals will be issued to the students and the staff to be studied within the reading room of the library. The books and journals shall have to be returned to the Library before the closure of the working hours. The students must surrender their identity cards to the counter-in-charge before borrowing referable books and journals.

NO REFERENCE BOOK, JOURNAL, AND STLLABUS ETC. CAN BE TAKEN OUTSIDE THE READING ROOM.

12. Students must return all books at the Library before they fill up their forms for term end final examination and obtain clearance certificate from the Library.

13. A borrower against whom any over due or other charge is outstanding shall not be allowed to borrow books from the library.

14. Any book issued to students must be returned to library on requisition of the librarian.

15. If any borrower keeps a library book in his/her possession for more than the time allowed no more books will be issued to him/her until the book is returned to the Library, or ten times cost of the book is paid.

16. Students are advised to maintain silence in and around the library. Noise or shouting of any kind is strictly prohibited.
17. NO STUDENT IS ALLOWED TO ENTER INTO THE LIBRARY. ALL TRANSACTIONS ARE TO BE MADE AT THE COUNTER ON.Y.
18. All requisitions slips must be submitted to the librarian before 2.00 P.M. on working days to get the books issued on the next day. (G.O. No. 62415 (91)/HE. Dt. 09-10-2001)
19. Identity card and the Library card are to be presented at the counter for transaction. In case of loss of the library card, another card will be issued on payment of Rs. 2.00 only.
20. Library card will be issued to a student on production of his/her last fee receipt.
21. The following is the extent to which a borrower entitled to borrow books from library.

a)	Members of the teaching staff	10 each
b)	Non - teaching staff	3 each
c)	Honours students	3 each
d)	P.G. Student	5 each

Note

1. Members of the Teaching staff can retain the books for 30 days, non teaching staff for 15 days and students for 15 days. Or expiry of the due date for return of books a default fine of Rs. 10/- per book per day will be charged.
2. Ten-times of the cost will be realized in case lost/ damage of books.
3. Books issued to a Particular can be reissued only for 2 Successive occasions during a Particular Session.

3:2 LIBRARY COMMITTEE

Library Committee is the Committee responsible for the management of a Library. In other words it is the government of a library. A Library committee is also called Library Board, Board of Directors, Library Trusties, Advisory Committee etc. The main functions of a Library Committee is of legislative character. The Librarians are to carry out its .decisions. The general policy in administration of a Library is laid down by the Committee. The Librarian is responsible for seeing that the policy is carried out. For better results the committee should not interfere with the methods adopted by the Librarian to carryout the determined policy. In co-operation with the librarian the Library committee concerns itself with formation of a library policy in relation to the development of resources for instruction and research, advising in the allocation of book. Funds to the Library, advising on the policy of reproduction unique materials, collaborating ondecisions regarding the Library space needed by departments of instruction developing a general programme of Library service for all the interests of the university. These is no hard and fast rule with regard to the constitution of a Library committee. It generally depends upon the nature of a Library and the social and political environments in which it is situated. For example in a premier college of Western Orissa, Rajendra College Balangir the Library Committee is constituted with -

1. Principal - Chairman (Ex-Officio)
2. All Heads of Departments - Members
    a) Botany
    b) Chemistry
    c) Commerce
    d) Computer Science

e) Economics
f) English
g) Geography
h) Hindi
i) History
j) Mathematics
k) Oriya
I) Philosophy
m) Political Science
n) Sanskrit
o) Statistics
p) Zoology.

3. all Librarian &
all Assistant Librarian — Member
4. Prof-in- change U.G.C. — Member
5. QIC Library. — Member Secretary

3:3 APPOINTMENT OF LIBRARIANS AND OTHER STAFF OF LIBRARY

Organized human effort is essential for the successful culmination of the desired aims of an institution. Library is the cultural center of a society. Therefore it has to render literary services to a community. It is the house in which the members like their professional lives and parttake of the characteristics of a happy home. It should be well regulated smooth running, cooperative, comfortable in which each member of the staff may find his rightful place.. To achieve this cherished aim a library should be governed by certain principles while recruiting its personnel who have to perform some specialized cultural and educational duties.

The recruitment policy of libraries influenced by the nature of its service. There are various types of libraries. Particularly for the Libraries of colleges the minimum basic and professional qualifications should remain uniform. Therefore the recruitment policy of a College Library, a University Library should differ from a Public Library or a School Library. Besides the professional staff each Library requires non professional staff. They include assistants, steno, typists, clerks, binder, Janitors, peons, messengers, watch man, choukidar etc. The non professional work in Libraries differs from the routine work of an office. Thus it is always in the interest of a library if the non professionals have a refresher course of at least four weeks in the general routines of Library work.

3:4 SELECTION PROCEDURE OF LIBRARY

The usual method of selection and appointment of Library staff is to invite applications by advertisement for the posts and prescribing the qualifications, categories, experience and the pay scale. The advertisement is made either through Employment Exchange or inserted in professional journals and newspapers. The Govt. of Orissa has prescribed a.yard stick for creation of posts for the colleges.

Usually four to oix weeks are allowed for the candidates to submit their applications so received are sorted out and the synopsis of the qualifications and experiences of the candidates who fulfil both the essential and desirable qualifications are prepared and out up to members of the Selection Committee generally comprises the Head of the institution as its Chairman, one expert member, two or three other members of the library committee out of which a lady member is there. The suitable candidates are called for interview out of whom the committee might select the one they consider suitable for the job. Sometimes a panel of names are recommended so that, one. No doubt it is difficult to estimate intelligence through interview but it is not difficult to know a candidate's interests, hobbies, forcefulness, .brightness in conversation and any disagreeable mannerisms.

3:5 DUTIES OF THE LIBRARIAN

The following type of duties and jobs are required to be done by the Librarian in addition to Administrative work.

.... PROFESSIONAL WORK-

1. Selecting and ordering books and journals.
2. Processing books
3. Compiling reading lists
4. Training in use of books
5. Guiding students in relation to library material for seminars/assignment work.
6. Interpreting the card catalogue to students and reference service.
7. Planning exhibits and informal displays annual stock taking

CIRCULATION WORK

1. Lending books to readers.
2. Renewing books
3. Issuing reminders and collecting fines
4. Handling reserve book routine
5. Shelving books.
6. Searching missing books.
7. Filling cards.

8. Preserving damaged book
9. Shorting books for binding
10. Realization of outstanding books.

The librarian should regard the Library work as social service work. He should be a jack of all trades. He should be able to do all kinds of work in the library from shelving to issue at reminders return of books from students and staff .He should see the shelves and chairs are kept clean and that new books are displayed in the Library every day to make the place attractive. Beside the Librarian should possess binding knowledge so that he can supervise the binding work properly.

'Every reader his book' enjoins a duty on the Librarian to provide much required reference service and the third law of Library Science 'Every book its reader' makes it obligatory for the Librarlan to use all publicity methods to bring books in the hands of potential readers. He must know that the books in the Library is not only to be preserved but they should also be put to use by the readers. The Librarian also owes a duty to himself. He must acquaint himself thoroughly with the reading material in the library in order to serve the readers well.

3:6 CONDUCT OF THE LIBRARIAN

A Librarian of a college or a university should keep burning the prescribed by Dr. R.L. Mittal. They are

Impersonal Book Selection.

While selecting books, a Librarian should do it without any prejudice. He should not accept the book if they are below standard and should not reject them on the basis of his personal dislike under the garb at declaring them as below standard.

Service before self.

It should be the motto of the Librarian. He is in the Library not for himself but he is a means to an end. That means he is in the Library for the fulfillment of the reading requirements of his readers.

Split mind as well as an active mind

A Librarian should have a split mind. He should be capable of retaining the unfulfilled demands of his readers alive in his mind for ever and should strive hard to fulfill the same at an opportune time. Further he should be capable of attending to more than one inquires at a time. He must have an active mind.

Sympathetic behaviour and Love

A Librarian should have a very sympathetic attitude towards the readers and should try to inculcate self-confidence amongst the readers. He should treat his readers in such a manner so as to make him a lovable personality.

Tact

A Librarian without tact will find it difficult to succeed since he deals with various types of students and unless he tackles them in a tactful manner he is sure to bring bad name to the profession.

Preservance

A Librarian job is not a bad of roses. It demands hard labour as preservance. Those who cannot put their learnt and soul into the profession should knack at some other door.

Scholarship

A Librarian must be a scholar himself first, so that he may become a guide for others in true sense of the word 'Guide' he should be fully conversant with the reading material in his Library in order to inspire confidence amongst his readers.

3:7 FINANCE

U.G.C. AND GOVT. GRANTS

A good library in Colleges depends on finance. The college authorities must, therefore, be fully alive to the value of better Libraries and willing to spend what ever is necessary for providing such a service. Recurring as well as non-recurring grants should be provided for the college Libraries. Besides contingent grants for consumable articles needs to be provided for better functioning of the college Library.

At present the Government colleges of a state receives financial assistance for purchase of books and Library equipments from the U.G.C. and state Government. Generally reference books are purchased out of the U.G.C. funds and text books from the State Government allotment. It is a well determined fact that a successful Library is the one that has a definite annual appropriation. The appropriation should ever binding, equipment, supplies and stationery at the Library.

3:8 LIBRARY FUND

The Library fee collected from the students in a college / University should not be amalgamated with general fund of the institution for meeting other items of expenditure but credited to the Library fund and spent exclusively for the development of the Library and reading room.

3:9 AUTOMATION

The software technology has knocked down the walls of the conventional academic Library by introducing online database, CD-ROM, Video Disk and other exotic media. At present databases are accessible to near beyond the confines of national boundaries. Extensive net works make possible wide geographic courage. CD-ROM technology allows the storage of large quantum of information an compact durable and highly portable medium. Now a days this is the state of art in live library systems. Therefore institutions of higher education should modernize their libraries if they are to meet effectively the information requirements of the academic community. To enable this; firstly head of the College Library should be prepared to respond to the new environment in an informed and positive way.

Management information for the librarian, which has earlier been characterised by disparate sources presented in a variety of incompatible formats will become a sophisticated and integrated support system in a computorised Library. This will make information on the performance of the Library more available to the Librarian and the Principal and will help further planning and programmes for development of services found more relevant to the users. Statistic that will become available in the computer system, on book issue like subject groups, document type, utilization of services etc. will help the review and analysis of Library's acquisition policies. It can also help assessing the costs and benefits of introducing new or replacement services together with the implication of with drawing others. A computerized library can facilitate the following.

1. Accurate and reliable management information.
2. Availability of more sophisticated techniques for review and analysis.
3. Quick and effective decision
4. Efficient coordination
5. Need based further development.

An efficient book acquisition system in a college should collect information on all new publications relating to the subject taught in the college; in the pre-acquisition stage. This information should be classified according to subjects and transferred to concerned subject departments for comments. The titles also should be checked with the catalogue or database, of the available titles and the current order file in order to ascertain that the items are not available in the Library and that they are not already ordered. The acquisition system should also keep full details of vendors, files of subject interests of the colleges and should be able to create purchase orders and chase the vendors with case. Using a manual system of acquisition of books in the present situation will require additional staff, stationeries and completion of the technical processing of the available materials. A computerized acquisition system forming part of automated library can undertake

1. preparing a database of available materials
2. Maintaining of accurate and up to date record of orders
3. Duplicate checking before placing orders
4. Printing of purchase orders.
5. Sending timely reminders.
6. Maintaining of up to date fund account.

7. Maintaining of complete vendor file.
8. Preparing of current activity report.
9. Preparing vendor performance report
10. Invoice accounting and listing of invoices for audit
11. Economy of staff.

While the library gets computerized it will become essential to create a database of the materials available in the library. Fields from this database can be used for examining and correcting the improper book numbers allotted to the items stacked in the library. Computers can also be used for annual stack verification with speed and efficiency. Accessioning the item by transferring the order file to the question file with additional information required is possible. Instead of manually supplicating the earlier stock registers; from the data available materials fed into the computer for-automating library services print outs at stock registers can be generated. In this process registers of nearly accessioned books also can be printed. So to say computerised stock recording can allow us.

1. To up to date record of the collection to stack verification.
2. Can give opportunity to review loses.
3. Inventory file can replace accession register or serve as a shelf list.
4. Current file can be maintained as a part of the automated circulation.
5. Current file can be maintained as a part of the automated circulation.

Computers can support and supplement classification system. Classification system using the computers can help the classificationist to:

1. Select isolate terms and groups them and arrange

them in their scalar sequence.

2. Synthesize the class number.
3. Save time avoiding the referring of the schedules of classification scheme.
4. Improve accuracy and speed in classification.

Like-wise classified catalogue can be generated and maintained using computers and this can be used for online information search. Computerised indexes can be maintained as a retrieval tool to provide various access points through which the uses can identify the document of his interest. A computorised cataloguing system can facilitate:

1. Efficiency in cataloging
2. Speed in cataloging
3. Economy of staff and services
4. Improved updating of the catalogue
5. Variety of outputs.
6. More bibliographical detail and depth of subject cataloging.
7. Multiple access to using large files from remote locations through on line.
8. Improved information accessibility through increased access points.
9. Speed in locating and retrieving information
10. Search of items by combination of index terms.

Again automation service is also helpful in circulation system as because it provides efficient circulation through Manuel systems like Browne or Newark. A computerised circulation system can do charging, discharging, overdue control, reservation and file maintenance.

The college at present subscribes to only less

than a hundred periodicals and newspapers and are supplied by local vendors. The college uses registers for recording the receipt of these items. There is no fool-proof system for watching the receipt of all issues, sending reminders for issues not received etc. But the college being a centre for research; when the library services are vitalised according to the needs of the users it will become essential for subscribing to a minimum number of journals on all subjects taught in the college. To ensure the availability of what is actually required; library will have to subscribe to many journals directly from publishers or their authorised distributors established at different far away places in or outside India. A system that can efficiently control the recording of receipt of journal issues, sending reminders for issues not received, renew subscription in time, and maintain details of completed volumes sent for binding etc. will become essential. A computerised serials management system can undertake the following functions.

- provide accurate and up to date record of subscription and holdings.
- Print subscription renewal and reminder letters.
- maintain complete supplier file, and give supplier performance notice.

At present the collection lacks sufficient source materials for providing different kinds of reference service that will be essential in the environment of a college supporting post graduate studies and research. So as a part of library revjatalisation projects a good reference collection consisting of popular dictionaries, encyclopaedias, handbooks, yearbooks etc. should be acquired. The reference collection of a library is normally built up by the effort and funds of many years. But here due to unscientific collection development methods reference collection as required has not come into existence. The acquisition of materials required for a basic reference collection at one instant will be very costly and no college can afford that. But if the library is getting computerised general reference sources or specialised sources in subjects of interest to the college can be acquired for the reference section in non print mediums at 50 to 75% less cost than in print materials.

Computerised library can provide all types of reference service with speed and efficiency. The Current Awareness Services (CAS) of an automated library can do the following.

- review the select publications immediately upon receipt.
- select the items of relevance to the programme of the teaching departments of research projects undertaken by teaching staff.
- notify the items to the departments to whom they are related or to the teachers who are working on those topics.

A computerised library can provide Selective Dissemination of Information (SDI) service as part of the reference services. Computerised SDI system can construct document profiles, can match them and provide selected information to the user, can assess feedback from users and modify users profiles it becomes essential. Such an SDI system can perform the following functions.

- continuously watch the documents being admitted into the system.
- evaluate the relevance of each document from the point of view of user's interest.
- form comprehensive idea of users' requirements.
- save users' search time.

- prepare individual notifications.
- continuously interact with users through feed backs.

3:10 ANNUAL VERIFICATION OF LIBRARY BOOKS

It is necessary that stock at books in the Library is physically checked and verified. This may be conveniently done after the annual examinations are over. Generally book issue work is practically closed after filling of forms for annual examinations by the students in a college. So it is better to conduct the Annual Physical verification of books at a Library during the summer vacation. The use of shelf list and Accession Book is necessary in stock-taking work. In an open-shelf system some loss is natural and inevitable despite strict enforcement of Library rules and supervision of the Library staff. A list of missing books may be drawn up and very effort should be made to locate or trace them out. The loss of books, of any, from the Library stock should be reported to the principal who is competent to write off some books every year in accordance with the modern Library practice, the university grants commission has recommended that at least three books per thousand of stock or issue should be written off. In the process of physical stock verification, the worn out books as well as out- moded volumes should be removed from the shelves. The worn out books which can be got repaired'should be rejuvenated and renovated and then again placed on the shelves. The books which have been worn out beyond repairs and those which have become out of date should be needed out of the stock and their value got written off by the competent authority. The entries in accession book and card catalogue should also be corrected accordingly.

Practical side of the verification

1. The authority should select members to verify the stock of books in the Library by a notification.
2. All the employees of the Library should be directed to remain present in the Library and assist the verifying officers.
3. During the verification all queries of the verifying officers should be explained by the Librarians.
4. The verified shelves should be marked with rate of verification and name of verifying officer so that duplication can be avoided.
5. Provision for refreshment should be more by the Liberian for verifying officer during the period at verification.
6. The individual verifying officer should draw the following list at the five of his/their verification
    1) Missing books
    2) Damaged books for binding
    3) Complete damaged books
    4) Books not returned by the borrowers
7. At the final stage the chief at the verification team should prepare a detailed report for verification which should incorporate the following
    1) Name of the college Library
    2) Year of Establishment
    3) Name and designation of the officer inspecting
    4) Date of commencement of the present inspecting
    5) Date of completion of the present inspecting
    6) Date of submission of the inspection note
    7) Name and designation of the affair respecting the Library last year

8) Whether action has been taken on all points raised by the inspecting officer
9) Whether any other superior authority verified the Library last year
10) Who are the Gazetted officers placed in charge at the Library
11) Date at assumption of charge
12) Name of the Library staff
13) Total number of books in the Library
14) Total number of books in the previous year
15) Loss of books
16) How the catalogue been maintains properly
17) Is the catalogue checked annually and loss of books reported
18) Has the Annual check been made for the last year
19) Was any discrepancy noticed during the last 3 years? If to steps taken to recoup the loss
20) Is the time limit for return of books insisted upon
21) Are cares of non return brought to the notice of the office in charge
22) When was the last annual stock taking made
23) Does the last Annual verification report mention the condition of the old books and suggestions for their repair.
24) Are repairs taken in time?
25) Present state of repairing of books.
26) Statistics relating to loss of books during the current year
27) Is there any action taken for disposal of absolute are resellers books

28) Check and note if these are still in the Library some absolute or useless books for disposal
29) When was the last disposal made
30) Financial statement : Grants received and utilizing during the year______

The Convenor of the Physical verification of books should append list of missing books, complete damaged books, Books to be repaired etc. with the verification report.

It should be the duty of the Librarian to chanelise the report to the authority and keep a record of it for compliance of audit verification.

CHAPTER - IV

(Executive Instructions and Codal Provision)

4.1 Letter No. 4522 dated 15.2.74 of D.P.I. (H.E.) Orissa on Professional training of Librarians.

4.2 Letter No. 32095/EYS dated 2.12.1974 of the Government of Orissa Education and Youth Services Department on Yardstick for entertainment of class III and class IV staff in Libraries of Government colleges.

4.3 Letter No. 26018 / EYS dated 28.7.1977 of the Government of Orissa Education and Youth Science Department on Professional Training of existing Librarian and fresh appointment of trained candidates as Librarians.

4.4 Govt. of India notification date forfulbright scholarship nominations.

4.5 Executive Instructions No. 45546 dated 18.10.1986 of the Directorate of Higher Education, Orissa on Return of Library book by the Borrowers.

4.6 Copy Letter No. F.I. 96 / 81 (CPP- I) dated 5th May 1987 of the Deputy Secretary, U.G.C. for upgradation in salary scale of Librarians in colleges.

4.7 Letter No. 542 date. 3.1.1998 of Govt. of Orissa Home Department on Fixation of criteria for promotion to the rank of Librarian / Appointment to the post ofAsst. Librarian in the Orissa Secretariat Library.

Copy of the letter No. 4522 dated 15.2.74 from the D.P.I. (M.E.) to the Principals of all Government Colleges including Training college in the state.

Sub : Professional training of Librarians.

State Government, in a recent communication sent to the Directorate have pointed out that libraries in Government colleges do not function properly and books disappear due to lack of supervision and suitable methodology adopted for running a library. They have therefore, felt that it is necessary to depute the untrained librarians for professional training according to a systematic and phased programme.

I, therefore, request you the enclosed proforma the particulars of the existing librarians working in your college, so as to reach this Directorate before the 15th February, 1974.

You may how encourage the untrained librarians of your college take initiative in this matter and apply through proper channel for seats in recognised Universities / Institutions of their choice that offer Degrees / Diploma / Certificates in Library Science. After they are assured of seats you may forward their application for deputation.

II. In connection with the observations of Government that our Libraries do not function properly and books disappear due to lack of supervision and suitable methodology adopted for running a library, I am to say that this matter was considered in some of the conferences of the principals where particularly requested to be ensure regular annual stock verification, prompt stock entry of all books and journals either purchased or cost thereof from the defaults. If such measures are not regulars adopted and stick supervision is not exercised it may result in rapid stock depletion and serious mismanagement of Govt. assets.

You are requested to take such steps as you may deem proper to streamline the administration of your college library at an early date make suitable arrangement for regular supervision of its day to day working and timely stock verification. As per the decision taken in the Principals Conference 1972, copy of the annual stock verification Reports with your comments should invariably be sent to this office for examination and suitable invariably be sent to this office for examination and suitable action./ these reports along with Annual stock verification Reports relating to laboratories and college and hostel furniture may be addressed to the Accounts officer, Directorate of Public Instruction (H.E.) Orissa, Bhubaneswar.

Sd/-B. Das

14.02.74

Director of Public Instruction (H.E.)Orissa.

Government of Orissa

Education and Youth Services Department.

No. 32095 /Eys. Dated. 2.12.74

IVE. A. 268/74

From,

Shri K. Roy, I.S,

Deputy Secretary to Government.

To,

The Director of Public Instruction (H.E) Orissa, Bhubaneswar.

Sub : Yardstick for entertainment of Class III and class IV staff in the libraries of Government Colleges.

Sir,

In continuation of G.O. No. 30303. E dt. 3.10.70

I am directed to say that Government have been pleased to lay down the following yardstick for entertainment of class III and class IV staff in the Libraries of Government colleges of the state. The status of Post Graduate and degree colleges except

Training and Evening Colleges, Training colleges and Evening colleges, have been taken separately.

1 For Post-Graduate and colleges other than

Training and Evening Colleges.

i) Graduate Librarian with diploma / degree in Library Science- Rs. 475-750/-

There shall be a post of Graduate Librarian with diploma / degree in Library Science in the scale of Rs. 475/- 750/- for (a) every Post-Graduate College irrespective of students strength and (b) degree college having student strength of more than 1500.

If Graduate Librarians with diploma / degree in Library Science are not available, a Graduate Librarian in the scale of Rs. 375-620/- may be appointed in lieu.

ii) Graduate Librarian: - .... 375-620 / -

There shall be one Graduate Librarian in the scale of Rs. 375-620/- for students strength up to 1000 in all Government colleges including post- Graduate colleges. For every additional students' strength of 700 or part thereof subject to a minimum of 300, there shall be one more Graduate Librarian. In addition to this, one additional post shall be allowed to colleges where there is Post-Graduate teaching for reference and research section.

iii) Under Graduate Librarian :- Rs. 300-410/-

There shall be one Under Graduate Librarian having minimum qualification of Intermediate or equivalent thereof in the scale of Rs. 300-410/- in colleges where there is facility of teaching upto degree stages.

iv) Library Assitant.

There shall be a Library Assistant having minimum qualification of matriculation in the scale of Rs. 255-360/- in colleges where the students strength exceeds 1,500/-

v) Library Attendant:- .... Rs. 215-265/-

There shall be one Attendant having read up to class X in the scale of Rs. 215-265/- in colleges for students strength upto 1000 in all Government Colleges including P.G. Colleges. For every additional student strength of 500 or part thereof, subject to a minimum of 200, one additional post will be sanctioned.

vi) Library Peon ....Rs. 200-250/-

There shall be one watchman in the scale of Rs. 200-250/- in colleges where the number of students exceeds 1000.

vii) Watchman :- 200-250/-

There shall be one watchman in the scale of Rs. 200-250/- for every Government College to keep watch over the reading rooms.

viii) Book-Binder-cum-Daftry .... Rs. 215-265/-

There shall be one Book-Binder-cum-Daftry in the scale of Rs. 215-265/- in colleges where the number of students exceeds 1000-

Under Certificate of Posting

GOVERNMENT OF ORISSA

EDUCATION AND YOUTH SERVICES DEPARTMENT.

No. IV. / M. II / 77:26018 (47) EYS dated 28.7.77.

From,

Sri. B. K. Das, O.S.S.

Asst. Secretary to Government.

To,

The Principals of all Government Colleges.

Sub : I, Professional Training of existing Librarian and ii., Fresh appointment of trained candidates as Librarians.

Ref: D.P.I. (H.E)'s letter No. 4522 dt. 15.2.74 addressed to all Principals and Govt. Memo No. 51910 dated 18.12.76.

Sir,

Government have been emphasizing the desirability of having professionally trained hands as Librarians in the educational institutions in order to ensure better management and maintenance of the Libraries.

The Director of Public Instruction (H.E), in his had instructed that the existing untrained librarians of the colleges should be impressed upon to seek admission in recognised universities/institutions that offer Degree/Diploma in Library Science. Government have been granting study leave to such in service librarians who are selected by the Universities recognised institutions that offer Degree/Diploma in Library Science. Government have been granting study leave to such in service librarians who are selected by the Universities/recognised institutions and this should be taken advantages of by the Untrained Librarians.

Further in G.O. No. 51909 (2) EYS dated 18th December 1976 it has been laid down that for the purpose of fresh appointment candidates having Degree/Diploma or any recognised specialisation of Library science should be given preference for the posts of Librarians of different categories. There should not be any deviation in this regard.

I am directed to request that necessary action should be taken by all Principals in pursuance of paragraph 2 and 3 supra. Receipt of this government order may kindly be acknowledged.

Yours faithfully,

Sd/-

Asst. Secretary to Govt.

Memo No. 23019 / dt. 28.7.77.

Copy forwarded to the Director of Public Institution (H.E), Orissa for information with reference to his memo No. 443 dated 15.2.74.

Sd/-

Asst. Secretary to Govt.

Memo No. 26020 (2) EYS dt. 28-7-77.

Copy endorsed to codes Section / Guard File No. IVE / A. 387/76 for record.

Sd/-

Asst. Secretary to Govt.

Copy of letter NO. F-27 -12/86 - 1.4, dated the 1st Oct'86 from S.K. Sengupta, under Secretary to the Govt. of India, Ministry of Human Resource development (Deptt. of Education) New Delhi, addressed to the

Chief Secretaries, All the State Government and others.

Sub :- Nominations for Intern ships in Library Science.

I am directed to say that the United States Educational Foundation in India, New Delhi has invited nominations for the necessary information about the terms and conditions of this programme is enclosed.

Nominations of suitable officers having experience in the specific area may please be sent to this Ministry in the prescribed application form (copy enclosed) in duplicate latest by 10th November, 1986.

Nominations of Officers whose cadre controlling Authority is the Department of personnel & Administrative Reforms, New Delhi should be sent to that Department latest by 5th November, 1986, in the first instance for obtaining their clearance and other nominations not falling within the obtaining the approval at the appropriate level. Nominations received after the last date will not be considered in any case. Nominations of academicians working in the universities colleges and schools may be sent direct to the United States Educational Foundation in India, Fulbright House, 12-Hailey Road, New Delhi- 110 001, with the prior permission of their Heads of the Institution.

It is for the sponsoring authorities to seek clearance of the concerned Cadrex controlling Authorities in respect of the nominations sponsored by them.

Advanced copies of applications will no be entertained. Hindi version is attached.

DIRECTORATE OF HIGHER EDUCATION : : ORISSA : BHUBANESWAR.

Memo No. 4A. 80.86-C1 //47917 //Date 12/11/86

Copy along with the enclosures forwarded to the Principals of all Govt. Colleges for information. They are requested to send their recommendation, if any in time.

LB 51186 Dy. Director (General) Orissa.

THE UNITED STATES EDUCATION FOUNDATION IN INDIA

"Fulbright House", 12 Hailey Road,

New Delhi- 110001.

INTERNSHIP IN LIBRARY SCIENCE / LIBRARY MANAGEMENT.

Applications for three internships in Library Science. Awarded under the Fulbright - Hays Act of the U.S. Congress providing maintenance in the U.S. and round-trip travel, will be received till November 15, 1986. The internships are for 5 months and are offered will have an opportunity to observe and learn the use of modern technology in an American library. This is not a degree program but it may be possible for an intern to audit a course in Library Science. The emphasis of this program is on PERIOD : One Semester.

ELIGIBILITY EQUIREMENTS:

1. Must have a degree or post-graduate diploma in Library Science.
2. Must be permanently employed and be eligible for leave.
3. Mist be below 45 years of age.
4. Must be an Assistant Librarian (or equivalent in rank) at an educational research institution or Public Library, which has a holding of at least 20,000 volumes.
5. Must not have visited the U.S. for study purposes during the last four years.

6. Be an Indian citizen and be present in India at the time of application.
7. Be in good health.
8. Have a good command of English language and be prepared to take TOEEL test (test of English as a Foreign Language)

Foundation does not encourage scholars who have been to the U.S. for study or for training in Library Science to apply for these internships.

GENERAL INFORMATION

Application forms will be sent to those who write to the Foundation stating their age, designation and enclosing a stamp (one rupees) and self addressed envelope of the size 23 CM. S x 10 cms. (Approx). applications will be available from any of the USEFI offices (addresses given below) after Sept. '15' 1986.

1. U.S. EDUCATIONAL FOUNDATION IN INDIA.

   Fulbright House

   12 HaileyRoad

   New Delhi 110001.

   (Head Quarters)

for states ofjammu & Kashmir, Himachal Pradesh, Punchab, daryana, Uttar Pradesh, Rajasthan and all Union Territories in North India.

2. U.S. EDUCATIONAL FOUNDATION IN INDIA.

   Regional Office

   "Sundeep"

   4 Now Marine Lines

   Bombay 400 020.

   For states of Gujarat, Maharastra, Madhya Pradesh.

and all Union Territories in West India.

3. U.S. EDUCATIONAL FOUNDATION IN INDIA.

Regional Office

8 short Street

Calcutta 700 017.

For States of Assam, Tripura, Meghalaya, Manipur, Nagaland, West Bengal, Sikkim, Bihar, Orissa and all union. Territories in East India.

4. U.S. EDUCATIONAL FOUNDATION IN INDIA.

Regional Office

Americal consulte Building

Mount Road

Madras 600 006.

For States of Andhra Pradesh, Karnataka, Tamilnadu, Kerala and all union Territories in South India.

Applications must be submitted in duplicate, complete in all respects through appropriate administrative authority Educational Foundation in India at 12 Hailey Road, New Delhi 110001. Application must indicate how service of the application will be utilized on return and whether leave with pay will be granted.

In the case of central or State Government officials both copies of applications should be sent through proper channel to the under Secretary (U.4) Department of Education, Ministry of Human Resource Development, Govt. of India, Shastri Bhawan, New Delhi -110001.

Candidates will be called for interview at Delhi some time in December, 1986. Decision Communicated to the candidate on behalf of the selection committee will be final.

THE UNITED STATES EDUCTIONAL FOUNDATION IN INDIA

"Fulbright House" 12 Holiday Road, Now Dehli -110001.

APPLICATIONN FOR INTERNSHIP IN LIBRARY MANAGEMENT.

IMPORTANT : These applications must be capable of being reproduced by a photographic process, Therefore answer must be typewritten with fresh black ribbon or hand write in block letters in black ink and must be limited to space provided.

NAME : Mr. /Mrs. /Miss. ....

Dateof Birth: ....Place of Birth................

EDUCATION : List educational institutions attended.

Degree	Name of University Rank	Subject	Duration Of study.	Class	%Mark

Present Position and brief outline of responsibilities:

Occupational Experience :

Designation.	Name & Address of the Employer	Nature of Duties	Period From to

Please Describe work of an innovative / experimental nature which you have tried to introduce in your library.

Name.........................

Professional societies of which you are a member.

Describe the program you with to pursue in the U.S. on this internship and how you propose to utilise your experience in the U.S. on return.

Dose your library have any special collection books? If yes, please describe.

Publications if any.

Brief statement about your-self, Name.......

Forwarding comments by Librarians / Head (Please comment on candidate is work and how the internship experience will be useful)

Signature......................

Name..........................

....

Designation.......................

....

Forwarding Comments : By Registrar/Director/ Administrative Head.

Please state whether salary will be paid to the candidate if he is selected.

Official Seal Signature Designation.

Marital Status : Single :

Number of Children, if any, and their ages :

Address to which correspondence is to be sent:

Name and Address with relationship of person to be contacted in India in case of emergency :

Extra- curricular activities (list):

List Scholarships or Fellowships or other distinctions :

Have you appeared earlier before USEFI's Selection Committee ? When ?

Have you taken TOEEL ? Are you prepared to take test now ?

Have you travelled abroad ? Mention places, purpose, duration of stay and years :

Have you in your possession (1) the original mark-sheets and (ii) Certificates / degree is used by the University Institution for the examinations you have taken ? Please list the copies attached with this application. Your application will not be considered unless copies of (1) the mark sheets of all examinations taken and (ii) degree/ diplomas received are attached.

Date : ....**Signature of the Applicant**

Directorate of Higher Education :

Orissa, Bhubaneswar.

No.2G-29-86.C2 45546 / Dated. 18-10-86.

To,

The Principals of

All Government and non-Government

Colleges in the State.

Subject:- Return of Library Books by the Borrowers.

Sir,

It has been brought to the notice of the undersigned that a large number of Library Books of the Colleges are lost due to non-return of Library Books by the Borrowers from the Library of the Institutions. As a result it not only transfer the Teaching of the Institution but also causes great loss of the Public property. In order to overcome such difficulties. The following principles should be adopted by the Principals for realising the Books from the Borrower's of their Colleges.

1. In case of loss of the Books three times the cost of the Books which are out of print and out of market or the present price for the books which are available in the market should be realised. It must be insisted that Books be replaced as far as practicals.
2. In case of transfer of the Employees or students the documents like L.P.C. T.C. Mark sheets should not be issued unless a clearance certificate is received from the Librarian.
3. In case of retirement, no financial benefits like sanction of G.P.F. of Final-with-drawals, Pension, Papers should be held up unless the clearance certificate is received from the Librarian.

Yours faithfully,

Deputy Director (General): Orissa

Copy of the letter No. F. 1-96 / 81 (CPP- !), dated 5th May, 1987, from C.M. Ramachandran, Deputy Secretary, University Grants Commission, Bahadur Shah Zafar Marg, New Delhi, addressed to the Registrar, Sambalpur University, Jyoti Vihar, Burla.

Sub :- Upgradation in salary scale of Librarians in colleges.

I am directed to say that the Government of India, Ministry of Human Resource Development (Department of Education) and the University Grants Commission have been receiving representations from College Librarians and their Organisations for a relaxation in the following qualifications prescribed for placing the existing Librarians in the pay scale of Rs. 700-1600/-

"First or second class BA/B.Sc./B. Corn degree plus a first or second M. Lib. Sc. Degree.

or

First or Second Class MA/M.Sc. / M. Corn. degree and a first or second class B. Lib. Sc. Or a diploma in Library Science".

These representations have been considered by the Govt. of India, Department of Education, Ministry of Human Resource Development in consultation with the University Grants Commission and on the recommendation of the University Grants Commission, it has now been decided by the Government of India that the existing incumbents of the posts on or before 31.12.72 may be sanctioned the upgraded scale of Rs. 700.1600 in relaxation of the prescribed qualifications as referred to above without insisting on a first or second class in the degree, diploma or other prescribed educational qualifications.

The above relaxation is however subject to the condition that the college concerned is satisfied that the experience and quality of work of the college Librarians justify their being placed in the upgraded salary scale of Rs. 700-1600.

In case of persons appointed on posts created after 31.12.1972, the prescribed qualifications would apply without any modifications.

The relaxation indicated above would have retrospective effect from 1st April, 1980.

A copy of the circular letter No. F. 2-3/84- U.I dated 16th January, 1987 issued to the Education Secretaries of the State Governments by the Government of India in this regard is enclosed.

The above decision may please be communicated to the colleges affiliated to your university which are receiving assistance from the Commission.

Sd/-

(C.M. RAMAC HAND RAN)

(DEPUTY SECRETARY)

****

SAMBALPUR UNIVERSITY

JYOTI VIHAR : BURLA

13880

Memo No. ..../Dev. Dated . : 3/7/87

Copy along with the copy of the enclosure forwarded to the Principals of all the affiliated colleges / Section Officer, Establishment I Section / Section Officer Estt. II, Section for information and necessary action.

DEVELOPMENT OFFICER

COPY OF LETTER NO . 2-3 / 84 -U.1 dated 16th January , 1987 received from Shri C.R. PILLAI, Deputy Secretary to the Government of India , Ministry of Human Resource Development (Department of Education) referred to the Education Secretary , copy endorsed to the secretary , University Grants commission , with reference to his letter NO. 3-1 / 85 (L) dated 23rd September, 1986 regarding up gradation in salary scale of Librarians Directors / Instructors of

Physical Education and Documentation officers in universities and colleges .

I am directed to refer to this Ministry 's letter No. 2-1 /82 U.1 dated 15.12 ,82 on the subject noted above and to say that this Deptt , ahs been receiving representations from college librarians and their organisations for a relaxation in the qualifications proscribed in Annexure I to that letter which prescribed the qualifications for placing the existing Librarians in the pay scale of Rs . 700 -1600 . These presentations have considered in consultation with the University Grants Commission . It has now been decided on the recommendations of the UGC, that the existing incumbents of the posts of librarians in colleges who have been appointed to these posts on or before 31. 12 . 72 may be sanctioned the upgraded scale of Rs . 700 -1600 in relaxation of the qualification prescribed in Annexure I referred to above without insisting on a first or second class in the degree , diploma or other prescribed educational qualification.

This relaxation is however subject to the condition that the university /college concerned is satisfied that their experience and quality of work justify their being placed in the upgraded salary scales.

In case of persons appointed on posts created after 31 . 12. 72 the prescribed qualifications would apply without any modifications.

The decision in para 2 would have retrospective effect from 1 April, 1980.

Yours faithfully ,

SD/-

(C.R. PILLAI)

DEPUTY SECRETARY TO THE

GOVT. OF INDIA

Government of Orissa Home Department

RESOLUTION

No.542/ Bhubaneswar, the 3.1.98.

Sub : Fixation of criteria for promotion
To the rank of librarian /appointment
To the post of Asst. Librarian in the
Orissa Secretariat Library.

The question of fixation of criteria for promotion to the rank of librarian and appointment to the post of Asst. librarian in the secretariat library will be as follows pending finalisation of the cadre rule regulating recruitment and condition of service of the staff of Orissa Secretariat:

LIBRARIAN

1 The post librarian in the scale of pay of Rs.1640-2900/- as per Orissa Revised pay scale Rules. 1989 and O.R.S. (Amendment) Rule, 1990 will be filled up by way of promotion from the rank of Asst. librarian .

2 In order to be a eligible for the post of librarian the officer must have rendered continuous service at least for a period of 5 (five) years as on Asst. Librarian in the scale of pay of Rs.1400-40-1800-EB -50 -2300/ - in the secretariat library.

3 There shall be a departmental promotion committee /selection Board headed by the Addl. Secretary of the Debarment and joint secretary/ Debuts Secretary in charge of office establishment and secretariat library and under Secretary in charge of O.E. as members to consider the promotion to the post of librarian.

ASSISTANT LIBRARIAN

1 THE POST OF Asst. Librarian in the scale of pay of Rs. 1400 -40 -1800 -3B -50 -2300 /- shall be filled up by direct recruitment.

2 A. In order to be eligible for the post of Asst. librarian, the candidate must be a graduate with degree in library and information science.

   B. In service candidate having graduate without diploma in library science having experience in Secretariat Library are eligible to apply.

3. The age limit is between 18 to 32 years. The upper age limit is relaxable in case of the in service candidate, SC/ST and other candidates socially and Educationally Backward Classes, Physically Handicapped. Ex-Service man, sports men as prescribed by Government from time to time.

4. The Criteria fixed under Orissa Civil Services (criteria for promotion) Rules, 1992 and the Orissa Civil application in these cases.

5. This order shall be come into force from the date of issue.

6. This has been concurred in by G.A. department in their U.O.R. No. 776/GA Dt. 25.9.97.

ORDER

Ordered that the resolution be published in the extra ordinary issue of Orissa Gazettee and copies there of be forwarded to all Departments of Government / All Heads of Departments / A.G. (A&E) Orissa, Bhubaneswar.

By order of the Governor

S. C. Hota

Principal Secretary to Government.

OFFICE OF THE DIRECTOR OF HIGHER EDUCATION ORISSA, BHUBANESWAR :

Memo No. : M-2, XV-98 6041 // Dt. 4.2.98

Copy forwarded to all subordinate Officers / All Officers / All section officers / P.S. to D.H.E. Orissa for information and necessary action.

Establishment Officer (HE), Orissa

CHAPTER - V

(SPECIMEN OF FORMS AND CORRESPONDENCE)

5:1 Specimen of a Book Selection card.
5:2 Specimen of a Book Selection list.
5:3 Specimen of a Quotation letter.
5:4 Specimen of an allocation Register.
5:5 Specimen of an order letter.
5:6 Specimen of Discrepancies in supply form.
5:7 Specimen of an Accession Register.
5:8 Specimen of an Accession Stamp.
5:9 Specimen of Spine Label.
- 5:9.1 Specimen of Owner slip.
- 5:9.2 Specimen of Ownership Stamp.

5:10 Specimen of Date slip
5:11 Specimen of Book Card
5:12 Specimen of Book Card.
5:13 Specimen of Location Marks.
5:14 Specimen of Binding Register / Card.
5:15 Specimen of Accession Register.
5:16 Specimen of Stock Taking Register
5:17 Specimen of Stock Taking sheets
5:18 Specimen of shelf list
5:19 Specimen of stock taking
5:20 Specimen of letter Bills for payment

5:21 Specimen of contingent Bill

5:22 Specimen of Application for a remittance in foreign currency

5:23 Periodical order work

5:24 Periodical register

5:25 periodicals register

5:26 Specimen of ledger for periodicals

5:27 Specimen of card system

5:28 Specimen of verso at the law

5:29 Specimen of register law

5:29:1 Specimen of check law

5:30 Specimen of classified index

5:31 Specimen of bottom law

5:32 Specimen of the bottom law

5:33 Specimen of the top card

5:34 Specimen of routing slip

5:35 Specimen of group routing slip

5:36 Specimen of membership register

5:37 Specimen of Reservation Slip

5:38 Specimen Letter for procurement of books on interlibrary loan basis

5:39 Specimen Letter intimating the borrower for demand book

5:40 Specimen Letter for inter library loan

5:41 Maintenance of record

5:42 Specimen Letter for clear Library dues

5:43 Specimen Letter for recovery of dues report

5:44 Specimen Letter for report of dues recovery

5:45 Specimen Letter for Loss of Library pass book-cum-identity

5:46 Specimen application for loss of books.
5:47 Specimen Letter for loss of token
5:48 Specimen Letter for withdrawal of lockers
5:49 Specimen Letter to curb library malpractice
5:50 Specimen application for consultation facilities
5:51 Specimen consultation slip
5:52 Specimen an clearance application form
5:53 Specimen an clearance certificate
5:54 Specimen N.D.C.
5:55 Specimen Ledger system
5:56 Specimen day book register
5:57 Specimen ledger system
5:58 Specimen date slip
5:59 Specimen book pocket
5:60 Specimen book send
5:61 Specimen borrower's ticket
5:62 Specimen Date slip
5:63 Specimen book pocket (inner back side)
5:64 Specimen book card containing essential information
5:65 Specimen borrower's card/identity card
5:66 Specimen membership-cum-identity card.
5:67 Borrower's card with metal plate
5:68 Specimen records of books
5:69 Specimen of an allocation register
5:70 Specimen of a Bill register
5:71 Specimen of visitors register
5:72 Specimen of annual report
5:73 Specimen of the statistical table on classification
5:74 Specimen on cataloguing.

5:75 Specimen of accession statistics
5:76 Specimen on statistics of periodically
5:77 Specimen of statistical table
5:78 Specimen of visitors register
5:79 Specimen of daily attendance statistics
5:80 Specimen of issue statistics
5:81 Specimen of issue statistics Language wise
5:82 Specimen of issue statistics registration
5:83 Specimen of classified issue statistics
5:84 Specimen of statistics of books consulted
5:85 Specimen of reference queries
5:86 Specimen of statistics of Income and expenditure
5:87 Specimen of staff statistics
5:88 Specimen of classing issue statistics
5:89 Specimen of issue statistics material-wise.

5:1 SPECIMEN OF A BOOK SELECTION CARD

(RECTO)

Call No. Acc. No.

Author

Title

Edition Publisher Year

Published price No. of copies required

Signature of the recommending authority

Librarians orders

(Verso)

Supplier

Cost in foreign currency (if any) in Indian currency

Checking

date Order No. dated

Receipt date

Bill No. date

Passed for amount amount

vounder No.

& date77

5:2 SPECIMEN OF A BOOK SELECTION LIST

Sl. No.	Author	Title	Edition	Publisher	Price

5:3 SPECIMEN OF A QUOTATION LETTER

Name of the Library

To

____

____

Dear Sir,

Please let this Library know by ___________, the rates at which you can supply books to this library. Kindly specify the rates as stated below.

a. Foreign Books — Conversion rates

1. Pound
2. Dollar
3. Other foreign currencies

b. Indian books

1. English — Discount
2. Hindi — Discount
3. Sanskrit — Discount
4. Other languages — Discount

c) Postage and other freight charges

Yours faithfully,

Officer in Charge Library

5:4 SPECIMEN OF AN ALLOCATION REGISTER

Subject y/Department amount allocated

For year

Sl. No.	Date	Voucher No.	Amo-unt	Total	Balance available	Remarks

5:5 SPECIMEN OF AN ORDER LETTER

Name of the Library...

No....................   Dated...........200.....

To

M/s ....

....

....

Dear Sir,

Please refer to your letter No...........dated............ regarding supply of books.

Please supply of books Please supply the following book/books given in the list enclosed to this library within a fortnight/month of the above-mentioned date, on the following conditions. Please note that if any discrepancy is found in supply, you will be responsible for it and you will have to bear the cost of returning the books:

1. Only one copy of each book is to be supplied, except mentioned otherwise.
2. Books of the latest edition are to be supplied, except mentioned other wise.
3. The prices charged must be printed / quoted, as the case may be.
4. The price should be indicated in the original currency. These should be converted in accordance with the approved conversion rates of this library/ quoted by you which-ever have been agreed to.
5. The supply must be made through Railway Parcel and the freight must be pre-paid.
6. If supply is made by post, the books should be sent per registered post. V.P.P. will not be accepted.
7. The books supplied must be physically in order,

otherwise these will be returned to you at your own cost.

8. Other conditions, if any.

Kindly acknowledge the receipt of this letter.

Yours faithfully

Librarian

(A copy of this order is sent to the Head of the Department or the person who recommended the books for purchase. This is done for informing him that the books mentioned therein have been ordered for purchase. The specimen of the endorsement which is added to the second and third copies of the order form is given below.)

No...................... Dated..........200....

Copy to the Head of the..........Department...........
....(or the person who recommended the books in question) for information and record.

Yours faithfully,

Librarian

5:6 SPECIMEN OF DISCREPANCIES IN SUPPLY FORM

Name of the Library..

No............................Dated....................19............

To

M/s ....
....
....

Dear Sir,

Please refer to your Bill No.......... Dated...........for

Rs............. for supplied books to this library in response to this office book order No........................ dated......................... Please note that the following discrepancies in supply have been detected. Kindly supply necessary information by return mail so that your bill can be passed. In the meantime, please note that the bill : has been passed for Rs................ Instead of Rs...................... The rest of the amount of the bill will be passed ofter requisite information along with a fresh bill for the items in question is received from you:-

1. Title of the book is different from the ordered one.
2. Authors of the book are different from those ordered for.
3. The binding of the book is defective.
4. The paging of the book is defective.
5. The book is shop soiled.
6. Short supply has been made i.e. the following books are missing from the bundle:

   i)

   ii)
7. The prices charged for the following books are more than the published ones. Please supply a documentary proof and send a bill in respect of these items.

   i) ii) iii)
8. The edition of the following books is not the latest.

   i) ii) iii)
9. The following books are not of library edition as was ordered otherwise,

   i) ii) iii)

10. Any other defects.

Please acknowledge the receipt of this letter.

Your faithfully,

Librarian

Encls

5:7 SPECIMEN OF AN ACCESSION REGISTER

Date	
ACC. No.	
Author	
Title	
Edition	
Place and publisher	
Vol. No.	
Binding and size	
Name and address of supplier	
Price	
Vr. No. and date of payment	
Call No.	
Withdrawal date	

Note : The assistant responsible for accessioning arranges the books in same order in which the books are listed in the bill and goes on entering in the Accession Register consecutively. He allots the accession Number to the books in a consecutive order. The assistant puts the relevant accession Number on the verso of the title page of the books and on a secret page decided by each individual library. The Accession Number is books in a consecutive order. The Assistant puts the relevant Accession Number on the verso of the title page of the books and on a secret page decided by each individual library. The Accession Number is put on the bill against the concerned item. Some libraries have the practice of tracing i.e. noting down the source of supply and the price of the book on the next page following the contents pages i.e. the first page of introduction, foreword, contents etc. In other libraries, a special kind of stamp is put on the verso of the title page and the relevant information is given therein. The specimen in given below.

5:8 SPECIMEN OF AN ACCESSION STAMP

Name of the Library ....

Accession Number..

Date of Receipt ....

Supplier ....

Price ....

Accession Assistant's Initials ....

5:9 LABEL PASTING

After the preparation of all the catalogue cards, the books are handed over to semi-professionals or unskilled workers who pasted the labels in the books. The following labels are generally pasted in the books:-

1. Spine Label: Gummed white cloth is cut into round or square pieces of about 1.25" each. This label is pasted or square pieces of about 1.25" each. This label is pasted one inch above the bottom of the spine of the book. This is done so that the Call Number may be properly visible to the readers when the book is shelved in a book rack. Symmetrical arrangement can also be ensured. It the width of the book is much less and the spine label cannot be pasted on the spine, it should be pasted at the same level on the front card board. The specimen is given below :-

Class No. Book No.	Spine Label.	Class No. Book No.

5:9:1

2. Ownership Slip Mark , (a) One ownership Slip is generally pasted on the inner side of the front card board at left hand top most corner. The size of this slip may be about 3" x 2.5". The slip may be made of glazed paper. The specimen of the slip is given below :-

Ownership Slip

Name of the Library:
Class No. :-
Book No. :
Acc. No. :

5:9:2

b) Other Ownership marks are put at various places of the book by rubber stamps or embossing machines. A stamp, which contains the name of the library is put on the title page and another on the secret page, to be decided by each library. Third stamp may be put at the end of the book.

Its specimen is given as under:

OWNERSHIP STAMP

Name of the library

Location Place

3. **Date Slip :** One date slip is pasted on the top most portion of the front or back fly-leaf of each book. But for Reference Books, manuscripts and other books which are not to be issued, this slip is not pasted, otherwise this would be a sheer wastage of time, energy and stationery. The size of the said slip may be 5" x 3". It specimen is given below :

5:10DATE SLIP

<table>
<tr><th>Call No.</th><th colspan="2">Name of the Library</th><th>Acc. No</th></tr>
<tr><td colspan="4"></td></tr>
<tr><td></td><td></td><td></td><td></td></tr>
</table>

4. **Book Pocket :** On the bottom of the inner right of the front or back card-board cover, a book pocket of 5" x 3" size is pasted. It specimen is given below:

BOOK POCKET

Open flap
Name of the Library
Brief Library Rules

For reference and other non-issuable books, this pocket is not pasted.

5. **Book Card :** One printed book card of 5" x 3" size is put in the book pocket of each book. But in case of reference and other non-issuable books, this card in not slipped in the book pocket. The specimen of this card is given below.

5:11BOOK CARD

<table>
<tr><td colspan="4">Call No. Acc. No.
Name of the Library
Author.......................................
Title ....</td></tr>
<tr><td colspan="4">This book was issued is due on the date last stamped or marked</td></tr>
<tr><td></td><td></td><td></td><td></td></tr>
</table>

The size and shape of the book card may be reduced and changed in form in case Browne Charging System is to be followed.

Because in that system, no issue or return dates are marked on the Book Card. Its specimen is given below :

5:12 BOOK CARD

Call ....
Acc. No. ....
Authers. ....
Title ....

5:13 LABEL WRITING AND ASSIGNING LOCATION MARKS

The pasted labels are written in ink. Superior type of ink and nibs are used for this purpose. Junior staff members are deputed for his repetitive job. But this job is a very important one because if the labels are not accurately written, the book is likely to be misplaced. So the employees who are entrusted with this job should have a good handwriting and should be accurate enough. The spine labels contain the Call

Number and the location mark of the book. These are written on the left-hand upper portion of the label. Such marks may be either Reference, Rare, Text Book, Reports etc. these words are abbreviated and followed consistently. Their specimens are given below:

Rare			R			R		P
	025			025			025	
W	563	P	W	563	P	W	563	P

For a rare Book   *For a Reference Book*   *For a Report used as a reference Book*

5:14SPECIMEN OF A BINDING REGISTER/CARD

Name of the Library and Place ____________________

Sl. No.	Date of Desp-atch	Call No.	Author	Title	Kind of Bind-ing	Date of Rece-ipt	Cost of Bin-ding Rs. P.	Pay-ment vou-cher No. & Date

5:15 ACCESSION REGISTER

Acc. No.	Author	Title	Publisher	Source of Supply	Ed.	Price Rs.	Call No.	Remarks

5:16 STOCK TAKING REGISTER

Acc. No.	1999	2000	2001	2002	2003	2004	Remarks

5:17SPECIMEN STOCK-TAKING SHEETS.

1.	11.	21.	31.
2.	12.	22.	32.
3.	13.	23.	33.
4.	14.	24.	34.
5.	15.	25.	35.
6.	16.	26.	36.
7.	17.	27.	37.
8.	18.	28.	38.
9.	19.	29.	39.
10.	20.	30.	40.

5:18SHELF LIST

025.7 C666B	**Cockerell, Douglas**
5728	Book-binding and the care of books; with drawings by Noèl Rooke. 4th ed. London, Isaac Pitman 1948 332 P. 17 cm. X 22 cm. Illus. (The Artistic crafts series of technical hanc Jbooks, edited by W.R. Lethaby) 1999 2000 2001 2002 2003 2004 2005 2006

5:19 STOCK TAKING

0257.7 C666B	Cockerell, Douglas
5728	Book binding and the care of book; with drawings by Noel Rooke. 4th ed. London, Isaac Pitman, 1948. 332 P. 17 cm. X 22 cm. Illus. (The Artistic crafts series of technical handbooks, edited by W.R. Lethaby)

5:20

To

The

....

....

....

Sub : Bills for payment.

Sir,

Please find enclosed herewith the under mentioned contingency bill [Our Bill Register Nos...........to............. duly verified for payment in favour of M/s ....Kindly make it convenient to arrange payment at the earliest.

Bill NO	Dated	Amount

Yours faithfully,

Librarian

Encl; As above

No /Pay./2004.........................Dated..................

1. Copy t communicated to the M/s..................

for information

Librarian.

5:21 CONTINGENT BILL

Bill Register No.................

Details of the Bill for Contingent Charges of ....
.... Department for the month of 200

Head of Charge	Serial No. of Sub-Voucher	Desciption of charge and authority for special sanctions, if any.	No. of Voucher Amount	
			Rs.	P.
		in favour of Cried over		

		Brought Forward	Rs P
		Budget Head .... Budqet .... Allotment .... Expenditure sought in the Present Case .... Progressive Total of Expenditure .... Balance .... Total Rs. (in words) Received contents (i.e., amount contained)	

(1) Also certified that the expenditure charged in this bill could not with due regard to interests of the University / Institute be avoided.

(2) I have satisfied myself that the charges supported by vouchers entered in this bill have been really

paid with the exceptions note below, which exceed the balance of the permanent advance and will be paid on receipt of the money drawn in this bill.

Dated.................... Librarian,

OFFICE PAY ORDER Name of the

University / Institution

Budget provision exists - Yes/No

Pay Rs ....

Examined ....

Assistant (Accounts) ....

Entered in the Budget Register ....

Dated ....

Cheque No.................. Dated............. Finance Officer

5:22

FORM A

APPLICATION FOR A REMITTANCE IN FOREIGN CURRENCY

I/We wish to purchase ....

....

Through ....

For payment to

For the purpose specified below :

I/We declare that the statements made by me/ us on this form are true, and that I/We have not applied for an authorisation through any other Bank.

Name of applicant(s) ....

Nationality ....

Address ....

....

....

Date............. Signature of aaplicant(s) ....

A. IN PAYMENT OF GOODS IMPORTED INTO THE REPUBLIC OF INDIA (The declaration on the reverse should also be completed).							
Invoice Value (State Currency	Quantity	Description of goods	Country of origin of goods	Country whence goods are consigned	Name of carrying steamer (if known)	Full NO. with prefixes and suffixes and date of the import Licence after this remittance	Balance outstanding on the Licence after this remittance

(The Declaration on the reverse should be signed by the traveller where necessary).

B. FOR TRAVELLER PURPOSES

I We desire to travel to....................via ....

for the purpose of ....

Passage has been booked through ....

Form in which

Exchange is Notes and Coin .... Tr. Chqs........

Dft.....................I/C required.

C. ANY OTHER PURPOSE FOR WHICH FOREIGN EXCHANGE IS REQUIRED

*Reason for payment..

Signature of Applicant(s)

Documentary evidence of the reason for payment must be attached to the form for submission to the Reserve Bank of India. In case, remittance is made under a permit issued by the Reserve Bank of India, the number and date of the permit and the purpose for which the remittance is being made must be stated.

**For use of the Reserve Bank of India.

Declaration to be signed by the applicant if the remittance is in payment of imports.

I/We declare that the goods to which this application related were imported into Republic of India on about .... or will be imported into the Republic of India and that

*(i) The goods fall under item.................................
Part.................... Schedule.......................of open Central Licence No...

(ii) and Exchange Control copy of import Licence has been obtained ;

(iii) The import is on behalf of (Central / State Government Department or a Company owned by Central / State Government Statutory Corporation etc. should be stated).

I/we attach or hereby undertake to produce to the Reserve Bank of India within three months the relative certificate / copy of the Custom Entry form or in the case of goods received by parcel post, the relative post parcel receipt or parcel wrappers.

Signature of applicant (s)

CERTIFICATE BY AUTHORISED DEALER

We hereby certify that :-

a) We have seen satisfactory documentary evidence in support of this application as stated below, viz.

b) In respect of the goods mentioned in section A overleaf the relative Bill of Exchange and / or Shipping Documents have been received by us and paid by consignee of draw.

c) This payment is : (strike out clause not applicable)

   i) in retirement of bills under Letter of Credit,

   ii) against delivery of shipping documents.

   iii) on advance remittance.

   iv) against goods imported on a consignment basis.

d) any other comments by authorised dealer.

Stamp and Signature of Authorised Dealer

Date........................ through whom the application is made.

SPACE FOR USE BY THE RESERVE BANK OF India

Note :- Where the application is for an estimated or approximate amount' (e.g. an importer not knowing the exact amount until he receives invoice or shipping documents, etc.) the authorised dealer whose stamp appears on this application is responsible for seeking that the excess amount applied for is cancelled and is not used for any other purpose.

Strike out item not applicable

Strike out if not applicable.

Name of the University / Institute

To,

....

....

....

Dear Sir,

A Draft No ....

dated ....for ....

....

....

is sent herewith against your Bill No ....

.... (Copy enclosed)

towards renewals subscription of the Journals entitled"

....

....

....

....

....

....

Vol............................Sub. No ....

for the period .... in favour of

....

....

.................................payable at ....

....

issued by (Name of the Bank) ....

....

Kindly acknowledge its receipt and send your next invoice for the year ....The delay is regretted but we expect full co-operation from you for getting the supply expedited on the aforementioned subscription, changes if any, in subscription period or volume no. may kindly be intimated.

The following issues are still missing which may kindly be supplied at the earliest.

Sr. No.	Title	Vol. No.	Period	Agent.

An early reply is highly appreciated. If missing issues cannot be supplied, please extend the subscription period accordingly or refund the proportionate amount and confirm.

Yours faithfully,

Librarian.

End.:-As above.

Draft .... for ....

No .... Dated..........................

Copy to the Finance Officer, with the information that the Draft No..
Dated............................... has been transmitted to the publisher concerned as detailed above.

Librarian

5:23 PERIODICAL ORDER WORK

The periodicals order work involves the following

1. New periodicals ordering.
2. Renewals ordering.
3. Backsets of periodicals ordering.

As regards new periodicals it is better to procure few sample copies before placing regular orders because only worthwhile journey should be subscribed to.

In case of discrepancy of subscription rates or evidence conversion rate letter is written to the vendor for supplying a documentry evidence which may either be the original announcement of the concerned publisher or his original invoice issued in the name of the vendor concerned. At the time of passing bills, certain records are kept so that duplicate payment may be avoided and proper account may be made possible and punctual supply of the ordered management may be ensured. A periodicals record should invariably provide following information.-

1. Number and names of the periodicals received in library.
2. Number and names of periodicals subscribed to.
3. Number and names of periodicals received gratis.
4. Amount of subscription of each periodical.
5. Total amount of subscription paid for one year.
6. Check record in order to gauge as to whether the subscribed magazines are received punctually, regularly and good condition.
7. Of how many periodicals the backsets were available were procured during a particular period.
8. Name and address of the publishers of periodicals.

Name of the Library ....

(Place)............................. Date.......................

To,

....

....

....

Dear Sir,

Kindly supply the following magazines to the library in addition to the ones already subscribed. The supply should begin with effect from the first issue of vol. ...., year......................... Please ensure that each issue is supplied regularly and punctually. Please also supply the title page, contents and index as soon as these are published so that complete volumes get bound in time.

This order may be considered as a standing order unless countermanded or revised.

Please note that if any issue is not received by this library, it will be intimated to you within a reasonable time i.e. within three months of the due date of receipt, and you will please make arrangements to supply the same without any extra payment.

As regards payment of subscription, an annual bill system will followed. Please arrange to send the bill in triplicate for the current volumes ordered as above.

Kindly acknowledge the receipt of this letter.

1. ....
2. ....
3. ....
4. ....
5. ....
6. ....

Yours truly,

Librarian.

5:24 PERIODICAL REGISTER

NAME OF THE LIBRARY:

FOR THE YEAR :

Sl. No.	Title	Vol. and year	Publisher	Supplier	Period Jan./Feb./Dec.	Subscription Bill No. & Date	Remarks
1.	India Today						
2.	National Geography						
3.	Women's Era						
4.	Career Digest						
5.	Reader Digest						
6.	Jhankara						
7.	Sucharita						
8.	Caravan						
9.	Kalyan						
10.	Gruhasabha.						

5:25 PERIODICALS REGISTER

(For dailies and weeklies)

Name of the Library................Place...................

Title ....

Publisher..

Supplier ....

Vol. and year ....

Subscription, Bill No. and Date...........................

Sl. No.	Month	Days						Remarks
		1	2	3	4	5	31	
	Jan.							
	Feb.							
	Mar.							
	Apr.							
	May.							
	June.							
	July							
	Aug.							
	Sept.							
	Oct.							
	Nov.							
	Dec.							

5:26LEDGER FOR PERIODICALS

Name of the Library________________________

Title.........................Frequency of Publication ...

Publisher.................... Supplier.........................

Subscription Amount ....

Year and Vol.	Jan.	Feb.	Mar.	Apr.	May	June	July	Aug.	Sept.	Oct.	Nov.	Dec.	Bill No. & Date	Remarks
1998 v. 15														
1999 v. 16														
2000 v. 17														
2001 v. 18														
2002 v. 19														
2003 v. 20														
2004 v. 21														

5:27 CARD SYSTEM

(SIZE 6" X 4")

Name of the Library.....................Place...............

Title................. Frequency of Publication ....

Publisher.................... Supplier.........................

Vol. and Year	Jan.	Feb.	Mar.	April	May	June	July	Aug.	Sept.	Oct.	Nov.	Dec.
1997 v. 15												
1998 v. 16												
1999 v. 17												
2000 v. 18												
2001 v. 19.												
2002 v. 20.												
2003 v. 21.												
2004 v. 22.												

5:28VERSO OF THE CARD

Title..

Vol. No. and Year	Subscription Amt.	Bili No. and Date	Voucher No. and Date	Reminders Sent	Bound upto...	Remarks
1997 v. 15						
1998 v. 16						
1999 v. 17						
2000 v. 18						
2001 v. 19.						
2002 v. 20.						
2003 v. 21.						
2004 v. 22.						

5:29 THREE CARD SYSTEM OF DR. RANGANATHAN

Dr. S. R. Ranganathan has evolved a new system known as "Three Card system. "Regarding its working in the Madras University Library he states that, "The amount of saving that has resulted from it can be inferred from the fact that although the fact that although the number of periodical publications taken in the library has risen from 240 in 1924 to 1200 in 1934, there has been no increase of staff in the Periodical Publications Section. It still continues single handed. Perhaps, it may be possible to carry on the work without additional staff, until the number reaches about 1000. In the earlier years when the library was using bound volumes for records, there was tight work even though there were only 240 periodical publications current. But the introduction of the "Three Card System" secures the maximum staff."

Three cards of 5" x 3" size known as Register Card, Check Card and Classified Index Card are used in this system. The specimen of each card is given below :-

REGISTER CARD

<table>
<tr><td colspan="4" rowspan="4">Title

Vendor

Cl. No. Period in weeks   Order No. and Date

Grace Weeks</td><td colspan="2">Payment</td></tr>
<tr><td>Vol. or Year</td><td>Voucher No. and Date</td></tr>
<tr><td></td><td></td></tr>
<tr><td>Annual Subscription</td><td></td></tr>
<tr><td>Vol. and No.</td><td>Date of Publication</td><td>Date of receipt</td><td>Vol. and No.</td><td>Date of Publication</td><td>Date of Receipt</td></tr>
<tr><td></td><td></td><td></td><td></td><td></td><td></td></tr>
</table>

5:29:1 CHECK CARD

Heading..................................

Period..................................

Grace Weeks.......................

Vol. of finance	Due week	Week of Rem.	L's initials	Vol. of issue	Due week	Week of Rem.	L's initials	Vol. of issue	Due week	Week of Rem.	L's initials	

5:30 CLASSIFIED INDEX CARD

Cl. No.	Annual Subscription	Per. In weeks.
Title Vendor Publisher Vol. Available Indexes, etc. Supplements, etc.		

Note.: **Function of Three Cards**

The Register Card is meant to record information about the name of the journal subscribed, its publisher, frequency, publication, amount of subscription, vouchers number and date of payment, and the complete data showing the receipt or non-receipt of particular issues of a journal. It also provides information as to when a particular issue was received, whether it was delayed or was received in time, whether any reminders were sent or not, so on and to forth. It enables a reader to know as to whether a particular magazine is subscribed to by a library. Register cards are arranged in an alphabetical manner.111

Which are visible indexed. The unit is motor-driven, with hand operated controls for use in emergencies. It should be noted that the 13'4 sq. ft. figure for floor space includes the operator's chair the price if $ 1.875 and there is a possibility of a 10 percent excise tax. This appears to be the file clerk's utopia.

For smaller and medium-sized libraries this apparatus seems be a costlier one, especially in case of Indian libraries.

5:31 BOTTOM CARD

At the time of ordering journals, one bottom card is prepared for each journal and title and other particulars are typed or written on the lower portion of the said card. This card, in addition to the usual information, contains the following columns :-

1. Library has :-
2. Library lacks :-
3. In Bindery.
4. Nature of Bindings.

All these columns provide very useful information about the journals. The columns Library has and "Library lacks" are very important as a research scholar is enabled to know as to how many and which volumes of a particular journal are in the library. It is also a very quick and handy guide for the persons who are responsible for acquiring complete volumes and/or stray numbers because the 'want list' remains always ready. By consulting this card, particular volumes of any periodicals can be located since the card shows as to whether a particular volume of a periodical is in the bindery or on the shelves. Certain volumes may be ascertained even by knowing the descriptive details of the binding. This card also serves as a check card because date columns are provided opposite the title of the periodical. After setting the card in the punched holes of the card holder, a coloured plastic tab is kept because otherwise typing of the title of the periodical becomes difficult.

The Remington Rand of India takes the responsibility of printing the cards in accordance with the needs of the library. The same of the library is printed on the top of the card. This card is printed on both sides. It can record 20 volumes of the periodical in question.

5:32SPECIMEN OF THE BOTTOM CARD

Name of the Library :-

	Vol.	Jan.	Feb.	March	April	May	June	July	August	Sept.	Oct.	Nov.	Dec.	I.C.I.	Index

Frequency.	Current Vol. expires with	Vols per Year	Department
Name of Binding	In Bindery.	Library has	Library lacks
Title.		Jan. Feb. Mar..............Dec.	

....

Type along the dotted line, then fold back or detach this stub.

TOP CARD

The second card called Top Card' is fitted opposite to Bottom Card i.e., on the verso of the next card holder in such a manner that when any card holder is lifted for finding out certain information both the cards face each other. This card, in fact, serves the purpose of keeping records of payments made to the suppliers of periodicals.

It also provides adequate information regarding the follow-up connected with the receipt of periodicals i.e. issuing of reminders keeping a record of the same.

It also serves as a classified card. It cannot serve all the functions which are performed by a card in the single card system because the single cards are handy and are arranged in a classified sequence whereas the cards in this system cannot be made to serve those functions because these cards which are arranged in an alphabetical order. These cards are also printed on both sides and these contain the requisite information for 20 volumes or years as the cards contain 10 columns on both sides of the card.

5:33 SPECIMAN OF THE TOP CARD

Title. Call No.

Publisher.

Agent	Period covered	Vol. No.	Amount of subscr-iption	Bill No.	Date	Reminder sent for non-receipt of an issue.

Routing Slip Method

The first simple method of circulating periodicals is to issue the periodicals to one member of the staff who is to pass it on to the other turn by turn without the need of returning the periodical to the library each time. One routing slip is to be attached on the title page of cover pate of the periodical. This slip contains detailed instructions as regards the duration for which a particular person has to keep the periodical. This slip contains detailed instructions as regards the duration for which a particular person has to keep the periodical with him and the order or circulation i.e. to whom the periodical is to be circulated next. If the circle is a long one, it seems somewhat difficult to locate it.

The specimen of such a Routing Slip may be as under :-

5:34ROUTING SLIP

Name of the Library ....
Title ....
Date upto which periodical will remain in the Library..........
Period for which each reader will remain in the Library..........
Date of issue.

Name of the Reader	Order of circulation	Date of Return	Remarks
Alphabetical Or Classified order	1 5 3 7 9 10		

5.35 GROUP ROUTING METHOD

Another method of circulation of periodicals which is superior in operation and location to the former is to issue a periodical to groups of readers, preferably belonging to one department or club etc. the periodical is circulated by the members of the group among themselves and on a fixed date it has to be returned to the library, from where it is issued to another group and so on and so forth. This method implies the provision of one Assistant in the Periodicals. Section so that proper record may be kept.

The specimen of "Group Routing Slip" Which is to be pasted on the title page or the back cover page may be as under :-

GROUP ROUTING SLIP

Name of the Library ....

Title ....

Date upto which the periodical must remain in the Library ....

Period for which each group or department can keep the periodical ....

Name of the Reader	Name of the Deptt. or Group	Date of issue	Date of passing on to next Reader	Date of Return to the library	Initials

5:36 MEMBERSHIP REGISTER

Keeping in view the purposes of registration, the registration procedures should be thought out. In other words, the permanent record which can be used easily should be kept. The generally accepted procedures include the filling up of a membership form preferably in 5" x 3" card from which will contain the would-be member's name, permanent and present addresses, occupation and the name and address of the guarantor. A specimen of the membership form is given below:-

RECTO

To

The Librarian,

....

....

Sir,

Kindly enroll me as a member of your library. I give below all my relevant particulars. I promise to abide by all library rules which m - y be made applicable from time to time. I would be liable to pay any dues, which I may owe due to my negligence or infringement of library rules. I certify that I am not already a member of this library in any capacity.

Name (Block letters) ....

Present Local Address ....

Class /Roll No...

Department / College / School ....

Permanent Address..

Signature of the Guarantor.

Address. Signature of the applicant.

VERSO

(For office use only) Receipt No. and Date (For Cash Deposit, if any) ....
....
Particulars checked found in order.
(Initials of the Counter Assistant).
Librarian's Orders ....
Date of enrolment ....
Signature of the applicant with date ....
Date of cancellation of the card and reason thereof
....
....
Clearance certificate issued on ....
Refund of cash deposit, if any ....
Initials of the Assistant.
Librarian's Signature.

As already mentioned, these application forms should be in the form of 5" x 3" cards so that these may be arranged in a tray alphabetically. In this way, it is easier to find out any information regarding a member. If these application forms are kept in a file, it is difficult to consult the same because every time a new member is enrolled, the order in the file will be disturbed if it is to be maintained in an alphabetical order. If it is not kept in an alphabetical order, it becomes difficult to consult. Some libraries maintain this record in a register form just like an accession register. It is difficult to consult it. But some libraries prefer to keep a duplicate record i.e. on cards and registers. This can be resorted to in special circumstances provided staff is enough. Otherwise, it will be merely is duplicate record and may not serve any useful purpose.

Reservation Card

RECTO

Call No. Acc. No.

Author ....

Title ....

To

The Librarian,

....

....

Dear sir,

Kindly reserve the above-mentioned book for me and inform me as soon as it is available for issue.

Yours faithfully,

(Signature of the member.)

Dated.

VERSO

Dear Sir,

Stamp

Please collect the book the particulars of which are given on reverse up to................otherwise it will be issued to other members.

Address of the member ....

....

Librarian.

In order to ensure that the books are issued to all the readers in proper order of their reservation, the relevant information should be kept by the Issue Counter either in a separate card or in a counterfoil a sunder :-

RECTO

Name of the Library ....

Date and time of Deposit of Reservation Card .....

Name of the Reader ....

His Membership No ....

FOR STAFF USE ONLY

SHELF CHECKED

Found/Not Found   Initials of the Stack Attendant.

Dated....................................

ISSUE RECORDS CHECKED

1. Reserved for ....
2. Not found ....
3. Issued to ....
4. Due on ....

VERSO

Recalled on ....

Reminders sent vide office letter No ....

Referred to Librarian on ....

Librarian's orders ....

Further action ....

5:37 RESERVATION SLIP

Call No............Author..............Acc. No. ....

Title...

Issued currently to ....

Address: ....

Due date of return...

Date of reservation ....

Date of receipt of the book ....

Date of sending intimation the book to
the reader for issuing the book ....

Librarian / Deputy Lib./
Circulation Incharge.

Assistant.

5:38

To

The Librarian

....

....

Sub :- Procurement of books on interlibrary Loan Basis.

Sir/Madam,

The following book/books are required by me for my research. These are not available in this Library. Kindly oblige by procuring the same from some other

Library on Inter-Library Loan basis : -

1. ....
2. ....
3. ....
4. ....

Thanking you

Yours faithfully

Dated................ Name and address of the Applicant

5:39 NAME OF THE LIBRARY

....

....

No...................... Dated........................

To

Mr./Miss/Mrs ....

....

....

Dear Sir/Madam,

The book/books required by you has /have been received in the library. Please arrange to procure the book / books for consultation in the library premises from the incharge circulation Section / Reference Section/Text Book Section. Please keep the book with care. Please note that if the book is mutilated or lost, you will be responsible for its replacement.

Yours faithfully,

Librarian

NAME OF THE LIBRARY

No.................... Dated......................

To

....

....

....

....

Sub: - Inter - Library Loan

Dear Sir/ Madam,

Please refer to the item (s) (✓) marked below :

1. We shall be thankful if you kindly send us the under mentioned publication (S) per bearer/ per registered post on Inter-Library Loan for a period of one month.
2. We are sending per bearer/in a separate registered cover the following title (s) as requested by you. Kindly acknowledge receipt and return the publication (s) on due date. Other publication (s) required by you is /are available and can be sent later on/but can't be sent out of the Library.
3. The under mentioned publication (s) which you so kindly sent us on Loan is/are returned per bearer/per registered post. Kindly acknowledge receipt.
4. We thankfully acknowledge the receipt of the following publication (s), which you so kindly sent us on Loan/ which we have received back in this library.
5. Please refer to our letter No........................ dated....................for the loan of the below noted publication (s). An early action is solicited.
6. Please refer to your letter No.................

dated.......................... kindly extend the period of loan upto .... as the publication (s) is/are still needed by the scholar.

7. Your request for the extension in loan period up to.......................... is granted/cannot be granted. Kindly return the under mentioned material immediately.

8. The under mentioned publication (s) loaned to you has / have not been returned as yet. Kindly return it/ them as these are urgently needed by us.

9. This is to inform you that the following publications has/have been procured on Loan from .... as requested by you and kept in the text books section for consultation.

   i) ....
   ii) ....
   i) ....
   iv) ....
   v) ....
   vi) ....

Your faithfully,

Librarian

5:41 MAINTENANCE OF RECORDS

The maintenance of circulation records is very important because these become the sound basis for preparing various comparative statements. These ultimately serve as reliable sources for drawing a conclusion and comparison of the services of one library with those of the other. The detailed account of circulation records is given in the chapter on 'Library Records'.

Miscellaneous Jobs

The other jobs which are involved in the circulation Section include the following :-

1. Issue of Reminders / Recovery of over-due books.
2. Replacement / Payment of Lost Library a Books / Cards.
3. Replacement Payment of Lost Books.
4. Administration of Property Counter.
5. Replacement of Lost Tokens.
6. Provision of Lockers / Carrels.
7. Taking Precautions against mutilation and loss of books.
8. Allowing consultation facilities.
9. Issue of clearance certificates.

The following forms and procedures may be followed for performing the above-mentioned miscellaneous jobs in the Circulation Section of a Library.

5:42 NAME OF THE LIBRARY

No..................... Dated....................

To,

....

....

....

Dear Sir,

Our records indicate that you have not cleared the dues for over-due book(s). You are requested to please clear the dues immediately.

Yours faithfully

Librarians.

5:43 NAME OF THE LIBRARY

Ref No. Dated..................200

The Finance Officer,

Name of the University / Institute

....

Subject: Recovery of Dues Report.

Dear Sir,

Our records show that book costing.................... is outstanding against Mr. / Miss .... of ....

You are requested to please recover this amount from his/her salary/Library Security. Intimation of recovery may please be sent to the undersigned on the form appended below.

Yours faithfully,

Librarian,

5:44 NAME OF THE INSTITUTE

Finance Section

No................. Date..............

To,

The Librarian

....

....

....

Subject:- Report of Dues Recovery.

Dear Sir,

The Dues amounting to Rs............................. have been recovered from Shri/Miss .... of..vide voucher No...........................Dt.......................

Yours faithfully,

Finance Officer,

5:45

The Librarian

....

....

....

Subject:- Loss of Library pass Book-cum-Identity card.

Dear Sir,

I here-by report the loss of Library Pass Book-cum-Identity card No..........................issued to me and request you for the issue of duplicate Library Pass Book-cum-Identity Card. I agree to pay the necessary charges according to the rules. Further, I hold myself responsible for any misuse of the Library Pass Book-cum-Identity card which I am reporting as lost.

Signature................................

Dated...................... Class.....................

Allowed. Department...........

Librarian

Duplicate Library Pass Book-cum- Identity Card issued on................................

Incharge Circulation Counter.

5:46 NAME OF THE LIBRARY

(Application for loss of books)

The undermentioned book issued to me has been lost and I want to replace it / deposit the replacement copy/charges may kindly be accepted.

Signature of the Applicant

Name......................................

Date Class / Department....................

1. Particulars of the book :
   i. Call No............................Acc. No ....
   ii. Author ....
   iii. Title ....
   iv. Edition..............Year of Publication ....
   Due Date ....
2. i. Whether accompanying replacement copy may be accepted? Yes/ No
   ii. Price of the book : (if in print only);
   a) Price (as in Ace. Reg.) ....

b) Price at present (As in Bibliographical sources) ....

c) Incidental charges ....

Total price (b+c) to be realised ....

(Incharge Acquisition section)

Dated...........197 Approved.

Librarian.

3. An amount of ....realised vide receipt No........ Date....................................

Dated................................ Office Clerk.

4. With draw record from the Public Catalogue and shelf List done.

(Incharge Technical Section)

Dated................................

5:47

To,

The Librarian

....

....

....

Subject:- Loss of Token

Dear Sir,

I have lost my Token No..................The particulars of my belongings kept at the readers' Property Counter against that number are as follows:-

I hold my self responsible for any dispute arising on account of ownership of the aforesaid articles. These may kindly be returned me after identification.

Yours faithfully,

Signature ....

Name ....

Date Class / Department ....

An amount of Rs. .... has been realised vide receipt No................ his belongings may be returned after identification.

Office Clerk.

Reference & Circulation incharge

I have received my aforesaid belongings in order. Delivered by.......................................

Signature.................................

Date............ Name.......................................

Replacement charges of Rs. 5/- plus late fine of Rs. only for the loss of Token No..................../ Late fine may be accepted to arrange return of his belongings after identification.

Office Clerk. Librarian.

5:48NAME OF THE LIBRARY

No.................. Dated.....................

To,

....

....

....

Dear Sir,

It has come to the notice of the undersigned that the facility of lockers provided in the Library is being misused by the readers to who these lockers have been allotted. Instances have also come to notice of the undersigned that a large number of books are stored the in these lockers for a long period. This practice if not only against the interest of the genuine readers but also against the spirit of Library Rules.

In view of this, it has been decided to withdraw the facility of lockers provided in the Library with immediate effect. As such, you are requested to open the locker in your possession in the presence of the incharge Reference Section and hand over the key to him latest by......................................

Yours faithfully,

Librarian.

Ref. No.................. Dated.........................

1. Copy forwarded to the Head, Department of ....for information.

5:49 (NAME OF THE LIBRARY)

CONFIDENTIAL D.O.

No........................ Dated ....

My dear, ...

It has been brought to my notice that some students have been indulging in tearing off pages from books and periodical sand stealing books from the Library which is a very serious matter In order to curb this evil, I seek your cooperation if the matter and request you to issue an appeal personally to the students of your Department to desist from such irresponsible and un-student like activities.

It fact, only a few delinquent students act in such a manner that results in a loss of valuable Library books and periodicals and puts the entire student community to an irreparable loss besides bringing a bad name to them.

I am confident that your appeal will elicit desirable results.

However, if this evil persists, the individual cases will be brought the notice of the higher authorities for strict disciplinary action which may lead to even rustication from the University.

Yours sincerely,

Librarian.

All Heads of Teaching Departments.

5:50 NAME OF THE LIBRARY

"Application for Consultation Facilities"

1. Name......................................(in Block Letters)

   Address :

   a) Permanent ______________________________

   ____

   b) Local : ______________________________

   ____

2. Particulars of the Institution where working : -

   a) Name of the institution ....

   b) Dept. / Section / Division etc ....

   c) Designation of the person ....

   (in case of students, the course of study)

3. Introduction / Recommendation from the institution stated at 3 above ; Yes/No

4. Period for which consultation facilities required:

   From..to...................................

5. Whether certificate for consultation required : Yes / No

Signature

Consultation facilities granted. Please issue consultation slip.

Librarian

Consultation slip No.................................Issued.

Dated................: (Registration Assistant)

In case a certificate for the consultation of this Library is required, please initial the register daily kept with Reference Desk at the Gate. The certificate will be issued on the basis of this register.

5:51 NAME OF THE LIBRARY

No...................... Date ....

"CONSULTATION SLIP"

No...................... Date ....

Name ______________________________

Address ______________________________

____

Librarian.

Note : No books will be issued against this slip.

5:52 "CLEARANCE APPLICATION FORM"

THE LIBRARIAN

Dear Sir,

I request you to issue a 'Clearance Certificate' to me. In this connection I give my particulars below:-

Name ______________________________

Designation __________________________

Borrowers No. ______________________________

I return my pass Book/Card in original / duplicate (For non-members only) OR I never got my self enfold as a member of the Library

Yours faithfully,

Signature.

Name ______________________________

Designation ______________________________

Department ______________________________

(For lost or duplicate Pass Book / Card holders only)

I take responsibility of any books if latter found issued on the Card/Pass Book of Shri______________

Signature.

Name ______________________________

Designation ______________________________

Clearance Certificate No. ________________ issued.

Signature.

5:53 NAME OF THE LIBRARY

CLEARANCE CERTIFICATE

Provisional Clearance Certificate is issued in favour of Shri ____________ Deptt. of ____________________ __________________________________ His Roll Number may be issued However. He/She is required to obtain "CLEARANCE CERTIFICATE" within two days after the completion of his/her Examination.

5:54 NAME OF THE LIBRARY

"CLEARANCE CERTIFICATE"

Certified that nothing is due from .... Borrower No...................................... Department / Branch so far as this library is concerned.

Periodical Section :

Circulation Section :

Accounts Section :

5:55 LEDGER SYSTEM

But when the number of Libraries and books increased and number of readers rose due to the spread of education, the need for some better method of keeping the record felt. He next step in the development of issue methods the introduction of the ledger system which implied the transfer of the daily transactions from the day book to a Ledger which consisted of numbered pages. One page allotted to each borrower. The following some of the columns of such ledgers :

Name of the Borrower ________________________

Sl. No.	Date of Issue	Author	Title	Date of return	Librarian's initials

This sample page shows that a permanent record was possible and full information could be found out at any time.

5:56 DAY BOOK REGISTER

Day Book System

This system, as mentioned in the earlier part of this chapter, was probably the first issue system. This system was very simple since it required one register only in which all the transactions were recorded. The specimen entries were in the following fashion :-

Date	Name and address of the borrower	Particulars of the book issued	Remarks

5.57 LEDGER SYSTEM

Since the Day Book System was very crude and did not suit the library staff and the readers in any way, so an improvement upon this system was made by the introduction of Ledger System. In it

1. A numbered register was maintained.
2. The borrower did not have any identity Card or Readers Card.

3. Every Reader was allotted one page.
4. An index to Borrowers' names was provided.
5. Transactions were first recorded in the Day Book and then transferred to the Ledger. (This system was later on abandoned and the transactions were recorded direct in the Ledger itself).

The specimen page of the Ledger was as under:

Name of the Borrower : Shri Adress :					Page No.	
Date of Issue	Accession No.	Author	Title	Signature of the borrower	Due date	Date of Return

5:58 REQUISITE MATERIALS

A. *For the book*

1. *Date slip.*

One 5" x 3" slip is pasted opposite to the page facing the card board back / front cover of the book.

<table>
<tr><td colspan="3">Call No. Acc. No.
Name of the Library
The following books were issued / are due o the below mentioned dates.</td></tr>
<tr><td>Date of issue
Due Date</td><td>Date of issue
Due Date</td><td>Date of issue
Due Date</td></tr>
<tr><td></td><td></td><td></td></tr>
</table>

5:59 BOOK POCKET

One 5" x 2" Book Pocket is pasted on the Inside back/ front cover cardboard of the book.

Brief Library Rules and instructions

5:60 BOOK CARD

One 4" x 2" Book Card of Manila or Xylonite is prepared for each book and is inserted inside the book pocket of the book. The book card contains call No., Acc. No, Author and Title.

Call No.	Acc. No.
Author	
Title	

5:61 FOR THE BORROWERS

1. Borrower's tickets or pockets. Each borrower is given as many ticket is in the shape of a pocket of 3" X 2" Size. It opens on two sides i.e. the upper and the lift or right portions. This pocket contains the name and address of the borrower, books. This ticket is in the shape of a pocket contains the name and address of the borrower, the date of expiry of membership, the signature and stamp of the Librarian. On the back of it, the seal of the library is printed/embossed.

Name Address Date of expiry   **Signature of the borrower.**

For the Counter Staff

1. Registration cards of borrowers.
2. Date stamp and ink pad.
3. Date guide cards.
4. Charging Trays of steel or wood of 1' × 1½' size with four drawers.
5. Stationery articles including pencils, printed lines sheets for circulation statistics, reminder cards and reservation cards.

5:62 REQUISITE MATERIALS

A. For the Book

1. *Date Slip.* One paper slip 5" x 3" size is pasted on the fly leaf (page facing the back or front card board cover of the book). The date slip has the following columns :-

<table>
<tr><td colspan="4">Call No. Acc. No.
Name of the Library :
This book was issued / is due on the date last stamped/marked,</td></tr>
<tr><td></td><td></td><td></td><td></td></tr>
</table>

5:63

2. *Book. Pocket.* A book pocket of slightly harder paper is pasted on the inner back side of front / back card board cover of the book in order to hold the book card size of this pocket is such that it can hold the book card easily. Its size is 5" x 3". The specimen is given below :-

Open flap.
Name of the Library. Brief Library Rules : 1. 2. 3. 4. 5.

5:64

3. Book Card. A book card of Manila or Xylonite is required for each book. It contains the essential information about the book. Its size is 4" x 2" and it is placed in the book pocket.

Name of the Library :		
Call No.		Acc. No.
Author		
Title		
This book was issued/is due on the date last stamped or marked		

B. For Borrowers

1. Borrower's Card / identity card. Every borrower at the time or registration is provided with a borrower's card. In a modified system a membership-cum-identity card is issued. The specimen of each of these two cards is given below. :-

5:65 SPECIMEN OF A BORROWER'S CARD.

Name of the Library :

<table>
<tr><td colspan="4">Borrower's No...
Date of Expiry...

Non-transferable

The following books were issued to me.

Signature</td></tr>
<tr><td>Due date/ Date of issue.</td><td>Date of return.</td><td>Due date/ Date of issue.</td><td>Date of return.</td></tr>
</table>

(These columns are repeated on the verso of the card)

5:66 SPECIMEN OF MEMBERSHIP-CUM-IDENTIFY CARD.

<table>
<tr><td>Name of the Library ....

Non-transferable...

Membership-cum-Identity Card.</td></tr>
</table>

Due date/ Date of issue.	**Date of return**	**Due Date/ Date of issue**	**Date of return**

(At least 2 leaves are provided in this Pass Book type card).

5:67 REQUISITE MATERIALS

1. *For the Book* - The equipment required for the book in this system includes due date cards like those of Detroit Self-Charging System and book cards and book pockets like those of Newark System.

2 *For the Readers* - Borrowers' cards or identity cards equipped with a metal plate containing the number of the member which is attached to the borrower's card with a hinge.

Specimen

Embossed Membership No.

Meta Plate

Membership No ....

Name and Address ....

....

Name of the library ....

3. *For the staff.* -
   1. Mechanical book charger machine.
   2. Metal plates with embossed dates.
   3. Double registration files i.e. alphabetical and numerical.
   4. Other miscellaneous stationery articles as required in the Newark System.

5:68 RECORDS OF BOOKS

Date	Accession No.	Author.	Title.	Publisher and Place of Publication.	Price.	Vol.	Collation.	Binding.	Course of supply.	Bill No. Date and Amt.	Call No.	Remarks

5:69 SPECIMEN OF AN ALLOCATION REGISTER

This register may be ledger type and a few pages may allotted to each department or subject :-

Name of the Dept./Subject.............................Total Amount Sanction

....

Name and Head of the Grant..............................

Sr. No.	Bill No. and Date	Name of the supplier.	Amount of the Bill.	Deduction. if any.	Total Amount of the Bill.	Total Grant of the Dept.	Balance available.

5:70 SPECIMEN OF A BILL REGISTER

Sr. No.	Date of passing for payment	Bill No. and date.	Name of the supplier.	Amount of the Bill.	Dept. to which debited.	Total Grant	Balance available.

5:71 SPECIMEN OF VISITOR'S REGISTER

Date	Sr. No.	Name of visitor	Addr ess	Occup- ation	Purp- ose	Rema- rks

5:72 ANNUAL REPORT

For the year.......................................

A. *General*

1. Name of the Library..............................
2. Nature of the Library ....
3. Date of establishment............................
4. Area / Population served ....
   Rural / Urban..
5. Working hours ....
6. No. of days closed in the year ....

B. *Clientele*

1. Total number of members ....
2. Male ....
3. Female ....
4. Children ....
5. Total No. of active members ....
6. New members added during the period ....
7. Conditions of membership ....
8. Ratio of members to the total population..
   ....

C. *Book Stock*	*Books*	*Bound Periodicals / Other*

1. Total No. of volumes at the beginning of the year.
2. Number of volumes added during the year.
3. Number of volumes with drawn during the year.
4. Total No. of volumes at the close of the year.
5. Total No. of current periodicals subscribed.

6. Total No. of Vols. In stock per head of population.146

D. *Technical Services*

1. Whether the Book Stock is classified or not ....
2. Classification Scheme in use ....
   Dewey / Colon / Others
3. Catalogue scheme in use ....
   Dictionary / Classified / Other.
4. Physical form of the catalogue ....
   (a) Card/Book/Shelf ....
   (b) Manuscript / typed / printed ....

E. *Staff*

1. Total No. of employees..........................
2. Professional..
3. Semi-Professional ....
4. Unskilled ....

F. *Public Services*

1. Issue system in vogue : Network / Browne / Others ....
2. Total number of books issued and returned during the year. ....
3. Average number of books issued daily .....
4. No. of books issued according to subject..
   Fiction______Non-Fiction ______Biography ___________

1\ *Reference Section*

1. Total No. of Reference Vols. in stock ....
   General______Specific subjects___________
2. No. of Books consulted daily ....

3. No of inquiries received daily ....
4. Total No. of readers who used the reference section during the period ....
5. Types of inquiries received for answering. (Type-wise).
   (a) Fact - Finding.
   (b) Directory.
   (c) Dictionary.
   (d) Research type.

III. Indexing, Abstracting & Documentation.

1. No. of Indexes made ...
2. No. of Indexes used ...
3. No. of Periodical articles abstracted ...
4. No. of Periodical articles documented ...

IV. Mobile Library Services.

a) No. of villages / deposit centres / stations visited...
b) No. of average working hours per week...
c) No. of books issued and returned during the period.

G. Finance

a) Expenditure Budget

1. *Recurring*
   a) Books and back sets.
   b) Current Periodicals.
   c) Staff Salary.
   d) Wages
   e) Binding etc.
   f) Building repairs.
   g) Heating and cooling charges
   h) Postage, telephone, etc.

i) Stationery and equipment,
j) Mobile vans
k) Special grant for books.
l) Other services.

3. *Non-Recurring*
4. *Total*

b) *Revenue*
   1. Library rates
   2. State Govt. grants.
   3. Endowments.
   4. Others.
   5. Total Surplus or deficit.148

H. *Cost Accounting*
   1. Cost of service per book ...
   2. Cost of service per reader...
   3. Budget provision per reader / per capita...

I. *Miscellaneous*
   1. General condition of the library...
   2. New Service rendered ...
   3. Extra-mural activities...
   4. Inter-Library co-operation ...
   5. Publications, if any ...
   6. Any other suggestions.

Signatures of the Librarian/

Chairman of Library Committee.

Dated.................................200.............

5:73 SPECIMEN OF THE STATISTICAL TABLES OF THE TECHNICAL SECTION

Classification

Month..................Year.............

Sr. No.	Name of the incumbent & designation	No. of Books Classified .... Days of the month											
		1	2	3	4	5	6	7	8	9	10	11	Total
1	Sh .... Classifier												
2	Sh .... Classifier												
3	Sh .... Classifier												
4	Sh .... Classifier												
5	Sh .... Classifier												

5:74 CATALOGUING

Month....................................Year

No. of Books catalogued and No. of cards prepared

....

<table>
<tr><th rowspan="2">Sr. No.</th><th rowspan="2">Name of the incumbent & designation</th><th colspan="12">No. of Books Classified ....
Days of the month ....</th></tr>
<tr><th>1</th><th>2</th><th>3</th><th>4</th><th>5</th><th>6</th><th>7</th><th>8</th><th>9</th><th>10</th><th>11</th><th>Total</th></tr>
<tr><td>1</td><td>Sh ....
Classifier</td><td colspan="11"></td><td></td></tr>
<tr><td>2</td><td>Sh ....
Classifier</td><td colspan="11"></td><td></td></tr>
<tr><td>3</td><td>Sh ....
Classifier</td><td colspan="11"></td><td></td></tr>
<tr><td>4</td><td>Sh ....
Classifier</td><td colspan="11"></td><td></td></tr>
<tr><td>5</td><td>Sh ....
Classifier</td><td colspan="11"></td><td></td></tr>
</table>

5:75 SPECIMEN OF ACESSION STATISTICS

Month.................... Year......................

Reading Material	**000**	**100**	**200**	**300**	**900**	**Total**
By Purchase :						
Books						
Pamphlets						
Others						
Total						
By Exchange :						
Books						
Pamphlets						
Others						
Total						
By Gift :						
Books						
Pamphlets						
Others						
Total						
Grand Total						

5:76 STATISTICS OF PERIODICALS

Month.......................... Year...................

Frequency of publication	No. of periodicals received	No. of periodicals registered	No. of reminders written	No. of reminders despatched
Daily ...				
Weekly ...				
Fortnightly ...				
Monthly ...				
Quarterly ...				
Yearly ...				
Others ...				
Total ...				

5:77 SPECIMEN OF STATISTICAL TABLE

Week No............Month............Year...........

Subject	No. of periodicals indexed	No of articles abstracted	No of articles reproduced
000			
100			
200			
300			
400			
500			
600			
700			
800			
900			
Total			

5:78 CIRCULATION SECTION

The Circulation Section is one of the most important sections of library dealing with the public directly. It is the most proper form to know the tastes, antipathies and reactions of the readers. To know these reliable statistics should be maintained. At the entrance gate of the library, there must be kept a Visitor's Register with the columns as under: -

Date	Sl. No.	Name and address of visitor	Occupation or Class	Sex	Age Group	Signature

From this register a statement should be prepared daily in the following manner

5:79 DAILY ATTENDENCE STATISTICS

Date	No. of readers who visited the library	Occupation or class	Sex	Age Group

5:80 ISSUE STATISTICS

Date	Subjects	No. of Books	No. of books returned	No. of books renewed	No. of books reported lost
	Poetry				
	Drama				
	Novel				
	Short stories				
	Other literature				
	Biographies				
	Useful arts				
	History and travels				
	Other non-fiction				
	Total				

We should also keep another kind of statistics by which we can have an idea of the languages which are popular with the readers.

5:81 ISSUE STATISTICS LANGUAGE WISE

Date	**Language**	**No. of Books Issued**
	English ...	
	Hindi ...	
	Punjabi ...	
	Urdu ...	
	Southern Languages ...	
	Bengali ...	
	Oriya ...	
	Others ...	
	Total	

5:82ISSUE STATISTICS READER WISE

Date	Nature of Readers	No. of Books Issued
	Adult ... Mail ... Female ... Children ... Blind ... Sick ... Others ... Total	

THE FOLLOWING STATISTICS SHOULD BE MAINTAINED WEEKLY:

Date	No. of new members enrolled	No. of with drawing members	Total No. of members	Total No. of active members

In case of academic libraries i.e. University, College and School Libraries, the statistics should be maintained on the following pattern: -

5:83 CLASSIFIED ISSUE STATISTICS

Date	Subjects	No. of Books Issued
	100	
	200	
	300	
	400	
	500	
	600	
	700	
	800	
	900	
	Total	

5:84 STATISTICS OF BOOKS CONSULTED

Date.	No. of Books consulted										
	000	100	200	300	400	500	600	700	800	900	Total

5:85 STATISTICS OF REFERENCE QUERRIES

Another kind of statistics to be maintained in the reference department relates to the actual reference service rendered to the readers.

Date.................Month...............Year.................

No. of readers directed	No. of shortage enquiries answered	No. of long range	No. of enquiries unanswered	Total

Another method for having statistical data regarding the regular users of the Reference Department is to have a sample survey on certain days of the week, at least twice or thrice a day in order to give margin to weather or other local conditions.

Miscellaneous Statistics

The library must know the number of its prospective clientele or the total number of people served. It can be found out from the latest census report. The figures giving total expenditure, book fund and periodicals fund should be maintained properly so that an accurate assessment of the library service rendered be made.

5:86 STATISTICS OF INCOME AND EXPENDITURE

Item	Book fund	Periodicals fund	Staff fund	Others	Total
Income					
Expenditure					

5.87 STAFF STATISITCS

Name of posts	No. of Posts filled	No. of Posts lying vacant	Amount spent on salaries	Amount saved on staff salaries

5:88 CLASSWISE ISSUE STATISTICS

Date	Class	No. of Books Issued
	Higher Secondary ...	
	Graduate ...	
	Post-Graduate ...	
	Teachers ...	
	Research Scholars ...	
	Others ...	
	Total ...	

PERSPECTIVES IN SPECIAL EDUCATION

PERSPECTIVES IN SPECIAL EDUCATION

Arul Jothi
M.Sc., M.Ed.
Principal, Arcot Sri Mahalakshmi Women's Teacher Training Institute,
Villapakkam, Vellore Dist.-632521 T.N.

Dr. D.L. Balaji
B.Com., M.A., M.Phil., D.Lit.,
Correspondent, Arcot Sri Mahalakshmi Educational Institutions,
Villapakkam, Vellore Dist.-632521 T.N.

Meena Kumari
Lecturer, Deptt. of Education,
Nalanda Open University,
Nalanda

CENTRUM PRESS
NEW DELHI-110002 (INDIA)

CENTRUM PRESS
H.O.: 4360/4, Ansari Road, Daryaganj,
New Delhi-110 002 (India)
Ph.: 23278000, 23261597

B.O.: No. 1015, Ist Main Road, BSK IIIrd Stage
IIIrd Phase, IIIrd Block,
Bangalore - 560 085 (India)
Tel.: 080-41723429
Visit us at: www.centrumpress.com

Perspectives in Special Education

First Edition, 2009

PRINTED IN INDIA

Printed at Balaji Offset, Delhi

Contents

Preface (*vii*)

UNIT-I : Perspectives in Disability 1
Definition and Classification of Disabilities • History of Special Education • Concessions and Rights of the Disabled • Recent Trends in the Field of Special Education • Awareness and Attitudinal Changes Towards the Disabled

UNIT-II : Blindness and Low Vision 37
Definitions and Identification • Incidence and Prevalence • Characteristics • Causes and Prevention • Intervention and Educational Programmes • Plus Curriculum

UNIT-III : Hearing Impairment 73
Definitions and Identification • Incidence and Prevalence • Causes and Prevention • Types of Hearing Loss and Characteristics • Communication Approaches • Sign Language and Educational Programmes

UNIT-IV : Mental Retardation and Mental Illness 97
Definition and Identification of Mental Retardation • Incidence and Prevalence • Causes and Prevention • Characteristics • Mild • Moderate • Severe • Profound • Types and Classification of Mental Retardation and Mental Illness • Mental Illness • Intervention and Educational Progremmes

UNIT-V : Locomotor Disabilities 131
Definition and Identification • Incidence and Prevalence • Causes and Prevention • Types, Classification and Characteristics • Intervention and Educational Programmes • Cerebral Palsy and Barrier Free Environment

UNIT-VI : Learning Disabilities, Austism and Other Associated Disorder 176
Definition and Identification of Learning Disabilities • Autism and Other Associated Disorders • Epilepsy • Behavior Disorders • Emotional Disorders • Multiple Disabilities • Incidence and Prevalence • Causes and Prevention • Types and Characteristics • Intervention and Educational Programmes

UNIT-VII : Family and Disability Management 238
Role of Mothers • Crisis Management • Counseling • Intervention by Multi-disciplinary Team • Referral Services

UNIT-VIII : Vocational Training and Community Based Rehabilitation 249
Concept of Sheltered Workshop • Transitory Employment • Self-employment • Extended Employment • Community Based Rehabilitation (CBR)

UNIT-IX : Students Awareness on Disability 271
Planning • Organizing and Conducting Programmes in the Community • Media Selection for Role Play • Drama • Puppetry • Dance • Exhibition • Postal Display • Folk Art • Psychology of Awareness • Reporting

UNIT-X : Policies and Legislation 296
Policies and Legislative Measures Pertaining to the Disabled • PWD Act, 1995 The Persons with Disabilities (Equal Opportunities, Protection of Rights and Full Participation) Act, 1995 • Rehabilitation Council Act of India Act 1992 • The National Trust for Welfare of Persons with Autism, Cerebral Palsy, Mental Retardation and Multiple Disabilities Act, 1999 • Services and Programmes for the Disabled

Bibliography 380

Index 383

Preface

Special education is the individually planned and systematically monitored arrangement of teaching procedures, adapted equipment and materials, accessible settings, and other interventions designed to help learners with special needs achieve a higher level of personal self-sufficiency and success in school and community than would be available if the student were only given access to a typical classroom education. Students with special needs, such as learning differences, mental health issues, specific disabilities and giftedness are those whose needs are addressed within the classroom setting. However generally, the term "special education" refers specifically to students with learning disabilities, mental conditions, and other disabling conditions. Beginning in 1952, Civitas were the first to provide widespread training for teachers of developmentally disabled children.

Special education in India was present since the pre independence time, with very few schools or NGOs helping intellectually impaired children. Today India has come a long way and made a good progress in the field of disability rehabilitation. Presently India has four national institutes for effective implementation of this special education through various government schemes.

Special education takes on added importance in view of the fact that inclusion of children with disabilities into regular classes leads to an absence of social acceptance by their peer group. Most children with disabilities need to be taught how to relate to others, quite as much as students without disabilities need to be taught tolerance and understanding of those who are different from themselves. In India, special education is an emerging discipline and an essential part of the modern education system. It includes all aspects of education, which are necessary to successfully run the courses and training programmes for abnormal students.

This book covers all aspects of special education and may prove to be a perfect guide for teachers and educators.

— *Meena Kumari*

UNIT-I

Perspectives in Disability

Definition and Classification of Disabilities

A disability is a condition or function judged to be significantly impaired relative to the usual standard of an individual or group. The term is used to refer to individual functioning, including physical impairment, sensory impairment, cognitive impairment, intellectual impairment mental illness, and various types of chronic disease.

Disability is conceptualized as being a multidimensional experience for the person involved. There may be effects on organs or body parts and there may be effects on a person's participation in areas of life. Correspondingly, three dimensions of disability are recognized in ICF: body structure and function (and impairment thereof), activity (and activity restrictions) and participation (and participation restrictions). The classification also recognizes the role of physical and social environmental factors in affecting disability outcomes.

Classification of Disabilities

Types of disabilities include various physical and mental impairments that can hamper or reduce a person's ability to carry out his day to day activities. These impairments can be termed as disability of the person to do his or her day to day activities. These impairments can be termed as disability of the person to do his day to day activities as previously. "Disability" can be broken down into a number of broad sub-categories, which include the following:

a) *Mobility and Physical Impairments:* This category of disability includes people with varying types of physical disabilities including:

Upper limb(s) disability.

Lower limb(s) disability

Manual dexterity.

Disability in co-ordination with different organs of the body.

Disability in mobility can be either an in-born or acquired with age problem. It could also be the effect of a disease. People who have a broken bone also fall into this category of disability.

b) *Spinal Cord Disability:* Spinal cord injury (SCI) can sometimes lead to lifelong disabilities. This kind of injury mostly occurs due to severe accidents. The injury can be either complete or incomplete. In an incomplete injury, the messages conveyed by the spinal cord is not completely lost. Whereas a complete injury results in a total dis-functioning of the sensory organs. In some cases spinal cord disability can be a birth defect.

c) *Head Injuries :* Brain Disability: A disability in the brain occurs due to a brain injury. The magnitude of the brain injury can range from mild, moderate and severe. There are two types of brain injuries:

Acquired Brain Injury (ABI)

Traumatic Brain Injury (TBI)

ABI is not a hereditary type defect but is the degeneration that occurs after birth.

The causes of such cases of injury are many and are mainly because of external forces applied to the body parts. TBI results in emotional dysfunctioning and behavioral disturbance.

d) *Vision Disibility:* There are hundreds of thousands of people that suffer from minor to various serious vision disability or impairments. These injuries can also result into some serious problems or diseases like blindness and ocular trauma, to name a few. Some of the common vision impairment includes scratched cornea, scratches on the sclera, diabetes related eye conditions, dry eyes and corneal graft.

e) *Hearing Disability:* Hearing disabilities includes people that are completely or partially deaf, (Deaf is the politically correct term for a person with hearing impairment).

People who are partially deaf can often use hearing aids to assist their hearing. Deafness can be evident at birth or occur later in life from several biologic causes, for example Meningitis can damage the auditory nerve or the cochlea.

Deaf people use sign language as a means of communication. Hundreds of sign languages are in use around the world. In linguistic terms, sign languages are as rich and complex as any oral language, despite the common misconception that they are not "real languages".

f) *Cognitive or Learning Disabilites:* Cognitive Disabilities are kind of impairment present in people who are suffering from dyslexia and various other learning difficulties and includes speech disorders.

g) *Psychological Disorders:* Affective Disorders: Disorders of mood or feeling states either short or long term. Mental Health Impairment is the term used to describe people who have experienced psychiatric problems or illness such as:

Personality Disorders- Defined as deeply inadequate patterns of behavior and thought of sufficient severity to cause significant impairment to day-to-day activities.

Schizophrenia: A mental disorder characterized by disturbances of thinking, mood, and behavior.

h) *Invisible Disabilities:* Invisible Disabilities are disabilities that are not immediately apparent to others.

It is estimated that 10% of people in the U.S. have a medical condition considered a type of invisible disability.

The Evolution of a Movement

Historically, disabilities have often been cast in a negative light. An individual thus affected was seen as being a "patient" subject either to cure or to ongoing medical care. His condition is seen as disabling; the social reactions to it are justified, and the barriers unavoidable. This position is known as the medical model of disability.

Over the past 20 years, a competing view known as the social model of disability has come to the fore. In this model, disability is seen more as a social construction than a medical reality. An individual may be impaired by a condition that requires daily living adaptations, but the bulk of his problem-his disability- can be found in the attitudinal and physical barriers erected by society.

Both the medical and social models agree, to a point, that facilities and opportunities should be made as accessible as possible to individuals who require adaptations. Dismantling physical barriers, or setting up adaptations such as wheelchair ramps, is known as "fostering accessibility".

The Language and Terminology of Disability

The term disability has replaced the older designations spastic, handicapped, and crippled. While these two designations can be used interchangeably, proponents of the social model of disability have appropriated the latter term to describe those social and economic consequences of the former. An individual with a physical or intellectual disability, then, is said to be "handicapped" by the lowered expectations of society.

A person may also be "impaired" either by a correctable condition such as myopia, or by an uncorrectable one such as cerebral palsy. For those with mild conditions, related impairments disappear with the application of corrective devices. More serious impairments call for adaptive equipment.

In the United Kingdom, people within the disability rights movement commonly use the term "Disabled" to denote someone who is "disabled by society's inability to accommodate all of its inhabitants."

The Person First Movement has added another layer to this discourse by asking that people with disabilities be identified first as individuals. "Person First Language" -- referring, for example, to a "woman who is blind," rather than to "a blind woman"- is a form of political correctness designed to further the aims of the social model by removing attitudinal barriers.

Some people with disabilities support the Person First Movement, while others do not. People who are Deaf in particular may see themselves as members of a specific community, properly called the Deaf culture, and so will reject efforts designed to distance them from the central fact of their identity.

A human rights based approach has been adopted by many organizations of and for disabled people. In 2000, for example, the United Nations Assembly decided to start working on a comprehensive convention for the rights of disabled people.

History of Special Education

In 1975, Congress passed the Education for All Handicapped Children Act, better known at the time as Public Law 94-142, to change what was clearly an untenable situation. Despite compulsory education laws that had been in place nationwide since 1918, many children with disabilities were routinely excluded from public schools. Their options: remain at home or be institutionalized. Even those with mild or moderate disabilities who did enroll were likely to drop out well before graduating from high school.

The Civil Rights Movement and the 1954 *Brown v. Board of Education* decision which extended equal protection under the law to minorities, paved the way for similar gains for those with disabilities. Parents, who had begun forming special education advocacy groups as early as 1933, became the prime movers in the struggle to improve educational opportunities for their children.

Public Law 94-142 proved to be landmark legislation, requiring public schools to provide students with a broad range of disabilities- including physical handicaps, mental retardation, speech, vision and language problems, emotional and behavioral problems, and other learning disorders- with a "free appropriate public education." Moreover, it called for school districts to provide such schooling in the "least restrictive environment" possible.

Reauthorized in 1990 and 1997, the law was renamed the Individuals with Disabilities Education Act (IDEA) and spawned the delivery of services to millions of students previously denied access to an appropriate education. Thanks to IDEA, these students were not only in school, but also, at least in the best case scenarios, assigned to small classes where specially trained teachers tailored their lessons to each student's individual needs. Schools also were required to provide any additional services- such as interpreters for the deaf or computer-assisted technology for the physically impaired- that students needed in order to reach their full potential. And, in more and more cases, special education students began spending time every day in regular classroom settings with their non-special education peers.

According to the Department of Education, approximately 6 million children (roughly 10 percent of all school-aged children) receive special education services. Educating those children was expected to cost nearly $51 billion last year, according to the Department of Education's Center for Special Education Finance, with the yeoman's share- more than $44 billion- coming from states and local school districts. That, despite the promise made by the federal government in 1975 to cover 40 percent of the additional costs incurred by districts to educate students with disabilities. Even though federal spending for special education continues to rise (from $3.1 billion in 1997 to $6.3 billion in 2001), the federal government has never paid more than 15 percent of the total costs.

Concessions and Rights of the Disabled

Scheme 1: Children's Educational Allowance

As per office Memorandum No. 21011/21/88 Est. (Allowances) dated. 17.10.1988, issued by the Ministry of Personnel, Public Grievances and Pensions (Department of Personnel and Training), grant of children educational allowance, reimbursement of tuition fee etc. to Central Government employees will be covered by the Central Civil Services (Educational Assistance) orders, 1988. Under this order, the reimbursement of tuition fee in respect of physically handicapped and mentally retarded children of the Central Government employees has been enhanced to Rs. 50 p.m. (from class I to XII) in comparison with general category where is restricted to only Rs. 20/ -. The **disabled** children will however, get other assistance under this scheme as per rates prescribed for the normal children.

Scheme 2: Income Tax Act

The most significant development is amendment to section 80 DD of the Income Tax Act as presented in the Union Budget 99-2000 finance bill. Section 80 DD has substituted the earlier section 80 DD, the assesse of the Hindu Undivided Family (HUF) would be entitled to a deduction of Rs. 40,000 in respect of any expenditure for medical treatment (including nursing), training and rehabilitation of handicapped dependent. If this amount is not spend on the treatment but deposited under any scheme by LIC or UTI for the maintenance of the handicapped children, then also this deduction would be permissible, during the accounting year 2000-2001.

On advocacy by parents having children with mental retardation Shri. D. K. Manavalan vide his letter no. 1325. SECY (SJ & E) / 99 dated February 16, 1999 to chairman, Central Board of Direct taxes, New Delhi made a request that parents need not submit supporting vouchers on medical bills for having incurred expenditure on medical treatment of their mentally handicapped ward. The Central Board of Direct Taxes vide its letter dated March 26, 1999 issued a clarification that it would be sufficient to furnish a medical certificate from a

Government doctor and a declaration in writing duly signed by the assessee certifying the actual amount of expenditure on account of medical treatment including nursing, training and rehabilitation of the disabled dependent, and receipt/acknowledgement of the amount paid or deposited in the specific schemes of LIC or UTI will be sufficient. The circular to the Drawing and Disbursing officers clearly indicated that they need not insist on production of vouchers or medical bills by the employees for having incurred expenditure on medical treatment of their disabled dependent for allowing the deduction under Section 80 DD for the Purpose of computing tax deductable at source.

Income Tax Concessions: The Government of India has recently announced the following additional concessions for individuals or Hindu Undivided families who have a relative who is physically disabled. If an assessor who is resident in India, being an individual or Hindu Undivided Family has a relative who has permanent physical disability and the assessor has, during the previous year, incurred any expenditure for medical treatment (including nursing), training and rehabilitation of the disabled person, he/she shall be allowed a deduction of Rs.6,000/-. This deduction will not be allowed where the income exceeds Rs. 1,00,000/-

Deduction from the total income of disabled persons under section 80-U of the Income Tax Act has been raised from Rs. 20,000/- to Rs. 40,000/- A deduction of Rs. 20,000/- from the taxable income of the parents or guardians of disabled children has been allowed, provided this amount is deposited in any approved scheme of LIC, UTI etc.

Scheme 3: Employees Provident Fund

The Central Government has made amendments in the Employees Pension Scheme, 1995; called employees pension (Amendment) scheme, 1999. According to this scheme "If a member dies leaving behind a family having son or daughter who is permanently and totally **disabled**, such son or daughter shall be entitled to Payment of monthly children pension or orphan pension, as the case may be, irrespective of age and number of children in the family in addition to the pension provided under clause (d) of sub para 3, Section 6a.

Scheme 4: Life Insurance Corporation of India

LIC has introduced a new plan "JEEVAN VISHWAS" for the benefit of the physically / mentally handicapped dependants. For the benefit of handicapped dependants "JEEVAN AADHAR" plan was introduced with effect from 17th January 1996. The plan was specially designed so that an individual or member of Hindu Undivided Family can take an assurance on his / her own life to provide for lump sum and an annuity to the handicapped dependant. The provision is in the nature of a limited payment whole life assurance policy. The payment is made to the nominee under the policy, who will be either the handicapped dependant or any other person or a trust, to be utilized for the benefit of the handicapped dependant.

The premiums under Jeevan Aadhar are eligible for tax benefit under Sec. 80DD of Income Tax Act, 1961. The definition of disability under rule 11A of Income Tax Rules, 1962, for this purpose is rather stringent in Jeevan Aadhar as such is thus not catering to the needs of those handicapped dependants whose degree of handicap is lower than the specified levels. Keeping in mind the guardians of such lives who may be willing to provide for the dependants even without the benefit under Sec. 80DD of Income Tax Act, it is decided to introduce JEEVAN VISHWAS with effect from 1st December 1999. While developing the plan, feedback received from various sources on the benefit structure of Jeevan Aadhar is taken into account. The plan is Endowment without Profit with guaranteed and loyalty additions. For further details, you can contact any office of Life Insurance Corporation of India in your city.

Scheme 5: Subsidies and Concessions

Scheme of Subsidy for Purchase of Petrol: Physically handicapped owners of motorized vehicles granted exemption from the payment of road tax by State Government / Union Territory Administration, are eligible to claim refund upto 50% of the expenditure incurred by them on purchase of petrol /

diesel from recognized dealers subject to a ceiling as indicated below;

- o Vehicle upto 2HP – 15ltr per month
- o Vehicle more than 2 HP – 25 its per month

Only physically handicapped persons having an income upto Rs. 2,500/- from all sources would be eligible for the grant of subsidy on purchase of petrol / diesel. The scheme is operative through District Welfare Officers or Tehsildar / Equivalent officer.

- Telecommunication (Preference In Allotment of STD booths / PCO) Educated unemployed disabled persons are eligible for allotment of STD booths / PCOs. The educational qualification required for the applicants is VIII or Middle School pass from rural areas and at least Matriculation or High School from urbanareas.
- Hotel *Discounts* : India Tourism Development Corporation (ITDC) has decided that in all its hotels across the country, it will offer the following two discounts to people with disabilities:
  - o 50% on room rent, accompanying person / attendant shall not be charged extra *i.e.* ITDC shall charge 50% on single room tariff for double room.
  - o 30% discount on food on the a-la-carte menu.

They are also taking steps to ensure that all the existing hotels are made accessible and disabled friendly. Infact, many have already made ramps, like Hotel Kanishka and Ashok Yatri Niwas in Delhi and the Ashoka Hotel in Bhopal. To be sure, many more hotels may have already got the ramps made and others too will soon follow. A decision has also been taken that at least one room in every fifty rooms should be made accessible and disabled – friendly.

- *Concession on Railways:* Railways allow disabled persons to travel at concession fares up to 75% in the first and second classes. Escorts accompanying blind, orthopedic ally and mentally handicapped persons are also eligible to 75% concession in the basic fare.

- *Air Travel Concessions:* Indian Airlines allow 50% concession fares to blind persons on single journeys.
- Postage

Payment of postage, both inland and foreign, for transmission by post of 'Blind Literature' packets is exempted if sent by surface route.

- *Customs / Excise:* Braille paper has been exempted from excise and customs duty provided the paper is supplied direct to a school for the blind or to a Braille press against an indent placed by the National Institute for the Visually Handicapped, Dehradun. All audio cassettes recorded with material from books, newspapers or magazines for the blind are exempt from custom duty. Several other items have also been exempted from customs duty if imported for the use of a disabled person.
- *Award of Dealership by Oil Companies:* The Ministry of Petroleum and Natural Gas has reserved 7.5 per cent of all types of dealership agencies of the public sector companies, for the orthopaedically handicapped and blind persons. Similarly, the Ministry has also reserved 7.5 per cent of such dealership/agencies for defense personnel, severely disabled either in war or while on duty in peacetime.
- *Economic Assistance by Public Sector Banks:* All orphanages, homes for women and persons with physical handicaps as well as institutions working for the welfare of the handicapped, are given loans and advances at very low rates of interest (4%) and a subsidy of 50% up to a maximum of Rs. 5,000/- is also admissible. State Governments/Union Territories also give concessions/ facilities such as reservation in jobs, scholarships, old age pension, free travel in buses, etc.

Know Your Rights!

A handicap is a disadvantage for a given individual, resulting from an impairment or disability that limits or prevents the fulfillment of a role that is normal (depending on age, sex, social and cultural factors) for that individual. The concept of disability is also subjective and situational, in that different functional organizations of the United Nations have evolved different definitions. The ILO defines a disabled person as an individual whose prospects of securing, retaining and advancing in suitable employment are substantially reduced as a result of duly recognized physical or mental impairment.

Provisions under Indian Constitution

There are ample constitutional provisions with regard to protection and safeguarding the rights of the individuals with disabilities. The Indian Constitution, has several provisions for the under privileged and marginalized sections of our society, which are enshrined in Articles 14,41,45 and 46 in our constitution. These are as under :

Article 14

The state shall not deny to any person equality before the low or the equal protection of the law within the territory of India.

Article 41

The State shall within the limits of its economic capacity and development, make effective provision for securing the right to work, to education and to public assistance in case of unemployment, old age, sickness and disablement and other cases of undeserved want.

Article 45

The State shall endeavor to provide within the period of ten years from the commencement of this constitutions, for free and compulsory **education** to all children until they complete the age of 14 years.

Article 46

The State shall promote with special care, the educational and economic interest of the weaker sections of the people and in particular Scheduled Castes and Scheduled Tribes and shall protect them from Social injustice and all forms of exploitation. These articles provide equal treatment to all citizens irrespective of caste, creed, colour, religion and disablement etc. Thus Article 14 can be interpreted to mean that the state is under an obligation to equalize the opportunities to the individuals with disabilities through affirmative action. Under Article 41, State is supposed to provide free and compulsory education to all children including disabled children. Article 45 and 46 enjoin the State to provide assistance in the field of education, employment and financial assistance as well.

Legislation on Disabilities in India

Around 12% of the country's population is disabled, which is unable to take care of itself without proper guidance and training. They are entitled in all respects to the freedom recognized under the directive principles of Articles 14, 45, 46 and 47 of the constitution, to promotion with special care of the educational and economic interest and protection from social injustice and all forms of exploitation. There are a few major laws on disabilities in India. These are as under :

Mental Health Act 1987

This Act was introduced to consolidated and amend the law relating to the treatment and care of psychiatrically disabled people and to make better provisions with respect to their property affairs and for matter connected therewith or incidental thereto. But the Act 14 of 1987 defines' mentally ill person in section 2(1) as a person who is in need of treatment by reason of any mental disorder other than mental retardation. This act deals with establishment of psychiatric hospitals, psychiatric nursing homes, treatment care and protection of human rights of psychiatric disabled persons.

RCI Act 1992

The Rehabilitation Council of India was set up as a registered society in 1986. However, it was soon found that a Society could not ensure proper standardization and acceptance of the standards by other Organizations. The Parliament enacted Rehabilitation Council of India Act in 1992. The Rehabilitation

Council of India become Statutory Body on 22nd June 1993. The RCI Act was amended by the Parliament in 2000 to work it more broad based. The Act casts onerous responsibility on the Council. It also prescribes that any one delivering services to people with disability, who does not possess qualifications recognised by RCI, could be prosecuted. Thus the Council has the twin responsibility of standardizing and regulating the training of personnel and professional in the field of Rehabilitation and Special Education.

Objectives

- To regulate the training policies and programmes in the field of rehabilitation of persons with disabilities
- To bring about standardization of training courses for professionals dealing with persons with disabilities
- To prescribe minimum standards of education and training of various categories of professionals/ personnel dealing with people with disabilities
- To regulate these standards in all training institutions uniformly throughout the country
- To recognize institutions/ organizations/ universities running master's degree/ bachelor's degree/ P.G.Diploma/ Diploma/ Certificate courses in the field of rehabilitation of persons with disabilities
- To recognize degree/diploma/certificate awarded by foreign universities/ institutions on reciprocal basis
- To promote research in Rehabilitation and Special Education
- To maintain Central Rehabilitation Register for registration of professionals/ personnel
- To collect information on a regular basis on education and training in the field of rehabilitation of people with disabilities from institutions in India and abroad
- To encourage continuing education in the field of rehabilitation and special education by way of collaboration with organizations working in the field of disability.

- To recognize Vocational Rehabilitation Centres as manpower development centres
- To register vocational instructors and other personnel working in the Vocational Rehabilitation Centres
- To recognize the national institutes and apex institutions on disability as manpower development centres
- To register personnel working in national institutes and apex institutions on disability under the Ministry of Social Justice & Empowerment

Persons with Disability Act 1995 (Equal Opportunities, Protection of Rights and Full Participation)

According to this law, disability means a person who is unable to ensure by himself/ herself, wholly or partly, the necessities of a normal individual or social life including work, as a result of deficiency, whether congenital or not, in his/her physical or mental capabilities because of his / her being a person (i) who is blind (ii) speech and hearing impaired (iii) who is orthopaedically impaired (iv) who is mentally impaired.

This law provides for recognition by the State of the rights of persons with disabilities to enjoy equality of opportunities and full participation in national life and for matters connected therewith or incidental there to. It is a very comprehensive law, and covers aspects like prevention, early intervention, education, vocational training, employment, social security and the appointment of commissioners for persons with disabilities.

The National Trust Act 1999 for the welfare of persons with Autism, Cerebral Palsy, Mental Retardation and Multiple Disabilities

The National Trust for Welfare of Persons with Autism, Cerebral Palsy, Mental Retardation and Multiple Disabilities Act, 1999 No. 44 of 1999 (30th December 1999) is an act to provide for the constitution of a body at the national level for the Welfare of Persons with Autism, Cerebral Palsy, Mental Retardation and Multiple Disabilities and for matters connected therewith or incidental there to.

Special Education and the Rights of the Disabled to Equal Access

The Individuals with Disabilities Education Act (IDEA) prevents public schools from discriminating against students with disabilities, guaranteeing access to free, equal public education. Special education must meet the unique needs of the child and prepare him or her for further education and independent living. Services may include small group or individualized instruction, assistance technology, and rehabilitation aids such as speech therapy. While the education has to be appropriate for the district, it does not have to be the best available. Disabled children should not be unfairly isolated from their classmates. The law requires that they be educated alongside other children whenever possible.

Assessments of Your Child: Each state is responsible for carrying out the IDEA, and the school system is responsible for evaluating the child to see if the child qualifies for special education. Parents cannot force the school district to use an outside evaluation. A variety of disabilities entitle the child to special education, including learning disabilities such as AD/HD, behavioral problems, mental retardation, emotional disturbances, or hyperactivity, as well as some physical limitations such as sight or hearing loss.

The IEP and Placement Once the child qualifies for special ed, the school and the parents create an individualized education programme (IEP). Parents unhappy with their child's IEP are entitled to a hearing. If the court or administrative body determines the public school is not giving an appropriate education, it may be possible for parents to get reimbursement for a private school placement.

Disability Harassment Unfortunately, disabled children are sometimes victims of harassment from other students and surprisingly, sadly, even teachers. Harassment that interferes with learning may violate the child's civil rights and the Americans with Disabilities Act (ADA).

How Can a Lawyer Help? You may need a lawyer if you want a hearing regarding your child's IEP, if your child has been denied access to public schools, or is being harassed. Contact an education law attorney for specific advice about your situation.

Recent Trends in the Field of Special Education

Special education, as its name suggests, is a specialized branch of education. Claiming lineage to such persons as Jean-Marc-Gaspard Itard (1775–1838), the physician who "tamed" the "wild boy of Aveyron," and Anne Sullivan Macy (1866–1936), the teacher who "worked miracles" with Helen Keller, special educators teach those students who have physical, cognitive, language, learning, sensory, and/or emotional abilities that deviate from those of the general population. Special educators provide instruction specifically tailored to meet individualized needs, making education available to students who otherwise would have limited access to education. In 2001, special education in the United States was serving over five million students.

Although federally mandated special education is relatively new in the United States, students with disabilities have been present in every era and in every society. Historical records have consistently documented the most severe disabilities–those that transcend task and setting. Itard's description of the wild boy of Aveyron documents a variety of behaviors consistent with both mental retardation and behavioral disorders. Nineteenth-century reports of deviant behavior describe conditions that could easily be interpreted as severe mental retardation, autism, or schizophrenia. Milder forms of disability became apparent only after the advent of universal public education. When literacy became a goal for all children, teachers began observing disabilities specific to task and setting–that is, less severe disabilities. After decades of research and legislation, special education now provides services to students with varying degrees and forms of disabilities, including mental retardation, emotional disturbance, learning disabilities, speech-language (communication) disabilities, impaired hearing and deafness, low vision and blindness, autism, traumatic brain injury, other health impairments, and severe and multiple disabilities.

Development of the Field of Special Education

At its inception in the early nineteenth century, leaders of social change set out to cure many ills of society. Physicians and clergy, including Itard, Edouard O. Seguin (1812–1880), Samuel Gridley Howe (1801–1876), and Thomas Hopkins Gallaudet (1787–1851), wanted to ameliorate the neglectful, often abusive treatment of individuals with disabilities. A rich literature describes the treatment provided to individuals with disabilities in the 1800s: They were often confined in jails and almshouses without decent food, clothing, personal hygiene, and exercise. During much of the nineteenth century, and early in the twentieth, professionals believed individuals with disabilities were best treated in residential facilities in rural environments. Advocates of these institutions argued that environmental conditions such as urban poverty and vices induced behavioral problems. Reformers such as Dorothea Dix (1802–1887) prevailed upon state governments to provide funds for bigger and more specialized institutions.

These facilities focused more on a particular disability, such as mental retardation, then known as "feeble-mindedness" or "idiocy"; mental illness, then labeled "insanity" or "madness"; sensory impairment such as deafness or blindness; and behavioral disorders such as criminality and juvenile delinquency. Children who were judged to be delinquent or aggressive, but not insane, were sent to houses ofrefuge or reform schools, whereas children and adults judged to be "mad" were admitted to psychiatric hospitals.

Dix and her followers believed that institutionalization of individuals with disabilities would end their abuse (confinement without treatment in jails and poorhouses) and provide effective treatment. Moral treatment was the dominant approach of the early nineteenth century in psychiatric hospitals, the aim being cure. Moral treatment employed methods analogous to today's occupational therapy, systematic instruction, and positive reinforcement. Evidence suggests this approach was humane and effective in some cases, but the treatment was generally abandoned by the late nineteenth century, due largely to the failure of moral therapists to train others in their techniques and the rise of the belief that mental illness was always a result of brain disease.

By the end of the nineteenth century, pessimism about cure and emphasis on physiological causes led to a change in orientation that would later bring about the "warehouse-like" institutions that have become a symbol for abuse and neglect of society's most vulnerable citizens. The practice of moral treatment was replaced by the belief that most disabilities were incurable. This led to keeping individuals with disabilities ininstitutions both for their own protection and for the betterment of society. Although the transformation took many years, by the end of the nineteenth century the size of institutions had increased so dramatically that the goal of rehabilitation was no longer possible. Institutions became instruments for permanent segregation. Many special education professionals became critics of institutions. Howe, one of the first to argue for in stitutions for people with disabilities, began advocating placing out residents into families. Unfortunately this practice became a logistical and pragmatic problem before it could become a viable alternative to institutionalization.

At the close of the nineteenth century, state governments established juvenile courts and social welfare programmes, including foster homes, for children and adolescents. The child study movement became prominent in the early twentieth century. Using the approach pioneered by G. Stanley Hall (1844–1924; considered the founder of child psychology), researchers attempted to study child development scientifically in relation to education and in so doing established a place for psychology within public schools.

In 1931, the Bradley Home, the first psychiatric hospital for children in the United States, was established in East Providence, Rhode Island. The treatment offered in this hospital, as well as most of the other hospitals of the early twentieth century, was psychodynamic. Psychodynamic ideas fanned interest in the diagnosis and classification of disabili ties. In 1951 the first institution for research on exceptional children opened at the University of Illinois and began what was to become the newest focus of the field of special education: the slow learner and, eventually, what we know today as learning disability.

The Development of Special Education in Institutions and Schools

Although Itard failed to normalize Victor, the wild boy of Averyon, he did produce dramatic changes in Victor's behavior through education. Modern special education practices can be traced to Itard, and his work marks the beginning of widespread attempts to instruct students with disabilities. In 1817 the first special education school in the United States, the American Asylum for the Education and Instruction of the Deaf and Dumb (now called the American School for the Deaf), was established in Hartford, Connecticut, by Gallaudet. By the middle of the nineteenth century, special educational programmes were being provided in many asylums. Education was a prominent part of moral therapy. By the close of the nineteenth century, special classes within regular public schools had been launched in major cities. These special classes were initially established for immigrant students who were not proficient in English and students who had mild mental retardation or behavioral disorders. Descriptions of these children included terms such as steamer children, backward, truant, and incorrigible. Procedures for identifying "defectives" were included in the World's Fair of 1904. By the 1920s special classes for students judged unsuitable for regular classes had become common in major cities.

In 1840 Rhode Island passed a law mandating compulsory education for children, but not all states had compulsory education until 1918. With compulsory schooling and the swelling tide of anti-institution sentiment in the twentieth century, many children with disabilities were moved out of institutional settings and into public schools. However, by the mid-twentieth century children with disabilities were still often excluded from public schools and kept at home if not institutionalized. In order to respond to the new population of students with special needs entering schools, school officials created still more special classes in public schools.

The number of special classes and complementary support services (assistance given to teachers in managing behavior and learning problems) increased dramatically after World War II. During the early 1900s there was also an increased attention to mental health and a consequent interest in establishing child guidance clinics. By 1930 child guidance clinics and counseling services were relatively common features of major cities, and by 1950 special education had become an identifiable part of urban public education in nearly every school district.

By 1960 special educators were instructing their students in a continuum of settings that included hospital schools for those with the most severe disabilities, specialized day schools for students with severe disabilities who were able to live at home, and special classes in regular public schools for students whose disabilities could be managed in small groups. During this period special educators also began to take on the role of consultant, assisting other teachers in instructing students with disabilities. Thus, by 1970 the field of special education was offering a variety of educational placements to students with varying disabilities and needs; however, public schools were not yet required to educate all students regardless of their disabilities.

During the middle decades of the twentieth century, instruction of children with disabilities often was based on process training–which involves attempts to improve children's academic performance by teaching them cognitive or motor processes, such as perceptualmotor skills, visual memory, auditory memory, or auditory-vocal processing. These are ancient ideas that found twentieth-century proponents. Process training enthusiasts taught children various perceptual skills (*e.g.*, identifying different sounds or objects by touch) or perceptual motor skills (*e.g.*, balancing) with the notion that fluency in these skills would generalize to reading, writing, arithmetic, and other basic academic tasks. After many years of research, however, such training was shown not to be effective in improving academic skills. Many of these same ideas were recycled in the late twentieth century as learning styles, multiple intelligences, and other notions that the underlying process of learning varies with gender, ethnicity, or other physiological differences. None of these theories has found much support in reliable research, although direct instruction, mnemonic (memory) devices, and a few other instructional strategies have been supported reliably by research.

The History of Legislation in Special Education

Although many contend that special education was born with the passage of the Education for All Handicapped Children Act (EAHCA) in 1975, it is clear that special educators were beginning to respond to the needs of children with disabilities in public schools nearly a century earlier. It is also clear that EAHCA did not spring from a vacuum. This landmark law naturally evolved from events in both special education and the larger society and came about in large part due to the work of grass roots organizations composed of both parents and professionals. These groups dated back to the 1870s, when the American Association of Instructors of the Blind and the American Association on Mental Deficiency (the latter is now the American Association on Mental Retardation) were formed.

In 1922 the Council for Exceptional Children, now the major professional organization of special educators, was organized. In the 1930s and 1940s parent groups began to band together on a national level. These groups worked to make changes in their own communities and, consequently, set the stage for changes on a national level. Two of the most influential parent advocacy groups were the National Association for Retarded Citizens (now ARC/USA), organized in 1950, and the Association for Children with Learning Disabilities, organized in 1963. Throughout the first half of the twentieth century, advocacy groups were securing local ordinances that would protect and serve individuals with disabilities in their communities. For example, in 1930, in Peoria, Illinois, the first white cane ordinance gave individuals with blindness the right-of-way when crossing the street. By mid-century all states had legislation providing for education of students with disabilities. However, legislation was still noncompulsory.

In the late 1950s federal money was allocated for educating children with disabilities and for the training of special educators. Thus the federal government became formally involved in research and in training special education professionals, but limited its involvement to these functions until the 1970s. In 1971, this support was reinforced and extended to the state level when the Pennsylvania Association for Retarded Children (PARC) filed a class action suit against their Commonwealth. This suit, resolved by consent agreement, specified that all children age six through twenty-one were to be provided free public education in the least restrictive alternative (LRA, which would later become the least restrictive environment [LRE] clause in EAHCA). In 1973 the Rehabilitation Act prohibited discriminatory practices in programmes receiving federal financial assistance but imposed no affirmative obligations with respect to special education.

In 1975 the legal action begun under the Kennedy and Johnson administrations resulted in EAHCA, which was signed into law by President Gerald Ford. EAHCA reached full implementation in 1977 and required school districts to provide free and appropriate education to all of their students with disabilities. In return for federal funding, each state was to ensure that students with disabilities received non-discriminatory testing, evaluation, and placement; the right to due process; education in the least restrictive environment; and a free and appropriate education.

The centerpiece of this public law (known since 1990 as the Individuals with Disabilities Education Act, or IDEA) was, and is, a free appropriate public education (FAPE). To ensure FAPE, the law mandated that each student receiving special education receive an Individualized Education Programme (IEP). Under EAHCA, students with identified disabilities were to receive FAPE and an IEP that included relevant instructional goals and objectives, specifications as to length of school year, determination of the most appropriate educational placement, and descriptions of criteria to be used in evaluation and measurement. The IEP was designed to ensure that all students with disabilities received educational programmes specific to their "unique" needs. Thus, the education of students with disabilities became federally controlled.

In the 1982 case of Board of Education of the Hendrick Hudson Central School District v. Rowley, the U.S. Supreme Court clarified the level of services to be afforded students with special needs and ruled that special education services need only provide some "educational benefit" to students–public schools were not required to maximize the educational progress of students with disabilities. In so doing the Supreme Court further defined what was meant by a free and appropriate education. In 1990 EAHCA was amended to include a change to person-first language, replacing the term handicapped student with student with disabilities. The 1990 amendments also added new classification categories for students with autism and traumatic brain injury and transition plans within IEPs for students age fourteen or older.

In 1997, IDEA was reauthorized under President Clinton and amended to require the inclusion of students with disabilities in statewide and districtwide assessments, measurable IEP goals and objectives, and functional behavioral assessment and behavior intervention plans for students with emotional or behavioral needs. Because IDEA is amended and reauthorized every few years, it is impossible to predict the future of this law. It is possible that it will be repealed or altered dramatically by a future Congress. The special education story, both past and future, can be written in many different ways.

Trends in Special Education

Researchers have conceptualized the history of special education in stages that highlight the various trends that the field has experienced. Although some of these conceptualizations focus on changes involving instructional interventions for students with disabilities, others focus on the place of interventions. The focus on placement reflects the controversy in which the field of special education has found itself throughout history. Samuel G. Howe was one of the first to assert–in the nineteenth century–that instructional settings had inherent qualities that alone insured effective interventions. Belief in the essential curative powers of place spurred the late nineteenth century crusade for bigger and better institutions, as well as the mid-twentieth-century movement for deinstitutionalization. Exclusive focus on the importance of place distracted many professionals and prevented them from recognizing that dramatic changes in philosophy were accompanying the movement for deinstitutionalization.

In the late nineteenth century, social Darwinism replaced environmentalism as the primary causal explanation for those individuals with abilities who deviated from those of the general population, opening the door to the eugenics movement of the early twentieth century, and leading to the segregation and sterilization of individuals with mental retardation. At the beginning of the twentieth century, the debate had suddenly shifted from whether the disadvantaged should be helped to where these individuals should be served. As the institutionalization versus deinstitutionalization debate raged, many individuals were given custodial treatment, which is contrary to the mission of special education.

Almost a century after the placement debate began, special educators still focused on the importance of place. Many were calling upon the field to create not one perfect setting for the delivery of services, but a continuum of placement options that would address the needs of all students with disabilities. The civil rights movement had reconceptualized special education as a case of access of minorities to the educational privileges of the majority, and the least restrictive environment clause of EAHCA/IDEA prompted advocates for people with disabilities to call for mainstreaming–the return of students with disabilities to the regular classroom whenever and wherever possible.

In the 1980s the Regular Education Initiative (REI) was an attempt to return responsibility for the education of students with disabilities to neighborhood schools and regular classroom teachers. In the 1990s the full inclusion movement called for educating all students with disabilities in the regular classroom with a single, unified and responsive education system. Advocates for full inclusion, following in the footsteps of Howe, argued for appropriate instruction in a single, ubiquitous place, contrary to the mandate of IDEA.

Controversial Issues in Special Education

Special education has been the target of criticism throughout history. Some of the criticism has been justified, some unjustified. Some criticisms brought to light ineffective practices, such as the inefficacy and inhumanity of relegating all persons with disabilities to institutions. Other criticisms were distractions with disastrous repercussions, such as the singular focus on the importance of place while ignoring other inappropriate practices. The beginning of the twenty-first century found new criticisms being launched at special education.

Some argue that the use of diagnostic labels is potentially stigmatizing to students, others that minority students are overrepresented in some disability categories, and still others that education of students with disabilities in special classes and schools, even pulling students out for instruction in resource classes, is akin to race-based segregation. Some of these criticisms may expose ineffective practices, others may only distract educators from the effort of finding and implementing effective instructional practices. Professionals must develop the ability to learn from history and differentiate between unimportant criticisms and those with merit.

One valid criticism repeatedly launched against special education involves the implementation of ineffective educational interventions. Although great concern about the where of instruction was expressed in the 1980s and 1990s, little attention was given to the what of instruction. Throughout the twentieth century the field of special education repeatedly adopted instructional strategies of questionable efficacy–interventions that have little to no empirical basis. Additionally, special educators have adopted, with "bandwagon" fervor, many practices that have been proven ineffective and have thereby repeated the mistakes of history. If special education is to progress, professionals will need to address and remedy the instructional practices used with students with disabilities.

Special education has also been validly criticized for the way in which students with disabilities are identified. In the early nineteenth century, physicians and educators had difficulty making reliable distinctions between different disability categories.

In fact, the categories of mental retardation and behavioral disorders are inseparably intertwined. Many of the disability categories overlap to the extent that it is hard to differentiate one from the other. Additionally, some of the categories–learning disabilities and behavioral disorders, for example–are defined by the exclusion of other contributing disabilities. Thus, at the beginning of the twenty-first century, much work remains on the identification of students with disabilities.

University of Phoenix

Perhaps the largest, most pervasive issue in special education is its relationship to general education. The relationship of special to general education has been controversial since the beginning of universal public schooling. However, in the late twentieth and early twenty-first centuries, the question of whether special education should retain a separate identity or be fused with general education such that it has no separate identity (*e.g.*, budget, personnel) was made prominent by proponents of a radical restructuring of special education.

Proponents of radical restructuring and fusion argue that such integration is necessary to provide appropriate education for all students regardless of their disabilities and without stigma or discrimination. In their view, special education suffers primarily from structural problems, and the integration of two separate systems will result in a flexible, supple, responsive single system that will meet the needs of all students without "separating out" any. All teachers, according to this line of thinking, should be prepared to teach all students, including those with special needs.

Opponents of radical restructuring argue that special education's problems are primarily the lack of implementation of best practices, not structural. Moreover, they suggest, special education will not survive to serve the special needs of exceptional students if it loses its identity, including special budget allocations and personnel preparation. It is not feasible nor is it desirable, they contend, to prepare all teachers to teach all children; special training is required to teach students who are educationally exceptional. Arguments about the structure of education (special and general), who (if anyone) should receive special treatment, how they should be taught, and where special services should be provided are perpetual issues in special education.

These issues will likely continue to be debated throughout the twenty-first century. In the late twentieth and early twenty-first centuries, another issue became the basis for conceptual or theoretical bases for special education practices. Postmodern and antiscientific philosophies have been put forward in both general and special education. These ideas have been challenged by others who have noted the importance of the scientific method in discriminating among ideas and assertions. Likely, postmodern ideas and attempts to apply them to or refute them will be perpetual.

More than two hundred years after Itard began his work on the education of the wild boy of Aveyron, special educators are being asked to make decisions concerning such issues as placement and delivery of services. The inclusion debate, although important, has the potential to distract the field of special education away from issues of greater import–issues such as the efficacy of intervention and the accurate identification of students with disabilities.

If special educators are to avoid the mistakes of the past, they will need to make future decisions based upon reliable data, evaluating the efficacy of differing options. Since the inception of what is now known as IDEA, significant progress has been made in applying scientific research to the problems of special education. In the twenty-first century, special education need not remain a field of good intentions, but can fully employ the scientific child-study techniques begun in the late eighteenth century to provide free and appropriate educations to all children with disabilities.

Awareness and Attitudinal Changes Towards the Disabled

Attitude Formation and Motives for Change

Attitudes are directly influenced through questioning, personal experience and positive or negative reinforcement (Fossey, 1993; Sdorow, 1990, cited by Eby et al, 1998). Attitudes are indirectly influenced through social learning and observation or by learning through association (Fossey, 1993; Sdorow, 1990 cited by Eby et al, 1998).

The role of direct experience may be particularly important in attitude formation. Positive effects of contact have been demonstrated in many domains including attitudes towards the elderly, psychiatric patients and children with disability (Hewstone, 2003 citing Hewstone, 1996; Pettigrew, 1998 and Pettigrew et al, 2000).Attitudes formed through direct experience may be better predictors of later behaviour than attitudes formed through indirect experience. The superior predictive power of attitudes formed through direct experience is not necessarily a function of the amount of information about the attitude object available to the individual (Fazio et al, 1978 cited by Eby et al, 1998). Direct experience may affect the attitude formation process by altering the way in which available information is processed.

Hewstone (2003) attempts to answer how direct contact between groups work in changing attitudes and diminishing or banishing prejudices. He cites Pettigrew (1998) who proposes four major potential mechanisms: 1) learning about the other group, the "out group" 2) behaviour-driven attitude change *e.g.* forming more positive attitudes after cooperating in a learning task 3) "in-group" reappraisal and 4) generating affective ties. It is generating affective ties, including the formation of close friendships that seems to be most effective in reducing prejudice.

Direct contact is discussed further in the next section. Deal (2006) found that the contact hypothesis was not supported by his research on attitudes of people with disabilities to other people with disabilities and diverse functional impairments. However, he suggests that whether the contact between people with disabilities is voluntary or involuntary may be a significant variable.

Research has shown that the effects of attitude change depend on a host of individual and situational factors (Petty et al, 1998). A range of factors produces attitude change by different processes in different situations. There are multiple specific processes that can determine the extent and direction of attitude change (Petty et al, 1998). Based on the research evidence, Petty et al (1998) consider it useful to divide the processes responsible for modifying attitudes into those that emphasise effortful thinking about the main merits of the attitude object from those that do not. Such a framework allows understanding and prediction of the variables which will affect attitudes, by what processes in what situations and the consequences of these attitudes.

Attitudes that are changed as a result of considerable mental effort tend to be stronger than those changed with little thought and are more predictive of behaviour. Such attitudes are also more persistent and resistant to counter-persuasion than attitudes that are changed by processes involving little mental effort in assessing the main merits of the attitude object (Petty et al, 1998). Petty et al consider it useful to regard attitudes as falling along a continuum ranging from non-attitudes (see Converse, 1970) to strong attitudes (Fazio, 1986).

When studying interventions to tackle negative attitudes and their consequences the motives that generate attitude change and resistance are important. Wood (2000) reviewed the literature, focussing on the 2-year period from 1996 -1998 and found three central motives involved in attitude change. These involved 1) concerns with the self and with others 2) with the rewards/punishments they can provide and 3) with a valid understanding of reality.

The Contact Hypothesis

As mentioned above direct experience can be important in attitude formation. Allport (1954) in his classic volume, The Nature of Prejudice, expounded the contact hypothesis for future generations of policy makers and social psychologists (Hewstone, 2003). Yuker (1988) cited by Rao (2004) considered that attitudes to disability are complex and multifaceted and that the attitudinal consequences of contact with people with disabilities are mediated by the characteristics of both the person with a disability and without a disability and the nature of the interaction between the two.

Hewstone (2003), based on research evidence, outlines five key, facilitating conditions under which members of two "groups" should be brought together:

1. Under conditions of equal status
2. In situations where stereotypes are likely to be disproved
3. Where inter-group cooperation is required
4. Where participants can get to know each other properly
5. Where wider social norms support equality.

Hewstone (2003) argues that successful inter-group contact promotes more positive "out-group" attitudes, increases the perceived variability of the "out-group", which now appears less homogenous and inter-group contact can also promote increased "outgroup" trust. Hewstone (2003) demonstrates from research that contact works, how it works and when it works. Antonak (1981) showed that the most influential factor in the attitudinal scores in his study was the intensity of contact with people with disabilities. "Where there is evidence on what changes attitudes, it centres on the impact of contact between disabled and non-disabled people.

This seems to work more than any other method- more, for example, than big communications campaigns. However, contact must be on at least equal terms" (Massie, 2006 citing Hewstone, 2003). "Contact on equal terms can also be achieved through training, and evidence shows that training led by, for example, people with mental health problems, impacts on attitudes and that this change is sustained over time" (Massie, 2006 citing Employers Forum on Disability Equal Opportunities Review, 2005). Wai Au et al (2006) compared attitudes of students (n=511) and four groups of health professionals (n=489) toward people with disabilities using an international attitude scale. The quality of contact was found to be a dominant factor affecting the attitude scores. In addition, significant factors in determining the attitudes held by students and professionals include age, year of study, knowledge and educational level[2]. Wai Au et al (2006) cite other studies including Gelber (1993) and Elmaleh (2000) that also found that contact and knowledge factors influence the development of positive attitudes towards people with disabilities.

Disability Awareness Training, Knowledge and Understanding

Gleeson (2006) describes how, in a "Making Access Happen" training programme for librarians, the participants, including herself, the mother of a child with a disability, after naming several different factors which cause people with disabilities to be excluded, finally acknowledged and were shocked that they themselves did not consider disabled people to be normal. However, this allowed them to change: "Now we were able to see and discuss how social structures reflect individual thinking and how individual thinking is shaped by social structures in any given society at any given time. This unconscious thinking about 'normal' and 'not normal' was brought to the surface through the training approach without blame or guilt because the discussion clarified that the individual and society are intimately connected to the socialisation process from when we are very small children. Participants very quickly moved to being able to identify ways in which society and libraries are designed, constructed and 'programmed' out of 'normal' thinking" (Gleeson, 2006).

"Those promoting disability awareness should understand that most people, if challenged, would deny that they treat disabled people unfairly. They will usually express considerable goodwill towards a group they tend to regard as unfortunate victims who are, sadly, disadvantaged. However, this sympathy and goodwill often conceals a deep reluctance to accept disabled people on equal terms. This is often based on unquestioned, deeply held negative assumptions or stereotypes"

Shevlin and Moore (1999) showed how a mainstream school in Ireland facilitated interaction between profoundly intellectually disabled young people and a group of adolescents from the school who were uneasy around peers with intellectual disabilities. The results were that the adolescents became more comfortable with their disabled counterparts. By facilitating this interaction, the mainstream school that the able bodied young people attended was fostered inclusion and the development of respect for and recognition of different abilities (cited by Lodge et al, 2004, p. 97).

How disability awareness training is carried out is important and its impact must be evaluated. Gash (1996) cited by NDA (2004) reported on an educational programme designed to increase awareness of children with disabilities amongst primary school children in Ireland. The results were mixed. On the one hand, the programme encouraged children to treat children with disabilities in a "more ordinary" way. On the other hand, some children "hardened" their attitudes, even becoming dismissive of children with disabilities.

Disability Awareness Training and Education is required for all professionals. Mukerherjee et al (2000) as cited by Lodge et al (2004) point out that teachers need to have a full understanding of the implications of particular impairments for teaching and learning if the are to inform other students or supports students with impairments. The Task Force on Autism (2001) made similar observations with respect to the education of students with Autistic Syndrome Disorder. The Task Force on Dyslexia (2001) observed that teachers often failed either to identify or fully recognise a learner's disability or have an inadequate understanding of it (cited by Lodge et al, 2004). Rao (2004) reviewed the literature with regards the attitudes of university staff towards students with disabilities in higher education. Only two studies investigated the relationship between attitudes of staff and willingness to provide accommodations and the results of these studies did not show a clear relationship between the two but this is an area that needs further exploration. Rao concludes from the literature that faculty need to bc better informed about students with disabilities to improve their attitudes and that the attitudes of staff could be a vital ingredient in the success or failure of students with disabilities.

Rohland et al (2003) report on a collaborative training Project at the University of Rhode Island in the Sather primary goal was to work with faculty and administrators at the State's post-secondary institutions to develop more inclusive and supportive learning environments for students with disabilities. This project aimed to prepare at least one faculty member in each academic department and one administrator in each administrative unit to serve as a disability resource mentor to colleagues and as a liaison to Disability Services. In this way a multi-institutional network of disability resource mentors throughout the State would be developed. The project included a 4day workshop for the mentors that included exploring attitudes and active involvement in identifying how students with disabilities could be assisted to meet department and programme requirements. Mentors were given a resource manual and a resource website was also established. Each mentor then worked within their own unit with their colleagues. One of the assumptions underlying this approach is that departmental colleagues respect one another and therefore can be very influential in the process of changing attitudes. The immediate effectiveness of the training for participants as well as the long-term effect of the training on the postsecondary learning environment was evaluated. Long-term impact on the post secondary environment included policy changes and improved communication.

Remove Obstacles to Achieving Human Potential

Negative public and social attitudes are major obstacles to accessing the basic conditions required to achieve human potential because they develop, reinforce and solidify socio-environmental barriers to participation in work and other mainstream activities (Clarke et al, 2000 cited by Brostrand, 2006).

The basic conditions required for each person to develop their potential and to live as responsible, autonomous individuals are basic human rights. Understanding and promoting the values underpinning basic rights or the basic human conditions required for development- equality, autonomy, dignity and solidarity/social justice- is essential if governments and individuals are to commit themselves to ensuring that each and every person can access the conditions required to live as self-determining individuals.

The values underpinning human rights or the basic conditions required to fulfil human potential in each setting, be it the home, the school, the workplace or the wider society, need to be promoted. Quinn et al (2002) define the values of equality, autonomy/selfdetermination, dignity and social justice that underpin human rights as follows: Equality- the imposition of benefits or burdens, and the process of setting the terms of entry and participation in the mainstream, are to be set with all equally in mind, which may require accommodation towards some.Autonomy/self-determination- all persons are ends and not means to ends and can freely choose their own ends in life3. Dignity- every human being is of inestimable value regardless of difference. Social justice/ Solidarity- we owe something to one another in society in order to help people realise their self-fulfilment.

Morris (2005) outlines some of the development of thinking with regards these values such as the need to re-define self-determination to include situations where people need support to exercise autonomy.

* A need for support does not mean that someone cannot experience self-determination
* In order for people with disabilities to have equal opportunities to be full citizens, it is necessary to take action to remove barriers to self-determination, and, for some people with disabilities, it will be necessary to use resources to support self-determination
* The action to be taken must be determined by people with disabilities themselves.

Included implicitly in each of the values that underpin human rights is the value of difference. For people with disabilities to have equal opportunities, to participate and to contribute as equal citizens "we need a society where difference does not mean you cannot belong but where instead our common humanity is recognised and valued. We will all benefit if everyone can achieve their potential through participation and maximising their participation within and contribution to families, communities and society" (Morris, 2005). Diversity needs to be addressed in a wide variety of settings including educational curricula.

The public have an important role to play in welcoming diversity as an integral, important and enriching part of society. According to Massie (2006) it is the recognition of difference that makes the ADA legislation in the USA crucially different from other forms of anti-discrimination law." The Act's approach is to recognise that equality is not about treating everyone in the same way. It is about responding to different needs in the different ways that best suit them. The DDA is not about equal treatment, because to treat everyone the same is to ignore their essential differences with the perverse effect of creating or sustaining inequality. It can take different treatment to provide equal opportunities." To open up opportunities for all on an equal basis, differences need to be systematically taken into account and catered for. There needs to be an active acceptance, welcoming and accommodation of difference/ diversity rather than its' avoidance, elimination or denial.

UNIT-II

Blindness and Low Vision

Definitions and Identification

The categorization of visual impairment currently in use worldwide is based on the ICD 10th Revision 1st and 2nd edition. This is derived from a WHO Study group on the Prevention of Blindness that was convened in 1972 to provide a standardized definition. This was to facilitate the collection of population based data on prevalence of vision impairment and blindness in a uniform and comparable manner. At the time of this meeting four major causes of vision loss had been identified. These were Trachoma, Onchocerciasis, Xerophthalmia and Cataract. There was no consideration of refractive error as an underlying cause of visual impairment, if not blindness.

Case for Revision

There are five issues that dictate the need for consideration of a revision of the current definition and categorization. These are:

(1) The definition of visual impairment categories based on "best corrected" vision

(2) The nomenclature

(3) The categorization of Blindness

(4) The inconsistencies within H 54 subcategories

(5) The ICO Resolution on Revision of ICD 10

Recommendations of WHO Consultation on "Development of Standards for Characterization of Vision Loss and visual functioning".

(1) *Definition of Visual Impairment and Blindness:* The currently used definition includes the term "best Corrected Vision" in the better eye.

The methodology followed for measuring visual acuity, particularly in population based studies, is to use a "pin hole" in patients whose "presenting" vision is below a certain cut off point (currently 6/18). Many recent studies have shown that the use of "best corrected" vision overlooks a large proportion of persons with visual impairment, including blindness, due to uncorrected refractive error, a common occurrence in many parts of the world.

Uncorrected refractive error is now considered to be a major cause of visual impairment and estimations are under way to calculate the loss in terms of DALYs (disability-adjusted life years) resulting from this cause.

The correction of refractive error is a cost effective intervention and is one of the priorities under the disease control component of the Global Initiative for the Elimination of Avoidable Blindness (VISION 2020, the Right to Sight).

(2) *Nomenclature:* The current ICD uses the words "LOW VISION" for categories 1, 2 and 3 of Vision impairment.

In the practice of eye care "LOW VISION" has a specific meaning as defined by WHO.

This is as follows:

"A person with low vision is one who has impairment of visual functioning even after treatment and/or standard refractive correction, and has a visual acuity of less than 6/18 to light perception, or a visual field of less than 10 degree from the point of fixation, but who uses, or is potentially able to use, vision for planning and/or execution of a task."

Under this definition persons who would benefit from low vision care also exist among those who are currently categorized as blind. This has led to miscalculations in the estimation of persons requiring LOW VISION care.

(3) *Definition of Blindness:* The current definition does not make a distinction between those who have "irreversible" blindness (NO perception of light) and those that have light perception but are still less than 3/60 in the better eye.

The management of these two categories is different and categorization based on this would be useful.

Legal Blindness: In order to determine which people may need special assistance because of their visual disabilities, various governmental jurisdictions have formulated more complex definitions referred to as legal blindness. In North America and most of Europe, legal blindness is defined as visual acuity (vision) of 20/200 (6/60) or less in the better eye with best correction possible.

This means that a legally blind individual would have to stand 20 feet (6.1 m) from an object to see it—with vision correction—with the same degree of clarity as a normally sighted person could from 200 feet (61 m). In many areas, people with average acuity who nonetheless have a visual field of less than 20 degrees (the norm being 180 degrees) are also classified as being legally blind. Approximately ten percent of those deemed legally blind, by any measure, have no vision. The rest have some vision, from light perception alone to relatively good acuity. Low vision is sometimes used to describe visual acuities from 20/70 to 20/200.

By the 10th Revision of the WHO International Statistical Classification of Diseases, Injuries and Causes of Death, low vision is defined as visual acuity of less than 6/18 (20/60), but equal to or better than 3/60 (20/400), or corresponding visual field loss to less than 20 degrees, in the better eye with best possible correction. Blindness is defined as visual acuity of less than 3/60 (20/400), or corresponding visual field loss to less than 10 degrees, in the better eye with best possible correction.

It should be noted that blind people with undamaged eyes may still register light non-visually for the purpose of circadian entrainment to the 24-hour light/dark cycle. Light signals for this purpose travel through the retinohypothalamic tract (RHT), so a damaged optic nerve beyond where the RHT exits it is no hindrance.

Legal Blindness

In 1934, the American Medical Association (AMA) adopted the following definition of blindness:

Central visual acuity of 20/200 or less in the better eye with corrective glasses or central visual acuity of more than 20/200 if there is a visual field defect in which the peripheral field is contracted to such an extent that the widest diameter of the visual field subtends an angular distance no greater than 20 degrees in the better eye.

The United States Congress included this definition as part of the Aid to the Blind programme in the Social Security Act passed in 1935. In 1972, the Aid to the Blind programme and two others combined under Title XVI of the Social Security Act to form the Supplemental Security Income programme which currently states:

An individual shall be considered to be blind for purposes of this title if he has central visual acuity of 20/200 or less in the better eye with the use of a correcting lens. An eye which is accompanied by a limitation in the fields of vision such that the widest diameter of the visual field subtends an angle no greater than 20 degrees shall be considered for purposes of the first sentence of this subsection as having a central visual acuity of 20/200 or less. An individual shall also be considered to be blind for purposes of this title if he is blind as defined under a State plan approved under title X or XVI as in effect for October 1972 and received aid under such plan (on the basis of blindness) for December 1973, so long as he is continuously blind as so defined.

Kuwait is one of many nations that share the same criteria for legal blindness.

Epidemiology

In 1987, it was estimated that 598,000 people in the United States met the legal definition of blindness. Of this number, 58% were over the age of 65. In 1994-1995, 1.3 million Americans reported legal blindness.

In the November 2004 article Magnitude and causes of visual impairment, the WHO estimated that in 2002 there were 161 million (about 2.6% of the world population) visually impaired people in the world, of whom 124 million (about 2%) had low vision and 37 million (about 0.6%) were blind.

Causes of Blindness

Serious visual impairment has a variety of causes:

Diseases

Most visual impairment is caused by disease and malnutrition. According to WHO estimates in 2002, the most common causes of blindness around the world are:

- cataracts (47.9%),
- glaucoma (12.3%),
- age-related macular degeneration (AMD) (8.7%),
- corneal opacity (5.1%), and
- diabetic retinopathy (4.8%), among other causes.

People in developing countries are significantly more likely to experience visual impairment as a consequence of treatable or preventable conditions than are their counterparts in the developed world. While vision impairment is most common in people over age 60 across all regions, children in poorer communities are more likely to be affected by blinding diseases than are their more affluent peers.

The link between poverty and treatable visual impairment is most obvious when conducting regional comparisons of cause. Most adult visual impairment in North America and Western

Europe is related to age-related macular degeneration and diabetic retinopathy. While both of these conditions are subject to treatment, neither can be cured.

In developing countries, wherein people have shorter life expectancies, cataracts and water-borne parasites—both of which can be treated effectively—are most often the culprits (see River blindness, for example). Of the estimated 40 million blind people located around the world, 70–80% can have some or all of their sight restored through treatment.

In developed countries where parasitic diseases are less common and cataract surgery is more available, age-related macular degeneration, glaucoma, and diabetic retinopathy are usually the leading causes of blindness.

Abnormalities and Injuries

Eye injuries, most often occurring in people under 30, are the leading cause of monocular blindness (vision loss in one eye) throughout the United States. Injuries and cataracts affect the eye itself, while abnormalities such as optic nerve hypoplasia affect the nerve bundle that sends signals from the eye to the back of the brain, which can lead to decreased visual acuity.

People with injuries to the occipital lobe of the brain can, despite having undamaged eyes and optic nerves, still be legally or totally blind.

Genetic Defects

People with albinism often suffer from visual impairment to the extent that many are legally blind, though few of them actually cannot see. Leber's congenital amaurosis can cause total blindness or severe sight loss from birth or early childhood.

Recent advances in mapping of the human genome have identified other genetic causes of low vision or blindness. One such example is Bardet-Biedl syndrome.

Poisoning

Rarely, blindness is caused by the intake of certain chemicals. A well-known example is methanol, which ironically is only mildly toxic and minimally intoxicating, but when not competing with ethanol for metabolism, methanol breaks down into the substances formaldehyde and formic acid which in turn can cause blindness, an array of other health complications, and death. Methanol is commonly found in methylated spirits, denatured ethyl alcohol, to avoid paying taxes on selling ethanol intended for human consumption. Methylated spirits are sometimes used by alcoholics as a desperate and cheap substitute for regular ethanol alcoholic beverages.

Willful Actions

Blinding has been used as an act of vengeance and torture in some instances, to deprive a person of a major sense by which they can navigate or interact within the world, act fully independently, and be aware of events surrounding them. An example from the classical realm is Oedipus, who gouges out his own eyes after realizing that he fulfilled the awful prophecy spoken of him. In 2003, a Pakistani man named Mohammad Sajid was sentenced to be blinded under Islamic Qisas law, for blinding his fiancee after her parents called off the engagement.

Treatments

A 2008 study published in the New England Journal of Medicine tested the effect of using gene therapy to help restore the sight of patients with a rare form of inherited blindness, known as Leber Congenital Amaurosis or LCA. Leber Congenital Amaurosis damages the light receptors in the retina and usually begins affecting sight in early childhood, with worsening vision until complete blindness around the age of 30.

The study used a common cold virus to deliver a normal version of the gene called RPE65 directly into the eyes of affected patients. Remarkably all 3 patients aged 19, 22 and 25 responded well to the treatment and reported improved vision following the procedure. Due to the age of the patients and the degenerative nature of LCA the improvement of vision in gene therapy patients is encouraging for researchers. It is hoped that gene therapy may be even more effective in younger LCA patients who have experienced limited vision loss as well as in other blind or partially blind individuals.

Adaptive Techniques

Visually impaired and blind people have devised a number of techniques that allow them to complete daily activities using their remaining senses. These might include the following:

- Adaptive computer and mobile phone software that allows people with visual impairments to interact with their computers and/or phones via screen readers or screen magnifiers.
- Adaptations of banknotes so that the value can be determined by touch. For example:
    - In some currencies, such as the euro, the pound sterling and the Norwegian krone, the size of a note increases with its value.
    - Some currencies' banknotes have a tactile feature to indicate denomination. For example, the tactile feature is a system of raised dots in one corner, based on Braille cells but not standard Braille.
    - It is also possible to fold notes in different ways to assist recognition.
- Labeling and tagging clothing and other personal items
- Placing different types of food at different positions on a dinner plate
- Marking controls of household appliances

Most people, once they have been visually impaired for long enough, devise their own adaptive strategies in all areas of personal and professional management.

For corrective surgery of blindness, see acquired vision.

Tools

Designers, both visually impaired and sighted, have developed a number of tools for use by blind people.

Mobility

Many people with serious visual impairments can travel independently, using a wide range of tools and techniques.

Orientation and mobility specialists are professionals who are specifically trained to teach people with visual impairments how to travel safely, confidently, and independently in the home and the community. These professionals can also help blind people to practice travelling on specific routes which they may use often, such as the route from one's house to a convenience store. Becoming familiar with an environment or route can make it much easier for a blind person to navigate successfully.

Tools such as the white cane with a red tip- the international symbol of blindness- may also be used to improve mobility. A long cane is used to extend the user's range of touch sensation. It is usually swung in a low sweeping motion, across the intended path of travel, to detect obstacles. However, techniques for cane travel can vary depending on the user and/or the situation. Some visually impaired persons do not carry these kinds of canes, opting instead for the shorter, lighter identification (ID) cane. Still others require a support cane. The choice depends on the individual's vision, motivation, and other factors.

A small number of people employ guide dogs to assist in mobility. These dogs are trained to navigate around various obstacles, and to indicate when it becomes necessary to go up or down a step. However, the helpfulness of guide dogs is limited by the inability of dogs to understand complex directions. The human half of the guide dog team does the directing, based upon skills acquired through previous mobility training. In this sense, the handler might be likened to an aircraft's navigator, who must know how to get from one place to another, and the dog is the pilot, who gets them there safely.

Government actions are sometimes taken to make public places more accessible to blind people. Public transportation is freely available to the blind in many cities. Tactile paving and audible traffic signals can make it easier and safer for visually impaired pedestrians to cross streets. In addition to making rules about who can and cannot use a cane, some governments mandate the right-of-way be given to users of white canes or guide dogs.

Reading and Magnification

Most visually impaired people who are not totally blind read print, either of a regular size or enlarged by magnification devices. Many also read large-print, which is easier for them to read without such devices. A variety of magnifying glasses, some handheld, and some on desktops, can make reading easier for them.

The rest read Braille (or the infrequently used Moon type), or rely on talking books and readers or reading machines. They use computers with special hardware such as scanners and refreshable Braille displays as well as software written specifically for the blind, such as optical character recognition applications and screen readers.

Some people access these materials through agencies for the blind, such as the National Library Service for the Blind and Physically Handicapped in the United States, the National Library for the Blind or the RNIB in the United Kingdom.

Closed-circuit televisions, equipment that enlarges and contrasts textual items, are a more high-tech alternative to traditional magnification devices. So too are modern web browsers, which can increase the size of text on some web pages through browser controls or through user-controlled style sheets.

There are also over 100 radio reading services throughout the world that provide people with vision impairments with readings from periodicals over the radio. The International Association of Audio Information Services provides links to all of these organizations.

Computers

Access technology such as screen readers and Screen magnifiers enable the blind to use mainstream computer applications. Most legally blind people (70% of them across all ages, according to the Seattle Lighthouse for the Blind) do not use computers. Only a small fraction of this population, when compared to the sighted community, have Internet access. This bleak outlook is changing, however, as availability of assistive technology increases, accompanied by concerted efforts to ensure the accessibility of information technology to all potential users, including the blind. Later versions of Microsoft Windows include an Accessibility Wizard & Magnifier for those with partial vision, and Microsoft Narrator, a simple screen reader. Linux distributions (as Live CDs) for the blind include Oralux and Adriane Knoppix, the latter developed in part by Adriane Knopper who has a visual impairment. The Macintosh OS also comes with a built-in screen reader, called VoiceOver.

The movement towards greater web accessibility is opening a far wider number of websites to adaptive technology, making the web a more inviting place for visually impaired surfers.

Experimental approaches in sensory substitution are beginning to provide access to arbitrary live views from a camera.

Other Aids

People may use talking thermometers, enlarged or marked oven dials, talking watches, talking clocks, talking scales, talking calculators, talking compasses and other talking equipment.

Sports

Blind and partially sighted people participate in sports such as swimming, snow skiing and athletics. Some sports have been invented or adapted for the blind such as goalball, cricket and golf. The worldwide authority on sports for the blind is the International Blind Sports Federation (IBSA). People with vision impairments have participated in the Paralympic Games since the 1976 summer Paralympics in Toronto.

Low Vision

Definition: Low vision is a term that denotes a level of vision that is 20/70 or worse and cannot be fully corrected with conventional glasses. Low vision is not the same as blindness. Unlike a person who is blind, a person with low vision has some useful sight. However, low vision usually interferes with the performance of daily activities, such as reading or driving. A person with low vision may not recognize images at a distance or be able to differentiate colours of similar tones. Although low vision can occur at any stage in life, it primarily affects the elderly. However, low vision is not a natural part of aging. Although most people experience some physiological changes with age (presbyopia), these changes usually do not lead to low vision. Most people develop low vision because of eye diseases. Common causes of low vision, particularly with older adults, include macular degeneration, glaucoma, and diabetic retinopathy. When vision impairment is recognized early, treatment can be more effective, enabling people to maintain as much independence as possible.

You are legally blind when the best corrected central acuity is less than 20/200 (perfect visual acuity is 20/20) in your better eye, or your side vision is narrowed to 20 degrees or less in your better eye. People who are legally blind may still have some useful vision, just like people who have low vision. If you are legally blind, you may qualify for certain government benefits. It is estimated that approximately 17% of people over the age of 65 are either blind or have low vision.

Low Vision Exams

To determine the extent of your useful vision, you will need to have your eyes examined. The examination for low vision differs from typical eye examination. During a low vision examination, your doctor may administer the following tests:

- Refraction (to assess your vision and determine the prescription for your glasses, if glasses may be of any use)
- Visual field (to assess your peripheral vision)
- Ocular motility (to assess how well your eyes move)

Because low vision examinations may involve a variety of tests, they are often more time consuming than the standard examination. For instance, refraction may be done through a telescope or trial lens so you can judge which lens is best.

Symptoms

- Difficulty recognizing objects at a distance (street signs or bus signs)

- Difficulty differentiating colours (particularly in the green-blue-violet range)
- Difficulty seeing well up close (reading or cooking)

The symptoms described above may not necessarily mean that you have low vision. However, if you experience one or more of these symptoms, contact your eye doctor for a complete exam. Your eye doctor can tell the difference between normal changes which are common with age and changes caused by eye disease.

Treatment

The Kellogg Eye Center Low Vision and Visual Rehabilitative Services Clinic embraces a multi-disciplinary approach to the treatment of low vision. Ophthalmologists, optometrists and occupational therapists make up the team of health care professionals who will work with you starting with your vision examination, and continuing to work with you to identify treatment options, which include:

- Optical devices that will help you adapt, such as magnifiers, telephones or closed-circuit televisions.
- Techniques that will help you utilize your remaining vision.
- Environmental modifications to maximize your remaining vision.
- Adaptive non-optical devices, such as large-print cookbooks and talking watches.

Occupational therapy programmes may last as long as several months or be as brief as one session. Occupational therapy treatment is available at Kellogg. Sessions include an evaluation of your environment and suggestions for modifying your home to enable you to become more independent and to improve safety.

Low Vision Aids

Many types of assistive devices are available to assist people with low vision. These items include special glasses and other magnification devices, and large print reading materials, shown above. Other communication aids include computer software and various other technological devices.

These items include special glasses and other magnification devices, and large print reading materials, shown above. Other communication aids include computer software and various other technological devices.

Incidence and Prevalence

Statistical information such as prevalence, incidence, deaths, and other data is provided from numerous sources and is subject to numerous provisos. Nevertheless, it is hoped to be useful, if not completely accurate.

Prevalence versus Incidence: Prevalence and incidence are different measures of a disease's occurrence. The "prevalence" of a condition means the number of people who currently have the condition, whereas "incidence" refers to the annual number of people who have a case of the condition. These two measures are very different. A chronic incurable disease like diabetes can have a low incidence but high prevalence, because the prevalence is the cumulative sum of past year incidence rates. A short-duration curable condition such as the common cold can have a high incidence but low prevalence, because many people get a cold each year, but few people actually have a cold at any given time (so prevalence is low and is not a very useful statistic). To understand prevalence versus incidence, consider these examples (which over-simplify but are still hopefully useful):

- *Short-duration Disease:* A person who has a common cold for one day, would be added to the incidence statistics, but (theoretically anyway) shouldn't be on the prevalence list.
- *Newly Diagnosed Chronic Disease:* A person diagnosed with diabetes will be on the incidence numbers and prevalence numbers in that first year, but then only on the prevalence numbers for second or later years.
- *Deaths:* A person who dies from a disease stops being on the prevalence data for both later years and also the

current year (unless prevalence statistics include this time period). That person will be on the incidence numbers only for the year they were diagnosed, and not in the year they die if they had the disease more than a year. A death from a short disease like flu does get included in incidence, but not prevalence. A death after many years from a long-term disease like diabetes removes that person from prevalence numbers (and they should only have been on the incidence data their first diagnosis year).

Maximum of Prevalence or Incidence: Taking the maximum value of either of the prevalence and incidence numbers for a disease is a reasonably useful indicator that is used in certain places throughout this information. It is a kind of "people affected" measure that gives an approximate value to the number of people who would have to deal with a condition in any given year.

Problems with Prevalence Data: Prevalence attempts to measure the number of people affected by a condition at any given time. There are various possible problems with prevalence data:

- *Diagnosed versus Undiagnosed Prevalence:* Two estimates of prevalence are not necessarily comparable. Some estimates attempt to quantify the number of diagnosed people. Other prevalence estimates attempt to include undiagnosed people who unknowingly have the condition. Some prevalence numbers include only symptomatic conditions whereas others may include latent infections.
- *Different Methods of Gathering Prevalence Data:* Prevalence numbers may also have been computed via various estimate methods ranging from research studies to phone surveys.
- *Prevalence and "Cured" or "Remission" Conditions:* Conditions that go into "remission" but are not necessarily "cured", such as cancer, cause problems for prevalence data. Some such estimates use 5-year

prevalence or 10-year prevalence estimates, which includes only people who have had cancer 5 or 10 years previously (even if they are "cured"). This effectively assumes that a remission becomes a cure after 5 or 10 years, so the person is then excluded from the prevalence numbers.

Problems with Incidence Data: Incidence data attempts to measure the number of people who become affected with a condition each year. Incidence includes only new conditions, not ongoing treatment of existing conditions. The actual number of people affected by a condition in a year can be less than incidence reports in cases where people get multiple cases (*e.g.* common cold).

Two incidence rates are not necessarily comparable. Some incidence data uses government notifications, others based on physician or hospital diagnoses, and various other methods. Some estimates of incidence for under-diagnosed conditions attempt to justify a larger incidence rate than is reported by doctors or medical authorities, whereas other rates may use only the official reported rates.

Rates of Incidence/Prevalence Calcuations: This site attempts to manipulate prevalence and incidence data to give more relevant data, such as to report the percent of the population affected, total number of people affected nationally, or the odds in a "1 in 1000" format. These computations are based on population data for the relevant reporting region (usually the national USA). Details of abbreviations used for sources of statistics can be found on our sources page. Some computation rates use different base data: prevalence, incidence, or maximum of prevalence/incidence. In some cases where the data is reported as a word such as "common", "rare", "uncommon" or similar phrase, an arbitrary numerical percentage has been applied to this information. Data that is reported based on births, such as 1-in-3000 births, has either been left as is (for chronic conditions) or modified by an estimate of the number of births. Data reported as a percent of pregnancies or pregnant women has been calculated using an estimate of the number of pregnancies annually.

Lifetime Risk Data: Some conditions report a risk factor for having a condition in your lifetime. For example, cancer is widely reported to affect about 1 in 3 people in their lifetime. These rates are naturally much higher than either prevalence or incidence data, because they are effectively the cumulative risk of incidence/prevalence over multiple years.

General Problems with the Data: In addition to the above discussion, there are various general qualifiers with regard to prevalence, incidence, and any of the other types of data. Use of the data may incur the old apples-and-oranges comparison problem because of data differences. Problems with using the data include:

- *Unclear Sources:* there are numerous statistics reported in articles and on the internet, and determining the actual study or survey on which an estimate is based is often difficult, even for statistics reported by health authorities or government agencies.
- *Data Ranges:* where a rate is reported as a range, such as "3 to 5 million people", the lower number is arbitrarily chosen and used here. This is a conservative assumption, but may cause some estimates to be lower than they should.
- *Different Definitions of Prevalence:* some prevalence numbers use estimates of people diagnosed, others try also to include estimated of undiagnosed people, and some use different values like 5-year prevalence or 10-year prevalence data.
- *Different Sources:* data has been collected from numerous sources, and the reputability and accuracy of each source cannot reasonably be completely confirmed.
- *Different Study Methodologies:* the data comes from various studies that used different methodologies. Some data comes from government notification bodies, other from patient phone surveys, others using various methods of estimation, and so on. Many estimates are computed from a small sample and then extrapolated

to a larger population group, and this method has various inherent limitations to its accuracy.

- *Different Disease Categories:* some data may use different categorization arrangements to determine who has a particular disease. Some studies use the ICD categories, others do not, and there are actually small variations in the different ICD categorizations in any case. For example, should wheezing be part of asthma or separate?
- *Different Years:* data may come from numerous different years.
- *Different Locations:* data may come from different countries, states, or areas.
- *Different Age Groups*: data may refer to a particular age group, such as "3% of adults", and may not necessarily reflect the overall prevalence in the entire population of all ages.
- *Different Racial Factors:* some data may reflect a particular race more accurately and not apply to the entire population.
- *Inherent Reporting Bias:* although most reputable organizations use official indepedent statistics, some organizations may tend to quote higher numbers because either (a) they see the medical condition every day and assume it is highly prevalence, or (b) to make the conditions they monitor seem more important such as to justify funding levels or seek donations.
- *Country-specific Information:* Most of the data is reported from USA sources, and may be of limited value to other countries. For example, certain conditions have a much higher prevalence worldwide, especially in developing countries, than in industrialized nations like the USA.

Characteristics

Visual impairment can be divided into five categories: (1) functional limitation in seeing print, (2) severe functional limitation in seeing print, (3) severely visually impaired people of working age, (4) legally blind persons, and (5) legally blind persons who are totally blind. Functional limitation in seeing print has two levels: nonsevere, *i.e.*, difficulty in seeing letters in ordinary print even with glasses; and severe, *i.e.*, inability to see letters in ordinary print even with glasses.

Functional Limitation in Seeing Print

Nationwide it is estimated that 9.7 million adults have a significant functional limitation in seeing print. This is 4 percent of the adult population, or 4 of every 100 adults. Moreover, of these 9.7 million adults, 1.6 million individuals have "severe" functional limitations in seeing print. This is 0.6 percent of the adult population, or 6 of every 1,000 adults.2 There are high rates of visual impairment in the adult population of Illinois. It is estimated that 40,000 of the State's 6 million adults, 6.7 percent, have a significant functional limitation in seeing print.

Legal Blindness

In the United States there are 1.1 million legally blind persons, *i.e.*, clinical visual acuity of 20/200 in the better eye with best correction or a visual field of 20 degrees or less. This is a rate of 4.5 individuals per 1,000. Of those individuals considered legally blind, 220,000 have no useful vision, *i.e.*, their vision is limited to light perception or less. Of those individuals who have no useful vision, 110,000 are totally blind, *i.e.*, they have no light perception.

Incidence of Blindness/Visual Impairment

Every year approximately 200,000 persons in the United States acquire some form of visual impairment that is a severe functional limitation in seeing, an incidence rate of 1 per 1,000. In addition, there are 80,000 annual new cases of legal blindness, an incidence rate of 33 per 100,000.

Age-related Blindness/Visual Impairment

The elderly, those aged 65 or older, are those most affected by vision loss; two out of three persons who are blind or visually impaired in the United States are over the age of 65. In 1990 the number of elderly affected by blindness or visual impairment was 2,700,000. Prevent Blindness America reports the leading causes of blindness will double their impact in the coming years as the Nation's 76 million baby boomers reach older adulthood. By the year 2020, twice as many people will be blind as are today. Macular degeneration will continue to be the leading cause of blindness, and there will be a near doubling of the total cases of glaucoma.

A special problem borne by some individuals is the incidence of the dual disability, deaf-blindness. The dual disability is not as rare an occurrence as perceived by the general public. The number of children, *i.e.*, individuals 21 years of age or younger, in the United States who are both deaf and blind is estimated at 10,000, an incidence rate of 1.2 per 1,000 children.

Employment and Social Characteristics

Individuals who are visually impaired are disproportionately outside the labour force and not working. The labour force is considered to include all individuals between the ages of 16 and 64 who are either employed or unemployed yet seeking work. Nationwide, 67.3 percent of all adults are in the labour force. Among adults who are blind with a severe visual impairment, just 26 percent are in the labour force. This means that for adults who have sight, 67 of 100 are either working or actively looking for work; among those with a severe visual impairment, only 26 of 100 are either working or actively looking for work.

It is a common perception among the public that persons who are blind read Braille. Most persons who are legally blind do not use Braille as a reading medium. This includes students in educational programmes below college and adults. Among legally blind students registered as such by the American Printing House for the Blind, only 10 percent use Braille as their primary reading medium. It is estimated that 8 percent of all legally blind adults are able to use Braille.

Causes and Prevention

Aims: This survey was conducted on children in schools for the blind in Tehran (from 2002 to 2003) to determine the causes of severe visual impairment and blindness and to identify preventable and treatable conditions.

Methods: The study was performed on 362 students at different grades in three schools for the blind. Patient sex, age, family history of blindness or low vision, visual acuity, causes of blindness, and treatable and preventable conditions were studied.

Results: Of the 362 cases, 210 (58%) were boys and 152 (42%) were girls. Mean age was 13.5 (SD 4) years. Severe visual loss was seen in 80.9%. Retinal diseases were the most common cause for low vision (51%); cataract, optic nerve atrophy, corneal and anterior segment diseases, glaucoma, anophthalmia, and globe malformations were other major causes of blindness. Treatable aetiologies and positive family history of blindness were seen in 25.7% and 36% of the patients, respectively. The incidence of preventable diseases, excluding familial disorders, was low.

Conclusion: In addition to the prevention and treatment of some conditions, premarital genetic counselling and family planning control in families with inherited diseases could decrease the number of blind children in the future in Iran.

Keywords: severe visual impairment, blindness, visually handicapped children.

Childhood blindness is one of the most important priorities in the World Health Organization (WHO) vision 2020 programme. There are approximately 1.4 million blind children all over the world, two thirds of whom live in developing countries.

There are few published studies on the causes of blindness in Iran. The diagnosis of diseases, which affect vision in children, is important because some of these diseases are preventable and some are treatable. The prevalence of diseases leading to blindness is different in various populations, depending on geographical location, culture, race, socioeconomic status, etc.

Although not a major problem in terms of absolute number, childhood blindness accounts for a significant number of years with blindness. In planning to deal with causes of blindness in children in future, public health services have to be strengthened at all levels and collaboration with the government should be improved.

It is essential to study the epidemiological status of diseases in order to decide on important health programmes.

Diseases that lead to blindness are dependent on inheritance and environmental conditions. Some of them are preventable, some others are treatable, and some are untreatable. Currently, the way to deal with such problems is to improve the tactile and hearing senses in patients at low vision schools. This rehabilitation allows a return to normal life; however, if the causes of blindness remain unknown and no programme for their prevention is designed, the current facilities are not enough for such a large population.

Related studies have been performed in many countries. The prevalence of diseases, which affect vision and are unpreventable, is unknown in Iran, but one related study showed that retinal diseases were the most common cause of visual loss. There are treatable diseases that would not lead to blindness if some measures are taken. The pattern of the prevalence of these diseases at a young age would be helped by implementing a health programme and primary treatment.

Materials and Methods

This study was carried out via interview and examination in three blind educational centres in Tehran, Iran, from 2002 to 2003.

All students at Narjes educational centre and half of the students at Mohebbi educational centre (low vision schools) were examined at the eye clinic of the Labbafinejad Medical Centre. The rest of the students, together with students from Khazaeli, were examined at their schools. History taking and eye examination including visual acuity (VA), refraction if possible, anterior segment examination by biomicroscope, fundus examination by indirect ophthalmoscope, and IOP measurement were performed. Data were recorded on special forms, and causes leading to blindness were highlighted regarding the possibility of prevention and treatment. Findings were statistically analysed by software programmes.

Loss of vision in students was defined according to the blind educational classifications of the special education organisation: visual acuity between 20/200 and 20/80 in the better eye, so that the patient could read large optotypes with maximum correction and could educate at ordinary schools, was defined as mild visual loss. Visual acuity between 10/200 and 20/200 in the better eye, so that the patients could walk but not read large optotypes and should learn the Braille system, was defined as moderate loss of vision.

Visual acuity between no light perception and 10/200 in the better eye, so that the patient is absolutely blind, was defined as severe visual loss. These patients must learn the Braille system and other skills to increase individual abilities for orientation and learning.

Results

A total of 362 patients with mean age of 13.5 (SD 4) years (range 5–25 years) were included in this survey, 210 (58%) were male and 152 (42%) were female. Family history of blindness was reported in 131 (36%), which included 38.2% of the girls and 34.8% of the boys. Figure 1 shows the cause of decreased vision in the studied cases: more than 80% of patients had severe visual loss.

Retinal diseases were the most common cause of blindness, followed by cataract, optic nerve atrophy, and glaucoma. Phthisis bulbi in two, trauma in three, neoplasm in one, and uveal coloboma in six cases had a minimal role in causing blindness.

Leber's congenital amaurosis (LCA) was the most common disease, present in 160 cases (44.2%) and is untreatable and unpreventable. The most common preventable disease was secondary atrophy of the optic nerve with a prevalence of 5.8%. The most common treatable disorder was congenital cataract, with a prevalence of 13.5%, followed by congenital glaucoma with a prevalence of 7.5%. Retinal detachment, familial exudative vitreoretinopathy (FEVR), anophthalmia, cortical blindness and phthisis bulbi, congenital retinal detachment, Usher syndrome and corneal endothelial dystrophy, Ehler-Danlos syndrome, and retinoblastoma were other causes of blindness.

One hundred eighty five patients (51%) had retinal diseases; the most common disorder in this group was LCA with 160 patients (86.5%).

There are several causes for severe visual impairment in children and some of them are preventable. Secondary atrophy of the optic nerve, congenital toxoplasmosis, and cataract secondary to intrauterine infection were detected in 15 patients and comprised 4.1% of preventable causes of blindness. If inherited diseases are added to acquired diseases more frequency will be obtained; however, since the determination of inherited diseases needs a study with better facilities, this group of diseases was not included in the preventable diseases group. Therefore, most disorders were categorised as unpreventable. Ninety three patients (25.7%) had treatable disorders, which mostly included cataract, glaucoma, anterior segment diseases, secondary atrophy of the optic nerve and, rarely, retinal diseases.

Retinal diseases were the most common untreatable diseases (68% of cases).

Discussion

The prevalence of childhood blindness was reported as 0.17% in southern India. Blindness was caused by treatable refractive errors (33.3%) followed by preventable causes (16.6% the result of vitamin A deficiency and 8.3% the result of amblyopia after cataract surgery). The major remaining causes of blindness were congenital eye anomalies (16.7%) and retinal degeneration (16.7%). The authors concluded that the priorities for action to reduce childhood blindness in India are refractive error, cataract related amblyopia, and corneal diseases. We did not evaluate overall causes of childhood blindness in our population but only the prevalence of causes of blindness in pupils in schools for the blind. Regarding frequency of retinal diseases, LCA, with 160 patients (86.5%), was the most frequent disease; other retinal diseases were less frequent as indicated in table 2. Seventy seven (48.1%) patients with LCA had a positive family history of blindness.

Kello and Gilbert studied causes of severe visual impairment and blindness in Ethiopia and concluded that vitamin A deficiency and measles were the major causes of severe visual impairment/blindness in children in schools for the blind. Most causes are preventable during childhood through provision of basic primary healthcare services. This shows the role of socioeconomic conditions in epidemiology of blindness in underdeveloped countries.

We did not have any proved case of vitamin A deficiency in our series.

About 36.2% of the students had a positive history of blindness in their families and relatives. No significant difference was seen in family history of blindness in both sexes. To our knowledge, this variable has not been studied in other reports to date.

Severe visual loss was the most frequent type. There was no significant difference in loss of vision between boys and girls; in other words, boys and girls were distributed equally in the three groups of visual loss (mild, moderate, and severe).

Retinal disorders, with a frequency of 51.1%, were the most common cause of blindness: LCA is transferred in an autosomal recessive pattern. Amini reported that the most common diseases leading to blindness were retinal dystrophy followed by optic nerve atrophy and cataract.

In 1988, Schwab performed a study in two schools for the blind in Zimbabwe, which indicated that the cause of blindness in 75% of students was bilateral corneal opacity. In a study carried out in 1992 by Antonowicz, 100 patients aged 3–18 years were studied in a blind centre in a Polish city. The causes of blindness or low vision in order of frequency were as follows: refractive errors, optic nerve atrophy, congenital cataract, retinal and choroidal degeneration, neoplasia, anophthalmia or globe malformations, iris or choroidal coloboma, retinoblastoma, ocular trauma, and congenital glaucoma. In 1992 a study was performed at six schools for the blind in Ethiopia by Gebriel. Causes of blindness were corneal opacity or phthisis bulbi in 70% and cataract in 14%. In another survey conducted in southern Australia by Newland, data from 3520 patients under 6 years of age were collected and the cause of blindness was cataract in 85% of cases. A study carried out by Cook indicated that senile cataract and chronic glaucoma were the main causes of blindness.

Because of the low incidence of some diseases in some subgroups, it was not possible to determine the significance of the difference in both sexes; however, the sexual dominancy could be determined in any disease. Preventable causes of blindness were as follows: secondary atrophy of the optic nerve, cortical blindness due to trauma, congenital toxoplasmosis, retinal detachment, and cataract secondary to intrauterine infections.

Forty per cent of preventable causes were seen in males and 60% in females; thus the frequency of preventable causes was different in the two sexes. The frequency of treatable diseases was 25.7%, based on primary aetiology of blindness. Retinal diseases, with 185 patients (68%), are the most common untreatable cause of blindness. Cataract, glaucoma, corneal and anterior segment diseases, secondary atrophy of the optic nerve, and rare retinal diseases were among the treatable diseases. In Gilbert's study, treatable and preventable disorders in Chile, South Africa, and India were 54%, 70%, and 48%, respectively. The prevalence of treatable and preventable diseases in students from Tehran blind schools was 30.1%, which is lower than in Gilbert's study. Because retinal diseases are the most common untreatable diseases, particularly LCA, it seems that despite measures taken to treat and prevent such disorders, a considerable number of children had (about 70%) developed untreatable and unpreventable diseases.

In conclusion, severe loss of vision was the most common type of visual loss in schools for the blind in Tehran. Retinal diseases, mostly Leber's congenital amaurosis, are the most common disorders leading to blindness. These diseases mostly have an autosomal recessive pattern and parents transfer recessive genes to their offspring usually by consanguineous marriages. Other diseases such as congenital cataract, optic nerve atrophy, anterior segment and corneal diseases, and glaucoma had lower frequencies.

Intervention and Educational Programmes

Response to Intervention (RTI)- Why is Response to Intervention Needed?

Year after year, thousands of children with learning problems are referred for assessment in schools across the country to diagnose learning disabilities and determine special education eligibility.

Every parent awaits the test results with hope and apprehension. A large number of those students tested will not meet their state's criteria for eligibility for special education under the Individuals with Disabilities Education Act (IDEA) despite having continued problems in school.

Often, the news leaves parents worried. They may be relieved to learn their children may not have learning disabilities. However their children still have serious problems in school and show signs of learning disabilities that may not have been severe enough to qualify but continue to negatively affect their ability to learn and achieve.

Further, they will not receive special education services. Parents are very concerned about their children's futures and often feel abandoned by the system. Their children are sometimes referred to as slow learners, gray area kids, or kids who fell through the special education eligibility cracks. Until recent changes were made in federal laws governing special education programmes, there were few mandated options for help beyond continued struggle in the regular classroom for these students. Some schools provided temporary assistance to some students through existing intervention programmes such as Title I, which serves students from low-income homes who are not learning as they should. However, there were no formally mandated programmes requiring long-term support for all struggling learners, regardless of socioeconomic status. The fact is, many students with learning disabilities go undiagnosed and unserved simply because they aren't "behind enough" to qualify for services. For example, under most formulas, to meet special education eligibility requirements in reading, a nine-year-old student with average intelligence would have to be practically unable to read at all to qualify. He may not recognize letters or be aware of the sounds they represent. By this time, he would probably have been retained for one or two years without having any additional help or change in his educational programme.

Response to Intervention- What is RTI, and How Can it Help?

RTI stands for Responsiveness to Intervention. Simply put, it is an alternate means of determining whether a child has a learning disability and needs special education services. RTI was included in the 2004 revision of the IDEA as an alternative to the formula methods in use over the last 20 years.

How will Response to Intervention Help Children?

In previous years, the most commonly used method of determining eligibility required that a student have about an average or higher intelligence and a severe discrepancy, or weakness, in one or more areas of achievement as measured on standardized, norm-referenced tests. In practice, a student would have to lag behind his peers by two years or more before he could qualify for services in special education.

Students with learning disabilities rarely met criteria for placement in special education until they were in third grade or later. They needed to fail long enough before they were behind enough to qualify. Picture this. A beginning third grade student of average intelligence would need to be unable to read even simple words to qualify. Meanwhile, his peers would be be reading chapter books.

The aptitude/achievement discrepancy method caused many problems for learning disabled students who did not meet the cutoff test scores:

- They missed two or more important years of specially designed instruction at a time research indicates is the most important for early intervention;
- They were often humiliated and frustrated by their inability to perform as well as their peers;
- They were so behind others, the likelihood of catching up was very small, if not impossible;
- In many cases, students developed dislike of school. Some developed behavior and social problems;
- Some children with disabilities were never identified and never received services they needed. Instead, they were thought of as "just slow learners," incapable of learning as well as peers, but not severe enough to require special education;
- Many failed at school and dropped out; and
- Many had no post-secondary education and took low-paying jobs.

Response to Intervention- benefits children who have undiagnosed learning disabilities but have not met special education eligibility in previous testing under discrepancy method formulas. These kids are sometimes referred to as gray area kids or kids who fell through the cracks. These children were literally "falling through the cracks" of the school system because they couldn't get the help they needed in special education or from regular education.

Response to Intervention can help these low-achieving children who have been lost in the maze of special education eligibility laws under previous versions of the IDEA. It allows schools the flexibility to provide more individualized instruction to children who need it, based on demonstrated needs and not simply on test scores.

Responsiveness to Intervention (RTI) is a three step process that may help your child get the help he needs. The first step, or tier, of intervention is the regular classroom setting. All students would begin in this setting. As teachers introduce instruction, students' progress is monitored. Most students in this group will need additional help from time to time, and the teacher provides that guidance.

Tier two of RTI targets students who do not show progress with regular instructional intervention. In tier two, students receive more individualized instruction and intervention. They may work in smaller groups to allow one-on-one and small group instruction. During this process, teachers carefully evaluate the students' response to these interventions. Students who do well may be phased back into the regular classroom. Students who demonstrate the need for ongoing, intensive intervention will move into tier three.

Tier three is an ongoing, long-term programme of diagnostic and prescriptive teaching and could be thought of as special education. In this level, students receive individualized instruction for as long as is necessary for them to acquire the skills they need to progress in school.

Response to Intervention (RTI)- offers clear advantages over the former process of relying solely on evaluation to determine eligibility. First, the RTI process is instructional from beginning to end. At no point is the child left to experience the frustration of failure while waiting until his test scores show a severe aptitude/achievement discrepancy before he gets help. He receives instruction that gradually increases in intensity and individualization as he shows the need for it.

RTI eliminates the gap in instruction for the kids who cannot succeed in the regular classroom without help and those who qualify for special education. The lack of services for gray area kids, kids who fall through the cracks, and slow-learners should be minimized as all children get the instruction they need. Response to Intervention- While standardized assessment may not be needed to determine eligibility for special education programmes diagnosis of learning disabilities, it can still provide educators with important information for students' programmes, even with the RTI model of eligibility.

First, intelligence testing provides important details on how students process information and how they learn. This information can be used by regular and special education teachers to develop specially designed instruction that truly taps their strengths and encourages skill development in their areas of weakness.

Second, standardized achievement testing can offer a larger view of how the student is learning as compared to others his age across the nation. This serves as critical guidance to ensure students make ongoing progress and move toward their long-term educational and career goals. Achievement testing can also provide diagnostic information that enables teachers to identify specific areas of strength and weakness. This helps teachers refine instructional processes.

Learn about RTI in Your State

If your child has been tested and determined ineligible for special education services because he or she missed the cutoff scores, RTI may help. Contact your state's department of education office for special education to get more information on how RTI will be implemented in your state.

Plus Curriculum

Physical facilities, technology, media and materials, and human resources all contribute to the quality of what transpires in schools. Yet there remains great disparity in quality from community to community. And these disparities, in turn, yield uneven results for students from community to community. Such unevenness is particularly troubling when observed in communities with high concentrations of students from poor families, English language learners, or members of racial minorities. Also troubling is the achievement gap observed between disabled and non-disabled student populations (Benz, Lindstrom, & Yovanoff, 2000; Blackorby & Wagner, 1996). Standards-based reform and its reliance upon broad-scale assessment represents an attempt to improve overall performance of American students and to narrow the achievement gap observed in diverse student populations, including students with disabilities.

Pugach (2001) calls for a "curriculum-centered dialogue" that will enable general and special educators to confront several crucial and fundamental issues embedded in curriculum. These include the following:

1. The appropriateness and quality of the general education curriculum for all students.
2. The degree to which the general education curriculum meets the needs of students from various cultural, linguistic, and socioeconomic backgrounds.
3. The relationship of the curriculum to the disproportionate numbers of students of colour in special education.

All teachers inevitably ask what do my students need to know and be able to do? In order to answer these questions, teachers must identify, locate, or develop curriculum—that which is generally believed to constitute the "what" or substance of education. This substance of education can be taken apart and understood in many different ways. For example, curriculum can be divided into domains or subject areas. Some domains may be considered "core" or vital, while others may be considered "extra" or supplementary (*e.g.*, extra-curricular activities). Curriculum can also be examined in terms of its scope, depth, or sequence.

Today, the aims or purposes of curriculum are stated in the form of "standards." For each domain, that which students need to know is often referred to as content standards, and that which students need to be able to do in order to demonstrate what they know is frequently called performance standards. Standards are generally sequenced so that entry-level or prerequisite knowledge, skills, and dispositions can be specified along paths or strands for each domain. Standards may be broadly stated or narrowly defined. (When broadly stated, standards permit flexibility in the multiple ways in which a standard can be achieved. When narrowly defined, standards may permit more precise benchmarking for indicating within a particular standard the level a student has achieved.)

Unlike other nations, standards for educational attainment in the United States are not uniformly set because education is neither prescribed nor controlled by a central government

(Eisner, 2001). Rather, separate states set standards that frame the curriculum for local school districts to follow. States may vary in the precision with which they frame the curriculum. Thus, local communities may have more or less latitude in interpreting state standards.

State and federal legislation during the 1990s established a context for local refinement of curriculum. State improvement plans, school improvement councils, and district coordinating councils made up of stakeholders established a direction and a vision for the kinds of schools, services, and resources considered necessary to improve education at all levels. In the absence of a nationalized education system, communities can vary widely in what they offer students. In some instances, standards may be exhaustive and perhaps unrealistic in their attainability by all students (Marzano, 1999), or standards may be so limited as to constrain the scope and depth of what schools can offer (Kohn, 2000).

In the U.S., high quality education is everybody's concern. Thus, federal, state, and local communities, along with the private sector, share the cost of the operation of the American education enterprise. Concern during the early 1980s over America's capacity to compete in an increasingly global economy set the stage for a wave of reform initiatives in the form of federal legislation. For states and local communities to receive federal assistance for the improvement of education, states had to identify or develop content standards and assessment systems for reporting the outcomes of federal investments in school reform. As stated, IDEA '97 mandated participation by students with disabilities in various reform efforts in order to ensure their opportunity to benefit from all that recent school reform had to offer. Access to, participation in, and progress within the general curriculum is a tall order indeed, further exacerbated by ambiguity in the definition of the general curriculum.

Blending General and Specialized Curriculum

Hitchcock, Meyer, Rose, and Jackson (2002) define the general education curriculum as the overall plan for instruction adopted by a school or school system. Nolet and McLaughlin

(2000) acknowledge the uniqueness of the general education curriculum for each school system—and each student—when they recommend procedures for "finding" the general education curriculum. Wehmeyer (et al., 2002) acknowledges that the general curriculum is defined broadly because Congress intends for it to be determined locally. How students with disabilities ultimately access the general curriculum depends on the assessment, planning, and evaluation skills of their local IEP team members (consisting of both general and special educators).

They need to examine the content of what is taught to non-disabled agemates, select entry points to the curriculum, determine appropriate accommodations for instruction and assessment, and determine curriculum modifications and alternates for assessment. They also need to determine what, if any, specially-designed instruction in expanded areas or domains of the curriculum is necessary to address needs arising from disability that also limit access to the general curriculum. Individual protections that reside at the heart of IDEA remain in place, so while curriculum is of primary importance, individual students will continue to be the focus of a free, appropriate, and public education (Turnbull & Turnbull, 1998).

What curriculum would support, complement, or augment student access to the general curriculum? For students with significant developmental or multiple disabilities, compilations of specialized curriculum have been published by Browder (2001) and by Ryndak and Alper (1996; 2003). These and other sources have been reviewed for inclusion in the low-incidence categories below. In the end, what students with low-incidence disabilities need to know and be able to do will depend on the expectations and standards embraced by their IEP team. A quality education for students with low-incidence disabilities will be a blending of curriculum designed to address disability-specific or unique needs and curriculum designed for optimal functioning in a democratic society.

Blind/Low Vision

Curriculum for blind students was developed largely by residential schools during the 19th and early 20th centuries

(Frampton, 1940). Content mirrored the curriculum of the day with significant alteration in teaching practices and communication systems for conveying that curriculum. Most notable is the use of Braille. Today, IDEA presumes that all students with IEPs who have vision impairments shall use Braille as their primary literacy medium unless the team determines that print is more efficient. Braille, however, was not always held in such high esteem. It took over 100 years—a period known as "the war of the dots"—for Braille to become established as the reading medium of preference for the blind.

Curriculum for students with low vision began to appear in the early part of the 20th century when so-called "partially sighted" children were separated from schools for the blind for educational purposes (Jackson, 1983). Due to concern that students with very high myopia (nearsightedness) would lose more vision through eyestrain, curriculum materials were enlarged and supplemented by aural reading (listening). This "sight saving philosophy," (Hathaway, 1959) as it was known, persisted well into the 1960s until Barraga's 1964 discovery that efficiency of vision improved through use. The new resulting "sight utilization philosophy" persisted into the 1980s, when declining Braille literacy rates among blind students were observed to correlate with unemployment. Hand in hand with the sight utilization philosophy was an increase in public day school attendance by blind students. Children who may have learned Braille at residential schools were now using enlarged print or print with optical magnification. In the minds of many advocates, this over-emphasis on the importance of sight utilization deprived many severely visually impaired students of the opportunity to learn Braille. Hence, the 1990s ushered in a new era of curriculum emphasizing Braille literacy (Rex, Koenig, Wormsley, & Baker, 1994).

Just as literacy is the focus of most of the current reform initiatives because of its connection with employment, so Braille literacy has taken center stage with the observation that nearly three-fourth's of blind people today are unemployed (Rabbi & Croft, 1989). In fact, fluent Braille users are among the most successfully employed blind sub-group. Reasons for the decline in Braille literacy among blind and visually impaired individuals are complex, but IDEA now requires that IEP teams undertake a learning media assessment (LMA) (Koenig & Holbrook, 1995) to determine the most efficacious approach to learning and literacy.

During the 1950s and 1960s, public day school programmes for blind and visually impaired students expanded rapidly. Resource models, itinerant teaching services, and teacher-consultation models emerged and soon overtook residential school placement as the preferred approach for meeting blind students' educational needs. Prior to IDEA, advocates for public school programming downplayed or, at least, de-emphasized the unique and challenging needs of these students when entering the general educational environment. They argued that blind students needed the same curriculum as every other student and that teachers could supply just a few additional skills and resources (Abel, 1959). These additional skills and knowledge areas became known as the "plus curriculum." Today, the plus curriculum is known as the "expanded core" curriculum, to emphasize that it must go hand-in-hand with the "common core" curriculum (Hatlen, 1996a).

UNIT-III

Hearing Impairment

Definitions and Identification

Hearing plays an important role in student development and daily performance. Hearing impairment occurs when there's a problem with or damage to one or more parts of the hearing mechanism. It is identified as one of the ten most prevalent causes of disability in the United States. The U.S. Department of Health and Human Services (1991) reported that five percent of children 18 years and under have a hearing loss. A student with a hearing impairment is part of a heterogeneous group whose one common characteristic is some degree of hearing loss. To effectively teach students with hearing impairment, teachers need to become familiar with hearing related concepts. The purpose of this chapter is to briefly outline the nature of hearing impairment and provide you with useful current definitions. The chapter will provide you with information on how we hear, how hearing is assessed, ways of identifying students with hearing impairments in the classroom and discuss their learning characteristics. Some information on the several types of professionals who can be of assistance in diagnosing and educating students with a hearing impairment will also be provided.

The Individuals with Disabilities Education Act (IDEA), defines "hearing impairment" and "deafness" separately. Hearing impairment is defined as an "impairment in hearing, whether permanent or fluctuating that adversely affects a child's educational performance." Deafness is defined as a "hearing impairment that is so severe that the child is impaired in processing linguistic information through hearing, with or without amplification."

Components of the Ear

The organ of hearing is the ear and it is composed of three major parts: the outer, middle and inner ear. It is important to understand the basic anatomy of each part and how it works before reading about the different types of hearing impairments. Refer to for a diagram of the ear. The anatomy and contribution of each part of the ear has been described below:

Outer Ear

Includes the external visible part of the ear (pinna) and the ear canal.

What Does it Do?

1. Sound waves are received by the pinna from the environment.
2. Sound waves travel through the ear canal.
3. Sound waves make their way to the beginning of the middle ear called the ear drum (thin membrane that separates the outer ear from the middle ear).

Middle Ear

Includes the eardrum, ossicles or three tiny bones(hammer/ malleus; anvil/incus; stirrup/stapes) and Eustachian tube.

What Does it Do?

1. Sound waves reach the eardrum.
2. Ear The ear drum begins to vibrate and makes the three tiny bones / ossicles to move together.
3. These bones help sound move into the inner ear.

The middle ear is filled with air and for optimal hearing the air pressure inside the middle ear and outside of the ear needs to be the same. The Eustachian tube connects the middle ear to the back of the nose. The Eustachian tube helps keeps the air pressure in the middle ear equal to the air pressure in the environment.

Inner Ear

Includes a snail-shaped, fluid filled structure called the cochlea, tiny hair cells (cilia) and the auditory nerve, which travels from the inner ear to the brain.

What Does it Do?

1. The vibration of the sound waves causes the cilia to move.
2. This movement creates electrical impulses or signals that are sent to the brain via the auditory nerve.
3. The hearing centers in the brain interpret these signals as sound and help give them meaning.

Some Definitions

A hearing impairment results when there is a problem in one or more components of the hearing mechanism. When describing hearing impairment, three attributes are considered:

1. Type of hearing loss (part of the hearing mechanism that is affected)
2. Degree of hearing loss (range and volume of sounds that are not heard)
3. Configuration (range of pitches or frequencies at which the loss has occurred).

Definition

Hearing loss is any reduction in a person's ability to detect sound.

Description

Hearing is a complex process that consists of many steps. It begins when sound waves strike the outside of the ear. Sound waves are vibrations that occur in air. When sound waves hit the ear, they cause tissue in the ear to start vibrating.

The ear consists of three major sections: the external ear, the middle ear, and the inner ear. The external ear acts like a small sound-collecting tube. Sound waves enter the ear and pass down a narrow canal called the auditory canal. At the end of the canal, the sound waves strike a thin membrane called the tympanic (pronounced tim-PA-nik) membrane, or ear drum. They cause the tympanic membrane to begin vibrating.

Hearing Loss: Words to Know

Audiometer: An instrument for testing a person's hearing.

Auditory Canal: A tube that leads from the outside of the ear to the tympanic membrane.

Auditory Nerve: A bunch of nerve fibers that carries sound from the inner ear to the brain.

Conductive Hearing Loss: Hearing loss that occurs in the external or middle ear.

Eustachian Tube: A passageway that connects the middle ear with the back of the throat.

Ossicles: A set of tiny bones in the middle ear responsible for transmitting sound vibrations from the outer ear to the inner ear.

Otosclerosis: A disorder in which the bones of the middle ear become joined to each other.

Sensory Hearing Loss: Hearing loss that occurs in the inner ear, auditory nerve, or brain.

Tympanic Membrane: A thin piece of tissue between the external ear and the middle ear.

Just beyond the tympanic membrane is the middle ear. The middle ear contains three bones called ossicles (pronounced AH-sih-kulls). Vibration of the tympanic membrane is passed along to the ossicles. They too begin to vibrate.

The ossicles are connected to the inner ear. The inner ear is filled with a clear, watery fluid. As the ossicles vibrate, they create another wave inside the watery fluid in the inner ear. This wave is similar to a water wave on a lake or the ocean.

In the last stage of hearing, the water wave in the inner ear collides with the auditory nerve. The auditory nerve picks up these vibrations and transmits them to the brain. The brain "reads" these vibrations as a sound.

Hearing loss can occur at any stage of this process. For example, sound waves may be blocked as they try to pass down the auditory canal. Or they may not be able to pass through the ossicles in the middle ear. Or they may not be transmitted through the liquid of the middle ear or along the auditory nerve. Finally, the brain may lose its ability to make sense out of the vibrations it receives from the auditory nerve.

Hearing loss is usually defined as being either conductive or sensory hearing loss. Conductive hearing loss is caused by damage to the external or middle ear. Sound vibrations are unable to pass down the auditory canal, across the tympanic membrane, and through the ossicles. Sensory hearing loss occurs in the inner ear and the auditory nerve. Sound waves may reach the inner ear, but they are not transmitted successfully to the brain.

Incidence and Prevalence

Central Auditory Processing Disorder (CAPD)

Central auditory processing disorder refers to limitations in the ongoing transmission, analysis, organization, transformation, elaboration, storage, retrieval, and use of information contained in audible signals.

- The body of literature on CAPD indicates that the disorder is not uncommon. Several groups of patients have been identified with CAPD such as children with language-learning problems, people with known lesions of the central auditory system, people complaining about an apparent inability to hear well in difficult listening situations, and people with age-related changes in the central rather than the peripheral auditory system.
- Prevalence data for CAPD are lacking. Although reports have appeared consistently in the literature describing

auditory perceptual and auditory processing deficits associated with a variety of conditions, no authoritative estimates of the prevalence of CAPD are available.

- Age-related CAPD abnormality has been described in many studies with widely varying prevalence reported. To date, there has been only one population study to report prevalence of this age-related condition, and these rates were significantly lower than in reports from clinical studies.

Conductive Hearing Loss

- According to one study within a population of individuals with Rett Syndrome, the prevalence of hearing loss was increased in older participants and in those with seizures requiring the use of anticonvulsants.
- Hearing loss, both sensorineural and conductive, has been reported in patients with rheumatoid arthritis (RA). Sensorineural hearing loss of the cochlear variety is a common finding in patients with RA, whereas conductive loss, although seen, is much less common. Increased laxity of the middle ear transducer mechanism is the likely cause of the conductive element.

Hyperacusis

Hyperacusis may be defined as an unusual intolerance of ordinary environmental sounds presented at normal levels.

- Little research has been done on hyperacusis. One study suggests that the prevalence of hyperacusis in the general population is probably underreported when it occurs with medically recognized symptoms such as tinnitus, headache, or depression.
- Hyperacusis is mainly a consequence of the noise level in the 21st century, owing to dramatic changes in people's lifestyles. Of every 100 people affected with otological complaints (*e.g.*, tinnitus and hyperacusis), 20 are affected by hyperacusis. Because of its high incidence, this symptom has long been the subject of investigation.

- Hyperacusis is associated with concentration difficulties, use of ear protection, avoidance, tension, and sensitivity to light/colours. According to one study, hyperacusis is a common problem.

Mixed Hearing Loss

Authoritative data concerning the general incidence and prevalence of mixed hearing loss are unavailable in the allied health or medical literature.

Sensorineural Hearing Loss

Sensorineural hearing loss (SNHL) describes abnormalities of the inner ear and/or nerve pathways beyond the inner ear to the brain.

- Sudden hearing loss is infrequent, with an estimated 5-20 cases yearly per 10,000 individuals.
- Sudden sensorineural hearing loss (SSHL) is a symptom of cochlear injury resulting from idiopathic causes. It is defined as a sensorineural hearing loss of 30dB or more over at least three contiguous audiometric frequencies that develops over a period of a few hours to three days.
- In SSHL, many hypotheses have been proposed to explain the etiology: viral inflammation, vascular occlusive disease, allergic reactions, rupture of intralabyrinthine membranes, local histamine production, and autoimmune disease.

Hearing Aid Use and Cochlear Implants

- According to a study conducted 2004, there were 24.1 million individuals with a hearing loss who do not own a hearing aid device. This is in contrast to 12.5 million individuals who own hearing instruments, and 11.1 million individuals who use their instruments.
- About 6 out of 10 hearing instrument owners and non-owners are male.
- The overall prevalence of device nonuse, according to one study, was noted to increase slowly with time. The

role of psychological factors in contributing to the decision of an individual to elect to opt out of device use remains unproven.

- Both hearing loss and the use of hearing aids are widely reported as unacceptably different from normal, or stigmatizing. Perceptions of stigmatization often result in denial of hearing problems and lack of adherence to professional recommendations to use hearing aids.
- Barriers to hearing aid use are complex and multifactorial involving, among other things, a lack of system commitment to utilization of hearing aids and hearing aid design, fit issues, and price of aid.
- Overall customer satisfaction with new hearing instruments is 77%, placing this product in the top-third of products and services in the United States.
- Cochlear implants are electronic devices that contain a current source and an electrode array that is implanted into the cochlea; electrical current is then used to stimulate the surviving auditory nerve fibers. Worldwide, about 60,000 cochlear implants have been placed during the past 20 years, approximately one half of them in adults and one half in children.
- Data vary as to how many individuals in the U.S. are potential candidates for receiving cochlear implants. These figures range from 250,000 to 1 million people.

Causes and Prevention

- Causes of Hearing Impairment
- Prevention of Hearing Impairment

Causes of Hearing Impairment

Before Birth:

- Family history of childhood deafness – Deafness in family members
- Consanguinous marriages-Marriage between close relations such as uncle-niece, first cousin.

- Blood group complications or Rh incompatibility –
- Infectious diseases or illnesses during pregnancy (*e.g.* syphilis, German measles or Rubella with fever, mumps)
- Very poor physical condition of the expectant mother.
- Excessive alcohol or nicotine intake by the expectant mother.
- Intake of ototoxic drugs. (Ototoxic drugs are drugs that can damage the hearing mechanism if used indiscriminately. For e.g Gentamycin, amikacin, quinine preparations etc.)
- Excessive exposure to X-rays.

During the Birth Process:

- Birth Asphyxia (lack of oxygen supply to the new born due to inability to breathe normally resulting in blueness of baby due to various reasons).
- Delayed or feeble birth cry.
- Birth weight less than 1200 grams.

After Birth:

- Pre–maturity.
- Deformities of ear, nose, face & throat.
- Jaundice, high fever or convulsions immediately after birth.
- Infectious diseases (*e.g.* whooping cough, mumps, measles, syphilis, meningitis, viral fever, T.B.)
- Intake of antibiotics for a long duration. (especially those known to be ototoxic)
- Injury to the head and /or ear – (by accidents etc.)
- Continuous exposure to loud sounds. High blood pressure, diabetes.
- Aging
- Tumor on the auditory nerve.
- Middle ear infections, ear discharge etc.

Prevention of Hearing Impairment:

- Avoid marriages amongst close relatives.
- Immunize adolescent girls and women in child bearing age against Rubella.
- Ensure good health of the expectant mother – seek health check-ups at regular intervals.
- Expectant mother should avoid contact with persons suffering from infectious diseases.
- Make sure that the delivery is performed under the supervision of a trained person.
- Follow the child's immunization schedule properly.
- Maintain good ear hygiene:
    - o Keep the ears clean, free from dust, water, wax etc.
    - o Do not clean or scratch your ears with pointed objects like matchsticks, hairpins, pencils etc. It can rupture the eardrum or injure the ear canal.
    - o Avoid slap or blow to the ear as it can cause a hearing problem that may be irreversible.
    - o Keep a watch on young children playing with tiny objects like beads, seeds etc. If they put them in the ear, the eardrum may get ruptured or the ear canal may be injured.
    - o Do not put oil or any other liquid in the ear as they can result in pain, swelling and ear discharge. Keep your ears dry always.
    - o Do not swim in dirty water. Unclean water entering the ear can cause ear infection. While swimming always plug your ears with cotton, especially while diving. This prevents the water from directly entering your ear and rupturing the eardrum.
    - o Do not have your ears cleaned by roadside quacks. They use unclean instruments, which may cause infection. The eardrum too may get damaged. Clean your ears with cotton buds regularly or get them cleaned by a doctor.

- o Avoid using unwashed pillow covers, towels, etc., used by a person with ear discharge. This may cause infection in your ear too.
- o While feeding a baby keep its head raised otherwise milk may enter into the ear cavity (through the small passage connecting the throat and the ear). It can cause pain with swelling and ear discharge.
- o Avoid exposure to loud sounds.
- o Do not take medicines without the doctor's advice.
- o Use ear protectors while working in noisy places.

Many of the factors causing hearing impairment cannot be always controlled. But knowledge about these factors helps us in identifying 'at risk' individuals. A detailed hearing evaluation is recommended to start rehabilitative measures as early as possible to ensure a bright future for the individual.

Types of Hearing Loss and Characteristics

Conductive hearing loss is due to any condition that interferes with the transmission of sound through the outer and middle ear to the inner ear. This type of hearing loss can be successfully treated in most cases.

In cases of conductive hearing loss, sound waves are not transmitted effectively to the inner ear because of some interference in:

- The external ear canal
- The mobility of the eardrum (problems with the mobility of the eardrum are often caused by accumulation of fluid in the eustachian tube, the tube that connects the middle ear to the back of the throat)
- The three tiny bones inside the middle ear
- The middle-ear cavity
- The openings into the inner ear
- The eustachian tube

Modern techniques make it possible to cure or at least improve the vast majority of cases involving problems with the outer or middle ear. Even if people with conductive hearing loss are not improved medically or surgically, they stand to benefit greatly from a hearing aid, because what they need most is amplification.

Sensorineural Hearing Loss

In sensorineural hearing loss, the damage lies in the inner ear, the acoustic nerve, or both. Most physicians call this condition "nerve deafness."

The cochlea has approximately 30,000 hearing nerve endings (hair cells). The hair cells in the large end of the cochlea respond to very high-pitched sounds, and those in the small end (and throughout much of the rest of the cochlea) respond to low-pitched sounds. These hair cells, and the nerve that connects them to the brain, are susceptible to damage from a variety of causes.

- The term "sensory" hearing loss is applied when the damage is in the inner ear. Common synonyms are "cochlear" or "inner-ear" hearing loss.
- "Neural" hearing loss is the correct term to use when the damage is in the acoustic nerve, anywhere between its fibers at the base of the hair cells and the relay stations in the brain (the auditory nuclei). Other common names for this type of loss are "nerve deafness" and "retrocochlear" hearing loss.

Nice to Know: Sensorineural hearing loss is one of the most challenging problems in medicine. A large variety of hearing impairments fall under this category. Although the chances for restoring a sensorineural hearing loss are slim, a small number of cases can be treated, and some people experience dramatic improvements as a result. However, a great need for further research in this area still exists.

Central Hearing Loss

In central hearing loss, the problem lies in the central nervous system, at some point within the brain. Interpreting speech is a complex task. Some people can hear perfectly well but have trouble interpreting or understanding what is being said. Although information about central hearing loss is accumulating, it remains somewhat a mystery in otology (the medical specialty of ear medicine and surgery).

A condition called central auditory processing disorder frequently leads people to think they have hearing loss when their hearing is actually normal. Despite the fact that this problem is extremely common and present in many highly successful people, it is actually classified as a learning disability.

Basically, the problem involves a person's inability to filter out competing auditory signals. People with central auditory processing disorders have difficulties that include:

- Problems "hearing" when there are several conversations going on
- Inability to read or study with the radio or television on
- Problems reading if someone turns on a vacuum cleaner or air conditioner near them
- Generally missing the first sentence from people talking to them if they are involved in an auditory attention task (such as watching television)

Although such people (and their families and friends) frequently suspect that they have a hearing loss, the function of the ears is usually normal, and routine hearing tests are normal. Naturally, people with this condition may also develop hearing loss from other causes, and this can make it even more difficult for them to function under everyday circumstances.

There is no good treatment for central auditory processing disorders other than educating the person, family, and friends, and trying to control the environment. This is especially important for children, whose grades may go from F to A if they are provided with a silent place in which to do their homework.

Nice to Know: The test necessary to diagnose central hearing impairment must be designed to assess a person's ability to handle complex information. Most of the tests now available were not created specifically for this purpose. It requires a very experienced and almost intuitive judgment on the physician's part to make an accurate diagnosis.

Functional Hearing Loss

Functional hearing loss involves a psychological or emotional problem, rather than physical damage to the hearing pathway. Individuals with this type of hearing loss do not seem to hear or respond; yet, in reality, they have normal hearing.

The most important challenge for physicians is to classify this condition properly. It may be difficult to determine the specific emotional cause, but if the classification is made accurately, the proper therapy can begin.

Too often, a functional hearing loss is not recognized, and individuals receive useless treatments for prolonged periods. In turn, this process may aggravate the emotional element and cause the condition to become more resistant to treatment.

Mixed Hearing Loss

Frequently, a person experiences two or more types of hearing impairment, and this is called mixed hearing loss. This term is used only when both **conductive** and **sensorineural** hearing losses are present in the same ear. However, the emphasis is on the conductive hearing loss, because available therapy is so much more effective for this disorder.

What Causes Hearing Loss?

What problems can affect the outer ear?

What problems can affect the middle ear?

What problems can affect the inner ear?

What Problems Can Affect The Outer Ear?

Anything that completely blocks the ear canal can cause hearing loss. Blockage with earwax (also called cerumen) is common. A doctor can cure this easily by removing the wax either with specially designed instruments or by flushing with water. There are many over-the-counter wax control preparations that can be used at home. However, they sometimes can cause external ear infections.

Need to Know

Q: Is it a good idea to remove wax inside the ear with cotton-tipped swabs?

A: No. The ear has a natural self-cleaning mechanism. Ear skin normally sheds from the inside out. If you place a drop of ink on the eardrum and wait a few weeks, it will turn up near the opening of the ear. The ear canal is also a shaped like a funnel, with the narrow end near the eardrum. Cotton swabs generally push wax deeper into the ear than it normally is (wax forms only in the outer segment of the ear canal), and packs it into a mass. As long as there is even a pinhole opening in the packed wax, hearing is usually good. However, when the canal is completely blocked by wax, substantial hearing loss develops.

Many other problems can block the ear canal and lead to hearing loss. Such blocking causes a decrease in volume but does not generally produce distortion. These problems include:

- Infections with swelling that shuts the ear canal
- Foreign bodies in the ear
- An injury
- Birth defects
- A growth in the ear canal

Any of these, including blockage by wax, may result in conductive hearing loss. That is, it interferes with sound conduction and is generally correctable. It causes decrease in volume but does not generally produce distortion.

Communication Approaches

Opening Doors: Technology and Communication Options for Children with Hearing Loss

Parents of children with hearing loss can find helpful information and resources in a publication produced for the Office of Special Education and Rehabilitative Services (OSERS) by the Academy for Educational Development (AED). Opening Doors: Technology and Communication Options for Children with Hearing Loss provides background on early intervention, the use of technology and other support available to children and their families.

A Note: Every child and every family is unique. It is not the intent of this website to promote any particular approach to language learning. Our intent is to simply provide information.

Most parents assume their child will naturally learn to speak the same language as they do. It can be a great shock, and a source of profound feelings of loss, to learn that a deaf or hard of hearing child will need an entirely different approach to learning language. (Unless the parents are deaf themselves, in which case the child will learn ASL like the rest of the family).

While most hard of hearing children can benefit from amplification and spoken language training, parents of children with a severe to profound hearing loss will be faced with additional considerations. Whether or not a child should receive a Cochlear Implant further impacts communication decisions (see our Cochlear Implant section)

For a more complete discussion of the various educational and communication approaches available for deaf and hard of hearing children see our Education section.

For an excellent overview of the primary communication methods see the article: Communication Choices with Deaf and Hard of Hearing Children.

Following is a brief summary of communication approaches.

Oral Method

Sometimes called the Oral/Aural method, this approach to language learning utilizes residual hearing and speech training. Hand signs are not used in the purely Oral method. Using intensive speech therapy, the emphasis is on teaching children to use spoken language for communication.

Cued speech is a method that uses hand movements to reinforce spoken language communication. It does not use

American Sign Language (ASL) signs. Rather Cued speech helps the child become aware of mouth movements used in pronunciation that are not visible on the lips.

For additional resources, see the following:

Alexander Graham Bell Association: The Alexander Graham Bell Association for the Deaf and Hard of Hearing is an international membership organization and resource center on hearing loss and spoken language approaches and related issues.

John Tracy Clinic: John Tracy Clinic is a private, non–profit deaf education center. Its mission is to offer hope, guidance and encouragement to families of infants and preschool children with hearing losses by providing free, parent–centered services worldwide. The Clinic has 60 years of expertise in the spoken language option.

Cued Speech Discovery Home Page: This is the online Bookstore of the National Cued Speech Association. Besides books and other learning tools, the site provides a basic overview of Cued Speech.

READ Education Center: READ's goals include empowering parents of children who are deaf or hard of hearing through full awareness of all the issues and options related to choosing the mode of communication and educational settings appropriate for their children. The programme serves Chicago and the Mid–west.

Total Communication or Simultaneous Communication: Total Communication is a philosophy that uses amplified hearing, speech, and signing to communicate and educate each child in the manner in which they learn best. Signs used are based on ASL and may have English modifiers (*i.e.*, ing, ed, pre) to aid in teaching English. Click here to read an in–depth article on this philosophy.

Bilingual–Bicultural: This approach assumes that a Deaf child will develop ASL language most quickly, naturally, and completely. This strong base of visual language is a foundation for learning English as a second language through writing, reading, and spoken language. Exposure to fluent ASL is essential to this approach. The following links provide more information about this approach.

Choices

The development of language in children with hearing impairment will usually follow the same language acquisition process as for hearing children, through meaningful interaction and conversation. Although language may be delayed due to a hearing impairment, for the majority of children with a hearing impairment language acquisition will match other aspects of the child's development. However, individual children with a hearing impairment have a variety of communication needs, and these may change over time. The SCS, together with partner agencies, provides parents of newly diagnosed children with information about methods of communication.

Parents can then make an informed choice regarding the approach that is most appropriate for their child's learning and emotional needs.

Broadly speaking communication approaches can be categorised under three main headings: Auditory/Oral, Manually Coded English, and Sign Bilingualism.

The future aims of parents undertaking these approaches might be:

Auditory/Oral

We want our child to speak, write and understand spoken and written English. To attain these will we need to make optimum use of our child's residual hearing and to interact with him/her using spoken language.

Manually Coded English (MCE)

We also want our child to speak, write and understand spoken and written English but we think using a supplementary manual system we can establish a means/ease of communication. Eventually we hope this will lead to fluent verbal conversations.

Sign Bilingualism

I want my child to have his/her easiest/preferred/natural way of communicating, so that they have access to the Deaf Community and functional (perhaps written) use of English. BSL will be their choice for language and communication.

Child's First Language

The majority of children with hearing impairment are born to hearing families and the role of the TOD is to promote opportunities to access and acquire the language of their family, their immediate community and the English language.

It is acknowledged that this approach may not be appropriate for all, and some children may be better suited to alternative means of communication. This will depend upon a variety of factors that can include parental preference, age of onset/diagnosis, degree of hearing impairment and additional difficulties.

The selected approach should be based on the child's communication needs, parental preferences following detailed assessment by all concerned with child's development.

In due course, as the child develops and matures, respect should be accorded to his/her view/choice of, and expressed preference for, a particular mode of communication.

Sign Language and Educational Programmes

During the last two decades bilingual-bicultural education programmes (programmes which recognize that children may come from a different culture and speak a different language in the home than in the school) have flourished in the United States as the ethnic composition of children attending public schools has become more diverse. In the late 1980's discussion of bilingual-bicultural education for children who are Deaf brought about new theories. (A capital D is used by bilingual-bicultural programmes to identify deafness as a cultural, rather than a medical, issue. According to Schirmer (1994) "the impetus for implementing bilingual-bicultural programmes for children who are deaf comes from two sources: (1) The Deaf community, who advocate for the right to pass on their language and culture to succeeding generations; (2) the overall disappointing achievement of youngsters who are deaf. (p. 98) Although small gains have been made in the levels of reading achieved by the average child who is deaf, overall achievement remains considerably lower compared to their hearing peers despite ardent attempts to teach Deaf children through Total Communication (see ERIC EC Digest E559) and oral approaches.

Additional impetus for bilingual-bicultural programmes comes from Sweden, where, in 1981, after years of grassroots activism by Deaf adults and parents of children who are Deaf, the Swedish Parliament passed a law stating that people who are Deaf need to be bilingual in order to function successfully in the family, school, and society (Mahshie, 1995).

What Does it Mean to Be Bilingual-Bicultural?

"A person who is bicultural can move freely within and between two different cultures. Biculturalism implies an understanding of the mores, customs, practices, and expectations of members of a cultural group and the ability to adapt to their expectations" (Finnegan, 1992). Bilingualism involves the ability to use two different languages successfully. Some individuals may be stronger in one language, some in the other, some may blend the two languages into a pidgin (Maxwell, 1991). Individuals who are Deaf are considered bilingual if they are able to communicate effectively in both American Sign Language (ASL) and English or the spoken language of their country. They are considered bicultural if they are capable of functioning in both the Deaf community and the majority culture.

Although there is no standardized formula defining bilingual-bicultural programmes, they are founded on a common set of principles. A basic premise of bilingual-bicultural education is that all children should develop communicative competency. This is a challenge because more than 90 percent of children who are Deaf have hearing parents or caregivers who must learn ASL as a second language.

Education programmes that follow the bilingual-bicultural philosophy work with parents/caregivers to help them realize the special linguistic, educational, and social needs of their child(ren) who are Deaf and to help them realize the importance of early language acquisition. Deaf children who develop language late are less proficient than those who develop an early first language (Newport & Sapulla, 1987). Helen Neville's research at the Salk Institute's Laboratory for Cognitive Neuroscience also shows that children must learn a language during their first five years or so, before the brain's neural connections are locked in place, or risk permanent linguistic impairment (Wolkomir, 1992). "What suffers is the ability to learn grammar. As children mature, their brain organization becomes increasingly rigid. By puberty, it is largely complete. This spells trouble because most deaf youngsters learn language late; their parents are hearing and do not know ASL, and the children have little or no contact with deaf people when young."

Since it is the grammar of languages that distinguishes them most significantly from one another (most spoken languages have similar pragmatic or social functions and similar sound systems), the early assault on the ability to learn grammar makes the development of a sound language system even more compelling.

Bilingual-bicultural programmes differ from other programmes most notably by their approach to first language acquisition. While bilingual-bicultural programmes have respect for both ASL and English, these programmes advocate for ASL to be the first language of children who are deaf. "Research has shown that effective language has to be fast and clear. ASL is an efficient language for visual learning and is easier for Deaf children to acquire as a first language than any form of English" (Finnegan, 1992). Johnson, Liddell, Ertling (1989) stated that ASL is the language choice of adults who are deaf, and it offers access to the school curriculum and other world knowledge. A solid foundation in a first language leads to better English performance over time, and skills transfer from one language to another.

Teaching ASL as the first language for Deaf children has additional benefits. ASL is the language of Deaf people throughout the United States. Proficiency in ASL automatically allows membership in the Deaf community and in cultural events that occur in communities where Deaf people live. This membership is vital to Deaf children because it promotes a healthy view of who they are as human beings and increases self-esteem and confidence in their abilities to interact in a wide array of situations. The bilingual-bicultural approach recognizes that ASL and English are two distinct languages in the same way that, for example, French and German are distinct languages. ASL is a complete language with its own grammar, syntax, and rules for interaction. Signing ASL and speaking English cannot be performed simultaneously with a great degree of success; therefore, when signing ASL one should not attempt to speak English. Speaking English when signing deteriorates the visual signal resulting in an inferior production of signs as well as inferior use of spoken English. The goal is clear and proficient production of ASL.

Proponents of the bilingual-bicultural approach believe that Deaf children are not deficient. Instead of being auditory learners, they are visual learners. Deaf children do not need remedial teaching strategies because the bilingual-bicultural programme provides a unique visual learning environment in which their linguistic, cultural, and social needs are met. Deaf teachers, administrators, and support staff are considered valuable components of the bilingual-bicultural programme. The bilingual-bicultural approach does not support mainstreaming Deaf children in regular education programmes. Many Deaf adults have shared their stories of isolation and academic deprivation while attending schools for children who can hear. The bilingual-bicultural approach holds that cognitive, linguistic, and social competence are best achieved in environments that provide full communicative access to the curriculum.

Who can Choose a Bilingual-Bicultural Option?

Proponents of the bilingual-bicultural option feel that all children, no matter what their degree of hearing loss, would benefit from a bilingual-bicultural option. However, it is most likely that these programmes will exist separate from the mainstream education agencies and buildings. Some may be residential, some may be day schools. Parents or caregivers who feel that this approach is appropriate for their child should call the residential school for Deaf children in their home state. Although a growing number of schools for children who are deaf have adopted bilingual-bicultural programming, families in rural areas may not have access to this approach.

What are the Benefits of a Bilingual-Bicultural Option?

There are several benefits of bilingual-bicultural education. Early access to comprehensible language fosters early cognitive development which, in turn, promotes increased literacy and greater academic achievement. Students who attend bilingual-bicultural programmes develop functional skills in two languages. The emphasis on early language acquisition and establishing a first language (ASL) provides a base upon which English is subsequently taught. Students in bilingual-bicultural programmes have increased self-esteem and confidence due to the healthy view of Deaf children, acceptance of who they are as human beings, and increased confidence to function in bilingual-bicultural environments.

What are the Limitations of a Bilingual-Bicultural Option?

Bilingual-bicultural programmes in the United States are still relatively new. Limited data are available regarding students' achievement in these programmes. As schools begin bilingual-bicultural programmes, schools may have difficulty recruiting native signers of ASL because their numbers are limited. Further, while staff may have excellent skills in signed English, they often do not have proficient ASL skills and must be retrained. Some opposition may result in this effort. At this time, most university education programmes continue to prepare teachers of the deaf in the philosophy of Total Communication. Generally, the level of sign language proficiency required by most universities, states, and certifying agencies is inadequate.

Lack of ASL classes for parents or caregivers, especially in rural areas, may severely restrict communication in the home. Without fluent language models, Deaf children's language will be developed neither optimally nor naturally.

Educational Programmes

During all states of the child's linguistic and educational development the programme provided by the Sensory Consortium Service is monitored and evaluated to ensure that the communication approach being offered is appropriate and that the child's potential is being maximized. This is achieved by:

- Regular discussion with parents and other professionals.
- Use of Early Support material.
- Multi-professional pre-school reviews, including Audiology and Speech and Language therapists.
- Individual case conferences.
- Regular liaison with schools.
- On-going assessment of progress using nationally recognised assessment tools.
- Attendance at Annual Reviews.
- Monitoring of National Curriculum assessments, tests and national examination results.
- Regular liaison with EA's through pre-school reviews and school meetings/annual reviews.

UNIT-IV

Mental Retardation and Mental Illness

Definition and Identification of Mental Retardation

Mental retardation in young children is often missed by clinicians. The condition is present in 2 to 3 percent of the population, either as an isolated finding or as part of a syndrome or broader disorder. Causes of mental retardation are numerous and include genetic and environmental factors. In at least 30 to 50 percent of cases, physicians are unable to determine etiology despite thorough evaluation. Diagnosis is highly dependent on a comprehensive personal and family medical history, a complete physical examination and a careful developmental assessment of the child. These will guide appropriate evaluations and referrals to provide genetic counseling, resources for the family and early intervention programmes for the child. The family physician is encouraged to continue regular follow-up visits with the child to facilitate a smooth transition to adolescence and young adulthood.

The diagnosis of mental retardation in young children is frequently missed. The three most common errors made by clinicians who overlook the possibility of mental retardation are (1) concluding that a child does not "look" retarded, (2) assuming that a child who is ambulatory is unlikely to be retarded and, (3) if retardation is actually considered, concluding that it is not possible to test young children.

The most common reasons for delayed diagnosis of mental retardation in young children include believing that normal appearance and ambulation are not compatible with mental retardation, assuming that testing is not possible in young children and failing to consider the diagnosis.

Incidence and Prevalence

Mental retardation is present in about 2 to 3 percent of the population. It can be defined as cognitive ability that is markedly below average level and a decreased ability to adapt to one's environment. The onset of the condition occurs during the developmental period, *i.e.*, gestation through age 18 years.

Mental retardation comprises five general categories: borderline, mild, moderate, severe and profound. Categories are based on scores obtained through use of age-standardized tests of cognitive ability *(Table)*. Mental retardation may occur as part of a syndrome or broader disorder but is most commonly an isolated finding.

The inclusion of concurrent related limitations in two or more adaptive skill areas was added to the definition of mental retardation in 1992 by the American Association on Mental Retardation. Because standardized testing in very young children is less predictive of future cognitive outcome, the term "developmental delay" has been used to characterize the developmental status of children under age three.

Etiology

A number of environmental, genetic or multiple factors can cause mental retardation. Unfortunately, in approximately 30 to 50 percent of cases, the etiology is not identified even after thorough diagnostic evaluation. Some persons have a congenital malformation of the brain; others had damage to the brain at a critical period in pre- or postnatal development. Acquired causes of retardation include near-drowning, traumatic brain injury and central nervous system malignancy.

Prenatal causes of mental retardation include congenital infections such as cytomegalovirus, toxoplasmosis, herpes, syphilis, rubella and human immunodeficiency virus; prolonged maternal fever in the first trimester; exposure to anticonvulsants or alcohol; and untreated maternal phenylketonuria (PKU). Complications of prematurity, especially in extremely low-birth-weight infants, or postnatal exposure to lead can also cause mental retardation.

Developmental Characteristics Related to Level of Mental Retardation (DSM-IV Criteria)

Mild retardation	**Moderate retardation**	**Severe retardation**	**Profound retardation**
75% to 90% of all cases of retardation	~10% to 25% of all cases of retardation	~10% to 25% of all cases of retardation	~10% to 25% of all cases of retardation
Function at one half to two thirds of CA (IQ: 50 to 70)	Function at one third to one half of CA (IQ: 35 to 49)	Function at one fifth to one third of CA (IQ: 20 to 34)	Function at < one fifth of CA (IQ: < 20)
Slow in all areas	Noticeable delays, especially in speech	Marked and obvious delays; may walk late	Marked delays in all areas
May have no unusual physical signs	May have some unusual physical signs	Little or no communication skills but may have some understanding of speech and show some response	Congenital abnormalities often present
Can acquire practical skills	Can learn simple communication	May be taught daily routinesand repetitive activities	Need close supervision
Useful reading and math skills up to grades 3 to 6 level	Can learn elementary health and safety habits	May be trained in simple self-care	Often need attendant care
Can conform socially	Can participate in simple activities and self-care	Need direction and supervision	May respond to regular physical activity and social stimulation
Can acquire vocational skills for self-maintenance	Can perform tasks in sheltered conditions	--	Not capable of self-care
Integrated into general society	Can travel alone to familiar places	--	--

Metabolic disorders are another possible cause of mental retardation. In some cases (*e.g.*, PKU, hypothyroidism), retardation is preventable with early treatment. Other disorders (*e.g.*, mucopolysaccharidosis, sphingolipidoses) are less responsive to early intervention. Molecular medicine has made it possible to diagnose a number of conditions referred to as mitochondrial cell diseases.

A number of single-gene disorders result in mental retardation. Many of these are associated with atypical or dysmorphic physical characteristics. Such conditions include fragile X syndrome, neurofibromatosis, tuberous sclerosis, Noonan's syndrome and Cornelia de Lange's syndrome. A complete list of syndromes associated with mental retardation is beyond the scope of this article, and the reader is referred to the reference list.

Although the etiology remains unknown in approximately one half of all cases of mental retardation, a chromosomal abnormality can be detected in as many as one quarter of affected persons.

As many as one fourth of persons with mental retardation have a detectable chromosome abnormality. Children with Down syndrome (trisomy 21) usually have highly recognizable physical characteristics, but features associated with other chromosomal abnormalities, such as Klinefelter's syndrome (47,XXY), may not be as obvious to family members or the physician. Other children may have a small deletion or duplication of a particular chromosome that is rarely reported; thus, the phenotype is still undetermined. Some chromosomal abnormalities are inherited from a parent but most occur de novo. Many previously described clinical syndromes have been found to have an associated chromosomal abnormality (*e.g.*, DiGeorge, Prader-Willi, Angelman and Williams syndromes).

The following case report highlights the importance of early diagnosis, in planning therapy for the child and in providing family planning information to the parents.

Illustrative Case

A 16-month-old boy was referred for developmental assessment because he was not yet talking.

He was born to a 30-year-old woman, gravida 2, para 2, living children 2. He was delivered at term by cesarean section with no prenatal, labour or postnatal complications. He was slightly blue at birth and required oxygen. Mother and infant went home in two days, and no other newborn problems were noted. Birth weight was 3.2 kg (7 lb, 1 oz). The infant was breast-fed for about 12 months. Solid foods were added at 10 months, but some difficulty was noted with chewing. The boy rolled over at three to four months, sat without support at seven months and crawled at seven to eight months. He began to walk at 16 months but still did not talk. The mother first became concerned about lack of speech when the child was 13 months old. The remainder of the medical history, the review of systems and the family history were noncontributory.

At 16 months, the child's height and weight were less than the 5th percentile; head circumference was at the 25th percentile. The child was pleasant, alert, active and cooperative. No vocalization of any kind was noted during the examination. Physical findings included a slightly prominent forehead with a depressed wide nasal bridge and a flat nose. The midface appeared depressed; the child's face closely resembled his mother's. The only other abnormal finding was a small left testis. The boy could stand for a few seconds without support and was able to take a few steps. His muscle tone was mildly low but within the reference range.

The physician's impressions included the following: midface hypoplasia, small stature, rule out hearing loss, speech and language delays and global developmental delay, hypoplastic left testicle, incoordinated swallowing, rule out genetic syndrome related to hypoplastic facial features, developmental delay, small stature and familial resemblance.

In the pediatric genetics dysmorphology clinic, the above dysmorphic features were confirmed. He also had distinctive blepharophimosis, ptosis, epicanthal folds, altered palmar creases and hyperextensibility of the fingers and knees. Ohdo blepharophimosis syndrome was diagnosed, based on a London Dysmorphology Database search. Chromosomal status was 46,XY.

At 17 months' chronologic age, his developmental quotient was 61, with most delay occurring in speech, which was at the five-month level. Motor skills were at the 11- to 12-month level. He was evaluated by subspecialists who addressed his various problems. Initial hearing assessment revealed moderate hearing loss. The child was referred to an early intervention programme.

Subsequent follow-up at 52 months of age revealed that the boy still had difficulty with feedings and was not yet toilet trained. His cognitive skills were at approximately a 27-month level, and genetic follow-up confirmed Ohdo blepharophimosis syndrome. The mother had subsequently given birth to a second child with the same syndrome.

Diagnosis

Parental concerns accurately target the majority of children with developmental problems.

The physician must have a high index of suspicion to consider the diagnosis of mental retardation in any child. Some helpful clues include delayed speech, dysmorphic features (minor anomalies), hypotonia generally or of the extremities, general inability to do things for self and, not least, expressed concern by the parents.

The first and most important step in the diagnosis of mental retardation is to obtain a comprehensive patient and family history. Previous gynecologic and obstetric history may reveal infertility or fetal loss. Assessment of maternal health status during pregnancy with the involved child should include questions regarding use of tobacco, alcohol and drugs (prescribed and illicit); lifestyle or other risks for sexually transmitted diseases; weight gain or loss; signs of infection; serious illness or injury; and surgery or hospitalization.

To establish a knowledgeable baseline history of the child, the physician should obtain information regarding length of pregnancy, premature onset of labour or rupture of the membranes, duration and course of labour, type of delivery and any complications. Apgar scores at one and (especially) five minutes should be reviewed, and birth weight, length and head circumference measurements obtained and plotted on appropriate growth charts. The parents should be asked about any illnesses, feeding or sleeping difficulties in the newborn period and problems with sucking or swallowing, as well as the baby's general disposition. Extremes in infant temperament are often the first clue to an atypical course in child development.

The systems review of the child should be complete, with special attention to growth problems, history of seizures, lethargy and episodic vomiting. A developmental screen should be used at all well-child visits to obtain information about the timing of the child's developmental milestones, any concerns by parents or caregivers and comparison of the child's developmental rate and pattern with those of siblings. Specific questions about the child's current developmental abilities should be asked at each visit.

The Revised Denver Prescreening Developmental Questionnaireis a useful screening tool that parents can readily complete to help determine the need for further evaluation with the time-honored Denver Developmental Screening Test.Another practical and reliable tool with which to monitor development in infants is the Kansas Infant Development Screen. The findings can be recorded and plotted just as with somatic growth charts and shared with parents. Other developmental screening tests are also available.

Delays in speech development are common and may become more obvious when contrasted with the speech development of a sibling. Inquiry should be made regarding concerns about hearing and vision. One cannot overemphasize the importance of addressing concerns voiced by a parent about a child's development, behavior and learning, because these expressed concerns accurately target the majority of children with developmental problems.

Information should be obtained about the family unit, parents' occupations and educational achievements, educational and developmental status of siblings, role of the patient in the family, discipline of the children and identity of the child's caregiver when the parents are not home. Family history of fetal loss, mental retardation, severe learning problems, congenital abnormalities and unexplained childhood deaths, as well as other serious illnesses in first- and second-degree family members, should be elicited.

A complete physical examination can begin with a review of growth curves since birth, if these are available. The head circumference should continue to be plotted. The examination should be thorough, with special attention to physical findings that are compatible with any risk factors obtained from the history.

The child should be examined closely for dysmorphic features or minor abnormalities, such as unusual eyebrow pattern, eyes that are widely or closely spaced, low-set ears or abnormal palmar crease patterns. Minor abnormalities are defined as defects that have unusual morphologic features without serious medical implications or untoward cosmetic appearance. Most minor abnormalities involve the face, ears, hands or feet, and are readily recognized even on cursory examination.The presence of three or more minor abnormalities in newborns is correlated with a 90 percent frequency of coexistent major abnormalities, suggesting close association with morphogenesis in utero. Thus, minor abnormalities may provide clues to developmental problems of possible prenatal origin.

Evaluation of the head, face, eyes, ears and mouth must include general assessment of visual acuity and hearing. Examination of the chest, heart, spine, abdomen, genitalia, extremities, muscles and neurologic reflexes can reveal abnormalities that may be associated with retardation.

Causes and Prevention

Down syndrome, fetal alcohol syndrome and Fragile X syndrome are the three most common inborn causes. However, doctors have found many other causes. The most common are:

* Genetic conditions. Sometimes disability is caused by abnormal genes inherited from parents, errors when genes combine, or other reasons. The most prevalent genetic conditions include Down syndrome, Klinefelter's syndrome, Fragile X syndrome, Neurofibromatosis, congenital hypothyroidism, Williams syndrome, Phenylketonuria (PKU), and Prader-Willi syndrome.

Other genetic conditions include Phelan-McDermid syndrome (22q13del), Mowat-Wilson syndrome, genetic ciliopathy. In the rarest of cases, abnormalities with the X or Y chromosome may also cause disability. 48, XXXX and 49, XXXXX syndrome affect a small number of girls worldwide, while boys may be affected by 47, XYY, 49, XXXXY, or 49, XYYYY.

* Problems during pregnancy. Mental disability can result when the fetus does not develop properly. For example, there may be a problem with the way the fetus' cells divide as it grows. A woman who drinks alcohol (see fetal alcohol syndrome) or gets an infection like rubella during pregnancy may also have a baby with mental disability.
* Problems at birth. If a baby has problems during labour and birth, such as not getting enough oxygen, he or she may have developmental disability due to brain damage.
* Exposure to certain types of disease or toxins. Diseases like whooping cough, measles, or meningitis can cause mental disability if medical care is delayed or inadequate. Exposure to poisons like lead or mercury may also affect mental ability.
* Iodine deficiency, affecting approximately 2 billion people worldwide, is the leading preventable cause of mental disability in areas of the developing world where iodine deficiency is endemic. Iodine deficiency also causes goiter, an enlargement of the thyroid gland. More common than full-fledged cretinism, as retardation caused by severe iodine deficiency is called, is mild impairment of intelligence. Certain areas of the world due to natural deficiency and governmental inaction are severely affected. India is the most outstanding, with 500 million suffering from deficiency, 54 million from goiter, and 2 million from cretinism. Among other nations affected by iodine deficiency, China and Kazakhstan have begun taking action, whereas Russia has not.

* Malnutrition is a common cause of reduced intelligence in parts of the world affected by famine, such as Ethiopia.

Prevention of Mental Disorders is a Public Health Priority

About 450 million people suffer from mental and behavioural disorders worldwide. One person in four will develop one or more of these disorders during their lifetime. Neuropsychiatric conditions account for 13% of the total Disability Adjusted Life Years (DALYs) lost due to all diseases and injuries in the world and are estimated to increase to 15% by the year 2020. Five of the ten leading causes of disability and premature death worldwide are psychiatric conditions. Mental disorders represent not only an immense psychological, social and economic burden to society, but also increase the risk of physical illnesses. Given the current limitations in effectiveness of treatment modalities for decreasing disability due to mental and behavioural disorders, the only sustainable method for reducing the burden caused by these disorders is prevention.

Mental Disorders have Multiple Determinants; Prevention Needs to be a Multipronged Effort

Social, biological and neurological sciences have provided substantial insight into the role of risk and protective factors in the developmental pathways to mental disorders and poor mental health. Biological, psychological, social and societal risk and protective factors and their interactions have been identified across the lifespan from as early as fetal life. Many of these factors are malleable and therefore potential targets for prevention and promotion measures. High comorbidity among mental disorders and their interrelatedness with physical illnesses and social problems stress the need for integrated public health policies, targeting clusters of related problems, common determinants, early stages of multiproblem trajectories and populations at multiple risks.

Effective Prevention Can Reduce the Risk of Mental Disorders

There is a wide range of evidence-based preventive programmes and policies available for implementation. These have been found to reduce risk factors, strengthen protective factors and decrease psychiatric symptoms and disability and the onset of some mental disorders. They also improve positive mental health, contribute to better physical health and generate social and economic benefits. These multi-outcome interventions illustrate that prevention can be cost-effective. Research is beginning to show significant long-term outcomes.

Implementation should be Guided by Available Evidence

For ethical reasons, and to make optimal use of the limited resources for prevention, priority should be given to preventive programmes and policies that show scientific evidence of their effectiveness. Building an evidence base is an incremental process. It should be culturally sensitive and use a wide range of research methods.

Successful Programmes and Policies should be Made Widely Available

Making effective programmes and policies widely available would provide countries and communities with a spectrum of preventive tools to tackle mental disorders.

It is therefore imperative to develop an accessible and integrated system of international and national databases to provide governmental and nongovernmental agencies with information on evidence-based programmes and policies, their outcomes and conditions for effective implementation.

Characteristics

Individuals with mild mental retardation (formerly referred to as "educable"):

* are likely to need only intermittent to limited support;
* typically do not "look" different from their non-disabled peers;
* often have only mild or moderate developmental delays, except in academics, which is often the major area of deficit;

* therefore, they are often not identified until they enter the school setting, where their cognitive disability is most apparent;
* in Minnesota, students with mild MR spend most of the school day in the regular classroom;
* they typically attain 3rd- to 6th-grade academic achievement levels by the time they finish high school;
* as adults, many, though not all, with mild MR will be able to obtain independent employment;
* many will marry, have children, and blend rather indistinguishably into the community; for those who achieve total independence, the label of mental retardation is no longer appropriate.

Individuals with moderate to severe mental retardation (formerly called "trainable"):

* will probably need limited to extensive supports;
* they are more likely to have a recognizable syndrome (such as Down Syndrome);
* therefore, may "look" different than their non-disabled peers;.
* their development is often significantly delayed;
* they are typically identified as infants or toddlers;.
* most begin receiving special education during the preschool years;
* they may be included in the regular classroom part of the school day (particularly here in Minnesota);
* but often spend much of the school day in a separate classroom where they learn adaptive living skills;
* as adults, most individuals with moderate to severe MR will not achieve total independence;
* rather, they are likely to continue to need limited to extensive support such as that provided in group homes or semi-independent living situations (SILs); some may continue to live with their parents;

* some individuals with moderate to severe MR may be able to succeed in modified competitive employment situations;
* however, many will work in supported, non-competitive settings such as sheltered workshops.

Individuals with profound mental retardation:

* will generally need services at the pervasive level, typically throughout their life;
* they are likely to have multiple disabilities, particularly in the areas of mobility and communication;.
* therefore, many use wheelchairs and alternate forms of communication;
* their communication deficits make it difficult to accurately assess their intellectual functioning;
* in educational settings, they may be placed along with students with moderate to severe MR or in their own classroom;
* some adults with this level of retardation remain in institutional settings, but most currently live in group homes.

Mild

Approximately 85% of the mentally retarded population is in the mildly retarded category. Their IQ score ranges from 50-75, and they can often acquire academic skills up to the 6th grade level. They can become fairly self-sufficient and in some cases live independently, with community and social support.

What Is Mild Intellectual Disability (MID) also Referred to as Mild Mental Retardation?

Many of the characteristics of MID correspond to those of Learning Disabilities. The intellectual development will be slow, however, MID students have the potential to learn within the regular classroom given appropriate modifications and/or accommodations. Some MID students will require greater support and/or withdrawal than others will. MID students, like all students demonstrate their own strengths and weaknesses. Depending on the educational jurisdiction, criteria for MID will often state that the child is functioning approximately 2-4 years behind or 2-3 standard deviations below the norm or have an IQ under 70-75. The intellectual disability may vary from mild to profound.

How are MID Students Identified?

Depending on the education jurisdiction, testing for MID will vary. Generally, a combination of assessment methods are used to identify mild intellectual disabilities. Methods may or may not include IQ scores or percentiles, adaptive skills cognitive tests in various areas, skills-based assessments, and levels of academic achievement. Some jurisdictions will not use the term MID but will use mild mental retardation.

Academic Implications

Students with MID may demonstrate some, all or a combination of the following characteristics:

* 2-4 years behind in cognitive development which could include math, language, short attention spans, memory difficulties and delays in speech development.
* Social Relationships are often impacted. The MID child may exhibit behavior problems, be immature, display some obsessive/compulsive behaviors and lack the understanding of verbal/non verbal clues and will often have difficulty following rules and routines.
* Adaptive Skill Implications. (Everyday skills for functioning) These children may be clumsy, use simple language with short sentences, have minimal organization skills and will need reminders about hygiene- washing hands, brushing teeth (life skills). etc.
* Weak Confidence is often demonstrated by MID students. These students are easily frustrated and require opportunities to improve self esteem. Lots of support will be needed to ensure they try new things and take risks in learning.

* Concrete to Abstract thought is often missing or significantly delayed. This includes the lacking ability to understand the difference between figurative and literal language.

Best Practices

* Use simple, short, uncomplicated sentences to ensure maximum understanding.
* Repeat instructions or directions frequently and ask the student if further clarification is necessary.
* Keep distractions and transitions to a minimum.
* Teach specific skills whenever necessary.
* Provide an encouraging, supportive learning environment that will capitalize on student success and self esteem.
* Use appropriate programme interventions in all areas where necessary to maximize success.
* Use alternative instructional strategies and alternative assessment methods.
* Help the MID student develop appropriate social skills to support friend and peer relationships.
* Teach organizational skills.
* Use behavior contracts and reinforce positive behavior if necessary.
* Ensure that your routines and rules are consistent. Keep conversations as normal as possible to maximize inclusion with peers. Teach the difference between literal/figurative language.
* Be patient! Assist with coping strategies.

Moderate

About 10% of the mentally retarded population is considered moderately retarded. Moderately retarded individuals have IQ scores ranging from 35-55. They can carry out work and self-care tasks with moderate supervision. They typically acquire communication skills in childhood and are able to live and function successfully within the community in a supervised environment such as a group home.

* IQ scores between 35 and 50
* Includes about 10 percent of the mentally retarded population
* Individuals in this group can often lead relatively normal lives provided they receive some level of supervision. Such individuals often live in group homes with other mentally retarded people.

Severe

About 3-4% of the mentally retarded population is severely retarded. Severely retarded individuals have IQ scores of 20-40. They may master very basic self-care skills and some communication skills. Many severely retarded individuals are able to live in a group home.

* IQ scores between 20 and 35
* Includes about 3 percent to 4 percent of the mentally retarded population
* Individuals in this category can often master the most basic skills of living, such as cleaning and dressing themselves. They often live in group homes.

Profound

Only 1-2% of the mentally retarded population is classified as profoundly retarded. Profoundly retarded individuals have IQ scores under 20-25. They may be able to develop basic self-care and communication skills with appropriate support and training. Their retardation is often caused by an accompanying neurological disorder. The profoundly retarded need a high level of structure and supervision.

The American Association on Mental Retardation (AAMR) has developed another widely accepted diagnostic classification system for mental retardation. The AAMR classification system focuses on the capabilities of the retarded individual rather than on the limitations. The categories describe the level of support required. They are: intermittent support, limited support, extensive support, and pervasive support. To some extent, the AAMR classification mirrors the DSM-IV classification. Intermittent support, for example, is support needed only occasionally, perhaps during times of stress or crisis. It is the type of support typically required for most mildly retarded individuals. At the other end of the spectrum, pervasive support, or life-long, daily support for most adaptive areas, would be required for profoundly retarded individuals.

* IQ scores of less than 20
* Includes about 1 percent to 2 percent of the mentally retarded population
* Individuals at this level can often develop basic communication and self-care skills. They often have other mental disorders.

Types and Classification of Mental Retardation and Mental Illness

Classification of Mental Disorders

The classification of mental disorders, also known as psychiatric nosology or taxonomy, is a key aspect of psychiatry and other mental health professions and an important issue for consumers and providers of mental health services. There are currently two widely established systems for classifying mental illness- Chapter V of the International Classification of Diseases (ICD-10) produced by the World Health Organization (WHO) and the Diagnostic and Statistical Manual of Mental Disorders (DSM-IV) produced by the American Psychiatric Association (APA). Both list categories of disorders thought to be distinct types, and have deliberately converged their codes in recent revisions so that the manuals are often broadly comparable, although significant differences remain. Other classification schemes may be in use more locally, for example the Chinese Classification of Mental Disorders. Other manuals are used by those of alternative theoretical persuasions, such as the Psychodynamic Diagnostic Manual. Generally there is a significant scientific debate about the relative merits of a categorical system or a dimensional system (also known as a continuum or spectrum system), as well as significant controversy about the role of science and values in classification schemes and the professional, legal and social uses to which they are put.

Definitions

In the scientific and academic literature on the definition of mental disorder, one extreme argues that it is entirely a matter of value judgements (including of what is normal) while another proposes that it is or could be entirely objective and scientific (including by reference to statistical norms); other views argue that the concept refers to a "fuzzy prototype" that can never be precisely defined, or that the definition will always involve a mixture of scientific facts (*e.g.* that a natural or evolved function isn't working properly) and value judgements (*e.g.* that it is harmful or undesired). Lay concepts of mental disorder vary considerably across different cultures and countries, and may refer to different sorts of individual and social problems.

The World Health Organization (WHO) and national surveys report that there is no single consensus on the definition of mental disorder/illness, and that the phrasing used depends on the social, cultural, economic and legal context in different contexts and in different societies. The WHO reports that there is intense debate about which conditions should be included under the concept of mental disorder; a broad definition can cover mental illness, mental retardation, personality disorder and substance dependence, but inclusion varies by country and is reported to be a complex and debated issue.

There may be a criterion that a condition should not be expected to occur as part of a person's usual culture or religion. However, despite the term "mental", there is not necessarily a clear distinction drawn between mental (dys)functioning and brain (dys) functioning, or indeed between the brain and the rest of the body.

Most international clinical documents avoid the term "mental illness", preferring the term "mental disorder" However, some use "mental illness" as the main over-arching term to encompass mental disorders. Some consumer/survivor movement organizations oppose use of the term "mental illness" on the grounds that it supports the dominance of a medical model. The term "serious mental illness" (SMI) is sometimes used to refer to more severe and long-lasting disorder while "mental health problems" may be used as a broader term, or to refer only to milder or more transient issues. Confusion often surrounds the ways and contexts in which these terms are used.

ICD-10

The International Classification of Diseases (ICD) is an international standard diagnostic classification for a wide variety of health conditions. Chapter V focuses on "mental and behavioural disorders" and consists of 10 main groups:

- F0 Organic, including symptomatic, mental disorders
- F1 Mental and behavioural disorders due to use of psychoactive substances
- F2 Schizophrenia, schizotypal and delusional disorders
- F3 Mood [affective] disorders
- F4 Neurotic, stress-related and somatoform disorders
- F5 Behavioural syndromes associated with physiological disturbances and physical factors
- F6 Disorders of personality and behaviour in adult persons
- F7 Mental retardation
- F8 Disorders of psychological development
- F9 Behavioural and emotional disorders with onset usually occurring in childhood and adolescence
- In addition, a group of "unspecified mental disorders".

Within each group there are more specific subcategories. The ICD includes personality disorders on the same domain as other mental disorders, unlike the DSM. The ICD-10 states that mental disorder is "not an exact term", although is generally used "...to imply the existence of a clinically recognisable set of symptoms or behaviours associated in most cases with distress and with interference with personal functions." (WHO, 1992).

The WHO is revising their classifications in this section as part of the development of the ICD-11 (scheduled for 2014) and an "International Advisory Group" has been established to guide this.

DSM-IV

The DSM-IV, produced by the American Psychiatric Association, characterizes mental disorder as "a clinically significant behavioral or psychological syndrome or pattern that occurs in an individual,...is associated with present distress...or disability...or with a significant increased risk of suffering." but that "...no definition adequately specifies precise boundaries for the concept of "mental disorder"...different situations call for different definitions" (APA, 1994 and 2000). The DSM also states that "there is no assumption that each category of mental disorder is a completely discrete entity with absolute boundaries dividing it from other mental disorders or from no mental disorder."

The DSM-IV-TR (Text Revision, 2000) consists of five axes (domains) on which disorder can be assessed. The five axes are:

Axis I: Clinical Disorders (all mental disorders except Personality Disorders and Mental Retardation)

Axis II: Personality Disorders and Mental Retardation

Axis III: General Medical Conditions (must be connected to a Mental Disorder)

Axis IV: Psychosocial and Environmental Problems (for example limited social support network)

Axis V: Global Assessment of Functioning (Psychological, social and job-related functions are evaluated on a continuum between mental health and extreme mental disorder)

The main categories of disorder in the DSM are:

Other Schemes

The Chinese Society of Psychiatry's Chinese Classification of Mental Disorders (currently CCMD-3)

The Latin American Guide for Psychiatric Diagnosis (GLDP).

Childhood Diagnosis

Child and adolescent psychiatry sometimes uses specific manuals in addition to the DSM and ICD. The Diagnostic Classification of Mental Health and Developmental Disorders of Infancy and Early Childhood (DC:0-3) was first published in 1994 by Zero to Three to classify mental health and developmental disorders in the first four years of life. It has been published in 9 languages. The Research Diagnostic criteria-Preschool Age (RDC-PA) was developed in 2000 to 2002 by a task force of independent investigators with the goal of developing clearly specified diagnostic criteria to facilitate research on psychopathology in this age group. The French Classification of Child and Adolescent Mental Disorders (CFTMEA), operational since 1983, is the classification of reference for French child psychiatrists.

Usage

The ICD and DSM classification schemes have achieved much widespread acceptance in psychiatry. A survey of 205 psychiatrists, from 66 different countries across all continents, found that ICD-10 was more frequently used and more valued in clinical practice and training, while the DSM-IV was more valued for research, with accessibility to either being limited, and usage by other mental health professionals, policy makers, patients and families less clear. A primary care (*e.g.* general or family physician) version of the mental disorder section of ICD-10 has been developed (ICD-10-PHC) which has also been used quite extensively internationally A survey of journal articles indexed in various biomedical databases between 1980 and 2005 indicated that 15,743 referred to the DSM and 3,106 to the ICD.

In Japan, most university hospitals use either the ICD or DSM. ICD appears to be the somewhat more used for research or academic purposes, while both were used equally for clinical purposes. Other traditional psychiatric schemes may also be used.

Mental Retardation

Doctors have found many causes of mental retardation. The most common are:

- *Genetic Conditions:* Sometimes mental retardation is caused by abnormal genes inherited from parents, errors when genes combine, or other reasons. Examples of genetic conditions are Down syndrome, fragile X syndrome, and phenylketonuria (PKU).
- *Problems during Pregnancy:* Mental retardation can result when the baby does not develop inside the mother properly. For example, there may be a problem with the way the baby's cells divide as it grows. A woman who drinks alcohol or gets an infection like rubella during pregnancy may also have a baby with mental retardation.
- *Problems at Birth:* If a baby has problems during labour and birth, such as not getting enough oxygen, he or she may have mental retardation.
- *Health Problems:* Diseases like whooping cough, the measles, or meningitis can cause mental retardation. Mental retardation can also be caused by extreme malnutrition (not eating right), not getting enough medical care, or by being exposed to poisons like lead or mercury.

Mental retardation is not a disease. You can't catch mental retardation from anyone. Mental retardation is also not a type of mental illness, like depression.

There is no cure for mental retardation. However, most children with mental retardation can learn to do many things. It just takes them more time and effort than other children.

What are the Signs of Mental Retardation?

There are many signs of mental retardation. For example, children with mental retardation may:

- sit up, crawl, or walk later than other children;
- learn to talk later, or have trouble speaking,
- find it hard to remember things,
- not understand how to pay for things,
- have trouble understanding social rules,
- have trouble seeing the consequences of their actions,
- have trouble solving problems, and/or
- have trouble thinking logically.

About 87% of people with mental retardation will only be a little slower than average in learning new information and skills. When they are children, their limitations may not be obvious. They may not even be diagnosed as having mental retardation until they get to school. As they become adults, many people with mild retardation can live independently. Other people may not even consider them as having mental retardation. The remaining 13% of people with mental retardation score below 50 on IQ tests. These people will have more difficulty in school, at home, and in the community. A person with more severe retardation will need more intensive support his or her entire life. Every child with mental retardation is able to learn, develop, and grow. With help, all children with mental retardation can live a satisfying life.

How is Mental Retardation Diagnosed?

Mental retardation is diagnosed by looking at two main things. These are:

- the ability of a person's brain to learn, think, solve problems, and make sense of the world (called IQ or intellectual functioning); and
- whether the person has the skills he or she needs to live independently (called adaptive behavior, or adaptive functioning).

Intellectual functioning, or IQ, is usually measured by a test called an IQ test. The average score is 100. People scoring below 70 to 75 are thought to have mental retardation. To measure adaptive behavior, professionals look at what a child can do in comparison to other children of his or her age. Certain skills are important to adaptive behavior. These are:

- Daily living skills, such as getting dressed, going to the bathroom, and feeding one's self;
- Communication skills, such as understanding what is said and being able to answer;
- social skills with peers, family members, adults, and others.

To diagnose mental retardation, professionals look at the person's mental abilities (IQ) and his or her adaptive skills. Both of these are highlighted in the definition of mental retardation provided between the lines below. This definition comes from the Individuals with Disabilities Education Act (IDEA). The IDEA is the federal law that guides how schools provide early intervention and special education and related services to children with disabilities.

Providing services to help individuals with mental retardation has led to a new understanding of how we define mental retardation. After the initial diagnosis of mental retardation is made, we look at a person's strengths and weaknesses. We also look at how much support or help the person needs to get along at home, in school, and in the community. This approach gives a realistic picture of each individual. It also recognizes that the "picture" can change. As the person grows and learns, his or her ability to get along in the world grows as well.

Mild Mental Retardation

Approximately 85% of the mentally retarded population is in the mildly retarded category. Their IQ score ranges from 50-75, and they can often acquire academic skills up to the 6th grade level. They can become fairly self-sufficient and in some cases live independently, with community and social support.

Moderate Mental Retardation

About 10% of the mentally retarded population is considered moderately retarded. Moderately retarded individuals have IQ scores ranging from 35-55. They can carry out work and self-care tasks with moderate supervision. They typically acquire communication skills in childhood and are able to live and function successfully within the community in a supervised environment such as a group home.

Severe Mental Retardation

About 3-4% of the mentally retarded population is severely retarded. Severely retarded individuals have IQ scores of 20-40. They may master very basic self-care skills and some communication skills. Many severely retarded individuals are able to live in a group home.

Profound Mental Retardation

Only 1-2% of the mentally retarded population is classified as profoundly retarded. Profoundly retarded individuals have IQ scores under 20-25. They may be able to develop basic self-care and communication skills with appropriate support and training. Their retardation is often caused by an accompanying neurological disorder. The profoundly retarded need a high level of structure and supervision.

The American Association on Mental Retardation (AAMR) has developed another widely accepted diagnostic classification system for mental retardation. The AAMR classification system focuses on the capabilities of the retarded individual rather than on the limitations. The categories describe the level of support required. They are: *intermittent support*, *limited support*, *extensive support*, and *pervasive support*. To some extent, the AAMR classification mirrors the *DSM-IV* classification. Intermittent support, for example, is support needed only occasionally, perhaps during times of stress or crisis. It is the type of support typically required for most mildly retarded individuals. At the other end of the spectrum, pervasive support, or life-long, daily support for most adaptive areas, would be required for profoundly retarded individuals.

Mental Illness

Language: Deaf people depend on gestures and body language to communicate. Thus, behavior which may appear overly animated may reflect a style of communication rather than an agitated state. English is often considered a second language for a culturally deaf person and when sign language is put into written form it can appear fragmented, concrete or confusing to a mental health clinician who is not a part of the deaf community. Therefore, distinguishing language limitations from confusion or thought disturbance is a complex clinical challenge. A recent study conducted in a specialty deaf inpatient psychiatric unit found that 75% of deaf individuals were non-fluent in American Sign Language (Black & Glickman, 2006). This finding may result from the fact that 90% of deaf children are born to hearing parents and these children may not have received any usable language input during critical language acquisition periods of brain development. Lacking language input during a child's earliest years and the underdevelopment of a formal language system can result in an adult without fluency or competence in any language, including ASL (Sacks, 1989).

Possession of a language system is necessary to facilitate abstract thinking. Without such a system some persons who are deaf may lack the ability to think abstractly or to generalize concepts. To further compound the issue, the average deaf adult reads English at a fourth grade level (Haskins, 2000). Differentiating between a language system attributed to neurological or psychiatric illness rather than social or experiential origins is extremely difficult for a diagnosing therapist. Misdiagnosing non-fluent (but otherwise healthy) deaf individuals (as psychotic) is not a new phenomenon. But what may be equally common are deaf individuals who are psychotic but whose illness is overlooked by clinicians who attribute symptoms to poor interpretation, deafness, or minimal language skills (Pollard, 2005).

How then are abstract English concepts such as "delusion" or "hallucination" to be explained or understood by a mentally ill deaf person? Standard psychiatric questions are very abstract and for a deaf person with a limited language system, these questions may lead to poor assessment resulting in barriers to treatment and ongoing appropriate intervention.

Psychosis

Deaf people who are psychotic can display disorders of thought form and or thought content. Disorders of thought content can be diagnosed by asking concrete questions (*i.e.*: are people following them, or is someone stealing their thoughts). Thought form disorders are more difficult to diagnose. Such disorders can include loose associations, flight of ideas, incoherence, tangentially and fragmentation (Haskins, 2000). One must consider that the ability to determine a thought disturbance can be compounded when a deaf person may have a limited language system.

Deaf people experiencing psychosis may have auditory hallucinations, such as hearing voices. This is noted to be possible even if they have been deaf from birth. Research conducted in a mental health setting revealed that 59% of deaf patients were able to give accounts of verbal auditory hallucinations (Briffa, 1999). Additionally, deaf people may also experience visual hallucinations described as seeing signing; such as Jesus signing or an image signing to them (Haskins, 2000).

These scenarios highlight the importance of having a diagnostic tool to effectively assess psychosis in deaf patients. This need was highlighted in a lawsuit stemming from two murders that took place at Gallaudet University in 2000-2001. The case required accurate knowledge of the deaf defendant's psychotic symptoms. The expert witness in the case was unable to explain the process for determining psychosis in deaf vs. hearing people as there was no such tool for making this type of assessment. As a result, a serious gap in mental health assessment was identified. Research and the development of a rating scale are currently in process at the University Rochester Medical Center and are expected to be completed in 2010 (Pollard, 2005).

Standards of care for mental health services to deaf and hard of hearing persons have been established (Myers, 1995). However, several studies continue to highlight problems with misdiagnosis; denial of appropriate services; lack of sustainable resources for clients; lack of appropriate medical care (assessment and treatment) and significant language and communication barriers. Several well documented ADA lawsuits reveal that it is not uncommon for deaf persons to have experienced forced hospitalizations, medication, etc. (Haskins, 2004 & Steinberg, Sullivan & Loew, 1998).

The reality is that deaf persons suffering from mental illness are at great risk of not receiving adequate treatment or may not be treated at all for milder, but still devastating mental health problems such as depression and anxiety. A lack of knowledge and effective tools leads to poor assessment and misdiagnosis of deaf persons with mental health needs. Valid detection and assessment of psychosis in deaf individuals and effective tools to assess risk related factors is a serious inequity in mental health services.

Diagnosis & Treatment

Historically, there were a variety of psychiatric myths about deaf people. One such myth was that deaf people could not suffer depression, as they didn't have enough of a superego to rise to the level of obsessional defenses (Altshuler, 1971). Psychiatry and research have evolved over the years and there are many recent case studies and research that dispute this way of thinking. Recent studies indicate a broader range of diagnosis of mental illness than in the past. Posttraumatic stress disorder is noted as being the most common diagnosis found in the deaf community. The study further revealed that deaf patients were less likely to be diagnosed with a psychotic or substance abuse disorder and more likely to be diagnosed with a mood, anxiety, personality, or developmental disorder. Furthermore, deaf patients presented at higher risks than hearing patients in areas of self-harm and risk of sexual offending (Black & Glickman, 2006). Acknowledgement that the deaf community struggles with significant mental health needs is noted. However, what remains is that professionals often have limited knowledge of deafness or deaf culture which seriously impacts their ability to accurately assess and intervene.

Oftentimes a person who is deaf or hard of hearing may enter the mental health system in the absence of severe mental illness. While the general population can be commonly treated for many mental health issues through private therapy, deaf or hard of hearing individuals have limited access to such services. This is due to that lack of communicative access. For example, mental health professionals are not skilled to effectively communicate with the deaf and oftentimes times there is an unwillingness for the private sector to provide a communicative resource (*e.g.* interpreters) (Myers, 1995).

Specialized psychiatric units which provide service to deaf people are uncommon in the United States. Many States do not have specialized services for persons who are deaf or a resource database available to deaf persons (Haskins, 2004). Offering services to psychiatric patients who are deaf, especially to persons who lack full language competency, requires clinicians to know sign language as well as the deaf culture. The ability to communicate is at the heart of good mental health. Deaf people face greater obstacles in establishing good communication with the mental health community and with most mental health services available. Without appropriate communication it will adversely affect the ability for deaf people to recover from mental health problems.

Conclusion

It is well known that mental health is generally under funded and socially marginalized across the country. Many specialized services have developed out of a critical incident that may or may not have resulted in a lawsuit. There continues to be a need for a milieu that includes interpretation and a strong understanding of deaf culture and language issues. Ongoing advocacy for mental health settings to become skilled in the diagnostic, cultural and language needs of deaf people will increase accuracy in diagnosis and enable better treatment planning for all deaf persons served.

Intervention and Educational Progremmes

Early Childhood Intervention and Education Branch

The Maryland Infants and Toddlers Programme/Preschool Services Branch provides oversight and support to local early intervention systems and local school system preschool special education programmes for children with disabilities from birth through age five.

The Programme Administration and Improvement Section coordinates funding, technical assistance, training, and monitoring activities for the state's early intervention system under Part C of the Individuals with Disabilities Education Act (IDEA). Family-centered early intervention services to enhance the development of children with disabilities from birth to age three and to support families' capacity to meet the special needs of their infants and toddlers are provided through 24 local interagency Infants and Toddlers Programmes.

The Preschool Services Section provides funding support and technical assistance for preschool special education programmes for children with disabilities from ages three thorough five in each local school system. Collaboration with other community-based early childhood programmes and local Infants and Toddlers Programmes is a major emphasis for preschool special education programmes at the state and local levels.

The branch coordinates support and information activities for families of children with disabilities from birth through age 21 through local Family Support Networks, Preschool Partners, and Partners for Success Resource Centers.

Programme Administration, Support, and Staff Development Branch

The Programme Manager supports the Assistant State Superintendent in administering special education programmes stat-wide and directing the Programme Administration, Support, and Staff Development Branch (PAS&SD). The Programme Administration Section is responsible for assisting local school systems and state-operated programmes in the implementation of programmes designed to improve the educational development of children and youth.

The Regional Administrator Section is responsible for supporting local school systems and state-operated programmes to ensure the delivery of special education and related services to students with disabilities.

The Staff Development Section is responsible for providing technical and programme assistance to local school systems and state operated programmes in maintaining a Comprehensive System of Personnel Development (CSPD) to assist in ensuring the appropriate and necessary educational services to children and youth with disabilities.

The Instructional Development Section conducts research and analysis of data pertaining to students with disabilities in the areas of assessment, instruction, and programme evaluation. The section works collaboratively with other instructional divisions in programme evaluation, staff development, and outcome-reporting activities supporting the division's approach to facilitate the inclusion of students with disabilities in general education programming.

School-based Programmes

Suicide education in school settings has failed to show any impact on suicide behaviours. There are even indications that such education may increase the number of students who consider suicide as a possible solution to their problems. Systematic direct screening of adolescents, using evidence-based suicide predictors, is considered an effective public health strategy to address adolescent suicide, however.

One school-based programme is the Suicide Prevention and School Crisis Management Programme implemented in a public school district in Florida in the USA, covering around 330 000 children and adolescents at elementary, middle and senior high schools.

This comprehensive programme encompasses the implementation of a suicide prevention school policy, teacher training and consultation, education to parents, stress management and life skills curriculum for students and the establishment of a crisis team in each school. In a five-year longitudinal study, a 63% reduction was found in the annual number of suicides among students and a 64% reduction in suicide attempts (Zenere & Lazarus, 1997).

Needs Assessment and Programme Development

Address community needs and evidence-based risk and protective factors:

> *Prevention policies need to be based on systematic assessments of public mental health needs.*
>
> *To be effective, programmes need to address evidence-based biological, psychological and social risk and protective factors and their interactions over the lifespan.*
>
> *To enlarge the impact of preventive interventions on the mental health of whole populations, interventions that have the capacity to have a large reach in such populations need to be developed.*

Base Prevention Programmes on Principles of Effectiveness

Although to date many effective prevention programmes exist, their effectiveness and cost-effectiveness need to be further improved. The long history of research and development in prevention has generated insight into strategies and conditions needed to develop effective prevention programmes and policies and to avoid failures.

For instance, more effectiveness can be expected from programmes that combine or coordinate multiple interventions addressing similar preventive targets, that are tailored to the needs of target populations and specific segments within them, that are timed at developmental periods sensitive to change, that make use of evidence- based principles of behaviour change and that have a large reach in populations at risk.

Programme developers and providers need to be guided by available knowledge on programme characteristics and other evidence-based principles and conditions that can increase effectiveness and cost-effectiveness.

Address Multiple Outcomes in Mental and Physical Health and Social Domains

Available evidence-based prevention programmes have also been found to improve positive mental health, to contribute to better physical health and to generate social and economic benefits. Such multi-outcome interventions illustrate that prevention can be cost-effective. One of the main problems in prevention science and policy is the compartmentalized approach to mental, social, educational, behavioural and legal problems. Many problems are related or share common risk factors that can be addressed simultaneously.

The accumulation of multiple proximal outcomes across domains of functioning can bring about more efficient strategies than collections of programmes with fragmented outcomes. Accumulation of outcomes across health and social domains will offer the most convincing arguments for multiple stakeholders to invest in prevention at national and local levels.

Programmes should address multiple outcomes, that is, they should have the potential to reduce the risk of multiple mental health problems and disorders, to improve simultaneously both mental and physical health and to generate social and economic benefits.

Programmes

The Education of All Handicapped Children Act of 1975 requires public schools in the United States to offer educational training and other services to all children, even those with profound mental retardation. These students often receive publicly funded education their entire lives.

Educational programmes for mentally retarded children under 6 years old focus on exploration, socialization, language acquisition, and developing basic living skills. Such programmes may be provided in settings ranging from specialized educational centers to the home.

Children of school age, typically from 6 to 18 years old, receive education that emphasizes basic academic and social skills. However, the specific skills taught to these children vary widely, especially across the levels of retardation. For example, students with mild retardation receive instruction in math, reading, writing, and social skills. Students with profound retardation receive training in more basic skills, such as bathing, brushing their teeth, and feeding or dressing themselves. Educational services for older students often emphasize the transition to adulthood. These programmes include teaching skills in developing friendships, self-sufficiency at home, and specific work skills.

The Education of All Handicapped Children Act of 1975 and subsequent laws known as the Individuals with Disabilities Education Act (IDEA) require that all children be placed in the "least restrictive" setting possible. Because retardation levels vary widely, educational services are not provided in any single type of setting for all these students. Students with mild levels of retardation may be educated in regular classrooms, with or without special education consultants. More restrictive settings include half-day placement in regular classrooms and in special education resource rooms, special education classrooms within regular schools, separate schools for students with special needs, and homebound or hospital educational programmes.

UNIT-V

Locomotor Disabilities

Definition and Identification

Impairment

An impairment in any loss or abnormality of psychological, physiological or anatomical structure or function in a human being.

Functional Limitations

Impairment may cause functional limitations which are partial or total inability to perform those activities, necessary for motor, sensory or mental function within the range or manner of which a human being is normally capable.

Disability

A disability is any restriction or lack (resulting from an impairment) of ability to perform an activity in the manner or within the range considered normal for a human being.

Locomotor Disability

Locomotor disability is defined as a person's inability to execute distinctive activities associated with moving both himself and objects, from place to place and such inability resulting from affliction of musculoskeletal and/or nervous system.

Categories of Locomotor Disability for Evaluation

- Guidelines for Evaluation of Permanent Physical Impairment of Upper Limb

- Guidelines for Evaluation of permanent physical Impairment in Lower Limb
- Guidelines for Evaluation of Permanent Physical Impairment of Trunk (Spine)
- Guidelines for Evaluation of PPI in cases of Short Stature/Dwarfism
- Guidelines for Evaluation of Permanent Physical Impairment in Amputees
- Guidelines for Evaluation of Permanent Physical Impairment of Congenital deficiencies of the limbs

Guidelines for Evaluation of Permanent Physical Impairment of Upper Limb

1. The estimation of permanent impairment depends upon the measurement of functional impairment and is not expression of a personal opinion.
2. The estimation and measurement should be made when the clinical condition has reached the stage of maximum improvement from the medical treatment. Normally the time period is to be decided by the medical doctor who is evaluating the case for issuing the PPI Certificate as per standard format of the certificate.
3. The upper limb is divided into two component parts; the arm component and the hand component.
4. Measurement of the loss of function of arm component consists of measuring the loss of motion, muscle strength and co-ordinated activities.
5. Measurement of loss of function of hand component consists of determining the prehension, sensation and strength. For estimation of prehension opposition, lateral pinch cylindrical grasp, spherical grasp and hook grasp have to be assessed as shown in Hand Component of Form A Assessment Proforma for upper extremity.
6. The impairment of the entire extremity depends on the combination of the functional impairments of both components.

Arm Component

Total value of arm component is 90%

Principles of evaluation of range of motion (ROM) of joints:

1. The value of maximum ROM in the arm component is 90%
2. Each of the three joints of the arm is weighed equally (30%)

Assesment Performa for Upper Extermity

Hand Component(Total Value 90%)		
30% prehension 1. Hand Component	**Movement**	**Normal Value**
A. Opposition B. Lateral Pinch (5%) C. Cylindrical grasp	1. Index 2. Middle 3. Ring 4. Little Key holding a. large object (4) b. Small object (1) a. Large object (4) b. Small object (1)Lifting bag	2 2 } 8% 225% 3}3} 6% 3}3} 6% 5%

Example

The intra articular fractures of the bones of right shoulder joint may affect range of motion even after healing. The loss of ROM should be calculated in each arc of motion as envisaged in the Assessment Form A.

Assessment Performa for Upper Extremity			
Arc of ROM	**Normal value**	**Active ROM**	**Loss of ROM**
Shoulder Flexion-	0-220	110	50%
Rotation	0-180	90	50%
Abduction-Adduction	0-180	90	50%

Shoulder movements constitute 30% of the motion of the arm component therefore the loss of motion for arm component will be 50 x 0.30 = 15%. If more than one joint of the arm is involved the loss of percentage in each joint is calculated separately as above and then added together.

Arm Component (Total Value 90%)

Summary value for upper extremity is calculated from component and hand component values.

Principles of Evaluation of Strength of Muscles

1. Strength of muscles can be tested by manual method and graded from 0-5 as advocated by Medical Research Council of Great Britain depending upon the strength of the muscles.
2. Loss of muscle power can be given percentages as follows:

Loss of Muscle Power	
Manual muscle Strength grading	Loss of strength in percentage
0	100%
1	80%
2	60%
3	40%
4	20%·
5	0%

The mean percentage of loss of muscle strength around a joint is multiplied by 0.30.

If loss of muscle strength involves more than one joint the mean loss of percentage in each joint is calculated separately and then added together as has been described for loss of motion.

Principles of evaluation of coordinated activities:

1. The total value for coordinated activities is 90%
2. Ten different coordinated activities should be tested as given in the ASSESSMENT PFROFORMA FOR UPPER EXTERMITY
3. Each activity has a value of 9%

Combining values for the Arm Component

The total value of loss of function of arm componet is obtained by combining the value of loss of ROM, muscle strength and coordinated activities, using the combing formula.

[A+B(90-A)/90]

where,

a = higher value

b = lower value

Example

Let us assume that an individual with an intra articular fracture of bones of shoulder joint in addition to 16.5% loss of motion in arm has 8.3% loss of strength of muscles and 5% loss of coordination. These values should be combined as follows:

Loss of ROM- 16.5%

$$\frac{16.5 + 8.3(90 - 16.5)}{90}$$

Loss of strength of muscles- 8.3% =23.33%

To add Loss of coordination- 5%

$$\frac{23.3 + 5(90 - 23.3)}{90} = 27.0\%$$

So the total value of loss of function in Arm component will be 27.0%

Hand Component

1. Total value of hand component is 90%.
2. The functional impairment of hand is expressed as loss of prehension, loss of sensation and loss of strength.

Principles of Evaluation of Prevention

Total value of prehension is 30%. It includes;

a. Opposition- 8%

Tested Against:

- o Index finger- 2%
- o Middle finger -2 %
- o Ring- 2 %
- o Little finger- 2%

b. Lateral pinch -5%- Tested by asking the patient to hold key between the thumb and lateral side of index finger.

c. Cylindrical grasp- 6% Tested for

i. Large object of 4 inches size -3%
ii. Small object of 1 inch size- 3%

d. Spherical grasp -6% Tested for Large object of 4 inches size- 3%
i. Small object of 1 inch size- 3%

e. Hook grasp- 5% -Tested by asking the patient to lift a bag

Principles of Evaluation of sensation:

1. Total value of sensation in hand is 30%
2. It should be assessed according to the distribution given below:

Complete loss of sensation:

- Thumb ray-9%
- Index finger-6%
- Middle finger-5%
- Ring finger-5%
- Little finger-5%

Partial loss of sensation: Assessment should be made according to percentage of loss of sensation in thumb/finger(s)

Principles of Evaluation of strength:

1. Total value of strength is 30%
2. It includes:
   i. Grip strength-20%
   ii. Pinch strength-10%

Strength of hand should be tested with hand dynamometer or by clinical method (grip method).

Additional weightage- A total of 10% additional weightage can be given to following accompanying factors if they are continuous and persistent despite treatment.

1. Pain
2. Infection
3. Deformity

4. Mal-alignment
5. Contractures
6. Cosmetic disfiguration
7. Dominant extremity -4%
8. Shortening of upper limb

First 1"- No weightage

For each 1" beyond first 1" -2%

The extra points should not exceed 10% of the total Arm Component and total PPI should not exceed 100% in any case

Combining Values of Hand Component

The final value of loss of function of hand component is obtained by summing up values of loss of prehension, sensation and strength.

Combining Values for the Extremity

Values of impairment of arm component and impairment of hand component should be added by using the combining formula

[A+B(90-A)/90]

A= higher value

B= lower value

Example

Impairment of Arm- 27%
therefore, [64+27(90-64)/90] = 71.8%

Impairment of hand- 64%

Identification

Timely identification of impairments, a secondary prevention, can reduce the impact of the impairment on the functional level of the individual and also in checking the impairments from becoming a disabling condition. Initially they need to be identified as soon as possible at home by the parents and outside (in the anganwadi centres/schools/sub-health centres/through camps), and then they need to be assessed by a team of specialists in order to plan necessary interventions.

Identification

A. At Home

Parents can observe and identify the children with disabilities by using the following checklist for early identification of disabilities:

I. Hearing Impairment

Screening new born:

1. Is there any one in the family with deafness since childhood.
2. Did the mother take an abortificient drug or any drug or any other medicine in large doses during the first three months of pregnancy?
3. Is the birth weight below 1500 gms.?
4. Did the child have a delayed cry after birth?
5. Did the child have significant jaundice (yellowness of eyes) during the first 10 days after birth?
6. Does the child have a cleft in the lip or palate, or a malformed pinna?

Screening children in the age group of 6 months to 2 years:

1. Does a child turn towards the source of sound which is located either at the back or towards one side of the body?
2. Does he/she has discharge from the ear?

Screening children above 2 years age:

1. Does he/she turn when called from behind?
2. Uses gestures excessively.
3. The child does not speak or has a defective speech.
4. The child does not understand the spoken language.
5. The child has an ear discharge.

II. Visual Impairment

1. The child does not follow an object moving before his eyes by one month's age.
2. The child does not reach for toys and things held in front of him by three months age.
3. One eye moves differently from the other; including squint.
4. Eyes are either red or have a yellow discharge, or the tears flow continuously.
5. The child has a tendency to bring pictures or books very close to the eyes.

III. Mental Retardation

1. Does the child respond to name/voice by fourth month?
2. Does the child smiles at others by sixth month?
3. Does the child hold the head steadily by sixth month?
4. Does the child sit without support by twelfth month?
5. Can the child stand without support by eighteenth month?
6. Can the child walk well by twentieth month?
7. Can the child talk 2-3 word sentences by third year?
8. Can the child eat/drink by himself by fourth year?
9. Can the child tell his name by fourth year?
10. Does the child has toilet control by fourth year?
11. Does the child avoid simple hazards?
12. Does the child get fits?

IV. Locomotor Disability

1. The child is not able to raise both the arms fully without any associated difficulties.
2. The child is not able to grasp objects without any associated difficulty.
3. The child has absence of any part of the limb.
4. The child has a difficulty in walking.

B. Outside

In the rural and tribal areas as well as in the urban-slums, early identification is usually done through door-to-door surveys, screening children at the anganwadis, schools, health centres, sub-health centres, rehabilitation centres or through camps usually organized by the voluntary workers.

1. Anganwadi Centre—ICDS

The Department of Women and Child Development under the Ministry of Human Resource Development, has been implementing the programme of Integrated Child Development Scheme (ICDS) since 1975. An anganwadi centre under the programme is located in each village and is run by an anganwadi worker. Some of the important objectives of the scheme include improvement of the nutritional status of the children in the age group of 0-6 years, providing nutrition and health education to every woman in the age group of 15-44 years, and improving the capability of the mothers to look after the normal health and nutritional needs of their children. An anganwadi worker is required to do early detection of the disabilities in children present at their anganwadi centres.

2. Primary Health Centres

India has a well established net work of Primary Health Centres, each catering to a population of 30 to 40 thousand. These have sub-health centres at the field level. Each sub-health centre caters to a population of around 3,000. Under the programme of the MCH (Mother & Child Health) the worker takes care of the children by providing immunization and vitamin A supplementation to the children below 6 years of age. She also identifies the health problems which may lead to disability and takes further preventive action.

3. Rehabilitation Services are Provided to All the Eligible Persons by the

Ministry of Social Justice and Empowerment through its Various Programmes:

(a) *Camps under District Rehabilitation Centres (DRCs) in 11 Districts:* Comprehensive rehabilitation services are provided to the rural disabled at their door steps mainly through camps organized by voluntary organizations. Grassroot functionaries like anganwadi workers, health workers, are also involved. These camps provide services such as prevention and early detection, medical intervention and surgical correction, fitting of artificial aids and appliances, therapeutic services such as physiotherapy, occupational and speech therapy, provision of training for acquisition of skills through vocational training, job placement in local industries, etc.

(b) *Composite Rehabilitation Services (District Centre):* Rehabilitation Services in more than 107 districts in the country are being provided at the door steps of persons with disabilities. These services include promotion of early detection and prevention of disability, fitting, follow- up and repair of assistive devices, provide vocational training and help in finding gainful employment. At the field level, grass-root functionaries—anganwadi workers, health workers and PRIs are helping in implementation of the programme.

(c) *National Programme for Rehabilitation Persons with Disabilities (NPRPD) :* The programme of NPRPD has recently been launched as a State Sector Scheme. Under the scheme there is a provision of two community based rehabilitation workers at each gram panchayat and two multi-purpose rehabilitation workers at block level. The focus at grass-root level would be prevention, early detection and information dissemination. Services at district level would be provided through various professionals like physiotherapists, occupational therapists, orthotic and prosthetic engineers, etc. At the state referral centre, higher level services would be provided.

4. School

Teachers in all the primary, upper primary and secondary government schools have a responsibility to identify children with disabilities. Check list for identification of children with special needs

(School teachers and parents should use this check list):

(i) Visual

(a) Watering of eyes.

(b) Recurrent redness.

(c) Frequent irritation.

(d) Frequent blinking.

(e) Squint.

(f) Inappropriate stumbling upon objects or bumping into other people.

(g) Titling of the head or closure of one eye.

(h) Difficulty in counting the fingers of an outstretched hand at a distance of one meter.

(i) Moving head side to side while reading.

(j) Difficulty in recognizing distant objects.

(k) Difficulty in doing fine work requiring perfect vision.

(l) Holding books too close or too far from the eyes.

(m) Frequently ask other children when taking down notes from the blackboard.

(n) Exhibit difficulty in reading from the blackboard.

(o) Hitting against the objects on the side.

Note: If any of the above four conditions are present, then the child should be properly examined by a qualified ophthalmologist to see if the existing condition can be improved by medical treatment or by using spectacles.

(ii) Hearing

(a) Malformation of the ear.

(b) Discharge from ear.

(c) Pain in ear.

(d) Irritation in ear.

(e) Trying to listen from a closer distance.

(f) Ask for the instructions repeatedly.

(g) Not able to write properly.

(h) Trying to listen to the echo reflection rather than to the speaker.

(i) Make errors while copying from blackboard.

(j) Frequently ask a colleague to show his workbook.

(k) Problems in paying attention in the class.

(l) Favour one ear for listening purposes.

(m) Problems when anyone speaks from behind.

(n) Child speaks loudly or too softly.

(o) Exhibit voice problem and mispronunciation.

(p) Tune the TV/Radio too loud.

(q) Irrelevant answers.

(r) The child keeps away from his age mates.

(s) The child is unable to respond when called from the other room.

(t) The child understands only after few repetitions.

Note : If any 3 to 4 of the above conditions are present, it indicates some kind of hearing/speech loss. Then the child should be carefully examined by a qualified ENT specialist an audiologist, and also by a speech therapist for complete evaluation. In case the child is below 4-5 years, a psychologist should also be consulted to identify and address any associated psychological problems which may not be overtly evident.

(iii) Speech

(a) Inappropriate sounds in speech.

(b) Stammering.

(c) Baby speech.

(d) Inability to learn correct sound, and use incorrect speech.

(e) Incomprehensible speech.

(iv) Physical Disabilities

(a) Deformity in the neck, hand, finger, waist or legs.

(b) Difficulty in sitting, standing or walking.

(c) Difficulty in lifting, holding or keeping things on floor.

(d) Difficulty in moving or using any part of body.

(e) Difficulty in holding a pen.

(f) Using a stick to walk.

(g) Jerks during walking.

(h) Lack bodily coordination.

(i) Epileptic movements of tremors.

(j) Joint pains.

(k) Any part of the body is amputated.

Note: If any of the above conditions is/are present, the child should be carefully examined by a qualified orthopaedic surgeon and referred to a physiotherapist &/or prosthetic/orthotic technician as needed.

(v) Mental Retardation

(a) If the child does not sit unassisted even after 12-15 months.

(b) Or does not walk even after 2½ years.

(c) Or does not talk even after 2 ½ years.

(d) If a child has undue problems in doing independently any of the following activities by the age of 6 years—

Eating —

Dressing —

Toilet activity

(e) Problems in holding a pencil/or using a pair of scissors.

(f) Unable to play with a ball or play 'guilli-danda' with the peers.

(g) Frequent tantrums, while playing with the peers.

(h) Usual inattentiveness to the spoken speech or addressal.

(i) Requires too many repetitions to remember simple things.

(j) Problems in naming even five fruits, vegetables or plants.

(k) Problems in naming the days of the week.

(l) Exhibit problems in expressing the needs in a clear language unlike the other peers.

(m) Unable to concentrate on tasks even for a short period of time.

(n) Inappropriate oral responses.

(o) Difficulty in learning new things.

(p) Poor comprehension of lessons taught in the school class.

(q) Difficulty in learning new things.

(r) Difficulty in conceptualization.

(s) Does not get well along with the children of same age group.

(t) More efforts are required in learning or practicing as compare to the peers.

(u) Takes an unreasonable amount of time in perfecting any work.

(v) Poor academic achievements.

(w) Show an undue dependency on visual clues or material for learning.

Note : If the responses to any of the above four indicators is positive when compared to the average school going peers of the same age group and class, then the child should be properly assessed by a qualified psychologist or a teacher who is specially trained to taken care of the mentally challenged children.

(vi) Learning Disabilities

(a) Difficulty in counting.

(b) Lack of concentration, or easily distracted by the surroundings, either at home or school.

(c) Difficulty in sitting quietly in the classroom.

(d) Does not write down the spoken words correctly.

(e) Inappropriate additions to the right word, *e.g.*, 'ischool' in place of school.

(f) Always confused between right and left.

(g) Unreasonable difficulty in remembering the verbal instructions.

(h) General difficulty in memorizing the things.

(i) Extreme restlessness in a child which significantly interferes with the timely completion of various tasks.

(j) Reverses letters or symbols too frequently while reading for example, b as d, saw as was, etc.

(k) Reverses numbers too frequently while reading, for example, 31 as 13, 6 as 9, etc.

(l) Excessive errors during reading like looses place/ repeat/insert/ substitute/omit words.

(m) Poor in mathematical calculations.

(n) Problems in accurate copying from the common sources like a book or a blackboard, even though the vision is normal.

(o) Write letters or words either too close or too far (spacing problems).

(p) The child appears to comprehend satisfactorily but is not able to answer the relevant questions.

Notes : I. If any of the above three to five conditions are present, the child should be examined by a qualified psychologist, pediatrician or a special educator for initial screening and further consultations. II.One of the main characteristics of children with learning disabilities is that their verbal skills are often much better than the writing skills. Therefore, they should be formally tested in order to elucidate their disability in detail. Incidence of disability declining says NSSO survey.

While there is reason to cheer, with the overall decline in disability in the country, there's also growing concern about rural areas that, compared to urban areas, show an increased rate.

The incidence of disability in India is declining says a recently released report by the National Sample Survey Organisation (NSSO). The prevalence of disability in the country came down from July-December 1991 when the last survey on disabled persons was conducted.

Around 18.53 million people are estimated to suffer some form of disability in the country. More than 10% of the disabled population suffer more than one form of disability. More people are affected in rural areas than in urban parts of the country, says the report.

Disability among people in rural areas is estimated at 1.85%—that's slightly more than their urban counterparts (1.5%). This is cause for concern. Results show that 2.12% of males in rural areas are affected by some form of disability compared to 1.67% males in urban India. Similarly, disability among females in rural areas is 1.56%, compared to 1.31% in urban areas.

Poor nutrition, limited access to vaccination programmes and health and maternity care, poor hygiene, bad sanitation, inadequate information about the causes of impairment and natural disasters are some of the causes for disability in rural areas. Most are easily preventable with proper care.

According to the World Health Organisation (WHO), as many as 50% of disabilities are preventable and directly linked to poverty. It is estimated that only 2% of people with disabilities in developing countries have access to rehabilitation and the appropriate basic services.

The NSSO, for the purpose of the survey, categorised disabilities into locomotor (lame/crippled), visual, hearing and mental disability. The results show that locomotor disability is the most prevalent, followed by hearing and visual disabilities. Mental illness, including retardation, was also seen among a significant number of people.

While locomotor disabilities affected about 1,008 people per lakh in the country, the rate for hearing disabilities was 300 per lakh people. Visual disability was seen to affect about 269 persons per lakh. Ninety-four people per lakh were found to be mentally retarded, and 105 people in a lakh suffered some form of mental illness. Illness during childhood was reported to be the reason for 42% of cases of mental retardation; about 87% were mentally disabled at birth.

According to the survey, the prevalence of disability is markedly higher among males across the country. For every 1 lakh people in the country, 1,755 were affected by some form of disability. Two thousand males, among 1 lakh people, were affected compared to 1,493 women. Among the individual disabilities too, visual disability was the only exception where the prevalence rate was higher among women.

At the state level, the prevalence of disability was highest in Himachal Pradesh (2,571 disabled people per lakh), followed by Lakshadweep (2,487), Orissa (2,459) and Kerala (2,235 disabled people per lakh). The survey also found that 55% of the disabled were illiterate; only 9% had completed higher secondary education. About 11% of disabled people in the age-group 5-18 years were enrolled in special schools in urban areas; in rural areas it was less than 1%.

Incidence and Prevalence

In the industrialised world, the incidence of cerebral palsy is about 2 per 1000 live births. The incidence is higher in males than in females; the Surveillance of Cerebral Palsy in Europe (SCPE) reports a M:F ratio of 1.33:1. Variances in reported rates of incidence across different geographical areas in industrialised countries are thought to be caused primarily by discrepancies in the criteria used for inclusion and exclusion. When such discrepancies are taken into account in comparing two or more registers of patients with cerebral palsy (for example, the extent to which children with mild cerebral palsy are included), the incidence rates converge toward the average rate of 2:1000.

In the United States, approximately 10,000 infants and babies are diagnosed with CP each year, and 1200–1500 are diagnosed at preschool age.

Overall, advances in care of pregnant mothers and their babies has not resulted in a noticeable decrease in CP. This is generally attributed to medical advances in areas related to the care of premature babies (which results in a greater survival rate). Only the introduction of quality medical care to locations with less-than-adequate medical care has shown any decreases. The incidence of CP increases with premature or very low-weight babies regardless of the quality of care.

Prevalence of cerebral palsy is best calculated around the school entry age of about six years, the prevalence in the U.S. is estimated to be 2.4 out of 1000 children

The SCPE reported the following incidence of comorbidities in children with CP (the data are from 1980–1990 and included over 4,500 children over age 4 whose CP was acquired during the prenatal or neonatal period):

- Mental disadvantage (IQ < 50): 31%
- Active seizures: 21%
- Mental disadvantage (IQ < 50) and not walking: 20%
- Blindness: 11%

The SCPE noted that the incidence of comorbidities is difficult to measure accurately, particularly across centers. For example, the actual rate of mental retardation may be difficult to determine, as the physical and communicational limitations of people with CP would likely lower their scores on an IQ test if they were not given a correctly modified version.

Apgar scores have sometimes been used as one factor to predict whether or not an individual will develop CP.

Symptoms

All types of CP are characterized by abnormal muscle tone(*i.e.* slouching over while sitting), reflexes, or motor development and coordination. There can be joint and bone deformities and contractures (permanently fixed, tight muscles and joints). The classical symptoms are spasticities, spasms, other involuntary movements (*e.g.* facial gestures), unsteady gait, problems with balance, and/or soft tissue findings consisting largely of decreased muscle mass. Scissor walking (where the knees come in and cross) and toe walking (which can contribute to a gait reminiscent of a marionette) are common among people with CP who are able to walk, but taken on the whole, CP symptomatology is very diverse. The effects of cerebral palsy fall on a continuum of motor dysfunction which may range from virtually unnoticeable to "clumsy" and awkward movements on one end of the spectrum to such severe impairments that coordinated movements are almost impossible on the other end of the spectrum.

Babies born with severe CP often have an irregular posture; their bodies may be either very floppy or very stiff. Birth defects, such as spinal curvature, a small jawbone, or a small head sometimes occur along with CP. Symptoms may appear, change, or become more severe as a child gets older. Some babies born with CP do not show obvious signs right away. Classically, CP becomes evident when the baby reaches the developmental stage at 6/12- 9/12 and is starting to mobilise, where preferential use of limbs, asymmetry or gross motor developmental delay is seen.

Secondary conditions can include seizures, epilepsy, speech (apraxia or dysarthria) or communication disorders, eating problems, sensory impairments, mental retardation, learning disabilities, and/or behavioral disorders.

Speech and language disorders are common in people with Cerebral Palsy. The incidence of dysarthria is estimated to range from 31% to 88%. Speech problems are associated with poor respiratory control, laryngeal and velopharyngeal dysfunction as well as oral articulation disorders that are due to restricted movement in the oral-facial muscles. There are three major types of dysarthria in cerebral palsy: spastic, dyskinetic (athetosis) and ataxic. Speech impairments in spastic dysarthria involves four major abnormalities of voluntary movement: spasticity, weakness, limited range of motion and slowness of movement. Speech mechanism impairment in athetosis involves a disorder in the regulation of breathing patterns, laryngeal dysfunction (monopitch, low, weak and breathy voice quality). It is also associated with articulatory dysfunction (large range of jaw movements, inappropriate positioning of the tongue, instability of velar elevation. Athetoid dysarthria is caused by disruption of the internal sensorimotor feedback system for appropriate motor comands, which leads to the generation of faulty movements that are perceived by others as involuntary. Ataxic dysarthria is uncommon in cerebral palsy.

The speech characteristics are: imprecise consonants, irregular articulatory breakdown, distorted vowels, excess and equal stress, prolonged phonemes, slow rate, monopitch, monoloudness and harsh voice. Overall language delay is associated with problems of mental retardation, hearing impairment and learned helplessness. Children with cerebral palsy are at risk of learned helplessness and becoming passive communicators, initiating little communication. Early intervention with this clientele often targets situations in which childrens communicate with others, so that they learn that they can control people and objects in their environment through this communication, including making choices, decisions and mistakes.

History

CP, then known as "Cerebral Paralysis", was first identified by English surgeon William Little in 1860. Little raised the possibility of asphyxia during birth as a chief cause of the disorder. It was not until 1897 that Sigmund Freud, then a neurologist, suggested that a difficult birth was not the cause but rather only a symptom of other effects on fetal development. Research conducted during the 1980s by the National Institute of Neurological Disorders and Stroke (NINDS) suggested that only a small number of cases of CP are caused by lack of oxygen during birth.

Prevalence

Among the many social problems, that of the disabled stands out prominently. Disabled persons are perceived only in the light of their infirmities. Around 10% of the world population is disabled. Some studies show more prevalence, others using stricter definitions show less prevalence. Usually only 4-7% of a developing country's population is listed as disabled in national surveys. Many studies based on census results give a rate of as little as 1%. Worldwide attempts to classify disability also pose problems. Causes overlap. So, studies of single factor may lead to double or triple counting. Very few studies have been conducted in India with regards to the magnitude of the prevalence of disability. Studies of such nature will be useful in developing appropriate intervention programmes. It was in this context that the present study was undertaken in a rural area.

Material and Methods

This study was carried out in the rural field practice area of Kasturba Medical College, Manipal. Two villages (Kadekar and Udyavava) were covered. People between 5-60 years of age were studied. Children above 5 years of age go to schools. Sometimes disability affects their studies. It is also difficult to assess all disabilities in children below five years of age in field conditions.

A door to door survey of disabled was undertaken. 1m315 houses in the two villages were visited within a period of four months. 38 houses were found to be locked. So, a total of 1,277 houses could be covered. People between age of 5-60 years were clinically examined to assess the nature and extent of abnormality as per the criteria laid down by WHO1. Detailed medical history was taken. Information regarding demographic, housing, education, occupation and socio-economic particulars was collected from all the households visited. A person was considered to be having partial visual impairment if the visual acuity was more than 6/60 after the best possible correction. Profound visual impairment was taken as visual acuity less than 6/60 in the better eye. Modified version of Udai Parikh socio-economic status scale2 was used.

Results

The prevalence of disability was highest in the 45-59 years age group which was significantly higher than the prevalence in other age groups ($p<0.001$). Among 67 cases of locomotor disabilty, 21 had paralysis and 26 had disabling arthirits. 70% of the arthritis patients were females. Total population covered was 8162. Number of people between 5 to 60 years of age was 6,708 [Males : 3,266 (48.70%), Females : 3,442 (51.30%)]. Total number of disabled people was 136, of whom 62 were males and 74 were females. The difference in prevalence of disability seen in males (1.89%) and in females (2.14%) (Total I) was not statistically significant. (Chi square = 0.53, $p>0.05$). The overall prevalence of disability was 2.02%.

Locomotor disabilities were the commonest, followed by visual disability.

Prevalence of Disability According to Age, Sex and Socio-economic Status.

	Population Surveyed	Disabled	Prevelance (%)
Sex			
Male	3,266	62	1.89
Female	3,442	74	2.14
Age Group in Years			
5 - 14	1,543	25	1.62
15 - 44	4159	37	0.88
45 - 59	1006	74	7.35
Socio-Economic Status			
Low	4883	84	1.72
Middle	1616	50	3.09
High	209	2	0.95
Total	6,708	136	2.02

Males and females showed almost similar pattern of disability distribution.

The prevalence of disability was lowest among high socio-economic group except in case of special disability, which was higher in high socio economic group. The lower prevalence in this group was found to be statistically significant (c2 = 12.78, $p<0.001$). More females had visual disabilities compared to males. Females constituted 60% of visually disabled. Visual disability showed association with socio-economic status. None of the 46 visually disabled were from high socio-economic status group. Chronic suppurative otitis media was the leading cause of hearing disability accounting for seven out of thirteen cases. Four of the hearing disabled were also dumb.

Discussion

Well documented studies to determine the prevalence and pattern of handicaps are few and far between. Most studies have been conducted in urban areas.

The widely differing prevalence rates of disability found in these studies are due to wide difference in the samples and definitions used. Some studies included only totally blind and completely deaf people as handicapped. In some studies, the data was collected by workers who because of their limited knowledge and training on the topic could not detect mild degrees of disability.

The overall prevalence of disability in this study was 2.02%. Anand Pandit et al had reported a prevalence rate of 10.01%. But their survey team included specialists like audiologists etc. and audiometry screening and IQ tests were also done. The prevalence of disability was highest in the 45 to 59 years of age group (Table I). This was mainly because cataract and arthritis- the two common causes of disability in this study, were more common in this age group.

The prevalence of disability was lowest among high socio-economic group. Disabilities like cataract which are liable to be corrected might have been promptly attended to in this group. Kumar et al also found that locomotor disability was the commonest disability. Prevalence of visual disability among females was higher compared to males. Similar findings were recorded in other studies. This has been attributed to higher prevalence of trachoma, conjunctivitis and cataract among females than males.

If meaningful rehabilitation is to follow a survey of this sort, it is of utmost importance to detect disabilities early. Many of the disabilities in rural people are correctable, viz. cataract. Medical intervention supported by educational and social integration of disabled people should be started early.

Causes and Prevention

Despite years of debate, the cause of the majority of cases of CP is uncertain.

While in certain cases, there is no identifiable cause, other etiologies include problems in intrauterine development (*e.g.* exposure to radiation, infection), asphyxia, hypoxia of the brain, and birth trauma during labour and delivery, and complications in the perinatal period or during childhood. CP is also more common in multiple births.

Studies at the University of Liverpool have led to the hypothesis that many cases of cerebral palsy, and other conditions that an infant has at birth, are caused by the death in very early pregnancy of an identical twin. This may occur when twins have a joint circulation through sharing the same placenta. Not all identical twins share the same blood supply (monochorionic twins), but if they do, the suggestion is that perturbations in blood flow between them can cause the death of one and damage to the development of the surviving fetus. It is common knowledge amongst obstetricians and midwives that a small dead fetus (fetus papyraceus) may sometimes be found attached to a placenta following birth. In the past, this has not been considered important and knowledge of the so called 'vanishing twin' has been suppressed to avoid triggering feelings of loss, grief, or guilt in mothers. The pathological consequences depend on the severity and the stage of development of the fetus when the imbalances in blood flow between the fetuses occur. It has been proposed that such pathology could account, not just for cerebral palsy, but for developmental abnormalities of the eye, heart, and gut, and other specific brain abnormalities such as neuronal migration disorders *e.g.* lissencephaly and holoprosencephaly, which occur during very early fetal development.

Between 40% and 50% of all children who develop cerebral palsy were born prematurely. Premature infants are vulnerable, in part because their organs are not fully developed, increasing the risk of hypoxic injury to the brain that may manifest as CP. A problem in interpreting this is the difficulty in differentiating between CP caused by damage to the brain that results from inadequate oxygenation and CP that arises from prenatal brain damage that then precipitates premature delivery.

Recent research has demonstrated that intrapartum asphyxia is not the most important cause, probably accounting for no more than 10 percent of all cases; rather, infections in the mother, even infections that are not easily detected, may triple the risk of the child developing the disorder, mainly as the result of the toxicity to the fetal brain of cytokines that are produced as part of the inflammatory response. Low birthweight is a risk factor for CP—and premature infants usually have low birth weights, less than 2.0 kg, but full-term infants can also have low birth weights. Multiple-birth infants are also more likely than single-birth infants to be born early or with a low birth weight.

After birth, other causes include toxins, severe jaundice, lead poisoning, physical brain injury, shaken baby syndrome, incidents involving hypoxia to the brain (such as near drowning), and encephalitis or meningitis. The three most common causes of asphyxia in the young child are: choking on foreign objects such as toys and pieces of food, poisoning, and near drowning.

Some structural brain anomalies such as lissencephaly may present with the clinical features of CP, although whether that could be considered CP is a matter of opinion (some people say CP must be due to brain damage, whereas people with these anomalies didn't have a normal brain). Often this goes along with rare chromosome disorders and CP is not genetic or hereditary.

Diagnosis

The diagnosis of cerebral palsy has historically rested on the patient's history and physical examination. Once diagnosed with cerebral palsy, further diagnostic tests are optional. The American Academy of Neurology published an article in 2004 reviewing the literature and evidence available on CT and MRI imaging. They suggested that neuroimaging with CT or MRI is warranted when the etiology of a patient's cerebral palsy has not been established- an MRI is preferred over CT due to diagnostic yield and safety. When abnormal, the neuroimaging study can suggest the timing of the initial damage. The CT or MRI is also capable of revealing treatable conditions, such as hydrocephalus, porencephaly, arteriovenous malformation, subdural hematomas and hygromas, and a vermian tumor (which a few studies suggest are present 5 to 22%). Furthermore, an abnormal neuroimaging study indicates a high likelihood of associated conditions, such as epilepsy and mental retardation.

Presentation

In order for bones to attain their normal shape and size, they require the stresses from normal musculature. Osseous findings will therefore mirror the specific muscular deficits in a given person with CP. The shafts of the bones are often thin (gracile). When compared to these thin shafts (diaphyses) the metaphyses often appear quite enlarged (ballooning). With lack of use, articular cartilage may atrophy, leading to narrowed joint spaces.

Depending on the degree of spasticity, a person with CP may exhibit a variety of angular joint deformities. Because vertebral bodies need vertical gravitational loading forces to develop properly, spasticity and an abnormal gait can hinder proper and/or full bone and skeletal development. People with CP tend to be shorter in height than the average person because their bones are not allowed to grow to their full potential. Sometimes bones grow to different lengths, so the person may have one leg longer than the other.

Prognosis

CP is not a progressive disorder (meaning the actual brain damage does not worsen), but the symptoms can become worse over time due to subdural damage. A person with the disorder may improve somewhat during childhood if he or she receives extensive care from specialists, but once bones and musculature become more established, orthopedic surgery may be required for fundamental improvement. People who have CP tend to develop arthritis at a younger age than normal because of the pressure placed on joints by excessively toned and stiff muscles.

The full intellectual potential of a child born with CP will often not be known until the child starts school. People with CP are more likely to have some type of learning disability, but this is not related to a person's intellect or IQ level. Intellectual level among people with CP varies from genius to mentally retarded, as it does in the general population, and experts have stated that it is important to not underestimate CP sufferer's capabilities and to give them every opportunity to learn.

The ability to live independently with CP also varies widely depending on the severity of the disability. Some individuals with CP will require personal assistant services for all activities of daily living. Others can live semi-independently, needing support only for certain activities. Still others can live in complete independence. The need for personal assistance often changes with increasing age and associated functional decline. However, in most cases persons with CP can expect to have a normal life expectancy; survival has been shown to be associated with the ability to ambulate, roll, and self-feed. As the condition does not directly affect reproductive function, some persons with CP have children and parent successfully.

According to OMIM, only 2% of cases of CP are inherited (with glutamate decarboxylase-1 as one known enzyme involved.) There is no evidence of an increased chance of a person with CP having a child with CP.

Treatment

There is no cure for CP, but various forms of therapy can help a person with the disorder to function and live more effectively. In general, the earlier treatment begins the better chance children have of overcoming developmental disabilities or learning new ways to accomplish the tasks that challenge them. The earliest proven intervention occurs during the infant's recovery in the neonatal intensive care unit (NICU). Treatment may include one or more of the following: physical therapy; occupational therapy; speech therapy; drugs to control seizures, alleviate pain, or relax muscle spasms (*e.g.* benzodiazepienes, baclofen and intrathecal phenol/baclofen); hyperbaric oxygen; the use of Botox to relax contracting muscles; surgery to correct anatomical abnormalities or release tight muscles; braces and other orthotic devices; rolling walkers; and communication aids such as computers with attached voice synthesizers. For instance, the use of a standing frame can help reduce spasticity and improve range of motion for people with CP who use wheelchairs. Nevertheless, there is only some benefit from therapy. Treatment is usually symptomatic and focuses on helping the person to develop as many motor skills as possible or to learn how to compensate for the lack of them. Non-speaking people with CP are often successful availing themselves of augmentative and alternative communication systems such as Blissymbols.

Early Nutritional Support In one cohort study of 490 premature infants discharged from the NICU, the rate of growth during hospital stay was related to neurological function at 18 and 22 months of age. The study found a significant decrease in the incidence of cerebral palsy in the group of premature infants with the highest growth velocity. This study suggests that adequate nutrition and growth play a protective role in the development of cerebral palsy.

Physical therapy (PT) programmes are designed to encourage the patient to build a strength base for improved gait and volitional movement, together with stretching programmes to limit contractures. Many experts believe that life-long physical therapy is crucial to maintain muscle tone, bone structure, and prevent dislocation of the joints.

Occupational therapy helps adults and children maximise their function, adapt to their limitations and live as independently as possible.

Orthotic devices such as ankle-foot orthoses (AFOs) are often prescribed to minimise gait irregularities. AFOs have been found to improve several measures of ambulation, including reducing energy expenditure and increasing speed and stride length.

Speech therapy helps control the muscles of the mouth and jaw, and helps improve communication. Just as CP can affect the way a person moves their arms and legs, it can also affect the way they move their mouth, face and head. This can make it hard for the person to breathe; talk clearly; and bite, chew and swallow food. Speech therapy often starts before a child begins school and continues throughout the school years.

Hyperbaric oxygen therapy (HBOT), in which pressurized oxygen is inhaled inside a hyperbaric chamber, has been used to treat CP under the theory that improving oxygen availability to damaged brain cells can reactivate some of them to function normally. Its use to treat CP is controversial. A 2007 systematic review concluded that the effect of HBOT on CP is not significantly different from that of pressurized room air, and that some children undergoing HBOT will experience adverse events such as seizures and the need for ear pressure equalization tubes; due to poor quality of data assessment the review also concluded that estimates of the prevalence of adverse events are uncertain.

Nutritional counseling may help when dietary needs are not met because of problems with eating certain foods.

Both massage therapy and hatha yoga are designed to help relax tense muscles, strengthen muscles, and keep joints flexible. Hatha yoga breathing exercises are sometimes used to try to prevent lung infections. More research is needed to determine the health benefits of these therapies for people with CP.

Surgery for people with CP usually involves one or a combination of:

- Loosening tight muscles and releasing fixed joints, most often performed on the hips, knees, hamstrings, and ankles. In rare cases, this surgery may be used for people with stiffness of their elbows, wrists, hands, and fingers.
- The insertion of a Baclofen Pump usually during the stages while a patient is a young adult. This is usually placed in the left abdomen. It is a pump that is connected to the spinal cord, whereby it sends bits of Baclofen alleviating the continuous muscle flexion. Baclofen is a muscle relaxant and is often given PO to patients to help counter the effects of spasticity.

- Straightening abnormal twists of the leg bones, *i.e.* femur (termed femoral anteversion or antetorsion) and tibia (tibial torsion). This is a secondary complication caused by the spastic muscles generating abnormal forces on the bones, and often results in intoeing (pigeon-toed gait). The surgery is called derotation osteotomy, in which the bone is broken (cut) and then set in the correct alignment.
- Cutting nerves on the limbs most affected by movements and spasms. This procedure, called a rhizotomy, "rhizo" meaning root and "tomy" meaning "a cutting of" from the Greek suffix 'tomia' reduces spasms and allows more flexibility and control of the affected limbs and joints.
- Botulinum Toxin A (Botox) injections into muscles that are either spastic or have contractures, the aim being to relieve the disability and pain produced by the inappropriately contracting muscle.

A new study has found that cooling the bodies and blood of high-risk full-term babies shortly after birth may significantly reduce disability or death.

Cord Blood Therapy: There are no published randomized controlled trials or meta-analysis of this treatment modality in cerebral palsy. In March 2008 a boy diagnosed with cerebral palsy appeared on the Today Show with his family. The parents noted that he could not walk on his own and appeared to be "swallowing his tongue" at times. He was eventually diagnosed with cerebral palsy and could only walk with the aid of a walker for a short time. Earlier that year he participated in a clinical trial involving his own cord blood that his parents had saved when he was born. His parents reported that within 5 days after the procedure he was walking on his own and talking, something his mother said he was not capable of on his own and it was doubtful he would ever be able to do on his own. They also reported that the doctors also told them that if his rate of progress continues uninterrupted until he is 7 he will be pronounced cured.

Conductive education (CE) was developed in Hungary from 1945 based on the work of András Petõ. It is a unified system of rehabilitation for people with neurological disorders including cerebral palsy, Parkinson's disease and multiple sclerosis, amongst other conditions. It is theorised to improve mobility, self-esteem, stamina and independence as well as daily living skills and social skills.

The conductor is the professional who delivers CE in partnership with parents and children. Skills learned during CE should be applied to everyday life and can help to develop age-appropriate cognitive, social and emotional skills. It is available at specialized centers.

Biofeedback is an alternative therapy in which people with CP learn how to control their affected muscles. Some people learn ways to reduce muscle tension with this technique. Biofeedback does not help everyone with CP.

Neuro-cognitive Therapy: A new approach to treating cerebral palsy from [Snowdrop]. It is based upon two proven principles. (1) Neural Plasticity. The brain is capable of altering its own structure and functioning to meet the demands of any particular environment. Consequently if the child is provided with an appropriate neurological environment, he will have the best chance of making progress. (2) Learning can lead to development. As early as the early 1900s, this was being proven by a psychologist named Lev Vygotsky. He proposed that children's learning is a social activity, which is achieved by interaction with more skilled members of society. There are many studies, which provide evidence for this claim. there are however, as yet no controlled studies on neuro-cognitive therapy.

Patterning is a controversial form of alternative therapy for people with CP. The method is promoted by The Institutes for the Achievement of Human Potential (IAHP), a Philadelphia nonprofit, but has been criticized by the American Academy of Pediatrics. The IAHP's methods have been endorsed by Linus Pauling, as well as some parents of children treated with their methods.

Prevention

Research Studies have shown that a large proportion of disabilities can be prevented. Further research indicates that the socio economic cost of prevention of disabilities are lower than the cost of rehabilitation. Three broad areas of preventive measures include:

Hygiene, Environmental Protection and Sanitation

Environmental sanitation and hygienic living conditions can immensely reduce the incidence of disabilities. For example, worm infection can cause anemia resulting in high mortality, morbity and disability among neonatals. Deficating in the open can lead to the growth of wild polio virus. Polluted water can cause growth of polio virus leading to poliomyelitis resulting in flacid paralysis. Similarly, uncleared water causes rota virus infection which results in diarrhea. Diarrhea is known to cause growth retardation. Flacid paralysis can also be caused by in-sanitary conditions which propogate the growth of poliomyelitis. In-sanitary conditions are known to cause trachoma in eyes which can lead to blindness. Even leprosy can be caused by in-sanitary conditions. Unhealthy and unhygienic food has been found to be cause of poliomyelitis.

Appropriate/balanced Nutrition

Balanced in take of nutrients especially, micro nutrients can help prevent disabilities. Malnutrition and deficiency of some micro-nutrients can cause anemia especially among pregnant women resulting in greater proneness of new borns to disease and disability. Vitamin `A' deficiency is a major cause of blindness among children. Studies indicate that Iodine deficiency is a major cause of blindness among children. Studies indicate that Iodine deficiency impairs brain development significantly. Various micro-nutrients deficiencies account for a large percentage of low birth weight in babies in India. The inadequate gestational weight gain is associated with poor mental and mortal development of surviving infants. Malnutrition during infancy and early childhood is believed to have adverse effects on both physical growth and intellectual performance in later life. Vitamin `A' deficiency is a major cause of blindness among children.

Immunization

Prevention is promoted through various National Health Programmes like programmes on blindness prevention, leprosy as well as various immunisation programmes like Pulse Polio, etc. Simple changes in life style, especially, towards a more cleaner environment and hygienic conditions, eating a balanced diet with adequate micro nutrients, timely following the prescribed immunisation cycles, especially for children and for pregnant women, can greatly reduce the incidence of disability.

Types, Classification and Characteristics

Types of Disability

The most commonly reported type of disability was locomotor disability. Overall, 12% of men and 14% of women reported having locomotor disability, of whom one in four men and one in three women reported a serious disability. Among those aged 75 and over, the prevalence of serious locomotor disability was higher for women than men. 32% of women aged 85 and over had serious locomotor disability as compared to 22% of men in the same group. The second largest prevalence was in personal care disability, with rates almost half those of locomotor disability for both sexes (men 6%, women 7%), followed by hearing disability (6%, 4%) and sight disability (2%, 3%). Few people reported having communication disability and it was also the least variable across the age groups.

Although differences by gender in overall prevalences of types of disabilities were relatively small, the large sample sizes mean that gender differences were significant at the 95% confidence level.

The relationship of the five types of disability to age and sex was very similar to that observed in HSE 95.As in 1995, the higher prevalence of hearing disability among men, particularly at age 55-74, resulted in slightly higher overall disability levels for men relative to women of the same age. But from age 75 onwards, the sustained and significantly higher prevalence of locomotor disability among women than men resulted in higher overall disability rates for women in the older age groups, as noted earlier.

Locomotor Disability

Informants were asked questions on the type of locomotor disability they experienced, including the ability to walk 200 metres, climb 12 stairs without resting and retrieve things from the floor. Both for walking 200 metres and for climbing up stairs, the prevalence of disability was higher in women aged 75 and over than in men of this age. For those aged 85 and over, two-thirds of women and just under half of men (46%) reported difficulty in walking 200 metres, and half of women, and a third of men, reported a problem with climbing stairs. There was no difference in the proportion of men and women reporting difficulty picking up things. For both sexes, the proportion with retrieval problems almost doubled between age 75-84 (about 16%) and 85 and over (about 30%).

Personal Care Disability

Inability to perform self-care tasks or ADLs without help is widely used in social surveys as a measure of physical dependency. However, differences between surveys in the tasks included, in question wording and, most importantly, in the treatment of aids and adaptations in the assessment of dependency, may result in widely different estimates of dependency among the population. In addition, because dependency is environment-related, change over time is intrinsically related to both changes in the underlying level of personal care disability and changes in the availability of supportive aids that allow more people to maintain their independence for longer.

6% of men and 7% of women had a personal care disability, with 1% unable to perform any of the six ADL tasks without help. The pattern of distribution is similar to that found in 1995: almost all personal care disability can be attributed to problems with bed and chair transfer and dressing for both sexes. The proportions needing help with washing, feeding and getting to or using the toilet were small (1%).

Hearing Disability

6% of men and 4% of women had a hearing disability. Below age 75, hearing disability was higher among men than women, particularly at age 55-74. Men and women aged 75 and over had similar levels of hearing disability.

Sight and Communication Disabilities

The prevalence of sight and communication disabilities was too low to allow meaningful comparison between groups. 2% of men and 3% of women reported a sight disability, with severity equally divided between those with a moderate and severe disability.

The proportion of people reporting a communication disability (1%) was the lowest of all types of disabilities recorded. These estimates could be affected by non-response bias in the survey, if those with communication difficulties were less likely to take part in surveys. Rates of communication disability were substantially higher amongst people aged 65 and over living in care homes (34%) than people of the same age in private households (2%). This suggests that people with a communication disability were also less likely to live in private households. Persons with Disabilities in India are defined according to The Persons with Disabilities (Equal Opportunities, Protection of Rights and Full Participation) Act of 1995 and are identified in seven categories of disability:

1. Blindness

Refers to a condition where a person suffers from any of the following conditions, namely:

- Total absence of sight
- Visual acuity not exceeding 6/60 or 20/200 (Snellen) in the better eye with correcting lenses
- Limitation of the field of vision subtending an angle of 20 degree or worse

2. *Low Vision*

- The total absence of visual function even after treatment or standard refractive correction. A person who has low vision or no vision uses appropriate assistive devices or is potentially capable of using vision.

3. *Leprosy-cured*

Means any person who has been cured of leprosy but is suffering from

- Loss of sensation in hands or feet as well as loss of sensation and paresis in the eye and eye-lid but with no manifest deformity
- Manifest deformity and paresis but having sufficient mobility in their hands and feet to enable them to engage in normal economic activity
- Extreme physical deformity as well as advanced age which prevents him from undertaking any gainful occupation, and the expression "leprosy cured" shall be construed accordingly

4. *Hearing Impairment*

- Loss of sixty decibels or more in the better ear in the conversational range of frequencies

5. *Locomotor Disability*

- Means disability of the bones, joints or muscles leading to substantial restriction of the movement of the limbs or any form of cerebral palsy

6. *Intellectually Disabled*

- Means a conduction of arrested or incomplete development of mind of a person which is specially characterized by sub-normality of the intelligence

7. *Mental Illness*

- Means any mental disorder other than intellectually disabled.

Intervention and Educational Programmes

Early Detection/Prevention

The Government recognizes that approximately 50% of disabilities are preventable and the costs of prevention are far lower than those of rehabilitation. The Government has therefore adopted the following campaigns:

- Pulse Polio Campaign
- Leprosy Eradication Programme
- National Programme for the Control of Blindness:
- Deficiencies of Vitamin A and Iodine
- Nutrition Mission by the Department of Woman and Child Development (malnutrition among pregnant women, mothers and infants)

In order to create an effective system of early identification of disability as well as early intervention, the National Programme for Rehabilitation of Persons with Disabilities is being implemented by State Governments. Through this programme, field level workers have undergone training on disability related issues and provide a referral chain from village to district and State centers.

To ensure that doctors in hospitals in rural areas can recognize disability and refer patients for appropriate medical intervention and rehabilitation services, doctors at Primary Health Centers are trained through a National Orientation Programme on Disability. To-date, 9,529 doctors have received training in the field of disability prevention and management. Recognizing that at-risk babies, like low birth weight and pre-term newborns, require specialized attention to prevent/ minimize impairments, neo-natal care facilities have been made available in over 130 districts to prevent/minimize the negative impact of birth insults and injuries before, during and after delivery.

Education

The Government has launched, Education for All (The Sarv Shiksha Abhiyan), with a particular focus on the education of

PWDs. Compulsory education has been enforced in four States and Union Territories at the primary stage of education while in eight States/UTs there is compulsory education covering the entire elementary stage of education. State Governments have issued directions to schools that no student may be denied admission on the basis of disability alone.

The CCC estimates that there are 2,500 special schools in India that include children with special needs in integrated and inclusive settings, or in non-formal education. These schools educate a total of 100,000 children with special needs. There are 15,000 schools which have enrolled a total of 60,000 children under the IEDC of the Ministry of Human Resource Development.

The IEDC provides benefits to children through the provision of scholarships, uniforms, books and transport facilities to get to school. Table 10 highlights the number of disabled students attending schools according to the MSJE.

Student with Disabilities in Schools

Student with Disabilities in Schools		
Education Options	Disabled Students	Regular Teachers
Integrated Education for the Disbled	133,000	?
District Primary Education Program	460,608	987,850
National Open Schools	1,800	?
Special Schools	160,000	?
Total	755,408	987,850

Source: *MSJE, Country Report- India*

Under the District Primary Education Programme, a World Bank funded programme, which covers 271 districts in 24 States, special attention has been paid to children with disabilities. This programme has resulted in approximately 350,000 additional children enrolling in school. To ensure that students with disabilities have fair access to higher and technical education, 3% of seats in educational institutions are reserved for them. The MSJE supports 500 scholarships for students with disabilities pursuing their studies at post school levels.

Educational Facilities

While disabled children are integrated into the regular school system there are additionally special schools established for disabled children. Voluntary organizations have also taken a major initiative in opening special schools throughout the country. Table indicates the number of educational institutions for the disabled:

Educational Institutions for the Disabled

Educational Institutions for the Disabled	
Education Options	Disabled Students
Residential Schools for Vusually Impaired	5
Residential Schools for Hearing Impaired	6
Residential Jr. for Visually Impaired	1
Residential Jr. Colleage for Hearing Impaired	1
Training Center for Teachers of Visually Impaired	1
IED Schools (Education Department)	161
Special Schools (Education Department)	11
Schools run by NGOs	144
Total	330

Source: *MSJE, Country Report- India*

The Department of Education provides financial assistance to organizations who establish special schools. Some of the special schools offer vocational training in trades like tailoring, carpentry and book binding. There are four national institutes in the area of visual, hearing, mental and locomotor disabilities which organize regular programmes for the training of teachers for the disabled.

Under the Integrated Education Scheme for Disabled, operated by the Department of Education, disabled children are sought to be integrated in the normal school system. Assistance is provided to States and UTs for education of children suffering from certain mild disabilities in regular schools with the help of necessary aids, incentives and specially trained teachers.

The following types of disabled children are covered under this scheme:

- Children with locomotor handicaps (orthopedic handicapped)
- Mildly and moderately hearing impaired
- Partially sighted children
- Intellectually disabled, educable group (IQ 50- 70)
- Children with multiple handicaps including, hearing impaired and orthopaedic, educable intellectually disabled and orthopaedic, visual impaired and mild hearing disabled
- Children with learning disabilities

The scheme provides the following allowances for children with disabilities:

- Books and stationery allowances of Rs. 400 per annum
- Actual expenses on uniforms up to Rs. 200 per annum
- Transport allowances of Rs. 50 per month
- Reader allowances of Rs. 50 per month in case of blind children after Class V
- Escort allowance for severely handicapped children with lower extremity disabilities of Rs. 75 per month
- Actual cost of equipment subject to a maximum of Rs. 2,000 per student for a period of five years.

Intervention

The MSJE supports 644 Institutions for running early intervention programmes, special education programmes, vocational training programmes under which 160,000 people are covered.

Cerebral Palsy and Barrier Free Environment

Cerebral palsy (CP) is an umbrella term encompassing a group of non-progressive, non-contagious conditions that cause physical disability in human development.

Cerebral refers to the cerebrum, which is the affected area of the brain (although the disorder most likely involves connections between the cortex and other parts of the brain such as the cerebellum), and *palsy* refers to disorder of movement. CP is caused by damage to the motor control centers of the developing brain and can occur during pregnancy (about 75 percent), during childbirth (about 5 percent) or after birth (about 15 percent) up to about age three. Further research is needed on adults with CP as the current literature is highly focused on the pediatric patient.

Cerebral palsy describes a group of permanent disorders of the development of movement and posture, causing activity limitation, that are attributed to nonprogressive disturbances that occurred in the developing fetal or infant brain. The motor disorders of cerebral palsy are often accompanied by disturbances of sensation, perception, cognition, communication, and behaviour, by epilepsy, and by secondary musculoskeletal problems.

There is no known cure for CP. Medical intervention is limited to the treatment and prevention of complications arising from CP's effects. A 2003 study put the economic cost for CP sufferers in the US at $921,000 per case, including lost income.

In another study, the incidence in six countries surveyed was 2.12–2.45 per 1,000 live births, indicating a slight rise in recent years. Improvements in neonatal nursing have helped reduce the number of babies who develop cerebral palsy, but the survival of babies with very low birth weights has increased, and these babies are more likely to have cerebral palsy.

Classification

CP is divided into three major classifications to describe different movement impairments. These classifications also reflect the areas of the brain that are damaged. The three major classifications are:

Spastic

Spastic cerebral palsy is by far the most common type, occurring in 70% to 80% of all cases. Moreover, spastic CP accompanies one of the other types in 30% of all cases. People with this type are hypertonic and have a neuromuscular condition stemming from damage to the corticospinal tract or the motor cortex that affects the nervous system's ability to receive gamma amino butyric acid in the area(s) affected by the disability. Spastic CP is further classified by topography dependent on the region of the body affected; these include:

- Spastic hemiplegia (one side being affected). Generally, injury to muscle-nerves controlled by the brain's left side will cause a right body deficit, and vice versa. Typically, people that have spastic hemiplegia are the *most ambulatory*, although they generally have dynamic equinus on the affected side and are primarily prescribed ankle-foot orthoses to prevent said equinus.
- Spastic diplegia (the lower extremities are affected with little to no upper-body spasticity). The most common form of the spastic forms. Most people with spastic diplegia are fully ambulatory and have a scissors gait. Flexed knees and hips to varying degrees are common. Hip problems, dislocations, and in three-quarters of spastic diplegics, also strabismus (crossed eyes), can be present as well. In addition, these individuals are often nearsighted. The intelligence of a person with spastic diplegia is unaffected by the condition.
- Spastic quadriplegia (all four limbs affected equally). People with spastic quadriplegia are the least likely to be able to walk, or if they can, to want to walk, because they are too tight and it is too much effort to do so. Some children with quadriplegia also have hemiparetic tremors, an uncontrollable shaking that affects the limbs on one side of the body and impairs normal movement.

Occasionally, terms such as monoplegia, paraplegia, triplegia, and pentaplegia may also be used to refer to specific manifestations of the spasticity.

Ataxic

Ataxia (ICD-10 G80.4) type symptoms can be caused by damage to the cerebellum. Forms of ataxia are less common types of Cerebral Palsy, occurring in at most 10% of all cases.

Some of these individuals have hypotonia and tremors. Motor skills like writing, typing, or using scissors might be affected, as well as balance, especially while walking. It is common for individuals to have difficulty with visual and/or auditory processing of objects.

Athetoid/dyskinetic

Athetoid or dyskinetic is mixed muscle tone—sometimes hypertonia and sometimes hypotonia (Hypotonia will usually occur before 1 year old; the muscle tone will be increased with age and progress to Hypertonia). People with athetoid CP have trouble holding themselves in an upright, steady position for sitting or walking, and often show involuntary motions. For some people with athetoid CP, it takes a lot of work and concentration to get their hand to a certain spot (like scratching their nose or reaching for a cup). Because of their mixed tone and trouble keeping a position, they may not be able to hold onto objects (such as a toothbrush or pencil). About one quarter of all people with CP have athetoid CP. The damage occurs to the extrapyramidal motor system and/or pyramidal tract and to the basal ganglia. It occurs in 40% of all cases.

Barrier-Free Enviornment

The PWD Act makes provisions to create a barrier free environment for all persons with disability and to encourage them to be fully participating members of the society. Broadly, the term 'barrier free environment' would mean removing obstacles and providing access to all.

Chapter VIII of the Act deals with the provisions relating to this principle. Some of the provisions in this Chapter include providing auditory signals on roads, taking special measures in the transport sector to make the rails, aircrafts and vessels easily accessible to wheel chair users, to provide ramps in public buildings, medical care and rehabilitation centres, Braille symbols and auditory signals in elevators and lifts.

Although such rights have been elaborately laid down under the Act, all the provisions have not been implemented. One possible reason could be that these provisions are not considered mandatory in nature. Most of these provisions direct the government to implement them only if it is within the 'economic capacity' of the state.

In this area, few interesting cases have come up before the Courts. For example, students with disability are accorded certain privileges and concessions depending on the nature of their disability and when this is violated then the Courts have ordered their implementation. In one such case, it was held that for certain competitive examinations, a visually handicapped candidate can arrange for a scribe at their own cost. According to the rules, the academic qualification of the scribe should be one level below the minimum educational qualification required for the post applied for by the disabled person.

It is heartening to note that in all instances, the courts have made efforts to favor the person with disability in the actualization of the demand made, to the maximum extent possible.

UNIT-VI

Learning Disabilities, Austism and Other Associated Disorder

Definition and Identification of Learning Disabilities

Recent consensus reports concur in suggesting major changes in the federal regulatory approach to the identification of learning disabilities (LD). These reports recommend abandoning the IQ-discrepancy model and the use of IQ tests for identification, and also recommend incorporation of response to instruction (RTI) as one of the identification criteria. These changes are also recommended to states in the current reauthorization of the U.S. Individuals with Disabilities in Education Act (IDEA). While not mandatory, states that follow these recommendations will experience major changes in identification and treatment of students served under the LD category. This paper reviews the basis for these recommendations, summarizing four recent consensus group reports on special education that concur in suggesting these changes. Seventeen commonly asked questions about these changes are presented, with responses. In order to ensure adequate instruction for students with LD, it is essential that identification practices focus on assessments that are directly related to instruction, that any services for students who are struggling prioritize intervention over eligibility, and that special education be permitted to focus more on results and outcomes and less on eligibility and process. Identification models that incorporate RTI represent a shift in special education toward the goals of better achievement and behavioral outcomes for students identified with LD, as well as those students at risk for LD.

In the past few years, increasing concern has been expressed in the United States about common definitions and procedures for identifying students with learning disabilities (LD). These concerns involve all four components of most definitions of LD, including the federal definition recommended in 1977 to states by the United States Office of Education (USOE, 1977). Three of these components-discrepancy, heterogeneity, and exclusioncan be found in the 1977 federal definition. Discrepancy in most definitions is indicated by the presence of a difference between aptitude and achievement, represented in the federal regulatory definition as a severe discrepancy between IQ and achievement test scores. Heterogeneity represents the multiple domains in which LD occurs: seven in the 1977 federal definition, including various disorders of reading, math, written expression, and language. The exclusion component reflects the orientation that LD should not be identified if the primary cause involves a sensory disorder, mental deficiency, emotional disturbance, economic disadvantage, linguistic diversity, or inadequate instruction. In addition, these three components-discrepancy, heterogeneity, and exclusion-are the basis for the fourth component of most definitions, the belief that LD is due to constitutional factors intrinsic to the student. Thus, a student who meets the criteria stemming from the first three components is presumed to have an achievement problem that is due to neurobiological factors. These components, which have served as the foundation for identifying students with LD since the inception of the construct, resulted from a general agreement that this was the best way to proceed, considering the lack of empirical evidence. These components of most definitions continue to prevail despite the emergence of a significant evidence base that suggests problems and alternatives to this consensus.

In the United States, recent efforts at educational reform have focused on the notion of accountability for results and the implementation of evidence-based instructional approaches. These efforts have specifically targeted improving reading instruction, reflecting the accumulation of research on how children learn to read and how to assist struggling readers. The impetus for reform and the emphasis on reading have multiple sources, the most salient being stagnant gains on different national and international assessments over the past 20 years. Of significant concern was the failure of schools to close the gap between achievement scores of economically advantaged, primarily nonminority students, and economically disadvantaged, predominantly minority students. These concerns eventuated in the reauthorization of the Elementary and secondary Education Act, or the No Child Left Behind Act of 2001, Public Law 107-110 (NCLB, 2002). Fundamental to NCLB is Reading First, which requires the implementation of approaches to reading instruction supported by scientifically based reading research documented in multiple consensus reports such as the 1998 National Research Council's Preventing Reading Difficulties in Young Children (Snow, Burns, & Griffin, 1998), the report of the National Research Panel (2000), and a report on reading comprehension by the RAND Reading Study Group (2002).

These same issues are affecting the major piece of special education legislation in the United States, the Individuals with Disabilities in Education Act (IDEA), which is presently being considered for reauthorization by Congress. This reauthorization was preceded by four consensus reports on special education: the National Research Council report on minority overrepresentation in special education (Donovan & Cross, 2002), a report entitled Rethinking Special Education by the Fordham Foundation and the Progressive Policy Institute (Finn, Rotherham, & Hokansen, 2001), the Learning Disabilities Summit by the U.S. Office of Special Education Programmes (Bradley, Danielson, & Hallahan, 2002), and the President's Commission on Excellence in Special Education (2002). Each of these reports was significantly influenced by reading research as well as research on the classification and identification of individuals with LD. All four reports suggested that the number of individuals identified with LD could be reduced if more effective reading instruction was in place, noting that many students placed in special education may not have received adequate instruction in general education. This lack of adequate instruction within general education also helps explain the disproportionate representation of minorities in special education. These reports also observed that current regulations for the identification of LD lacked a research base and constituted obstacles to the implementation of better instructional approaches for students with disabilities. Thus, in the reauthorization of IDEA, bills under consideration in both the House and Senate loosen the grip of the U.S. federal regulatory definition of LD, allowing states options for a) not using IQdiscrepancy or even not giving IQ tests as part of a standard identification process, and b) allowing states to include response to instruction (RTI) criteria as part of the identification process.

These changes have been embraced by many professionals and researchers, but viewed with considerable anxiety by others, including some professional organizations and practitioners involved in LD. At the same time, a recent national survey found that 54% of parents and 72% of teachers felt that current identification methods for LD took too long to identify students in need and to provide intervention (National Center for Learning Disabilities, 2002). Few teachers endorsed the view that current methods for identifying LD were effective and most (84%) felt that improvements could be made. Parents with a student who had been identified with LD were especially negative about the current system. This survey implies that those who want to preserve the current system are not listening carefully to parents and teachers.

The most common misconception is that the proposed changes in both bills involve mandatory replacement of IQdiscrepancy with RTI as a new approach to assessment and identification. In fact, RTI is not mandated and any changes in the use of IQ tests and discrepancy models are up to the individual states. Parents retain the right to request IQ tests. Moreover, RTI is not an alternative approach to accessing special education services, but rather only one of the criteria used in the identification process. It represents a method for assessing the "adequate opportunity to learning" exclusion already present in IDEA. Identification models that incorporate RTI represent an opportunity to provide early intervention and/or prereferral services to reduce inappropriate referral and identification, and to establish a prevention model for students to eliminate the "wait to fail" model in place in many schools. It is also an opportunity to move more quickly into intervention for older students who have not had the opportunity or simply not profited from early intervention.

Despite the existence of some promising models and encouraging data (Donovan & Cross, 2002), some parents and educators continue to warn against changes in current identification procedures, thus retaining an emphasis on IQ testing and the discrepancy model. Others argue that LD cannot be identified without some assessment of cognitive processes. The research base supporting these propositions is very limited. Perpetuating assumptions about LD on the basis of a discrepancy model would represent continuance of an identification model singled out as inadequate by all four of the consensus reports and by empirical research (Aaron, 1997; Steubing, et al., 2002). There is clear consensus that this traditional model has not led to improved instructional outcomes for children, neither those deemed eligible for special education nor those found ineligible, but who continue to struggle in school.

The authors served on one or more of the four recent consensus groups on special education. In this paper, we summarize components of these reports and recent empirical syntheses that have raised numerous issues concerning the reliability and validity of the federal regulatory definition of LD in the IDEA. These evidence-based reports show congruence in recommending abandonment of the IQ-discrepancy criterion, a significantly restricted role of IQ tests, and a focus on deficient achievement, exclusionary criteria, and RTI for identification of LD. We discuss the basis for these recommendations and respond to 17 questions raised by different groups in the LD community. This community urgently needs to consider these recommendations and responses. The LD category is in danger of expiation without a closer link with the research on LD from the past 30 years and the even more immediate problem of lack of progress of students with LD who are placed in special education.

Autism and Other Associated Disorders

Autism is a brain development disorder characterized by impaired social interaction and communication, and by restricted and repetitive behavior. These signs all begin before a child is three years old. The autism spectrum disorders (ASD) also include the related conditions Asperger syndrome and PDD-NOS, which have fewer signs and symptoms. Autism has a strong genetic basis, although the genetics of autism are complex and it is unclear whether ASD is explained more by multigene interactions or by rare mutations. In rare cases, autism is strongly associated with agents that cause birth defects. Other proposed causes, such as childhood vaccines, are controversial, and the vaccine hypotheses lack any convincing scientific evidence and are biologically implausible. The prevalence of ASD is about 6 per 1,000 people, with about four times as many males as females. The number of people known to have autism has increased dramatically since the 1980s, partly due to changes in diagnostic practice; the question of whether actual prevalence has increased is unresolved.

Autism affects many parts of the brain; how this occurs is not understood. Parents usually notice signs in the first two years of their child's life. Although early behavioral or cognitive intervention can help children gain self-care, social, and communication skills, there is no known cure. Not many children with autism live independently after reaching adulthood, though some become successful, and an autistic culture has developed, with some seeking a cure and others believing autism should be tolerated as a difference and not treated as a disorder.

Characteristics

Autism is a highly variable brain development disorder that first appears during infancy or childhood, and generally follows a steady course without remission. Symptoms tend to continue through adulthood, although often in more muted form. It is distinguished not by a single symptom, but by a characteristic triad of symptoms: impairments in social interaction; impairments in communication; and restricted interests and repetitive behavior. Other aspects, such as atypical eating, are also common but are not essential for diagnosis. Autism's individual symptoms occur in the general population and appear not to associate highly, without a sharp line separating pathologically severe from common traits.

Social Development

Social deficits distinguish autism and the related autism spectrum disorders (ASD; see Classification) from other developmental disorders. People with autism have social impairments and often lack the intuition about others that many people take for granted. Noted autistic Temple Grandin described her inability to understand the social communication of neurotypicals, or people with normal neural development, as leaving her feeling "like an anthropologist on Mars".

Unusual social development becomes apparent early in childhood. Autistic infants show less attention to social stimuli, smile and look at others less often, and respond less to their own name. Autistic toddlers have more striking social deviance; for example, they have less eye contact and anticipatory postures and are more likely to communicate by manipulating another person's hand. Three- to five-year-old autistic children are less likely to exhibit social understanding, approach others spontaneously, imitate and respond to emotions, communicate nonverbally, and take turns with others. However, they do form attachments to their primary caregivers. They display moderately less attachment security than usual, although this feature disappears in children with higher mental development or less severe ASD. Older children and adults with ASD perform worse on tests of face and emotion recognition.

Contrary to common beliefs, autistic children do not prefer being alone. Making and maintaining friendships often proves to be difficult for those with autism. For them, the quality of friendships, not the number of friends, predicts how lonely they feel.

There are many anecdotal reports, but few systematic studies, of aggression and violence in individuals with ASD. The limited data suggest that, in children with mental retardation, autism is associated with aggression, destruction of property, and tantrums. A 2007 study interviewed parents of 67 children with ASD and reported that about two-thirds of the children had periods of severe tantrums and about one-third had a history of aggression, with tantrums significantly more common than in children with a history of language impairment. A 2008 Swedish study found that, of individuals aged 15 or older discharged from hospital with a diagnosis of ASD, those who committed violent crimes were significantly more likely to have other psychopathological conditions such as psychosis.

Communication

About a third to a half of individuals with autism do not develop enough natural speech to meet their daily communication needs. Differences in communication may be present from the first year of life, and may include delayed onset of babbling, unusual gestures, diminished responsiveness, and vocal patterns that are not synchronized with the caregiver. In the second and third years, autistic children have less frequent and less diverse babbling, consonants, words, and word combinations; their gestures are less often integrated with words.

Autistic children are less likely to make requests or share experiences, and are more likely to simply repeat others' words (echolalia) or reverse pronouns. Joint attention seems to be necessary for functional speech, and deficits in joint attention seem to distinguish infants with ASD: for example, they may look at a pointing hand instead of the pointed-at object, and they consistently fail to point at objects in order to comment on or share an experience. Autistic children may have difficulty with imaginative play and with developing symbols into language.

In a pair of studies, high-functioning autistic children aged 8–15 performed equally well, and adults better than individually matched controls at basic language tasks involving vocabulary and spelling. Both autistic groups performed worse than controls at complex language tasks such as figurative language, comprehension and inference. As people are often sized up initially from their basic language skills, these studies suggest that people speaking to autistic individuals are more likely to overestimate what their audience comprehends.

Repetitive Behavior

Autistic individuals display many forms of repetitive or restricted behavior, which the Repetitive Behavior Scale-Revised (RBS-R) categorizes as follows.

- Stereotypy is apparently purposeless movement, such as hand flapping, making sounds, head rolling, or body rocking.
- Compulsive behavior is intended and appears to follow rules, such as arranging objects in a certain way.
- Sameness is resistance to change; for example, insisting that the furniture not be moved or refusing to be interrupted.
- Ritualistic behavior involves the performance of daily activities the same way each time, such as an unvarying menu or dressing ritual. This is closely associated with sameness and an independent validation has suggested combining the two factors.
- Restricted behavior is limited in focus, interest, or activity, such as preoccupation with a single television programme or toy.
- Self-injury includes movements that injure or can injure the person, such as biting oneself. A 2007 study reported that self-injury at some point affected about 30% of children with ASD.

No single repetitive behavior seems to be specific to autism, but only autism appears to have an elevated pattern of occurrence and severity of these behaviors.

Other Symptoms

Autistic individuals may have symptoms that are independent of the diagnosis, but that can affect the individual or the family. An estimated 0.5% to 10% of individuals with ASD show unusual abilities, ranging from splinter skills such as the memorization of trivia to the extraordinarily rare talents of prodigious autistic savants. Many individuals with ASD show superior skills in perception and attention, relative to the general population. Unusual responses to sensory stimuli are more common and prominent in autistic children, although there is no good evidence that sensory symptoms differentiate autism from other developmental disorders. Differences are greater for under-responsivity (for example, walking into things) than for over-responsivity (for example, distress from loud noises) or for sensation seeking (for example, rhythmic movements). Several studies have reported associated motor problems that include poor muscle tone, poor motor planning, and toe walking; ASD is not associated with severe motor disturbances.

Unusual eating behavior occurs in about three-quarters of children with ASD, to the extent that it was formerly a diagnostic indicator. Selectivity is the most common problem, although eating rituals and food refusal also occur; this does not appear to result in malnutrition. Although some children with autism also have gastrointestinal (GI) symptoms, there is a lack of published rigorous data to support the theory that autistic children have more or different GI symptoms than usual; studies report conflicting results, and the relationship between GI problems and ASD is unclear. At some point in childhood, about two-thirds of individuals with ASD are affected by sleep problems; these most commonly include symptoms of insomnia such as difficulty in falling asleep, frequent nocturnal awakenings, and early morning awakenings. Sleep problems are associated with difficult behaviors and family stress, and are often a focus of clinical attention over and above the primary ASD diagnosis.

Parents of children with ASD have higher levels of stress. Siblings of children with ASD report greater admiration of and less conflict with the affected sibling; siblings of individuals with ASD have greater risk of negative well-being and poorer sibling relationships as adults.

Conditions Comorbid to Outism Spectrum Disorders

There are many conditions comorbid to autism spectrum disorders, such as fragile X syndrome and epilepsy. In medicine and in psychiatry, comorbidity describes the effect of other diseases an individual patient might have other than the primary disease of interest.

About 10–15% of autism cases have an identifiable Mendelian (single-gene) condition, chromosome abnormality, or other genetic syndrome, and ASD is associated with several genetic disorders. However, autism and other autism spectrum diagnoses, including Asperger syndrome, are diagnosed strictly as a cognitive disability, as a brain disorder that begins in early childhood, persisting throughout adulthood, and affecting three crucial areas of development: communication, social interaction and creative or imaginative play.

Comorbid Conditions

Anxiety: Anxiety disorders are common among children with ASD, although there are no firm data. Symptoms are likely affected by age, level of cognitive functioning, degree of social impairment, and ASD-specific difficulties. Many anxiety disorders, such as social phobia, are not commonly diagnosed in people with ASD because such symptoms are better explained by ASD itself, and it is often difficult to tell whether symptoms such as compulsive checking are part of ASD or a co-occurring anxiety problem.

The prevalence of anxiety disorders in children with ASD has been reported to be anywhere between 11% and 84%; the wide range is likely due to differences in the ways the studies were conducted.

Bipolar Disorder: Bipolar disorder, or manic-depression, is itself comorbid with a number of conditions, including autism. Autism includes some symptoms commonly found in mood and anxiety disorders.

Bowel Disease: Some children with autism also have gastrointestinal (GI) symptoms, but there is a lack of published rigorous data to support the theory that autistic children have more or different GI symptoms than usual. It has been claimed that up to fifty percent of children with autism experience persistent gastrointestinal tract problems, ranging from mild to moderate degrees of inflammation in both the upper and lower intestinal tract. This has been described as a syndrome, autistic enterocolitis, by Dr. Andrew Wakefield; this diagnostic terminology, however, has been questioned by medical experts. Constipation, often with overflow, or encopresis, is often associated with developmental disorders in children, and is often difficult to resolve, especially among those with behavioral and communication problems.

Depression and Other Psychopathological Disorders

Phobias, depression and other psychopathological disorders have often been described along with ASD but this has not been assessed systematically.

Fragile X Syndrome

Fragile X syndrome is the most common inherited form of mental retardation. It was so named because one part of the X chromosome has a defective piece that appears pinched and fragile when under a microscope. Fragile X syndrome affects about two to five percent of people with ASD. It is important to have a person with autism checked for Fragile X, especially if the parents are considering having another child. If one child has Fragile X, there is a one-in-two chance that boys born to the same parents will have Fragile X (see Mendelian genetics). Other members of the family who may be contemplating having a child may also wish to be checked for the syndrome.

ADHD

A person cannot have both an ASD and attention-deficit hyperactivity disorder (ADHD), as the Diagnostic and Statistical Manual of Mental Disorders (4th edition) prohibits their co-diagnosis. However, clinically significant symptoms of these two conditions commonly co-occur, and children with both sets of symptoms may respond poorly to standard ADHD treatments, and may benefit from additional types of medications or from behavioral or other therapies.

Mental Retardation

The fraction of autistic individuals who also meet criteria for mental retardation has been reported as anywhere from 25% to 70%, a wide variation illustrating the difficulty of assessing autistic intelligence. For example, a 2001 British study of 26 autistic children found about 30% with intelligence in the normal range (IQ above 70), 50% with mild to moderate retardation, and about 20% with severe to profound retardation (IQ below 35). For ASD other than autism the association is much weaker: the same study reported normal intelligence in about 94% of 53 children with PDD-NOS. Conversely, a 2008 study estimated that 28% of adolescents with intellectual disabilities have autism. A 2007 study reported that autistics score relatively higher in Raven's Matrices than in Wechsler tests; a 2008 study found a similar effect, but to a much lesser degree and only for individuals with Wechsler IQs less than 85. By definition, the diagnosis of Asperger's excludes mental retardation.

A 2006 review questioned the common assumption that most children with autism are mentally retarded. It is possible that the association between mental retardation and autism is not because they usually have common causes, but because the presence of both makes it more likely that both will be diagnosed.

Neuroinflammation and Immune Disorders

The role of the immune system and neuroinflammation in the development of autism is controversial. Until recently, there was scant evidence supporting immune hypotheses, but research into the role of immune response and neuroinflammation may have important clinical and therapeutic implications. The exact role of heightened immune response in the central nervous system (CNS) of patients with autism is uncertain, but may be a primary factor in triggering and sustaining many of the comorbid conditions associated with autism. Recent studies indicate the presence of heightened neuroimmune activity in both the brain tissue and the cerebrospinal fluid of patients with autism, supporting the view that heightened immune response may be an essential factor in the onset of autistic symptoms.

Non-verbal Learning Disorder

Motor Clumsiness: The initial accounts of Asperger syndrome and other diagnostic schemes include descriptions of motor clumsiness. Children with ASD may be delayed in acquiring motor skills that require motor dexterity, such as bicycle riding or opening a jar, and may appear awkward or "uncomfortable in their own skin". They may be poorly coordinated, or have an odd or bouncy gait or posture, poor handwriting, or problems with visual-motor integration, visual-perceptual skills, and conceptual learning. They may show problems with proprioception (sensation of body position) on measures of apraxia (motor planning disorder), balance, tandem gait, and finger-thumb apposition.

Obsessive-compulsive Disorder

Obsessive-compulsive disorder is characterized by recurrent obsessional thoughts or compulsive acts.

Obsessional thoughts are ideas, images or impulses that enter the individual's mind again and again in a stereotyped form. They are almost invariably distressing (because they are violent or obscene, or simply because they are perceived as senseless) and the sufferer often tries, unsuccessfully, to resist them. They are, however, recognized as the individual's own thoughts, even though they are involuntary and often repugnant.

Compulsive acts or rituals are stereotyped behaviours that are repeated again and again. They are not inherently enjoyable, nor do they result in the completion of inherently useful tasks.

It must be recognized that this is different from the obsessions that are a feature of autism spectrum disorders in that the obsessions are not enjoyable or in any way beneficial, which can sometimes be the case with autism, for instance an obsession to study an interest.

Tourette Syndrome

The prevalence of Tourette syndrome among individuals with autism is estimated to be 6.5%, higher than the 2% to 3% prevalence for the general population. Several hypotheses for this association have been advanced, including common genetic factors and dopamine or serotonin abnormalities.

Seizures

ASD is also associated with epilepsy, with variations in risk of epilepsy due to age, cognitive level, and type of language disorder. One in four autistic children develops seizures, often starting either in early childhood or adolescence. Seizures, caused by abnormal electrical activity in the brain, can produce a temporary loss of consciousness (a "blackout"), a body convulsion, unusual movements, or staring spells. Sometimes a contributing factor is a lack of sleep or a high fever. An EEG can help confirm the seizure's presence.

Sensory Problems

Unusual responses to sensory stimuli are more common and prominent in autistic children, although there is no good evidence that sensory symptoms differentiate autism from other developmental disorders. The responses may be more common in children: a pair of studies found that autistic children had impaired tactile perception while autistic adults did not. The same two studies also found that autistic individuals had more problems with complex memory and reasoning tasks such as Twenty Questions; these problems were somewhat more marked among adults. Several studies have reported associated motor problems that include poor muscle tone, poor motor planning, and toe walking; ASD is not associated with severe motor disturbances.

Tuberous Sclerosis

Tuberous sclerosis is a rare genetic disorder that causes benign tumors to grow in the brain as well as in other vital organs. It has a consistently strong association with the autism spectrum. One to four percent of autistic people also have tuberous sclerosis. Studies have reported that between 25% and 61% of individuals with tuberous sclerosis meet the diagnostic criteria for autism with an even higher proportion showing features of a broader pervasive developmental disorder.

Epilepsy

Epilepsy is a common chronic neurological disorder characterized by recurrent unprovoked seizures. These seizures are transient signs and/or symptoms of abnormal, excessive or synchronous neuronal activity in the brain. About 50 million people worldwide have epilepsy, with almost 90% of these people being in developing countries. Epilepsy is more likely to occur in young children, or people over the age of 65 years, however it can occur at any time. Epilepsy is usually controlled, but not cured, with medication, although surgery may be considered in difficult cases. However, over 30% of people with epilepsy do not have seizure control even with the best available medications. Not all epilepsy syndromes are lifelong – some forms are confined to particular stages of childhood. Epilepsy should not be understood as a single disorder, but rather as a group of syndromes with vastly divergent symptoms but all involving episodic abnormal electrical activity in the brain.

Behavior Disorders

All kids misbehave some times, but behavior disorders go beyond mischief and rebellion. With behavior disorders, your child or teen has a pattern of hostile, aggressive or disruptive behaviors for more than 6 months.

Warning signs can include:

- Harming or threatening themselves, other people or pets
- Damaging or destroying property
- Lying or stealing
- Not doing well in school, skipping school
- Early smoking, drinking or drug use
- Early sexual activity

- Frequent tantrums and arguments
- Consistent hostility towards authority figures

If you see signs of a problem, ask for help. Poor choices can become habits. Kids who have behavior problems are at higher risk for school failure, mental health problems and even suicide. Classes or family therapy may help parents learn to set and enforce limits.

Emotional Disorders

Early recognition of social and emotional problems in infants and preschool children is necessary for best developmental outcomes. Social and emotional difficulties continue over time and are highly resistant to change. It is not surprising that a strong relationship exists between childhood behavior problems, delinquency, and later criminality. If left untreated, "early-onset" conduct problems (high rates of aggression, disobedience, oppositional behaviors and emotional impairment) place children at high risk for persistent social and emotional problems, underachievement, school drop out and ultimately delinquency. Research has demonstrated that a young child's ability to learn is assured by a sense of security and stability, and continuous relationships with adults, including their families and communities.

Early identification and intervention with social and emotional problems can have a significant impact on the developing child in three major areas. First, brain development, important early relationships and experiences can positively affect gene role, neural connections, and the organization of the mind, having a life-long positive effect. Positive early experiences lay the necessary foundation for the healthy growth of future behaviors and thought development. The development of emotional self being and social ability in the early years plays a critical part in shaping the way children think, learn, react to challenges, and develop relationships throughout their lives.

Social and Emotional Facts

- Kindergarten teachers say that about 20 percent of children entering kindergarten do not yet have the necessary social and emotional skills to be "ready" for school.

- Social and emotional development is important because it contributes to cognitive development.
- When children are young, the adults around them (parents, other adult caregivers, preschool teachers) are the most important influences on their social and emotional development.
- Preschool education can support early development with long term social and emotional benefits.

Understanding Social and Emotional Behaviors

Evaluating social and emotional capability in very young children can be difficult. Accuracy of the child's behavior often depends upon certain variables including the age of the child, when the behavior occurs, the setting where it occurs, and which adults are present at the time. Developmental and cultural variability, differences in adult and child temperament, and changing behavioral expectations are some factors that make social and emotional assessment particularly challenging. For example, one family may tolerate loud talking and throwing of play toys while another family may tolerate only quiet voices and no throwing of objects indoors. A two-year-old who throws herself on the floor at the supermarket and screams because she can't have a chocolate donut will not be labeled "unusual" while an eight-year old who does the same would be.

Very young children, for example, have to learn to understand and recognize their own feelings, but then they increasingly learn to associate verbal labels to those feelings, to learn that others have feelings too, and to begin to sympathize with others. As children grow older, they learn to manage their emotions to block feelings of anxiety, sadness, or frustration, and to delay gratification in order to achieve a goal.

Children need a combination of intellectual skills, motivational qualities, and social emotional skills to succeed in school. They must be able to understand the feelings of others, control their own feelings and behaviors, and get along with their peers and teachers. Children need to be able to cooperate, follow directions, demonstrate self-control, and "pay attention."

One of the most important skills that children develop is self-control- the ability to manage one's behavior so as to resist impulses, maintain focus, and undertake tasks even if there are other more tempting options available.

Self-control motivates the ability to take on every task, so that the outcomes are not just how children get along with one another but also how they can focus and learn in the classroom.

Social-emotional skills include the following:

- The child is able to understand and talk about his/her own feelings.
- The child understands the perspective of others and realizes that their feelings may be different from his/ her own feelings.
- The child is able to establish relationships with adults and maintains an ongoing friendship with at least one other child.
- The child is able to enter a group successfully.
- The child is able to engage in and stay with an activity for a reasonable amount of time with minimal adult support.

Social and emotional development involves the achievement of a set of skills. Among them is the ability to:

- Identify and understand one's own feelings.
- Accurately read and comprehend emotional reactions from others.
- Manage strong emotions and their expression in a constructive manner.
- Control one's own behavior.
- Develop compassion for others.
- Establish and maintain relationships.

Social and Emotional Behaviors in Preschool

Children with social and emotional problems enter kindergarten unable to learn because they cannot pay attention, remember information on purpose, or act socially in a school environment. The result is growing numbers of children who are hard to manage in the classroom. These children cannot get along with each other, follow directions, and are impulsive. They show hostility and aggression in the classroom and on the playground.

The problems begin before kindergarten. In some studies as many as 32 percent of preschoolers in Head Start programmes have behavioral problems. Children lacking social and emotional skills suggest that teachers spend too much time trying to restrain unmanageable children and less time teaching. Early childhood teachers report that they are extremely concerned about growing classroom management problems, and that they are unprepared to handle them. Kindergarten teachers report that more than half of their students come to school unprepared for learning academic subjects. If these problems are not dealt with, the result can be growing aggression, behavioral problems and, for some, delinquency and crime through the school years and into adolescence and adulthood.

Social and Emotional Aggression

Continual physical aggression, high-school dropout rates, adolescent delinquency, and antisocial behavior have all been associated with early childhood conduct problems. The preschool years are a vulnerable period for learning to control development of aggression. Children who display high levels of physical aggression in elementary school are at the highest risk for taking part in violent behaviors as adolescents. Researchers believe that children with difficult, disruptive behavior (poor social and emotional skills) are at risk for these later problems for at least three reasons: (1) teachers find it harder to teach them, seeing them as less socially and academically capable, and therefore provide them with less positive feedback; (2) peers reject them, which obstructs an important opportunity for learning and emotional support; and (3) children faced with this rejection from peers and teachers are likely to dislike school and learning, which leads to lower school attendance and poorer outcomes. Difficult behavior exhibits itself early, even before children begin kindergarten; the pattern of rejection and negative experiences begins early, too. The early experience of rejection can have lasting emotional and behavioral impacts beyond elementary school, creating the problem even more difficult to reverse.

Developing Social and Emotional Skills

Promoting social and emotional development and preventing problems caused by inadequate development is clearly important to individuals and to society. They begin with the relationships children form with the people around them, including parents, caregivers, and peers. One characteristic of a successful person is his or her ability to live and work peacefully and productively with others. Social capacity is the ability to interact positively within personal and family relationships, as well as the ability to demonstrate positive concern and consideration. Emotionally healthy children engage in positive behaviors, develop mutual friendships, and are more likely to find acceptance from their peers. Through play, children learn how to work in teams and cooperate with others. Their behavior and interactions influence the way in which teachers perceive them and the way they are treated by their peers. As early as preschool, the relationships children develop with one another can have a lasting impact on academic achievement, because they can contribute to more positive feelings about school and eagerness to engage in classroom activities, which can, in turn, lead to higher levels of achievement.

Social Emotional Problems and Peer Relationships

Social interaction with peers builds upon and improves the rules and customs of social interaction that children first encounter in their families. Although many adults assume that the influence of peers on adolescents is negative, the repercussions of peer relationships are often more positive than negative. Peer relationships can provide cognitive, social, and physical stimulation through mutual activities and conversations. Friendships in particular can provide emotional security and compassion and can often serve as an additional source of support outside of the family, especially in times of crisis.

Children must be provided an emotionally secure and safe environment that prevents any form of bullying or violence, where they can be effective learners and integrate the development of social and emotional skills within all aspects of school life. These skills include problem-solving, coping, conflict management/resolution and understanding and managing feelings. Gaining social and emotional skills enables children to learn from teachers, make friends, express thoughts and feelings, and cope with frustration. These kinds of skills, in turn, directly influence cognitive learning such as early literacy, numeracy and language skills.

Early rejection by peers has been associated with persistent academic and social difficulties in elementary school. That is why it is important to have skilled preschool teachers who can intervene when they see children having difficulties with peers and help the children learn how to resolve conflicts, control emotions, and respond to the feelings of others.

Social Emotional Problems in the Family

Parents and families play a huge part in determining a child's social and emotional development. Early relationships with parents lay the foundation on which social ability and peer relationships are built. Parents who support positive emotional development interact with their children affectionately; show consideration for their feelings, desires and needs; express interest in their daily activities; respect their opinions; express pride in their achievements; and provide support during times of anxiety. This encouragement significantly raises the probability that children will develop early emotional capability, will be better prepared to enter school, and less likely to display behavior problems at home and at school. This is why many preschool programmes include a focus on parent involvement and parenting education. Interactions with siblings are an important part of child development. These interactions influence the course of a child' s social and moral development, including the development of good citizenship and good character. In general, having an encouraging relationship with parents and siblings is important to positive adolescent development. Children who disconnect from parental influence are at particular risk for delinquent activities and psychological problems.

Social and Emotional Support

The results of early childhood social-emotional problems may be a response from child distress and suffering, difficulty with learning, trouble with play, poor peer interactions and sibling relationships, are all warnings of future mental health problems. Nationally, fewer than 25% of children with clinical mental health problems receive treatment. Promoting children's social and emotional wellbeing can help improve their physical and mental health, performance at school and assist with behavioral problems. A range of factors impact on how children feel, including their individual family background and the community they live in, everyone needs to work together to agree effective strategies as part of a team.

Children might need more focused instruction on skills such as: identifying and expressing emotions; self-control; social problem solving; initiating and maintaining interactions; cooperative responding; strategies for handling disappointment and anger; and friendship skills. Families of infants and young toddlers might need guidance and support for helping the very young child regulate emotions or stress and understand the emotions of others.

Parents should consult with school staff regarding the social and emotional behavioral needs of their children. Once you have contacted the school about concerns the following steps should be taken.

- A consultation with school staff regarding classroom and/or school approaches to behavior and to develop positive behavior supports and interventions.
- Screening, evaluation, identification and referral for children displaying emotional disturbances.

- Planning and implementing appropriate academic and other educational supports.
- Measuring progress and improvement both for individuals and also for programmes.
- Interventions for students with chronic behavior and emotional needs.
- Small group and/or individual counseling for such issues as social skills, anger control, etc.
- Development of expectations such as positive behavior and intervention, prevention of violence, crisis planning and intervention, etc.
- Coordination and referral of children and families to community service agencies, related to mental health needs.

When children have persistent challenging behavior that is not responsive to interventions, comprehensive interventions are developed to resolve problem behavior and support the development of new skills. The process begins with arranging the school staff that will develop and implement the child's individualized education plan. At the center of the team is the family and child's teacher or other primary caregivers. The next step is to conduct a functional assessment to gain a better understanding of the factors that are related to the child's engagement in challenging behavior. The individualized educational plan includes prevention strategies to address the triggers of challenging behavior; replacement skills that alternatives to the challenging behavior; and strategies that ensure challenging behavior is not reinforced or maintained. The individualized education plan is designed to address home, community, and classroom routines where challenging behavior is occurring.

Multiple Disabilities

Characteristics and Background Information for Students with Multiple Disabilities:

Children with multiple disabilities will have a combination of various disabilities that may include:

speech, physical mobility, learning, mental retardation, visual, hearing, brain injury and possibly others. Along with multiple disabilities, they can also exhibit sensory losses and behavior and or social problems. Children with multiple disabilities- also referred to as multiple exceptionalities will vary in severity and characteristics. These students may exhibit weakness in auditory processing and have speech limitations. Physical mobility will often be an area of need. These students may have difficulty attaining and remembering skills and or transferring these skills from one situation to another. Support is usually needed beyond the confines of the classroom. There are often medical implications with some of the more severe multiple disabilities which could include students with cerebral palsy and severe autism and brain injuries. There are many educational implications for these students.

Strategies and Modifications

What Can You Do?

- Early intervention is necessary- as soon as the child begins school.
- Involvement of the appropriate professionals, *i.e.*, occupational therapists, speech/language therapists, physio therapists, etc.
- A team approach at the school level involving external agency/community liaison who meet on a regular basis is essential.
- The physical arrangement of the classroom will need to best accommodate this child. Consideration of special equipment and assistive technology is essential.
- Integration among their peers is important to assist these students with social development. It's important to integrate multiply disabled children as much as is possible. Research does indicate that when these students attend their community school and participate in the same activities as their peers is social skills

develop and are enhanced. (Sometimes these students are place full time in a regular classroom with support, however, in the majority of cases, these students are place in a developmental skills type of classroom with some integration.

- Ensuring that all students demonstrates respect for the multiply disabled student becomes a teacher responsibility and needs to be taken seriously with ongoing activities that develop respect from the other students in the class.
- An Individual Education Plan will need to be carefully planned out and adjusted on a regular basis and will need to be aligned to the child.
- Remember, these children are often completely dependent upon others for most/all of their daily needs.
- Assistive technologies may assist this child and the support team will need to decide which assistive technologies will be most appropriate. (In the IDEA act: ASSISTIVE TECHNOLOGY. Consider whether the child requires assistive technology devices and services.
- A safety plan will need to be developed and is often included in the IEP.
- Care needs to be given in your expectations of this student to ensure the child doesn't not become frustrated.

Most importantly, these idenditifed children are to be given the same rights as non-identified school age children including screening, evaluation and an appropriate programme and services.

Incidence and Prevalence

What are Low-incidence Disabilities?

- Alternative Systems for Classification
- A Focus on Incidence

Alternative Systems for Classification

Students with disabilities can be classified in many ways. IDEA '97 continues to recognize disabilities in the form of more or less discrete diagnostic categories, such as mental retardation, specific learning disabilities, or emotional disturbance. Other approaches to classification include categorizing disabled individuals by degree of severity of their needs, or by how atypical an individual may be when compared to a norm. Still other approaches may emphasize the level of intensity of supports necessary for an individual to function optimally in home, school, community, and work settings.

Each of these approaches has advantages and disadvantages. The categorical approach taken by IDEA may emphasize learner characteristics for each disability, but, in so doing, it could also foster a self-fulfilling prophecy in which all members of a group sharing a categorical label, in a sense, become that label. A severity approach may emphasize developmental milestones at the expense of ignoring strengths in functional skills. An intensity approach may meaningfully focus on levels of needed support, but, at the same time, limit opportunities for an individual to move to a less restrictive setting. None of these systems of classifying individuals with disabilities are either entirely satisfactory or entirely lacking in merit. For educators, it is important to be aware that several systems of categorizing students with disabilities exist simultaneously, because eligibility criteria, placement alternatives, intervention strategies, and teaching credentials may all vary substantially from school to school, depending on which system of classification is currently being employed.

A Focus on Incidence

When the issue at hand for students with disabilities centers on the provision of services in local schools, the availability of qualified personnel and the technical sophistication of necessary resources must be carefully considered. In order to provide students with disabilities with a free and appropriate public education, it is useful to classify learners in terms of incidence, or how many students with any particular disability or combination of disabilities reside in a community. Under such a system, students with the most commonly-seen disabilities may be more appropriately served by local public schools while students with relatively rare disabilities may not find adequate resources or highly qualified personnel.

High-incidence *disabilities include*—

- communication disorders (speech and language impairments)
- specific learning disabilities (including attention deficit hyperactivity disorder [ADHD])
- mild/moderate mental retardation
- emotional or behavioral disorders

Low-incidence disabilities include—

- blindness
- low vision
- deafness
- hard-of-hearing
- deaf-blindness
- significant developmental delay
- complex health issues
- serious physical impairment
- multiple disability
- autism

None of the disabilities listed under low-incidence disabilities generally exceed 1% of the school-aged population at any given time. The relative rarity of students with these disabilities in public schools often poses significant challenges for local schools struggling to meet their needs. Since they encounter these students so infrequently, most local schools have little if any knowledge of how to best educate these students, of what technologies are available to assist them, and of how to obtain needed and appropriate support services from outside agencies. All students with low-incidence disabilities thus experience a commonality: they are difficult to serve in current local public school programmes.

Prevalence

As most categories in special education, LD has its roots in medicine. Histories of LD reveal origins in language and reading disorders emanating from neurological impairments. When LD was formally recognized as a category of special education, a tension arose between its medical origins and its educational context. A medical model of LD is sufficient for conceptualizing the abstract nature of the condition but fails to include real-world contingencies like school. After all, students with LD are referred, diagnosed, and classified within the context of school.

It is not difficult to imagine that without schools we would not have an LD category as we now know it. Thus, the field of medicine laid the foundation for LD but special education shaped its present form. Once removed from a strict medical foundation, LD was subject to social influences. LD is presently a behavioral phenomenon where there may be a medical foundation that becomes secondary to the individual - manifestations shaped by social forces in the environment. The problems in the LD field are primarily intellectual in nature and are evidenced in a failure to achieve a real understanding of LD (Kavale & Forness, 1995). This failure is not the result of a lack of the requisite information.

Although LD is a relatively new category, the concept is not new, and it is possible to answer the question: What was a learning disability supposed to be? Historical analyses of LD point to an important consideration: LD was originally conceived as a discrete classification whose parameters included, not generalized learning failure, but particular problems related to academic learning. Thus, LD was created as a discrete category to describe academic problems, particularly underachievement, that resulted from specific deficits. Conceptually, LD differed from MR with respect to IQ level (LD was not associated with below average intellectual performance) and an ability profile indicating both strengths and weaknesses rather than the flat and depressed profile associated with MR. The focus on academic problems, rather than behavior problems, differentiated LD from emotional or behavior disorders (E/BD). Thus, LD, as the newest category in special education, fit a niche by describing a classification of neurologically based learning disorders that resulted primarily from a variety of processing deficits. Thus, specific LD was a circumscribed category describing a particular form of underachievement and not a general form of low achievement.

A learning disability (LD) is a neurological disorder that affects the brain's ability to receive process, store and respond to information. The term learning disability is used to describe the seeming unexplained difficulty a person of at least average intelligence has in acquiring basic academic skills. These skills are essential for success at school and work, and for coping with life in general. LD is not a single disorder. It is a term that refers to a group of disorders.

Numerous definitions and conceptualizations of the term, learning disability have been offered. Since the inception of the area of learning disability, controversy has raged over how learning should be defined. Of the many proposed definitions none has been universally accepted. Different professionals from the different field have tried to define the term in their own way to suit to their own purpose or to suit to their own profession.

Because of the continued problems in the definition of learning disability and lack of consensus among the professionals a group of specialists from several organizations was convened. This group of specialists included representations from American Speech-Language Hearing Association, Council for Learning Disability, International Reading Association, Association for Children with Learning Disability, Division for Children with Communication Disorders and the Orton Dyslexia Society and they with a combined effort generated a definition which speaks, "Learning disability is a generic term that refers to a heterogeneous group of disorders manifested by significant discrepancies in the acquisition of use of listening, speaking, reading, writing, reasoning or mathematical abilities. These disorders are intrinsic to the individual presumed to be due to central nervous system dysfunction and may occur across the life span. Problems in self regulating behaviours, social perception and social interaction may exist with learning disability but do not by themselves constitute a learning disability. Although learning disability may occur concomitantly with other handicapping conditions (for example, sensory impairment, mental retardation, serious emotional disturbances) or with intrinsic influences (such as cultural differences, insufficient or inappropriate instruction) they are not the result of these conditions or influences".

The definition accepted by the United States Congress speaks that, "Those children who have a disorder in one or more of the basic psychological processes involved in understanding or in using language, spoken or written, which disorder may manifest itself in imperfect ability to listen, think, speak, read, write, spell or to do mathematical calculations. The term includes such conditions as perceptual handicaps, brain injury, minimal brain dysfunction, dyslexia and developmental aphasia. The term does not include a learning problem which is primarily the result of visual, hearing or motor handicaps, of mental retardation, of emotional disturbance, or of environmental, cultural or economic disadvantage."

From the point of view of education the term learning disability can be defined as a kind of behavioural deficit almost always associated with academic performance that can be remediated by precise individual instructional programming. Educationally a learning disabled is one whose achievement is less than his expected level of achievement.

Even though differences exist in the definitions offered by different individuals and organisations yet four common components are observed: ability-achievement discrepancy, psychological processes disorder, central nervous system dysfunction, and exclusion of other handicap categories. Learning disabilities can affect a person's ability in the areas of listening, speaking, reading, writing and mathematics.

Other features of a learning disability are:

- A distinct gap between the level of achievement that is expected and what is actually being achieved.
- Difficulties that can become apparent in different ways with different people.
- Difficulties that manifest themselves differently throughout development.
- Difficulties with socio-emotional skills and behavior.

A learning disability is not a disease, so there is no cure, but there are ways to overcome the challenges it poses through identification and accommodation. A student with a learning disability may show one or more of the following characteristics (Batshaw & Perret, 1992).

- *Specific Academic Skills Deficits:* For example, the student may have trouble with basic reading skills, reading comprehension, writing, written expression, spelling, mathematical calculation, and mathematical reasoning. Perceptual-motor impairments. The student may have trouble distinguishing shapes and sizes. He or she may have also difficulty with fine motor activities, such as writing, coloring and cutting. They may lack established handedness and may make letter, word, and/or number reversals.
- *Memory and Thinking Disorders:* The students may be deficient in the use of strategies for memorization and haphazard in their approaches to learning. They may have poor language skill, which hinder memory, difficulty with short-term auditory and visual memory, and a lack of awareness of skills and strategies needed to solve problems and perform tasks.
- *Speech and Language Disorders:* The student may have difficulty with the grammar (syntax), meaning (semantics), or social use (pragmatics) of language.
- *Attention Disorders:* The student may have difficulty concentrating and remaining "on task". He or she rarely finishes what is started, frequently jumps from one

activity to another, and is easily distracted by competing stimuli.

- *Hyperactivity:* The student has difficulty sitting still, is constantly in motion, is fidgety, and seems driven by an "inner motor."
- *Impulsiveness:* The student often acts without thinking, has poor planning and organizational skills, responds quickly and makes many errors, and lacks self-regulation skills.
- *Emotional Lability:* The student is moody and often isolated or rejected by his or her peers. He or she may have low self-esteem and is more likely to violate social norms. He or she may exhibit inappropriate ways of getting attention, elicits more negative reactions from others, and be lacking in social cognition skills. Also, he or she may have difficulty with reading nonverbal social cues and with motivation. He or she may be passive, rather than active learners.
- *General Coordination Deficits:* The student may be uncoordinated and have difficulty with fine and/or gross motor skills (*e.g.* tying shoes, running, hopping, skipping), and depth perception.
- *Neurological Soft Signs:* Poor fine motor coordination, balance, and tactile discrimination. The student may have strabismus and poor visual-motor coordination.

Discussion

One major aspect of the problem of learning disabilities is how to determine its prevalence. Because of variations in definition and criteria it is difficult to give accurate figures in this regard. Prevalence has been estimated to be as low as 1% and as high as 20% of school age children in the United States and the more severe cases probably present from 1% to 3% of the total school population (U. S. Congress Senate, Committee on Labour and Public Welfare, 1968). Estimates of the prevalence of learning disabilities vary widely depending largely on the criteria used to determine eligibility for services. The more stringent the identification criteria, the lower the prevalence rate and the more lenient the criteria, the higher the prevalence rate. The prevalence rate varies from 1% to 30% of the school population (Lerner, 1971). After specifying the difficulties involved in estimating the prevalence of learning disabilities, Kirk (1972) suggested that "the best guess is that from 1 to 3 percent at the least, and possibly 7% at the most, of the school population require special remedial education." The validity of this estimate has received some support from Wissink (1972), who surveyed one hundred "leaders" in the learning disabilities area. Out of one hundred thirty-nine responded regarding their estimates of the incidence of learning disabilities in school population. Half the respondents estimated the incidence to be 5% or less, though almost one-third thought it was 15% or higher. Several comprehensive surveys of school populations have tried to establish an exact incidence but have had little success in establishing a set figure.

After reviewing twenty-one studies on prevalence rate Bryant and McLoughlin (1972) concluded that the prevalence of learning disabilities ranged from 3 to 28%, with half of the studies reporting an incidence of above 13%. Based on PL 94-142 child count data reported by the states of U.S.A., the number of children with learning disabilities represented 4.5% of the total population of U.S. school children during 1988-89 school years (U.S. Department of Education, 1990).

In 1970, the National Centre for Educational Statistics (a branch of U.S. Office of Education) conducted a survey of approximately 2000 public elementary and secondary school principals. The sample was stratified to represent the nation's 81,000 public schools. Principals of the 2,000 schools filled out a questionnaire on the number of their students with specific learning disabilities, and the reported result was 2.6% (Silverman & Metz, 1973). When the sample schools were separated into low-versus high-income areas, the estimate separated into 3.5% and 2.0%. Although this must be considered the official count, there are many other estimates in the published literature. A 1973 summary is shown in following table.

Eisenberg (1966) noticed 28% LD in the 6 graders who were reading two or more years below grade level in a large metropolitan city. The prevalence rate of LD was observed 15% and there is wide geographical variations (HEW National Advisory Committee on Dyslexia and Related Reading Disorders, 1969). In Chicago suburbs it was between 7.5 to 15% as evidenced from a four year study of 3 and 4 grade children (Myklebust and Boshes, 1969). Rubin and Balow (1971) studied 967 1, 2 and 3 graders who were part of a medical research project in the Minneapolis- St. Paul area and found it 24 to 41%.

In 1977 fewer than 8,00,000 children or 1.8% of the enrolled school population received services under the category of learning disabilities. This percentage has increased to 5.27%, or over 2.4 million by the school year 1993-1994 (U. S. Department of Education, 1995). Figure:1 shows the percentage of students with learning disabilities enrolled in schools from 1978 to 1994 Gradually the number of students with learning disabilities is increasing (Gelzheiser, 1987; Adleman, 1990, Stevenson, 1993, Payette, 1994 & Wegner, 1976).

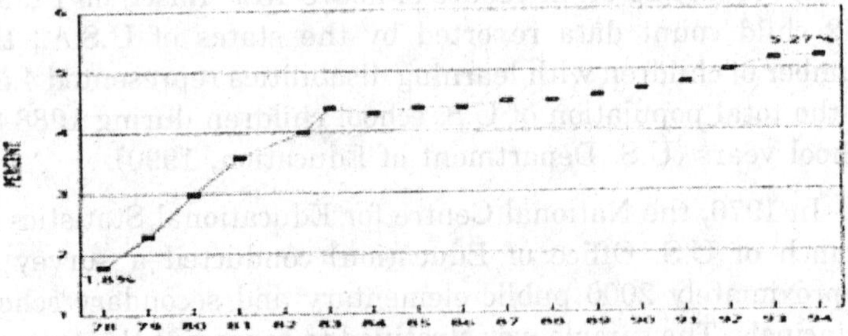

Percentage of ld Dtudents Enrolled in U.S. Schools

The following explanations are suggested for rapid increase in the learning disabilities category.

1. *More Awareness of the Category of Learning Disabilities*: Public awareness of the condition of learning disabilities has increased for which parents, educators and students are exerting additional pressure on the schools to

provide adequate services for students with learning disabilities.

2. *Improvement in Procedures for Identifying and Assessing Learning Disabilities:* Improved evaluation and assessment techniques have identified many children who previously would have gone unnoticed.
3. *Social Acceptance and Preference for the Learning Disabilities Classification:* Most parents and administrators prefer the classification of learning disabilities because it does not carry the stigma of other areas of disability. Some students who once would have been classified as having mental retardation or behaviour disorders are increasingly being classified under the rubric of learning disabilities.
4. *Cutbacks in Other Programmes and Lack of General Education Alternatives for Children Who Experience Problems in the Regular Class:* Due to decrease in funding of many programmes and a lack of adequate remedial programmes, such as remedial reading there is increase in learning disabilities category.
5. *Court Orders:* A number of court decisions found that the classification of minority children as mentally retarded was discriminatory. Some of these children may be identified under the classification of learning disabilities (U.S. Department of Education, 1991a). In Contrast with the increase in learning disabilities, there has been a long-term decrease in the number of relative proportion of children and youth identified with mental retardation.

The estimate rate of learning disabilities among prison population is as high as 80 or 90%. It is increasingly suspected that, the longer learning disabilities goes undetected the more severe do the emotional problems become. These problems, moreover, may be associated with, and possibly responsible for, deviant, antisocial or psychopathological behaviour in adolescents and adults. Many believe that there is a link between learning disabilities and juvenile delinquency.

According to the report prepared for the Office of Juvenile Justice and Delinquency Prevention, Law Enforcement Assistance Administration, by Murray et al. (1976a), there are two broad hypotheses linking learning disability and juvenile delinquency in a causal relationship. First, a child gets a reputation with parents, teachers and peers for being a slow learner, a disciplinary problem, an undesirable playmate.

In the next stage, a child so labeled develops a negative self-image "and is thrown together (informally, or through class assignments) with other problem students." The student then develops a felt need "to compensate for continued school failure" and develops a tendency towards absenteeism, suspension or drop-out from school. Then immediately preceding delinquent behaviour, the child has the psychological incentives, the economic incentives and increased opportunity (in the form of time on his hands) to commit delinquent acts.

The second and more direct line of argument linking learning disabilities and juvenile delinquency posits "that certain types of combinations of learning disabilities are associated with behavioural tendencies that facilitate delinquency". According to this so called "susceptibility" rationale, certain types of learning disabled children are generally impulsive, limited in their ability to learn from experience, and also limited in their ability to decipher social clues. "Together", Murray explains, "characteristics like these points to a child who is not wholly responsive to the usual systems of sanctions and rewards. Messages do not get through to him in quite the way they are intended, with the result that some of the factors which might restrain a normal child from committing a delinquent act might not restrain the learning disabled child. In short, this type of child starts out with one strike against him when exposed to opportunities for committing delinquent acts."

A survey commissioned by the General Accounting Office (GAO) in 1977 found that 26% of the juvenile delinquents tested by the survey's educational consultants in Connecticut and Virginia institutions had "primary learning problems" or learning disabilities (Comptroller General of U.S., 1977).

The GAO Report notes that, "overall, the results of the testing in Connecticut Virginia substantiate similar studies conducted in other states which also showed considerable academic underachievement in their delinquent populations", pointing out that, in a study conducted by the State of Colorado's Division of Youth Services, 90% of adjudicated delinquents tested "were diagnosed as having learning problems" and, in a Rhode Island Study, 70% of the delinquent youths tested "were found to have measurable disabilities significant enough to warrant professional attention " (Comptroller General of the U.S., 1977).

Estimates of the prevalence of learning disabilities among the school-age population range from 1% or less to 35% or more, although most assessments fall in the 3 to 16% range. Frank (1996) observed that learning disabilities occurs in 10-15% of the general population and 3-5% of the adult population. If the children population is removed this comes to 10%.

According to figures kept by the U.S. Government, the public schools have identified as learning disabled between 5 and 6% of students 6 to 17 years of age. Learning disabilities is by far the largest category of special education. More than half of the students identified by the public schools as needing special education are learning disabled. The size of the learning disabilities category has more than doubled since 1976-1977, when prevalence figures first started being kept by the federal government.

Many authorities maintain that the rapid expansion of the learning disabilities category reflects poor diagnostic practices. They believe that children are being over identified, that teachers are too quick to label students with the slightest learning problem as "learning disabled" rather than entertain the possibility that their teaching practices are at fault. Some, however, argue that the claim of over identification has been exaggerated and that there are logical explanations for some of the increase in students with learning disabilities. Some have pointed to social/cultural changes that have raised children's vulnerability to developing learning disabilities

(Hallahan, 1992). For example, an increase in poverty has placed children at greater risk for bio-medical problems, including central nervous system dysfunction (Baumeister, Kupstas & Klindworth, 1990). The number of children living in poverty, for example, has grown by 15 to 19% since the 1970s. (U.S. Department of Education, 1997). Furthermore, even families who are not in poverty are under more stress than ever before, which takes its toll on the time children have for concentrating on their school-work and on their parents' ability to offer social support.

Still others maintain that there is a causal relationship between the decrease in the numbers of students being identified as mentally retarded and the increase in the numbers of students being identified as learning disabled. There is suggestive evidence that school personnel, when faced with a student who could qualify as mentally retarded, often "bend" the rules to apply the label of "learning disabilities" rather than the more stigmatising label of "mental retardation" Macmillan, Gresham & Bocian, 1998).

Lack of agreement among studies on prevalence rate of learning disabilities can be traced back to the absence of an agreed-on, definitive and operational definition of the term "learning disabilities". Since educators who use a strict interpretation conceive of the category of the learning disabled as including little more than classically defined students who are more likely to be found in private schools or clinical settings than in public school operations, they believe that no more than 3% of the school population is learning disabled. To supporters of the liberal interpretation, an incidence figure of 15 to 30% seems minimal. In urban school districts with large concentrations of minorities and economically impoverished people, the figures reported by liberal interpretationists are sometimes higher.

Reports from clinics and schools show that four times as many boys as girls are identified as having learning disabilities. However, longitudinal and epidemiological studies suggest that actually there may be as many girls with learning disabilities as boys (Lyon, 1995a; Shaywitz et al., 1990; Shaywitz, Fletcher & Shaywitz, 1995). It is suspected that many of these girls are not being identified and therefore represent an undeserved group of children who are at significant risk for long-term academic, social and emotional difficulties (Shaywitz & Shaywitz, 1988; Vogel, 1990b).

Currently, almost 2.9 million school-aged children in the US are classified as having specific learning disabilities (SLD) and receive some kind of special education support. They are approximately 5% of all school-aged children in public schools. These numbers do not include children in private and religious schools or home-schooled children.

Studies show that learning disabilities do not fall evenly across racial and ethnic groups. For instance, in 2001, 1% of white children and 2.6% of non-hispanic black children were receiving LD-related special education services*. The same studies suggest that this has to do with economic status and not ethnic background. LD is not caused by economic disadvantage, but the increased risk of exposure to harmful toxins (lead, tobacco, alcohol, etc.) at early stages of development is prevalent in low-income communities.

Cooley (1991) and U.S. Department of Education (1992) estimate that the boys outnumber girls by about 3:1 in the learning disabilities category. Some researchers have suggested that the prevalence of learning disabilities among males is due to their greater biological vulnerability. The infant mortality rate for males is higher than that for females, and males are at greater risk than females for a variety of biological abnormalities. Other researchers have contented, however, that the higher prevalence of learning disabilities among males may be due to referral bias. They suggest that academic difficulties are no more prevalent among boys than among girls, but that boys are more likely to be referred for special education when they do have academic problems because of other behaviours that bother teachers, such as hyperactivity. Research on this issue is mixed (Clarizio & Phillips, 1986; Leinhardt, Seewald & Zigmond, 1982; Shaywitz, Shaywitz, Fletcher & Escobar,

1990). Because of the cultural factors more boys may be referred as boys tend to exhibit more disruptive behaviours that are troublesome to adults. Furthermore, the pressure to succeed in school may be greater for boys than for girls, making boys more vulnerable to the effects of stress.

Cone, Wilson, Bradley & Reese (1985); Kirk & Elkins (1975); Norman & Zigmond (1980); Shepard & Smith (1981) and Cone et. al (1985) examined the demographic, intellectual and achievement data for 1,839 students enrolled in K-12 learning disabilities programmes in Iowa. They found that males outnumber females by a 3:1 ratio across primary, elementary and secondary age levels. It is widely accepted in the field at this point that boys turn up with learning disabilities far more frequently than girls do, estimates range from 4 boys for 1 girl to ratios as high as 9 to 1. Trout says that she now sees equal numbers of both, possibly as a result of a shift towards greater expectations for girls than has been the case in the past. At this point it is safest to conclude that some bias does exist but that the biological vulnerability of males also plays a role. For example, the figures indicate that all disabilities are more prevalent in males, including conditions that are difficult to imagine resulting from referral or assessment bias, such as hearing impairment (53% are males), orthopedic impairment (54% are males) and visual impairment (56% are males) (Hallahan, Kauffman & Lloyd, 1999). Estimates of the prevalence of LD range from 2% to 10%. It is thought that around 5% of students in public schools in the US are identified as having a LD (Ingersoll & Previts, 2004).

The wide range of prevalence estimates of learning disabilities, from 1 to 30% (Lerner, 1971), reflects the uncertain state of affairs regarding identifying criteria. However, even the conservative estimate of 1 to 3% recommended by the National Advisory Committee on Handicapped Children (1968) recognizes that this elusive group of children constitutes a substantial segment of the school age population.

Pulliam (1975) reported an investigation of the incidence for child learning disabilities, as it is reflected in the literature of several disciplines and as a function of criteria by which LD has been defined. The literatures of medicine, psychology, special education and related disciplines were examined. Forty reports of incidence for LD or like conditions were found. In spite of some inconsistency, findings reflected a generally increasing level of incidence as defining criteria were increasingly broad, and as the level of severity assumed to be disabling declined. There was some agreement among studies suggesting a level of incidence around 10%, for LD defined in terms of either neurological impairment or of deficiency in relation to a learning expectancy. This level of incidence was found when the cutting point for severity was a learning performance below 90% of expectancy, based on ability and experience. Extreme high and low levels of incidence reported in the past appeared to be explained by extremely narrow and broad defining criteria used by researchers concerned.

Wegner (1976) viewed learning disabilities as an area of growing concern in school psychology. Increasing numbers of children referred to psychologists for emotional and behavioural problems are found to have concurrent learning disorders. Gradually, interest in learning disabilities has intensified and the demand for services for LD children has increased. These changes have produced confusion on the part of both psychologists and teachers concerning the extent to which the school psychologist's role should include a focus upon the learning aspects of children's problems. 63.52 percent of the total recommendations made by all psychologists were found to be learning disabilities related. It is needed to broaden and strengthen the role of the school psychologists.

Taylor (1977) observed variation in prevalence due to varying standards for identification of LD children and differing perceptions regarding the characteristics of LD population. However, the existing prevalence rate, noted by Taylor was 3%.

Criteria proposed by Bureau of Education for the Handicapped, Iowa's State Department of Education, Kentuky's State Department of Education, Widerholt, and Hammill's suggested criteria were employed by McNutt (1978) to determine the easiest set of criteria for identification of LD adolescents and to determine the incidence rate of LD. The sample for the study was 1,392 ninth and tenth graders. The result indicated that estimated incidence rates ranged from 5.5 to 6% of the total sample.

Acutt (1987) investigated the factors that went into the labeling of LD students in order to determine what criteria was used to label students LD and whether these factors conform to the federal definition which was set forth in the 1978 federal rules and regulations. The numbers went from an estimated 2% of the school population who may have specific learning disabilities to some districts that identified more than 20% of their students to be LD. Federal incidence figures estimate 2% of the school population as LD. Illinois, New York, and California are three states reporting incidence figures that exceeded 6% or three times greater than the federal projections.

Finlan (1991) observed a tremendous increase in the number of learning disabled children following the passage of PL 94-142. Decrease in the number of students with other exceptionalities, Chapter-I disadvantaged students and general school population was also noticed. Nearly half of the special education student population in 1988-89 was labeled as learning disabled. The author noticed the continuation of current practice of identifying LD for tremendous increase in the number of LD population. There seems to be a relationship between the existence of methods of determining a severe discrepancy and the percentage of LD students identified. The prevalence rate of learning disabilities in Orissa was thought to be 5.67%.

In recent years, an increasing number of student with learning disabilities have been studying in institutions of higher education. An examination of post secondary education in the United Kingdom revealed that students with learning disabilities represented 3.8% of all the first-year students. (Higher Education Statistics Agency, 1999). According to the American Council of Education (1995), the percentage of all students with disabilities entering college quadrupled between 1978 and 1991 from 2.2 to 8.8% of all students. In 1998, two out of five first year students who had some kind of disability reported having a learning disability. Although in recent years there has been an increase in the number of students with learning disabilities, who graduate, the graduation rate of college students with learning disabilities was only 3.6%, compared with 62.1% for students without disabilities (Murray, Goldstein, Nourse & Edgar, 2000).

In Israel, the Council for Higher Education reported in 1998 (Margalit, Breznitz & Aharoni, 1998) that between 1.5 and 3% of University students had learning disability. At the Open University of Israel, the number of students with learning disabilities increased from 500 in 1996-1997 to 750 in 2000-2001 (out of total of 29,000 registered students, 2.58%) and in 2000-2001; there were 1,593 students with learning disabilities out of a total enrolment of more than 32,000 students (4.98%).

Incidence figures for children with learning disabilities vary. The U.S. Department of Education (1999) reports that slightly less than 5% of school-age children are receiving special education services, with 2.7 million served in 1997-1998 school year (National Information Centre for Children and Youth with Disabilities, 2000). Fuchs, Fuchs, Mathes and Lipsey (2002) report an incidence of 7%. However, considering the special education population alone, the specific learning disabilities category contains the largest number of children, between 52 and 54% (Cramer & Ellis, 1996).

In its 19 Annual Report to Congress, the U.S. Department of Education (1999) states that 43% of students with specific learning disabilities are served in regular classrooms, 39% in resource rooms, 17% in separate classrooms, and less than 1% in separate schools, residential facilities or hospital.

Ninety-eight percent of the states exclude from the learning disability criteria children with mental retardation and low academic achievement due to environmental disadvantage. However, MacMillan and Speece (2000) reveals the evidence that between 52 and 70% of children identified by schools as learning disabled do not meet the standard established by state and federal criteria. Gottlieb, Alter, Gottlieb and Wisner (1994) note that in the urban areas they studied many of the children classified as learning disabled previously would have been classified as educable retarded because of their lower IQ scores. The estimate the prevalence rate of learning disabilities in the state capitals of Orissa and Bihar *i.e.*, Bhubaneswar and Patna is found to be 6.63% in Bhubaneswar and 6.21% in Patna.

Phipps (1977) while examining the perception of boys and girls with school learning and behaviour problems hypothesized that the boys would be perceived as being LD more often than the girls. The school records of LD children who had been placed in special programmes in southern California school district were examined to study the characteristics at the time of referral. Phipps found that the boys were referred much more than the girls for placement in LD programmes. The reason given most often for referral was that of behaviour problems than the academic problems.

Tomevi (1980) compared the ability and efficacy of two screening instruments, Meeting Street School Screening Test and the Dallas Pre-school Screening Test-Dallas to identify educationally high-risk children. Subjects of the study comprised 83 pre-KG children enrolling for KG classes, chronological age ranging from 4 years 7 Ms to 5 years 6 Ms. (mean age 61 months) at the time of screening. The subjects were tested on Meeting Street School Screening Test and the Dallas Pre-school Screening Test-Dallas within a two-week period of time. More boys than the girls were identified as educationally high-risk children. Dallas Pre-school Screening Test-Dallas was found to be more efficient and able in terms of time and space requirements than Meeting Street School Screening Test.

Cooley (1991) used regression estimate model and full regression model to evaluate the aptitude achievement discrepancy model to identify learning disabled students. The regression estimate model identified a greater proportion of minority students than their proportion in the general population whereas the full regression model showed no bias in this respect. Both the models identified the males at a rate of 3:1 over females. The male female ratio is 6:5 in LD population.

The male female ratio was found to be 8:5 in Bhubaneswar whereas it was 9:4 in Patna.

Causes and Prevention

Understandably, one of the first questions parents ask when they learn their child has a learning disorder is "Why? What went wrong?"

Mental health professionals stress that since no one knows what causes learning disabilities, it doesn't help parents to look backward to search for possible reasons. There are too many possibilities to pin down the cause of the disability with certainty. It is far more important for the family to move forward in finding ways to get the fight help.

Scientists, however, do need to study causes in an effort to identify ways to prevent learning disabilities.

Once, scientists thought that all learning disabilities were caused by a single neurological problem. But research has helped us see that the causes are more diverse and complex. New evidence seems to show that most learning disabilities do not stem from a single, specific area of the brain, but from difficulties in bringing together information from various brain regions.

Today, a leading theory is that learning disabilities stem from subtle disturbances in brain structures and functions. Some scientists believe that, in many cases, the disturbance begins before birth.

Errors in Fetal Brain Development

Throughout pregnancy, the fetal brain develops from a few all-purpose cells into a complex organ made of billions of specialized, interconnected nerve cells called neurons. During this amazing evolution, things can go wrong that may alter how the neurons form or interconnect.

In the early stages of pregnancy, the brain stem forms. It controls basic life functions such as breathing and digestion. Later, a deep ridge divides the cerebrum--the thinking part of the brain--into two halves, a right and left hemisphere. Finally, the areas involved with processing sight, sound, and other senses develop, as well as the areas associated with attention, thinking, and emotion.

As new cells form, they move into place to create various brain structures. Nerve cells rapidly grow to form networks with other parts of the brain. These networks are what allow information to be shared among various regions of the brain.

Throughout pregnancy, this brain development is vulnerable to disruptions. If the disruption occurs early, the fetus may die, or the infant may be born with widespread disabilities and possibly mental retardation. If the disruption occurs later, when the cells are becoming specialized and moving into place, it may leave errors in the cell makeup, location, or connections. Some scientists believe that these errors may later show up as learning disorders.

Other Factors That Affect Brain Development

Through experiments with animals, scientists at are tracking clues to determine what disrupts brain development. By studying the normal processes of brain development, scientists can better understand what can go wrong. Some of these studies are examining how genes, substance abuse, pregnancy problems, and toxins may affect the developing brain.

Genetic Factors—The fact that learning disabilities tend to run in families indicates that there may be a genetic link. For example, children who lack some of the skills needed for reading, such as hearing the separate sounds of words, are likely to have a parent with a related problem. However, a parent's learning disability may take a slightly different form in the child. A parent who has a writing disorder may have a child with an expressive language disorder. For this reason, it seems unlikely that specific learning disorders are inherited directly. Possibly, what is inherited is a subtle brain dysfunction that can in turn lead to a learning disability.

There may be an alternative explanation for why LD might seem to run in families. Some learning difficulties may actually stem from the family environment. For example, parents who have expressive language disorders might talk less to their children, or the language they use may be distorted. In such cases, the child lacks a good model for acquiring language and therefore, may seem to be learning disabled.

Tobacco, Alcohol, and Other Drug Use—Many drugs taken by the mother pass directly to the fetus. Research shows that a mother's use of cigarettes, alcohol, or other drugs during pregnancy may have damaging effects on the unborn child. Therefore, to prevent potential harm to developing babies, the U.S. Public Health Service supports efforts to make people aware of the possible dangers of smoking, drinking, and using drugs.

Scientists have found that mothers who smoke during pregnancy may be more likely to bear smaller babies. This is a concern because small newborns, usually those weighing less than 5 pounds, tend to be at risk for a variety of problems, including learning disorders.

Alcohol also may be dangerous to the fetus' developing brain. It appears that alcohol may distort the developing neurons. Heavy alcohol use during pregnancy has been linked to fetal alcohol syndrome, a condition that can lead to low birth weigh, intellectual impairment, hyperactivity, and certain physical defects. Any alcohol use during pregnancy, however, may influence the child's development and lead to problems with learning, attention, memory, or problem solving. Because scientists have not yet identified "safe" levels, alcohol should be used cautiously by women who are pregnant or who may soon become pregnant.

Drugs such as cocaine—especially in its smokable form known as crack—seem to affect the normal development of brain receptors. These brain cell parts help to transmit incoming signals from our skin, eyes, and ears, and help regulate our physical response to the environment. Because children with certain learning disabilities have difficulty understanding speech sounds or letters, some researchers believe that learning disabilities, as well as ADHD, may be related to faulty receptors.

Current research points to drug abuse as a possible cause of receptor damage.

Problems During Pregnancy or Delivery—Other possible causes of learning disabilities involve complications during pregnancy. In some cases, the mother's immune system reacts to the fetus and attacks it as if it were an infection. This type of disruption seems to cause newly formed brain cells to settle in the wrong part of the brain. Or during delivery, the umbilical cord may become twisted and temporarily cut off oxygen to the fetus. This, too, can impair brain functions and lead to LD.

Toxins in the Child's Environment—New brain cells and neural networks continue to be produced for a year or so after the child is born. These cells are vulnerable to certain disruptions, also. Researchers are looking into environmental toxins that may lead to learning disabilities, possibly by disrupting childhood brain development or brain processes. Cadmium and lead, both prevalent in the environment, are becoming a leading focus of neurological research. Cadmium, used in making some steel products, can get into the soil, then into the foods we eat. Lead was once common in paint and gasoline, and is still present in some water pipes. A study of animals sponsored by the National Institutes of Health showed a connection between exposure to lead and learning difficulties. In the study, rats exposed to lead experienced changes in their brainwaves, slowing their ability to learn. The learning problems lasted for weeks, long after the rats were no longer exposed to lead.

In addition, there is growing evidence that learning problems may develop in children with cancer who had been treated with chemotherapy or radiation at an early age. This seems particularly true of children with brain tumors who received radiation to the skull.

Prevention

Prevent Learning Disabilities by Stopping Alcohol Use- Drinking Alcohol Can Contribute to Learning Disabilities: There is no established "safe amount" of drinking during pregnancy and no single type of alcohol is safer than another, so it is best not to drink any type. Maternal alcohol use can cause Fetal Alcohol Syndrome (FAS), a birth defect that causes varying degrees of mental disabilities, behavior problems, and physical deformities.

Prevent Learning Disabilities by Stopping Smoking and Avoiding Second-Hand Smoke—When You Smoke, Your Baby Smokes Too: As with alcohol abuse, there is no established "safe amount" of smoking. Smoking can threaten your and your baby's life. It can cause bleeding that can lead to death of the baby and you. Smoking mothers are more likely to have miscarriages and give birth to under-weight babies and infants with birth defects. Sudden Infant Death Syndrome (SIDS) happens more frequently in babies of smoking mothers. Smoking has also been linked to learning disabilities and emotional/behavioral problems later in life.

Infants and children who live in homes where others smoke have more health problems than those who don't. They have more instances of pneumonia, ear, nose, and throat problems, sinus issues, bronchitis, asthma, and lung diseases. Studies have also linked second-hand smoke to cancer in non-smokers.

Children who have frequent illnesses and infections affecting their ears and sinuses are more likely to experience delays in language development, impaired early reading skills, and other learning disorders. This can lead to learning disabilities in reading and writing.

Preventing Learning Disabilities—Know the Dangers of Substance Abuse: Any abuse of drugs can lead to physical deformities, mental disabilities, and learning and behavior problems in infants and childhood. The effects of maternal and paternal drug abuse on children are nearly always disabling to some degree and are sometimes fatal. If you or someone you know is pregnant and abusing drugs, the earlier you seek medical assistance with stopping the abuse and caring for the unborn child, the better.

If you are thinking about becoming pregnant and you abuse drugs, get help now. See a doctor, be forthright about your substance abuse, and follow your doctor's treatment plan before becoming pregnant. Although much of the research and information on substance abuse targets mothers, there is some evidence to suggest that a father's drug abuse may also be linked to birth defects.

See Your Doctor About Recommended Vitamins and Nutritional Needs: A healthy diet and the right vitamins are important in the prevention of disabilities and increasing the chances of having a healthy baby. For example, folic acid, a type of B vitamin, has been shown to help prevent Neural Tube Defects, also called. Neural Tube Defects are deformities of the spinal cord that can cause mental and physical disabilities. Scientists estimate that as many as 70% of spina bifida cases are preventable by taking folic acid vitamins.

Screening of Newborns Helps Identify Disabilities for Early Intervention: It is important to have your baby screened for disabilities before discharge from the hospital at birth. Hearing problems are the most common sensory defect. It is estimated that three out of one thousand children are born with hearing difficulties and deafness.

Early identification of problems can enable quicker intervention. Early speech and language therapy and intervention for hearing impairments and deafness can dramatically increase the chances of successful learning in regular school environments later in life.

Early Eye Examinations are Important

Full eye examinations, not just vision screenings, are important for preschool aged children. An eye examination involves diagnosis of physical eye problems, not just a child's visual perception. Physical vision problems such as amblyopia can be treated and sometimes reversed through early treatment. Blindness associated with sexually transmitted diseases (STDs) can be prevented with appropriate medication at birth.

Ophthalmologists typically recommend examining children at least at six months and age five. Early intervention for vision problems can help prevent learning problems in school.

Naturally, undetected vision problems can affect a child's ability to form important visual concepts, to read, to write, and develop early number concepts. For children with visual impairments or blindness, it is critical they receive the appropriate early intervention services from a qualified early intervention specialist or special education teacher. Visual impairments and blindness affect all aspects of learning and living. They will require specialized instruction for academics, language, and safe movement and interaction in their environments to increase their future success in school and in life.

Types and Characteristics

Learning Disabilities (LD) are neurologically-based processing problems. These processing problems can interfere with learning basic skills such as reading, writing, or math. They can also interfere with higher level skills such as organization, time planning, and abstract reasoning.

The types of LD are identified by the specific processing problem. They might relate to getting information into the brain (Input), making sense of this information (Organization), storing and later retrieving this information (Memory), or getting this information back out (Output). Thus, the specific types of processing problems that result in LD might be in one or more of these four areas.

Input

Information is primarily brought into the brain through the eyes (visual perception) and ears (auditory perception). An individual might have difficulty in one or both areas.

Auditory Perception: (Also called Receptive Language) The individual might have difficulty distinguishing subtle differences in sound (called phonemes) or might have difficulty distinguishing individual phonemes as quickly as normal. Either problem can result in difficulty processing and understanding what is said. Individuals might have difficulty with what is called auditory figure-ground. They have difficulty identifying what sound(s) to listen to when there is more than one sound.

Visual Perception: One might have difficulty distinguishing subtle differences in shapes (called graphemes). They might rotate or reverse letters or numbers (d, b, p, q, 6, 9); thus misreading the symbol. Some might have a figure-ground problem, confusing what figure(s) to focus on from the page covered with many words and lines. They might skip words, skip lines, or read the same line twice. Others might have difficulty blending information from both eyes to have depth perception. They might misjudge depth or distance, bumping into things or having difficulty with tasks where this information is needed to tell the hands or body what to do. If there is difficulty with visual perception, there could be problems with tasks that require eye-hand coordination (visual motor skills) such as catching a ball, doing a puzzle, or picking up a glass.

Integration

Once information is recorded in the brain (input), three tasks must be carried out in order to make sense or integrate this information. First, the information must be placed in the right order or sequenced. Then, the information must be understood beyond the literal meaning, abstraction. Finally, each unit of information must be integrated into complete thoughts or concepts, organization.

Sequencing: The individual might have difficulty learning information in the proper sequence. Thus, he might get math sequences wrong, have difficulty remembering sequences such as the months of the year, the alphabet, or the times table. Or, she might write a report with all of the important facts but not in the proper order.

Abstraction: A person might have difficulty inferring the meaning of individual words or concepts. Jokes, idioms, or puns are often not understood. He might have problems with words that might have different meanings depending on how they are used. For example, "the dog" refers to a pet. "You dog" is an insult.

Organization: An individual might have difficulty organizing materials, losing, forgetting, or misplacing papers, notebooks, or homework assignments. She might have difficulty organizing her environment, such as her bedroom. Some might have problems organizing time. They have difficulty with projects due at a certain time or with being on time. (Organization over time is referred to as Executive Function.)

Memory

Three types of memory are important to learning. "Working memory" refers to the ability to hold on to pieces of information until the pieces blend into a full thought or concept. For example, reading each word until the end of a sentence or paragraph and then understanding the full content. "Short-term memory" is the active process of storing and retaining information for a limited period of time. The information is temporarily available but not yet stored for long-term retention. "Long-term memory" refers to information that has been stored and that is available over a long period of time. Individuals might have difficulty with auditory memory or visual memory.

One reads a sentence and hold on to it. Then the next and the next. By the end of the paragraph, he pulls together the meaning of the full paragraph. This is working memory. He continues to read the full chapter and study it. Information is retained long enough to take a test and do well. This is short-term memory. But, unless the information is reviewed and studied over a longer period of time, it is not retained. With more effort over time, the information might become part of a general body of knowledge. It is long-term memory.

Output

Information is communicated by means of words (language output) or though muscle activity such as writing, drawing, gesturing (motor output). An individual might have a language disability (also called expressive language disability) or a motor disability.

Language Disability: It is possible to think of language output as being spontaneous or on demand. Spontaneous means that the person initiates the conversation. Thoughts have been organized and words found before speaking. Demand language means that one is asked a question or asked to explain something. Now, she must organize his thoughts, find the right words, and speak at the same time. Most people with a language disability have little difficulty with spontaneous language. However, in a demand situation, the same person might struggle to organize her thoughts or to find the right words.

Motor Disability: One might have difficulty coordinating teams of small muscles, called a fine motor disability. He might have problems with coloring, cutting, writing, buttoning, or tying shoes. Others might have difficulty coordinating teams of large muscles, called a gross motor disability. She is awkward when running or jumping. Each individual will have his or her unique pattern of LD. This pattern might cluster around specific common difficulties. For example, the pattern might primarily reflect a problem with language processing: auditory perception, auditory sequencing/abstraction/organization, auditory memory, and a language disability. Or the problem might be more in the visual input to motor output areas. Some people with LD will have a mixture of both.

Characteristics

Learning Disability Characteristics and Your Child-Learning Disability Signs: Most students experience difficulty learning at various points during their school years. In fact, struggling with new material is a normal part of the learning process and can provide benefits to learners. The additional effort and concentration required to complete challenging tasks can strengthen problem solving skills, increase comprehension, and sustain the focus necessary to improve long-term memory. Consequently, not all learning problems are signs of learning disabilities.

Symptoms of Learning Disabilities- When to Suspect a Learning Disability: In early childhood, learning disabilities may first appear as developmental delays in some children. However, it is important to remember that many children with developmental delays may catch up with early intervention in special education programmes and will not develop learning disabilities.

In later school years, difficulty with school work and underachievement may signal a more serious learning problem. Students with learning problems that do not improve over time with appropriate interventions may have learning disabilities. Suspect a learning disability when students:

- Make poor grades despite significant effort;
- Need constant, step-by-step guidance for tasks;
- Cannot remember problem solving steps because they do not comprehend tasks or the logic behind them;
- Have poor memory of spoken or written material;
- Have difficulty mastering tasks or transferring academic skills to other tasks;
- Cannot remember skills and facts over time;
- Have strong general knowledge but cannot read as in dyslexia, write as in dysgraphia, or do math as in dyscalculia at that level;
- May have difficulty with communication and language processing, expressive, and receptive language;
- May be very frustrated with school and homework; and
- May have low self-esteem.

Learning Disabilities and Behavior- Behavioral Signs and Symptoms of Learning Disabilities: Knowing what behavioral signs and symptoms to look for helps parents get earlier intervention for children with learning disabilities. Common behavioral signs of learning disabilities fall within two categories, internalizing and externalizing behaviors.

Common Internalizing Behaviors of Students with Learning Disabilities: Students with learning disabilities who internalize show behaviors that mostly affect themselves and are sometimes overlooked by the adults around them. Students with externalizing behaviors have a more obvious effect on those around them and are usually recognized earlier as having problems. Both groups of students are at-risk for being seen as being problems rather than having problems.

Internalizing Learning Disabled Students: Students with internalizing behaviors are generally quiet and may be withdrawn. They are embarrassed by attention and worry about the possibility of their academic weaknesses being seen by others. These students may show a range of behaviors including:

- o Boredom and carelessness;
- o Disinterest in school or reluctance to go to school;
- o Withdrawal in class;
- o Disorganization, inattention;
- o Work that appears sloppy or poorly done;
- o Slow to response to questions; and
- o Physical symptoms of stress such as headaches or stomach aches.

Common Externalizing Behaviors of Students with Learning Disabilities

Students with learning disabilities who externalize are hard to miss. These students are often loud and disruptive. They seem to want attention, even if it is negative. They may enjoy joking about their poor work. They may take pleasure in annoying others because they feel it shifts the focus away from their weak academic skills. Inside, however, they may feel powerless and embarrassed. There are many ways that externalizers show problems. Some of these behaviors include:

- o Impulsive blurting out incorrect answers;
- o Breaking school rules and being referred for discipline because of behavior problems;
- o Behavior problems at home;
- o Aggression toward peers or adults;
- o Clowning around and inappropriate joking;
- o Attraction toward other underachievers; and
- o Delinquent behavior at home or in the community.

Most students with learning disabilities and attention deficit hyperactivity disorders(ADHD) are typically externalizers.

What to Do if You Suspect Learning Disability?

If you suspect a learning disability, keep a record of the problems you are having at home. List the strategies you are trying to address the problem. It is important to contact your child's teacher or counselor to discuss your child's problem behaviors and academic difficulty. Teachers can suggest other strategies to use at home and at school and can assist you with making a referral for formal evaluation if a disability is suspected. Learn more about the assessment process.

Diagnosis through evaluation is the first step in determining if your child meets eligibility requirements for learning disabilities under the Individuals with Disabilities Education Act. Children who qualify for IDEA services, also called special education programmes, will receive an Individualized education programme. As a parent of a child with a disability, you have specific rights under the IDEA.

Intervention and Educational Programmes

IDEA 04 offers states and localities the option of using "a process that determines if the child responds to scientific, research-based intervention as part of the evaluation process...," but it does not require that states or districts use Responsiveness-to-Intervention, often shortened to RTI. Although RTI is similar to the old pre-referral or problem-solving model first suggested by Dr. James Chalfant in the mid-70's as Teacher Assistance Teams (TAT), parents have begun to hear a lot about RTI as a "new" way to help students with learning disabilities.

What is an RTI?

Although there is no single RTI model, the many variations that are emerging use a two- to five-tiered model in the primary grades. The goal is early intervention for students having difficulty learning, so that achievement is improved for all students. Each tier provides increasingly individualized instruction, continuous monitoring of progress, and criteria for changing intervention and/or tier through a team decision-making process. In general, three tiers would include:

* Tier 1- high quality instruction and behavioral supports are provided in general education classrooms.
* Tier 2- more specialized instruction in a smaller group is provided when a student's progress and performance fall behind that of their classmates, schoolmates, or district.
* Tier 3- more individualized intervention is provided by special education personnel if referral and evaluation for special education determines eligibility for services.

Why should Parents Get Involved Now?

As states (SEAs) and districts (LEAs) begin exploring whether an RTI approach will be used, and if so, what form it will take, decisions will be made that affect students with learning disabilities. Unless parents become involved in the decisions of states and localities by asking questions and demanding clear answers, those decisions will be made without parent input. These questions include: 1) what components of RTI will be used, 2) when and how will parents participate, 3) what instruction will be provided and by whom, 4) what criteria will determine changes for a student, 5) who will be on decision-making teams, and 6) when and how will SLD identification and eligibility be determined?

What Components of RTI will Your State/District Implement?

While IDEA encourages the use of a process that documents how successfully a child responds to scientific, research-based interventions as part of the evaluation for SLD identification, there are many choices that SEAs and LEAs can make in developing an RTI approach. Some of the most commonly recognized components that should be part of any RTI process include:

* An early screening that is universal, or given to all children.
* Two to five stages or tiers that reflect instruction that increases in intensity, specialization and individualization.

* Requirements for parent/family notification and involvement when difficulties are initially noted and continuing until the student achieves age-appropriate academic progress or when evaluation for identification occurs.
* Scientific, evidence-based screening, instruction, monitoring and evaluation measures whenever possible.
* General and specialized teachers that can provide effective instruction needed by each child.
* Methods of regularly monitoring student progress that have been shown to be valid and reliable.
* A team decision-making process that includes parent participation and approval.
* Requirements that an evaluation for identification/ eligibility include multiple measures.

The way in which these and additional components are implemented should not lead to delay in serving students or to the misidentification of students. Thus, an RTI intended to serve students with SLD should recognize that intra-individual differences are typical and difficulties may occur in language arts areas other than basic reading, in academic areas such as mathematics or science, and/or in organizational, social, and attentional skills. However, neither lack of age-expected progress in basic reading skills nor academic underachievement alone is sufficient to identify SLD.

When and How will Parents Participate?

Parents and families must be meaningfully involved in RTI development, beginning with planning and continuing as implementation occurs at SEA and LEA levels, including participation in the activities of federally mandated, state and local Special Education Advisory Panels. As an RTI approach is shaped, procedures must guarantee that parents/families will be notified of and involved when student difficulties are first noted, and continued as team-decisions; adjustments in instruction; changes in educational, related service, or support personnel occur; and evaluation for identification are initiated.

Similarly, parents must ensure that schools are required to provide written information on a regular basis about their child's progress or lack of it.

Families should not be expected to initiate requests for such information. Just as IDEA empowers parents to initiate an evaluation, provisions should be included that allow a parent to initiate an RTI team meeting to consider tier or instruction/intervention changes.

What Instruction will be Provided and by Whom?

A crucial, but not unique, concern of RTI, is the quality of instruction. RTI broadens the focus of instructional effectiveness to include both general and special educators. As an RTI approach is developed, considering availability of resources will be important, but ensuring that teachers possess the needed instructional skills is also vital. More specifically, any RTI approach must make certain that:

* A range of instructional approaches and interventions are available to students.
* High quality general education instruction is supported by continuing professional development.
* High quality specialized intervention is supported by continuing professional development.
* The time, space, personnel and materials are available for short and long-term instruction.
* Supervision is provided to monitor the accuracy, or fidelity, of student instruction and intervention.

What Criteria will Determine Changes for an Individual Student?

The availability of timely, purposeful, and data-driven changes to inform instruction, determine tier placement, and meet individual student needs are key concepts of RTI. As RTI approaches are developed, both the intended and unintended consequences need to be carefully reviewed so that:

* The measures used for progress monitoring are evidence-based, and shown to be valid and reliable.

* Responsibility for administration, recording, and regular review of monitoring data is clearly described.
* Decisions are made about whether student progress will be compared with classmates, schoolmates, or with other groups.
* Guidelines are in place to specify the length of time required or permitted in order to determine if instruction is effective.
* The criteria for change in tier level are clear and based on scientific evidence from similar populations.
* Guidelines for team consideration of objective, quantified data and/or subjective, professional judgment are in place.
* Timelines are established for calling a team meeting and implementing a change in instruction or in tier placement
* Guidelines for change to a tier providing either more intensive or less intensive instruction are in place.

Who will be on Decision-making Teams?

Decision-making teams should be used in two different ways within an RTI approach. First, continuous progress monitoring data that meets established criteria for academic difficulty should trigger a team meeting to recommend changes in instruction and movement among tiers. Second, continued difficulty or initiation of parent or professional request for evaluation (under IDEA) should trigger team meetings consistent with IDEA.

In either case, at least one team member should have expertise in learning disabilities based on professionally accepted standards and/or competencies, which mild/moderate certification may not ensure. In addition, a parent should be a required and respected participant in both team processes. Guidelines for including a general education teacher and appropriate related and support service professionals are also important.

UNIT-VII

Family and Disability Management

Role of Mothers

The discussion about our mother always evokes strong emotions in us. And it should! After all, we lived in her womb for nine months even before we experienced the light of this world. When we try to appreciate her by telling others what she means to us or what a mother should be like or do, each of us has a different understanding and expression. In this article we will try to address some basic and general ways of understanding the unique role of the mother as relates to her children in the mother-child relationship.

As we emphasize the role of the mother, this is not to say that the father is not important or is less important. What the mother can give to her child and the extent to which she can give, very much depends on that which she can receive from her relationship with her spouse. If she receives support, joy, and peace from that relationship- that is what she will pass on.

If she only finds false expectations, empty promises, and frustrations- then that is what she will pass on. Thus, as we emphasize the mother's role, this in no way isolates or separates the mother from the father, nor does it place a greater emphasis on the mother's role as opposed to the father's one. Instead, it points to the mother's unique role within the family.

The Mother with the 'Good' Qualities

An important question that has preoccupied earlier generations and will continue occupying many future ones is the following: "What makes a 'good' mother-child relationship? Is it the mother's 'nature' (her inborn instincts) or is it her 'nurture' (the effect of the environment in which she is brought up)?" Of course, every culture and generation defines "good" in a different way, yet nature versus nurture discussion tends to be common to all.

For Christians, St. Mary in the Gospels best exemplifies the role of a 'good' mother. She shows that one has to naturally receive a blessing and then continue building upon that blessing. On the one hand, St. Mary is shown to be of a certain family and Jesus of the lineage of King David. [cf. Luke 1:27] Elizabeth, her cousin, calls her 'blessed among women.' [Luke 1:42-45] Certainly, St. Mary did not choose her parents or the blessings she received. However, along with the lineage and the blessings, the 'nature' aspect, she gives Christ all the 'nurture' that a mother can possibly give her child. St. Mary is next to him every step of the way- be it for joy or for suffering. She is the only human who is with Jesus from the time he is conceived into this world, to the time he is crucified, and even when the Holy Spirit descends at Pentecost. *In the earthly portion of the ministry of Christ, St. Mary represents the* ***only*** *thread of continuity in human relationships*. She demonstrates both the need for nature as well as nurture in the role of a 'good' mother in relation to her child.

Crisis Management

To Prevent Litigation, Prepare for Litigation

If you are like most parents, you do not need an attorney. The key to resolving special disputes is preparation, preparation and more preparation.

As a parent, your goals are to prevent problems when possible and to minimize the seriousness of those problems you cannot prevent.

Our Prevention Model of Special Education Advocacy is based on the "prepare for litigation" approach to civil litigation.

You do not initiate a battle to secure appropriate special education services until you have a good chance of prevailing and you can prevail without damaging your child.

Many parents say, "But look at the damage they are doing to my child. This must stop immediately!"

I reply, "To start a fight when you have no ammunition, your guns are unloaded, you have not assessed their weapons and location, and you don't know where the high ground is, is more damaging in the end."

To charge up the enemy's hill is foolhardy. Yet this is the course many parents take when they try to advocate for their children.

In most cases, children are stronger and more resilient than parents realize. If children know we believe in them, they can endure short-term pain to realize long-term benefit.

Managing a Crisis

A crisis hits! What should you do?

For the first few days, DO NOTHING!

At the beginning of a crisis, you will feel emotionally overwhelmed. You may believe you must DO SOMETHING! If you act, you are likely to shoot wildly from the hip before aiming, expending all your ammunition before the opposition fires a shot. When the opposition opens fire, you will be exposed and vulnerable.

SLOW DOWN! Think first, act later. Regroup. Analyze the battleground. Make rational decisions about the weapons you will use. Locate the high ground. Plot your strategy so you can take the hill and prevail, without firing a shot or taking casualties.

Your Long-range Planning

Use your energy to prepare. Focus on short-term solutions and long-range planning. Do your long-range planning first.

Begin Your Programme of Self-Study

You need to learn about the nature of your child's disability, how your child learns, and how your child should be taught. You also need to learn about your legal rights and responsibilities.

Learn About Legal Rights and Responsibilities

Using a highlighter, read and re-read the Individuals with Disabilities Education Act (IDEA). Attach sticky notes to the pages that relate to your child's situation.

Wrightslaw: *Special Education Law* is a legal reference book that includes the full text of the Individuals with Disabilities Education Act, IDEA regulations, Section 504 of the Rehabilitation Act, the Family Educational Rights and Privacy Act (FERPA), and decisions in special education cases from the U. S. Supreme Court.

You can download the special education regulations from the Wrightslaw site and from other sites, including the U. S. Department of Education website

Your State Department of Education

Call the Special Education Division of your State Department of Education. Use our Directory of State Departments of Education for contact information.

Ask for a copy of your state special education laws, regulations, and guidelines. Request that they send you all material they publish about special education, IEPs, and Section 504 programmes. Visit their web site.

Your State Protection and Advocacy Office

Your state has an independently operated and funded Protection and Advocacy Office that is not affiliated with the state Department of Education.

Contact your state P & A Office and request their publications about special education, IEPs, and parent rights and responsibilities.

Your Parent Training and Information Center.

Contact your state Parent Training and Information Center. Request their information about advocacy. Check our **Directory of PTIs** for the office nearest you.

Learn About Your Child's Disability and Educational Needs

You need accurate information about your child's disability, how your child learns, and how your child needs to be taught.

Meet with Educational Consultant

Schedule a consultation with a psychologist or educational diagnostician in the private sector. Provide your consultant with a copy of your child's file and test history. Ask your consultant to educate you about your child's disability and your child's educational needs.

Get a Comprehensive Private Sector Evaluation

Get a comprehensive evaluation of your child from an independent expert in the private sector. The purpose of this evaluation is to identify your child's problems and develop a comprehensive plan to address these problems. Before you can make decisions about your child's special education programme, you need accurate diagnostic information about the child's disability, strengths and weaknesses.

Use Tactics & Strategy

To resolve problems successfully, you need to understand how schools work and how school culture affects decision-making. You must learn to turn lemons into lemonade – how to turn a negative event into a positive opportunity to secure services for your child. For ideas about how to use tactics and strategy to get better services, read The Art of Writing Letters.

Control Your Emotions

You must keep your emotions under control! If you confide in school staff and share your feelings with them, you become vulnerable. If you obsess about unfairness and revenge, you will shoot yourself in the foot.

Spend your energy thinking, planning, and preparing. When you prepare, it is harder for you to shoot yourself in the foot.

Use your emotions as a source of energy and motivation. Your emotions will keep you moving, step by step, to high ground.

Short-Term Relief

Now, it's time to look at short-term relief. Put your child's self-esteem at the top of your list.

When children with disabilities struggle and fail, many decide that they are losers. Your child must feels your love and concern, even though some behavior is unacceptable.

During a school crisis, family stress is high. Many families consult with a psychologist, psychiatrist, or clinical social worker in the private sector. Your goals are to reduce stress, improve communication, and provide support to the family.

Examine Your Personal Beliefs

Examine your beliefs about your child and your child's disability. Do you feel sorry for your child? Do you feel guilt about your child's problems? As you try to protect your child from painful experiences, have you become over-protective?

Will pity, guilt, and over-protectiveness help your child become an emotionally healthy adults?

Children with disabilities learn differently. Because they learn differently, they must be taught differently. When they are taught correctly, they can and do learn.

Your Journey from Emotions to Advocacy

On your journey from emotions to advocacy, you'll learn about your child's disability, educational and remediation techniques, how to measure educational progress, IEPs, and how to artfully advocate. You are not alone. Other parents have traveled down this road. They walked on the same paths. Follow their footsteps.

Build a network of people who can help. Connect with other parents – they are always your best resource.

Counseling

The emerging importance of disability management within vocational rehabilitation Noun 1. vocational rehabilitation-providing training in a specific trade with the aim of gaining employment rehabilitation- the restoration of someone to a useful place in society and rehabilitation counseling rehabilitation counseling, *n* counseling started in the United States in 1920 to assist individuals disabled by industrial accidents; originally included physical, psychologic, and occupational training; expanded over the next 70 years and laid the has been recognized for over a decade (Bruyere & Shrey, 1991; Crystal, 1987; Gilbride, Stensrude, & Johnson, 1994; Habeck, Kress, Scully, & Kirchner, 1994; Kilbury, Benshoff, & Riggar, 1990; Matkin, 1987; McMahon & Matkin, 1983; Olsheski, 1996; Riggar, Crimando, Bordieri & Phillips, 1988; Rosenthal, 1997; Shrey & Mitchell, 1986). However, the degree of progress made in convincing employers that they are the most appropriate professionals to help manage disability at the work place remains debatable de·bat·a·ble *adj.*

1. Being such that formal argument or discussion is possible.
2. Open to dispute; questionable.
3. In dispute, as land or territory claimed by more than one country. and difficult to quantify Quantify- A performance analysis tool from Pure Software.. The following discussion highlights some of the concerns that affect the potential employment of rehabilitation counseling professionals in employer-based disability management programmes.

Concern one: The nature and quality of disability management programmes among employers are highly variable. Consequently, employers may not have consistent conceptualizations of the responsibilities and job requirements of a disability management specialist.

A primary concern within rehabilitation counseling has been an increasing emphasis on meeting employer needs in preventing and managing employees' disabilities. However, the connection between the rehabilitation rehabilitation: see physical therapy. counselor's skills and the disability management needs of the employer has not been made as directly or expeditiously ex·pe·di·tious *adj.*

Intervention by Multi-disciplinary Team

The growing acceptance and implementation of the team approach are not solely the results of federal mandates. They also reflect early intervention professionals' view of human development that regards a child as an integrated and interactive whole, rather than as a collection of separate parts (Golin & Ducanis, 1981). The team approach also recognizes that the multifaceted problems of very young children are too complex to be addressed by a single discipline (Holm & McCartin, 1978). The complexity of developmental problems in early life (Fewell, 1983) and the interrelated nature of an infant's developmental domains are prompting early intervention specialists to recognize the need for professionals to work together as a team.

Although different team models are in use, most are composed of professionals representing a variety of disciplines: special education; social work; psychology; medicine; child development; and physical, occupational, and speech and language therapy. All teams also involve the family in varying ways and degrees. Team members share common tasks including the assessment of a child's developmental status and the development and implementation of a programme plan to meet the assessed needs of the child within the context of the family.

What may best distinguish early intervention teams from one another is neither composition nor task, but rather the structure for interaction among team members. Three service delivery models that structure interaction among team members have been identified and differentiated in the literature: multidisciplinary, interdisciplinary, and transdisciplinary (Fewell, 1983; Linder, 1983; Peterson, 1987; United Cerebral Palsy National Collaborative Infant Project, 1976).

Multidisciplinary Teams

On multidisciplinary teams, professionals from several disciplines work independently of each other (Fewell, 1983). Peterson (1987) compared the mode of interaction among members of multidisciplinary teams to parallel play in young children: "side by side, but separate" (p. 484). Although multidisciplinary team members may work together and share the same space and tools, they usually function quite separately. Interaction among team members in the multidisciplinary approach does not foster services that reflect the view of the child as an integrated and interactive whole (Linder, 1983).

This can lead to fragmented services for children and confusing or conflicting reports to parents. Another concern about the multidisciplinary model is the lack of communication between team members that places the burden of coordination and case management on the family. In contrast, both the interdisciplinary and transdisciplinary approaches avoid the pitfalls of multidisciplinary service fragmentation by having the team develop a case management plan that coordinates both their services and the information that is presented to the family.

Interdisciplinary Teams

Interdisciplinary teams are composed of parents and professionals from several disciplines. The difference between multidisciplinary and interdisciplinary teams lies in the interaction among team members. Interdisciplinary teams are characterized by formal channels of communication that encourage team members to share their information and discuss individual results (Fewell, 1983; Peterson, 1987).

Regular meetings are usually scheduled to discuss shared cases. Representatives of various professional disciplines separately assess children and families, but the team does come together at some point to discuss the results of their individual assessment and to develop plans for intervention. Generally, each specialist is responsible for the part of the service plan related to his or her professional discipline.

Although this approach solves some of the problems associated with multidisciplinary teams, communication and interaction problems (*e.g.*, influence of "professional turf") may impinge upon the team process.

Transdisciplinary Teams

Transdisciplinary teams are also composed of parents and professionals from several disciplines. The transdisciplinary approach attempts to overcome the confines of individual disciplines in order to form a team that crosses and recrosses disciplinary boundaries and thereby maximizes communication, interaction, and cooperation among team members. Fundamental to this model are two beliefs: (1) children's development must be viewed as integrated and interactive, and (2) children must be served within the context of the family. Since they have the greatest influence on their children's development, families are seen as a very critical part of the transdisciplinary team and are involved in setting goals and making programmatic decisions for themselves and their children. All decisions in the areas of assessment and programme planning, implementation, and evaluation are made by team consensus.

Although all team members share responsibility for the development of the service plan, it is carried out by the family and one other team member who is designated as the primary service provider. Another characteristic of a transdisciplinary team is that team members accept and accentuate each other's knowledge and strengths to benefit the team, the child, and the family (Lyon & Lyon, 1980). Staff development in the form of mutual training may occur at three increasing levels of complexity: (1) sharing general information; (2) teaching others to make specific judgments; and (3) teaching others to perform specific actions. The first two levels pertain to the sharing of information while the third level pertains to the sharing of roles.

Referral Services

Disability is largely a neglected problem in the developing countries Part of the problem lies in the very erroneous structure of medical education which has all along been putting the onus of disability management on tertiary care services seemg no role for the primary care physician Over the years, the management of disability has become synonymous with rehabilitation The general practitioner, working in a rural set up, has conveniently been holding the ominous belief that he has no role to play in the management of disability The centralized, institution-based services, being expensive, have remained out of reach to the vast majority of the disabled populations Consequently, 98% of the disabled people in the developing world remain totally neglected

Contrary to the commonly-held belief, disability is a colossal global health problem, which cant be tackled by the tertiary, highly specialized, institutional services alone This has led to the worldwide awakening that all doctors working anywhere should be sensitized to disability and its management The Government of India established an autonomous body, the Rehabilitation Council of India which, in addition to its regulatory functions, undertook the huge task of orienting each and every doctor of the country to disability management In the J & K State the programme started in April 2000 and till March 2003, 510 doctors had already been oriented.

Each 3-day training sessioit begins with pre-evaluation of the trainees about various aspects of disability, analysis of which reveals their pre-orientation awareness, beliefs & attitudes The results are shared here to give an idea of the widely prevalent ignorance & wrong perceptions among the medical profession, which in turn shows the need and cost-effectiveness of such orientat.on trainings.

UNIT-VIII

Vocational Training and Community Based Rehabilitation

Concept of Sheltered Workshop

Sheltered workshops, founded by Mentally Retarded Citizens of Missouri are state supported vocational programmes designed to provide work for persons with mental retardation/ developmental disabilities. They were established under Senate Bill #52 in 1968 and provide employment for over 8,000 handicapped individuals in Missouri.

Value

Shelter Workshops provide basic needs for the handicapped and the community including:

"*Pay Check*" allows the handicapped to perform a service for society by earning a portion of their livelihood.

"*Responsibility*" gives them the responsibility of coming to work and doing a job.

"*Asset to Business*" performs a service to competitive industry in jobs that are labour intensive.

"*Socialization*" working side by side with their buddies.

In addition it's probably the greatest *Respite* programme ever designed for parents and guardians, because they have the peace of mind that their son or daughter is safe, secure and a productive member of society.

Funding Increased for Sheltered Workshops

The St. Louis County Productive Living Board gave sheltered workshops an additional $1.6 million at a recent meeting in response to a local parents group's request.

The Parents Advocacy Group (PAG) asked the PLB for a bigger share of the approximately $14 million in tax dollars collected from personal property and real estate taxes from county residents. That money is appropriated for sheltered 0workshops, residential facilities and other related services.

About $500,000 of the $14 million went to sheltered workshops, and PAG wanted more.

Before about 200 parents at the Nov. 15 meeting, the PLB unanimously approved giving sheltered workshops an additional $1.6 million for building acquisitions or improvements, bringing the total funds for sheltered workshops to about $2.1 million.

"Everything has resolved itself, but we will still watch them like hawks," said PAG president Bert Sterbenz.

Three facilities – Florissant Valley, Lafayette Industries in Manchester and ITE in Berkely – will each receive $467,000 for their facilities.

"We are very pleased with the way it came out" said Steve Frank, executive director of the Florissant Valley Sheltered Workshop, which employs 190 persons at two workshops.

Sheltered workshops employ developmentally disabled adults for a variety of subcontracting work, such as packaging, mailing and sorting services for area companies.

The employees work about 30 hours per week and are paid wages based on their abilities to produce compared to normal standards, Frank said.

Another facility, Canterbury Industries in Crestwood, will receive $250,000. Two other facilities, Work Activity Center in South County and Universal Sheltered Workshop in Jennings, are in much better shape and will wait in the wings for more money, Sterbenz said.

PLB member Laurie Donovan, a former state representative and long-time sheltered workshop supporter, was pleased with the meeting's outcome.

"I came away very satisfied." She said. "I didn't hear anyone complain/"

Donovan said she was impressed by the turnout of parents at the meeting.

"I was very, very moved by the testimony of the parents." She said. "They spoke so passionately and explained things in such a way that made it clear how important sheltered workshops are to their family members."

For over tow years, Mentally Retarded Citizens of Missouri has been working with the Greater St. Louis Parents Advocacy Group, Inc., St. Louis County Workshop Managers, Donna Mueller of Senator Schneider's office and Jim McHugh of Buzz Westfalls' office to facilitate the PLB allocating a "fair share" of its tax revenue to sheltered workshops. As you can see from this Nov. 25 reprint of the Citizen Journal, MISSION ACCOMPLISHED!

A Parent's View of her Mentally Retarded Son

There is no parent in this world who prays for a handicapped or mentally retarded baby. All prayers are for a baby with 10 fingers and 10 toes and everything to be all right.

Most parents are blessed with the answer to that prayer. However, some are blessed with a slightly different answer. Those parents become the parents of a special child. While that child is young, his differences do not seem so great, as the parents and family think: Our child will outgrow his problems. He will do better than the doctors think. Therapy will help. My child will improve significantly and be almost normal. He will have a normal future.

While the child is still little, funding is not too difficult to secure for his special needs. Doctors recommend agencies that can be of assistance. Besides, the child is so cute! As the child grows, a shuffle develops, perhaps a drool sets in, his attention span is short, things that should not be funny are. Persons notice the differences more. Whispers or snickers do not go unheard. Other children and teens pick on him and get him in trouble when he tries to stand up for himself. His ability to learn has reached its peak at third grad. Schools keep trying to teach him fractions, division, history, science, things that have no meaning for him. REALITY SETS IN.

This wonderful child who is your son or daughter is not going to be able to survive out in the competitive world. This child, who is so special to your is not special to others, but is taken advantage of, stared at, and avoided. He is going to need sheltered employment if he is to grow up to be a productive individual and feel good about himself. That is why parents a number of years ago formed into support groups and then worked for legislation to create sheltered workshops. Because those parents understood that the productive capabilities of their children were not as great as the productive capabilities of persons in competitive employment, they worked to pass further legislation to provide funding to establish sheltered workshops and keep them operating. They also sponsored the Senate Bill 40 tax levy that was authorized by the State Legislature to enhance these programmes.

I am so pleased and thankful that these programmes are available to my son.

Editor's Note: This is an excerpt of a press release to the Macon Chronicle-Herald from Janet Ryan, whose son worked at the Macon County Sheltered Workshop.

From the Citizen Journal, Thursday, November 25, 1999

Defense of Sheltered Workshops

There is currently a movement to change the mission of sheltered workshops. The Missouri Department of Mental Health is closing its workshop in St. Joseph and placing the workers in supportive employment. SB40 organizations are trying to distance themselves from their founders, sheltered workshops. Some workshop managers along with the Department of Elementary and Secondary Education want to hire normal workers for the workshop.

This changes the original concept form sheltered employment to integrated employment infusing the pressures of competition and productivity.

Supportive employment takes workers out of the full time work environment of the workshop and places them in fifteen hours per week part time employment. What do they do the rest of the time? Who watches over them? Do they get to socialize with their buddies?

What is even worse now that many have been moved into the community with inadequate support, they are "home alone" to be used and abused when they should be in a structured environment.

This is not acceptable. This defeats the purpose of the workshop programmes in the first place. The workshop was designed by parents to give their sons and daughters dignity, self worth and socialization with their peers.

Parents are not going to let theorists destroy the most successful programme in all the disability field!

It's tough to run hab centers, group homes, sheltered workshops, etc. It takes, brick and mortar, supervision, technical skill and work. That's right, plain old hard work. Parents are tired of bureaucrats and professionals designing programmes that are "easy" to administer *i.e.* "pass the money around." It's time they go back to work and design programmes for the mentally retarded. That's what they supposedly are paid to do!

It's time for professionals in the field of mental retardation to wake up! Place common sense back into your repertoire. Persons with mental retardation are not normal and they never will be. Quit trying to make them something they are not! Let's give the mentally retarded the help to attain their constitutional right of the pursuit of happiness instead of placing them in environments without adequate supports.

Workshops are for the Handicapped

House Bill 1415 allows normal workers into Sheltered Workshops. We oppose this measure because it will do irreparable harm to our sons and daughters. We have been advocates for them for over 40 years and have found through those many years of experience that the Sheltered Workshop is the only place where our sons and daughters are not pushed to be normal- the only place where they are not pressured to compete with normal persons and the only place where they are not used and abused. Sheltered Workshops brought the out of the Middle Ages!

While it is true that a small percentage of the mentally retarded can be successful in the normal workplace provided there are adequate supports, the vast majority of persons with Mental Retardation cannot function in normal settings.

Nothing can replace the smiles on our sons' and daughters' faces as they work and interact with their peers in a stress-free environment. Nothing can replace their pride in a job well done. Nothing can replace their self esteem at being the best!

Editor's Note: Following is a response by Majorie Zeller, a parent, to a letter supporting SB707 by the president of the Workshop Managers Association, Peggy Kutchback. March 4, 1996.

Peggy Kutchback, president of MASWM sent a paper to Missouri Sheltered Workshop manager in support of Senate Bill 707. She states that the only organized opposition to this bill is from "Missouri Association for Retarded Persons", a group she discounts. The Greater St. Louis Parents Advocacy Group for Mentally Retarded Citizens, Inc. opposes SB 707. We are not Mentally Retarded Citizens of Missouri. She further states that arguments against the bill are "insubstantial." We do not consider our carefully thought out objections to the bill unworthy of consideration.

She says that workshops were formed back when persons with disabilities were called retarded and needed protection against the risks and demands of the competitive world. The politically correct term "person with a disability" can mean everything from severe arthritis to colour blindness. We shall use the more precise word "retarded" to indicate mental slowness. Those with this characteristic still need a degree of help and protection. To deny them this is on a par with denying a wheel chair to those who cannot walk. Our children's shops provide encouragement, supervision, jobs they find exciting and challenging, the pride of accomplishing meaningful work, compatible peers and the all important pay check. In short; the rewards of a successful career.

Missouri Sheltered Workshops are now mandated to serve the mentally retarded. Kutchback displays great distaste for this arrangement, apparently overlooking the fact that no one is forced into a workshop. Other opportunities abound. In fact, many agencies steer clients away form workshops and toward supported employment and other costly options that siphon funds from traditional programmes.

Kutchback correctly states that workshop managers "support the voluntary movement of workshop employees" into competitive employment. The problem is that they often make it difficult to return after the humiliation of repeated firings.

Ms. Kutchback states that non-disabled workers will be role models. Does she really believe that wholesome stable workers will flock to sheltered workshops? She advises us to have no concern about "workers who would be detrimental" because the integrated programmes would be approved of and monitored by a governmental agency. The news is full of tragic stories of abuse which agencies could not prevent.

In another part of the paper, she states that there are not enough jobs for "workers who require a high level of support" and thoughtfully translates this to the understandable term "lower functioning employee." Yes, our workshop employees are low functioning which is why they need the help a workshop is mandated to provide. Many St. Louis area shops turn away employees and contracts because of space constraints. The inclusion minded PLB, the group that controls the revenue dollars marked "Sheltered Workshops" on St. Louis County tax bills, denies funds for expansion. Non-disabled workers entering one of these shops would displace retarded workers. There is not other possible scenario.

Workshops are not intended to be competitive and managers should be committed to the sometimes frustrating job of encouraging the lower functioning to be somewhat productive.

Ms. Kutchback condescendingly explains that any disagreement with her position is because "Parents are just afraid of change." This is thoroughly untrue. The point is that we don't want to change the things that make our children's lives happy and satisfying. A recent poll by the PLB reported 85% satisfaction with sheltered workshops as they now exist. Why did the "segregated" shops achieve such a high rating? Why did they achieve a higher rating than any other form of employment? We think it's because by the time retarded children reach adulthood, their families grow in another way. Dreams of "cures" and prestige jobs blossom into acceptance and appreciation of their children's happiness with their peers and their special place in life.

Peggy Kutchback may label our concerns insubstantial, but they are heartfelt and come from years of experience.

Transitory Employment

Schedule-2

Transitional Provlslons, Savings and Transitory Provlslons

Part I- Transitional Provisions and Savings General Transitionals and Savings

1. The substitution of this Act for the provisions repealed or revoked by this Act does not affect the continuity of the law.

2(1). Anything done, or having effect as done, (including the making of subordinate legislation) under or for the purposes of any provision repealed or revoked by this Act has effect as if done under or for the purposes of any corresponding provision of this Act.

2(2). Sub-paragraph (1) does not apply to the making of any subordinate legislation to the extent that it is reproduced in this Act.

3. Any reference (express or implied) in this Act or any other enactment, or in any instrument or document, to a provision of this Act is (so far as the context permits) to be read as (according to the context) being or including in relation to times, circumstances and purposes before the commencement of this Act a reference to the corresponding provision repealed or revoked by this Act.

4(1). Any reference (express or implied) in any enactment, or in any instrument or document, to a provision repealed or revoked by this Act is (so far as the context permits) to be read as (according to the context) being or including in relation to times, circumstances and purposes after the commencement of this Act a reference to the corresponding provision of this Act.

4(2). In particular, where a power conferred by an Act is expressed to be exercisable in relation to enactments contained in Acts passed before or in the same Session as the Act conferring the power, the power is also exercisable in relation to provisions of the Act which reproduce such enactments.

5. Paragraphs 1 to 4 have effect in place of section 17(2) of the Interpretation Act 1978 (but are without prejudice to any other provision of that Act).

Preservation of Old Transitionals and Savings

6(1). The repeal by this Act of an enactment previously repealed subject to savings (whether or not in the repealing enactment) does not affect the continued operation of those savings. 6(2). The repeal by this Act of a saving made on the previous repeal of an enactment does not affect the operation of the saving in so far as it remains capable of having effect. 6(3). Where the purpose of an enactment repealed by this Act was to secure that the substitution of the provisions of the Act containing that enactment for provisions repealed by that Act did not affect the continuity of the law, the enactment repealed by this Act continues to have effect in so far as it is capable of doing so.

Employment Particulars

7(1). In this paragraph "pre-TURERA employee" means an employee whose employment with his employer began before 30th November 1993 (the day on which section 26 of the Trade Union Reform and Employment Rights Act 1993 came into force), whether or not the provisions of sections 1 to 6 of the, Employment Protection (Consolidation) Act 1978, as they had effect before the substitution made by that section, applied to him before that date. 7(2). Subject to the following provisions of this paragraph, sections 1 to 7 of this Act do not apply to a pre-TURERA employee (but the provisions of sections 1 to 6 of the Employment Protection (Consolidation) Act 1978, as they had effect before the substitution made by section 26 of the Trade Union Reform and Employment Rights Act 1993, continue in force in his case). 7(3). Where a pre-TURERA employee, at any time- (a) on or after the day on which this Act comes into force, and (b) either before the end of his employment or within the period of three months beginning with the day on which his employment ends, requests from his employer a statement under section 1 of this Act, the employer shall (subject to section 5 and any other provision disapplying or having the effect of disapplying sections 1 to 4) be treated as being required by section 1 to give him a written statement under that section not later than two months after the request is made; and section 4 of this Act shall (subject to that) apply in relation to the employee after he makes the request. 7(4). An employer is not required to give an employee a statement under section 1 pursuant to sub-paragraph (3)- (a) on more than one occasion, or (b) if he has already given him a statement pursuant to paragraph 3(3) of Schedule 9 to the Trade

Union Reform and Employment Rights Act 1993. 7(5). Where- (a) on or after the day on which this Act comes into force there is in the case of a pre-TURERA employee a change in any of the matters particulars of which would, had he been given a statement of particulars on 30th November 1993 under section 1 of the Employment Protection (Consolidation) Act 1978 (as substituted by section 26 of the Trade Union Reform and Employment Rights Act 1993), have been included or referred to in the statement, and (b) he has not previously requested a statement under sub-paragraph (3) or paragraph 3(3) of Schedule 9 to the Trade Union Reform and Employment Rights Act 1993, subsections (1) and (6) of section 4 of this Act shall be treated (subject to section 5 and any other provision disapplying or having the effect of disapplying section 4) as requiring his employer to give him a written statement containing particulars of the change at the time specified in subsection (3) of section 4; and the other provisions of section 4 apply accordingly.

Monetary Limits in Old Cases

8. In relation to any case in which (but for this Act) a limit lower than set by Article 3 of the Employment Protection (Increase of Limits) Order 1995 would have applied in accordance with Article 4 of that Order, this Act has effect as if it reproduced that lower limit.

Shop Workers and Betting Workers to Whom Old Maternity Provisions Applied

9(1). This paragraph applies where an employee exercised a right to return to work under Part III of the Employment Protection (Consolidation) Act 1978 at a time when the amendments of that Part made by the Trade Union Reform and Employment Rights Act 1993 did not have effect in her case (so that her right was a right to return to work in the job in which she was employed under the original contract of employment). 9(2) Section 36(4) shall have effect as if for paragraph

(b) there were substituted:- "(b) under her original contract of employment, she was a shop worker, or a betting worker, but was not employed to work only on Sunday." 9(3). If the employee was employed as a shop worker under her original contract of employment, she shall not be regarded as failing to satisfy the condition in section 36(2)(a) or (c) or 41(1)(c) merely because during her pregnancy she was employed under a different contract of employment by virtue of section 6O(2) of the Employment Protection (Consolidation) Act 1978 (as it had effect before the commencement of section 24 of the Trade Union Reform and Employment Rights Act 1993) or otherwise by reason of her pregnancy. 9(4). In this paragraph, and in section 36(4)(b) as substituted by sub-paragraph (2), "original contract of employment" has the meaning given by section 153(1) of the Employment Protection (Consolidation) Act 1978 as originally enacted.

Validity of provisions deriving from certain regulations.

10. Any question as to the validity of sections 47,61, 62, 63 and 103 which derive from the Collective Redundancies and Transfer of Undertakings (Protection of Employment) Regulations 1995 made under subsection (2) of section 2 of the European Communities Act, shall be determined as if those provisions were contained in regulations made under that subsection.

Unfair Dismissal

11. Part X does not apply to a dismissal from employment under a contract for a fixed term of two years or more (not being a contract of apprenticeship) if:- (a) the contract was made before 28th February 1972, and (b) the dismissal consists only of the expiry of that term without its being renewed.

Redundancy Payments

12(1). Section 135 does not apply to an employee who immediately before the relevant date is employed under a contract for a fixed term of two years or more (not being a contract of apprenticeship) if the contract was made before 6th December 1965. 12(2). Section 197(3) does not apply if the contract was made before 6th December 1965.

Periods of Employment

13(1). The reference in section 215(2)(b) to a person being an employed earner for the purposes of the Social Security Contributions and Benefits Act 1992 in respect of whom a secondary Class 1 contribution was payable under that Act (whether or not it was in fact paid) shall be construed:- (a) as respects a week of employment after 1st June 1976 and before 1st July 1992, as a reference to a person being an employed earner for the purposes of the Social Security Act 1975 in respect of whom a secondary Class 1 contribution was payable under that Act (whether or not it was in fact paid), (b) as respects a week of employment after 6th April 1975 and before 1st June 1976, as a reference to a person being an employed earner for the purposes of the Social Security Act 1975, and (c) as respects a week of employment before 6th April 1975, as a reference to a person being an employee in respect of whom an employer's contribution was payable in respect of the corresponding contribution week (whether or not it was in fact paid). 13(2). For the purposes of the application of sub-paragraph (1) to a week of employment where the corresponding contribution week began before 5th July 1948, an employer's contribution shall be treated as payable as mentioned in that sub-paragraph if such a contribution would have been so payable had the statutory provisions relating to national insurance in force on 5th July 1948 been in force in that contribution week. 13(3). The references in subsection (4) of section 215 to the Social Security Contributions and Benefits Act 1992 include the Social Security Act 1975; and that subsection applies to any question arising whether an employer's contribution was or would have been payable as mentioned in sub-paragraph (1) or (2). 13(4). In this paragraph- "employer's contribution" has the same meaning as in the National Insurance Act 1965, and "corresponding contribution week", in relation to a week of employment, means a contribution week (within the meaning of that Act) of which so much as falls within the period beginning with midnight between Sunday and Monday and ending with Saturday also falls within that week of employment.

14(1). Subject to paragraph 13 and sub-paragraphs (2) and (3) of this paragraph, Chapter I of Part XIV applies to periods before this Act comes into force as it applies to later periods. 14(2). If, during the whole or any part of a week beginning before 6th July 1964, an employee was absent from work- (a) because he was taking part in a strike, or (b) because of a lock-out by his employer, the week counts as a period of employment. 14(3). Any week which counted as a period of employment in the computation of a period of employment for the purposes of the Employment Protection (Consolidation) Act 1978 counts as a period of employment for the purposes of this Act; and any week which did not break the continuity of a person's employment for the purposes of that Act shall not break the continuity of a period of employment for the purposes of this Act.

Part II- Transitory Provisions Occupational Pension Schemes

15(1). If sections 42 to 46 of the Pensions Act 1995 have not come into force before the commencement of this Act, this Act shall have effect with the omission of sections 46, 58 to 60 and 102 until the relevant commencement date. 15(2). The reference in sub-paragraph (1) to the relevant commencement date is a reference- (a) if an order has been made before the commencement of this Act appointing a day after that commencement as the day on which sections 42 to 46 of the Pensions Act 1995 are to come into force, to the day so appointed, and

(b) otherwise, to such day as the Secretary of State may by order appoint.

Armed Forces:

16(1). If section 31 of the Trade Union Reform and Employment Rights Act 1993 has not come into force before the commencement of this Act, this Act shall have effect until the relevant commencement date as if for section 192 there were substituted-

"Armed forces. 192. Section 191- (a) does not apply to service as a member of the naval, military or air forces of the Crown, but (b) does apply to employment by an association established for the purposes of Part XI of the Reserve Forces Act 1996." 16(2). The reference in sub-paragraph (1) to the relevant commencement date is a reference- (a) if an order has been made before the commencement of this Act appointing a day after that commencement as the day on which section 31 of the Trade Union Reform and Employment Rights Act 1993 is to come into force, to the day so appointed, and (b) otherwise, to such day as the Secretary of State may by order appoint.

17(1). If Part XI of the Reserve Forces Act 1996 has not come into force before the commencement of this Act, section 192 of this Act shall have effect until the relevant commencement date as if for "Part XI of the Reserve Forces Act 1996" there were substituted "Part VI of the Reserve Forces Act 1980" 17(2). The reference in sub-paragraph (1) to the relevant commencement date is a reference- (a) if an order has been made before the commencement of this Act appointing a day after that commencement as the day on which Part XI of the Reserve Forces Act 1996 is to come into force, to the day so appointed, and (b) otherwise, to such day as the Secretary of State may by order appoint.

18. (Disability Discrimination) is deleted by ERDRA 1998 sch 2 with effect from 1st August 1998- see Employment Rights (Dispute Resolution) Act 1998 (Commencement

No. 1 and Transitional and Saving Provisions) Order 1998, SI 1998/1658

Self-employment

Self-employment is where a person works for themselves rather than someone else or a company that they do not own. To be self-employed, an individual is normally highly skilled in a trade or has a niche product or service for their local community. With the creation of the Internet the ability for an individual to become self-employed has increased dramatically. The amount of money spent on self-help, self-improvement and training materials has reached the billions in the past decade.

Self-employed people can also be referred to as a person who works for himself/herself instead of an employer, but drawing income from a trade or business that they operate personally. To be self-employed is not the same as being a business owner: A business owner is not required to be hands-on with the day-to-day operations of his or her company, while a self-employed person has to utilize a very hands-on approach in order to survive.

Self-employment Law Germany

Taxation in the US: In the United States, a person is considered self-employed for tax purposes if that person is running a business as a sole proprietorship, independent contractor, as a member of a partnership, or as a member of a limited liability company that does not elect to be treated as a corporation. In addition to income taxes, these individuals must pay Social Security and Medicare taxes in the form of a SECA (Self-Employment Contributions Act) tax.

The self-employment tax in the United States is currently set at 15.30% which is the equivalent of the combined contributions of the employee and employer under the FICA tax. The rate consists of two parts: 12.4% for social security and 2.9% for Medicare. The social security portion of the self-employment tax only applies to the first $97,500 of income for the 2007 tax year. There is no limit to the amount that is taxable under the 2.9% Medicare portion of the self-employment tax. Half of the hypothetical self-employment tax is allowed as a deduction against self-employment income so only 92.35% of the self-employment income is taxable at 15.30%, an effective tax rate of about 14.13%. However, this benefit disappears if self-employment income exceeds $105,577, since the entire applicable amount of $97,500 will be taxed at 15.30%.

Self-employed persons are sometimes eligible for more deductions than an ordinary employee. Travel, uniforms, computer equipment, cell phones, etc., can be deducted as legitimate business expenses. Self-employed persons report their business income or loss on Schedule C of IRS Form 1040 and calculate the self-employment tax on Schedule SE of IRS Form 1040. Estimated taxes must be paid quarterly using form 1040-ES if estimated tax liability exceeds $1,000.

Many self-employed individuals choose to establish a corporate entity, in order to have more control over their tax liability. The advantage of a corporate structure is the ability to pay out profits as salary, which is subject to FICA tax, and dividends (called "distributions"), which are not subject to FICA tax. For example, if the business owner paid out 100% of profits to herself as a dividend, she could avoid approximately $14,900 in FICA taxes (both the employee and employer portions) on $100,000 in profits. However, since dividends are subject to double taxation at the corporate and personal level, it is advisable to seek professional tax advice on the most favorable distribution of profits.

Self-employed 401k Retirement Account

Self-employed workers cannot contribute to a 401k plan of the type with which most people are familiar. However, there are various vehicles available to self-employed individuals to save for retirement. Many set up a Simplified Employee Pension Plan (SEP) IRA, which allows them to contribute up to 25% of their income, up to $49,000 (2009) per year. There is also a vehicle called the Self-Employed 401k or SE 401k for self-employed people. The contribution limits vary slightly depending on how your business is organized but are generally higher than the other types of plans.

Self-employment Law in the United Kingdom

A self-employed person in the United Kingdom can operate as a sole trader or as an incorporated limited liability company. It is also possible for someone to form a business that is run only part-time or concurrently while holding down a full time job. This form of employment, while popular, does come with several legal responsibilities. When working from home clearance is required from the local authority to use part of the home as business premises. Should the business hold records of customers or suppliers in any electronic form it is required to register with the Information Commissioner's Office. Other legal responsibilities include statutory public liability insurance cover, modifying premises to be di. Free advice on the range of responsibilities is available from government operated Business Link centres.

Taxation in the UK

A self-employed person may be subject to more taxes than an average employee. In addition to both the employee and employer National Insurance contributions, there may be VAT, business rates and other taxes payable to central and local governments. Both in the US and the UK governments are cracking down on disguised employment, often described as the pretence of a contractual intra-business relationship to hide what is otherwise a simple employer-employee relationship.

Extended Employment

The Rehabilitation Act requires that CBVH conduct reviews and reevaluations of the status of individuals who have achieved an employment outcome in an extended employment setting. Reviews and reevaluations must take place for 2 years after the individual achieves their employment outcome and thereafter if requested by the individual or their representative.

Purpose of the Review

The purpose of the review is to determine the feasibility of a individual entering competitive employment and to provide assistance including the provision of vocational rehabilitation services, reasonable accommodations and other necessary support services wherever possible in the transition from extended employment to competitive employment (including supported and self-employment) through the provision of such services.

Scope of the Review

The review and reevaluation must include input by the individual, or if appropriate, the individual's representative. In addition, the review and reevaluation of the status of individuals closed in extended employment should include:

1. an examination of the individual's record of services including a review of the reasons for placement into extended employment,
2. a review of the individual's employment history in the community rehabilitation programme during the past year including productivity and work adjustment,
3. a determination as to whether any progress or change has occurred in the individual's readiness for competitive employment,
4. a determination as to whether the provision of additional rehabilitation services, reasonable accommodations and/ or other support services may lead to competitive employment.

A signed acknowledgment that the review and reevaluation has taken place must be obtained from the individual.

Other Factors to Consider During the Review

In addition to the above minimum review criteria, other issues to consider include new production techniques or equipment which may aid the individual in employment and the current job market.

Outcome of the Periodic Review

The periodic review of extended employment may result in:

1. continuation of the individual in extended employment, or

2. the provision of post-employment services, or
3. reopening the individual's case.

Note: In some instances, the counselor will require a vocational assessment when:

1. existing information is not sufficient for a determination of the individual's readiness for competitive employment, or
2. the counselor wants to know whether the provision of rehabilitation services is likely to make the individual ready for competitive employment.

This service will be provided as a post-employment service in Status 32.

Who Conducts the Review?

The senior counselor is responsible for determining who will conduct the review of extended employment. In most cases the reviewer will be a VR counselor.

How to Complete the Review?

To complete the review, the designated individual will interview the individual, community rehabilitation programme staff and where appropriate, the individual's representative and will review the individual's record of services. Available and appropriate information from the community rehabilitation programme may be used to assist the reviewer during the review process. Examples of such information are agency reviews, reports, and vocational assessment.

Number of Reviews

Individuals in extended employment will be reviewed for two consecutive years. If the two reviews indicate that no significant change has taken place in the individual's job readiness or prospect for competitive employment, succeeding reviews will take place only at the request of:

1. the individual,
2. the individual's representative, or
3. the community rehabilitation program's representative.

Recording the Review

The outcome of the review will be recorded on the form titled Periodic Review of Persons Placed in Extended Employment.

Where to File the Form

After appropriate signatures are secured on the form, it will be placed in the individual's file and become part of the record of services.

Reporting Requirement

The outcome of the periodic reviews of persons in extended employment is reported to the Rehabilitation Services Administration (RSA) by Central Office annually. District offices will be asked to report the outcomes of their reviews to Central Office at the end of each State fiscal year.

Community Based Rehabilitation (CBR)

It is a strategy within general community development for the rehabilitation, equalization of opportunities and social inclusion of all people with disabilities. The primary objective of CBR is the improvement of the quality of life of people with disability / marginalized persons. Key principles relating to CBR are equality, social justice, solidarity, integration and dignity CBR is not an approach that only focuses on the physical or medical needs of a person or delivering care to disabled people as passive recipients. It is not outreach from a centre. It is not determined by the needs of an institution or groups of professionals, neither it is segregated and separate from services for other people.

Conversely CBR involves partnerships with disabled people, both, adults and children, their families and careers. It involves capacity building of disabled people and their families, in the context of their community and culture. It is an holistic approach encompassing physical, social, employment, educational, economic and other needs. It promotes the social inclusion of disabled people in existing mainstream services. It is a system based in the community, using district and national level services. Institutional rehabilitation provides excellent services to address the problems of individual disabled person and is often available only for a small number at a very high cost. Moreover, the endeavor in an institution, is often out of context to the felt needs of the disabled person, and thus falls short of their expectations. In an institutional rehabilitation programme, the community is not linked with the process. Hence, when the disabled person returns home, it may become difficult for them to integrate into their community.

Disability often requires life-long management, therefore, activities aimed at enabling people with disability should be community based as much as possible. Sustainability is the ability of project or programme to continue to address needs as long as needs exist. The most basic rehabilitation activities can be carried out in the person's own community. A multi - sectoral / multi- disciplinary concept of CBR is to be adopted. This concept emphasizes working with and through the community. In response to this conceptual change, CBR is now defined as a community development programme that has seven different components –

I. Creation of a positive attitude towards people with disabilities
II. Provision of rehabilitation services
III. Provision of education and training opportunities
IV. Creation of micro and macro income – generation opportunities
V. Provision of long term care facilities
VI. Prevention of causes of disabilities
VII. Monitoring & Evaluation.

The core values of individual dignity, autonomy or self-determination, equality and the ethic of solidarity are fundamentals of human rights law that concern disability. To achieve this there is an increased focus on the participation and involvement of disabled people and their representatives

UNIT-IX

Students Awareness on Disability

Planning

Students find this site exciting and informative with fun articles about careers, recreation, education and skills. In Zones, hundreds of occupations are arranged by career cluster. Career Finder is a quick and easy self-assessment of interests and skills. Colorful graphics compare student's self-ratings of skills and interest to suggested occupations. Career Research Tool guides students through skills, values, interest and personailty inventories to generate career research leads. The sight license for CX Online allows for career exploration to be accessed both at school and at home on the Internet. Each suggested career can be explored in detail, and there are web links to professional associations, colleges that offer the required courses, and additional related articles. Ask the Career Center Coordinator for a username and password

Choices/College Selection

The Choices programme allows students to investigate over 6,000 two- and four-year colleges to develop an individualized list of colleges and universities according to personally selected criteria, such as location, size, majors, athletic and other special programmes, and financial aid availability. There are also direct links to the web pages for numerous colleges and universities listed and to online applications where these are available. Vocational/ technical schools can also be explored. Financial aid applications and scholarsihps available as well. This programme is available on the RMHS network. Students and parents are encouraged to make and appointment with Ms. Hull, Colege Career Coordinator, to do this college search. The internet version, Choices Planner, may be accessed at http://www.access.bridges.com using the same user name and password as for CX Online

Naviance (formerly called Tcci)

An internet-based programme designed to help counseling departments, students and parents navigate through the college application process. The Family Connection component allows students to do college searches, compare institutions, make contact with colleges in which they are interested and view scattergram data showing acceptance statistics of previous graduating classes of their own high school. Students can also use Naviance to build a resume, summarize post-secondary goals, and keep track of their college and scholarship applications. Students can obtain the web address for Naviance and their individual registration codes from their counselors or Ms. Hull.

Organizing and Conducting Programmes in the Community

"In democratic countries, knowledge of how to combine is the mother of all other forms of knowledge; on its progress depends that of all the others." — De Tocqueville

Once students are familiar with *colonias* either by viewing *The Forgotten Americans* video or through a class discussion, brainstorm a list of community problems in *colonias*. Ask your students if they feel that the problems outlined in the first part of the film can be solved. Ask them how optimistic they are about *colonias* families making changes to improve conditions in these South Texas communities. Select one or two video segments either the section about Rosie De Leija (13:43 to 17:08) or the segment about Veronica Cruz's work with *Proyecto Azteca* (29:17 to 31:31) or information about EPISO (31:32 to 34:11).

Remember you don't have to limit the discussion to *colonias*. Consider expanding the discussion to talk about Appalachian communities, Native American reservations or poor communities in your area. Check your local newspaper for a story about a community group who has organized and made a difference in your community. Use the glossary of terms and the discussion questions to help students understand grassroots organizing and some of the ways it has been done. Ask your students if they feel optimistic that these strategies can really make a difference. Ask what strategies your students think would work.

Once you feel comfortable that your students have a good understanding of grassroots organizing and community building, consider trying an experiment. Contact a local public official and let your students present their proposals to that official either at a community meeting or in the classroom. Have the official comment on the presentations. We encourage you to share your experiences from this discussion, class project, and essays. We also encourage you to give us feedback on what impact this unit had on your classroom and the experience of your students.

Media Selection for Role Play

To determine which medium we should use to advertise our product we must first understand our target market. This includes the following:

1. Knowing who they are. Are they consumers (all consumers (TurboTax, Quicken or Dell), or just select consumers (teenage to 35 year-old gamers (Sony Playstation)), Fortune 100, small business, etc. If they are all consumers, or a large part of the population, we can use mass market medium such as network TV, radio or general publications (weekly newspaper). If they are Fortune 100 or small business we might use specific trade publications that target our same markets.
2. Their buying process. Is the sale simple (a package of gum that is an instant decision), or complex--requiring

numerous complex presentations and layers of approvals (educational or government sales).

3. Who are the final decision makers, along with the primary and secondary influencers. For example, for a sales force automation decision, the final say may be the VP of Sales. However, the primary influencers may be the sales people and sales managers (who have to use it every day), plus the IT department (who has to support it). The secondary influencers may be the president (who wants more sales), the CFO (who has to finance it), and the secretary (who has to enter weekly leads).

   The percentage weight of influence of each person in the decision chain helps determine which medium and publications we may target. The VP of Sales may travel (so American Airlines magazine may work well). The Regional Sales Manager may be trying to move up (so Success Magazine may work). The IT department may need integration support (so CRM magazine may work), etc.

   I typically create a matrix showing the key decision and influencers within the market and have the most market--knowledgeable internal team members (product managers, sales managers, PR, etc.) come to a consensus as to which percentage weight we should assign to each group. This process is subjective, but usually yields fairly accurate results--when the numbers come in.

4. Where they buy. If the target buys from retail, we may use "Run of Press" ads (co-op ads with the retailers). If the target buys from VARs or Integrators, we may use VARBusiness to recruit more VARs (who in turn may use direct response mail to reach the targets). If they buy on-line--we may run direct response ads with an on-line or 800# call to action.

5. How they buy. If the customer buys on terms, our ads may mention financing options (cars, delayed payment).

6. What the competition is doing. We might use services such as AdScope (now TNS Media Intelligence) to compile a 12-month history of our competitor's campaigns so we can see their media targets and either apply a blocking campaign, were we match (and counter) a competitor's campaign, or use a separatist campaign, where we fish in a different pond entirely (assuming we know the market better than they do--which should be the case). Or we may choose to do some of both.
7. What has worked for us in the past (which media and ad format generated the most revenue?). This is one of the most difficult steps since most companies do not capture this information. If nothing is in place, then you must extrapolate the data from whatever sources you have. You must also fix this problem immediately and setup a complete tracking system--or you will not have the managerial information you need to determine which medium is working best (TV, Radio, Publications (and which of the publications is working best)--*i.e.*, are you fishing in the right pond, nor will you know which ad format and message is working best (do you have the right bait). See the later section within advertising on Tracking & ROI to see how to set this up.

Understanding your customer and being able to answer each of the previous questions is the hard part. Finding media that targets our same prospect is actually the easy part.

Selecting the Correct Media

The next step is to determine which medium type (TV, Radio, Display Ads) will reach your desired targets and generate the greatest ROI. It may be multiple types--if so, you should put a % weight value on each and consider your budget accordingly.

In the high-tech market (aside from consumer electronics (PlayStations, Dell, etc.)), the most widely used advertising medium is print. Within the print medium, the most common for high-tech is trade publications (rather than the general business and consumer publications like Newsweek, Fortune,

Popular Mechanics, Southern Living, etc.). Trade publications might include PC Magazine (general market), Network Computing (corporate networking), Videomaker (highly vertical video market), Gaming (obvious), etc.

The key is to find the right publication (the pond) that contains the most of your preferred target (type of fish).

Fortunately, there are several publications that can help you determine the demographics of various media and publications. For example, the Nielson Rating can tell you the audience demographics and ratings for specific network and cable stations and specific television shows. Other services like those from IAG Research can measure the performance of every ad. However, they often only measure recall within the channel, by brand, and the fit (how well it was integrated into the show). Based on these criteria, they rate as "most effective" those ads (brands) that are recalled by the most people. However, a more important indicator is not the recall scores, but the ads that actually sell and cause a change in brand preference.

You can find a fairly comprehensive on-line listing of TV, radio, newspapers, on-line, and trade magazines at Media Post. Registration is free and they even include a free on-line media scheduling tool.

If you are moving into a new market and don't know the most popular trade publications, then you will have to use media books (Bacon's is again helpful), internet resources, get help from alliances, and clients (ask what they read), or from a media buying company. If you are fairly certain of the publications you want to use, you can go to their web site (or call for a media kit) and get rates, demographics, circulation, frequency, etc.

If you talk to a rep, be cautions not to place too much merit when they say they cater to your market (I've had some sales reps try to sell me placement in a publication that was clearly not aimed at my target). The Editor in Chief understands the publication's target best since he/she must create content to appease that audience. This is one of the reason's I usually get PRs' assistance in the media selection--they know who covers your space by the type and number of articles produced for your desired target. The PR group also has the editorial schedule that helps identify the target audience.

The term role playing was originally coined in the 1920s by Jacob L. Moreno, a Viennese psychiatrist who surmised patients gained more from exploring their problems by acting them out than by talking about them. Moreno first tested out his ideas by forming the Theatre of Spontaneity acting company in 1921 and two years later publishing his theories in a book of the same name. When the practice became popular in business and educational institutions twenty years later the problem solving aspect shifted towards the learning of a professional role for later real life assumption.

"What astronauts do in their practice for missions; what pilots do in learning to navigate in flight simulators; what thousands of soldiers do in the course of military exercises—it's all role playing. Teaching salespersons to deal with customers, teaching doctors to interview patients, teaching teachers to deal with difficult situations, all these require some measure of actual practice and feedback."

After its inception into the realm of business, role playing has steadily flourished for over fifty years expanding into multiple areas of public and private life.. Formal examples include: teaching (especially in the development of social skills, communication skills, and interpersonal skills), self-help groups, organizational management, leadership training, professional training, scientific research in the social sciences, and even sports. Less formal examples have also arisen including: role playing games for entertainment, and sexual roleplaying practices. Now in the 21st century, role playing as a form of personal entertainment may be overtaking in numbers the more formal practice of educational roleplay.

Drama

Drama is the specific mode of fiction represented in performance. The term comes from a Greek word meaning "action" (Classical Greek: äñÜìá, *dráma*), which is derived from "to do" (Classical Greek: äñÜù, *dráô*). The enactment of drama in theatre, performed by actors on a stage before an audience, presupposes collaborative modes of production and a collective form of reception. The structure of dramatic texts, unlike other forms of literature, is directly influenced by this collaborative production and collective reception. The early modern tragedy *Hamlet* (1601) by Shakespeare and the classical Athenian tragedy *Oedipus the King* (c. 429 BCE) by Sophocles are among the supreme masterpieces of the art of drama.

The two masks associated with drama represent the traditional generic division between comedy and tragedy. They are symbols of the ancient Greek Muses, Thalia and Melpomene. Thalia was the Muse of comedy (the laughing face), while Melpomene was the Muse of tragedy (the weeping face). Considered as a genre of poetry in general, the dramatic mode has been contrasted with the epic and the lyrical modes ever since Aristotle's *Poetics* (c. 335 BCE)—the earliest work of dramatic theory.

The use of "drama" in the narrow sense to designate a specific *type* of play dates from the 19th century. Drama in this sense refers to a play that is *neither* a comedy nor a tragedy—for example, Zola's *Thérèse Raquin* (1873) or Chekhov's *Ivanov* (1887). It is this narrow sense that the film and television industry and film studies adopted to describe "drama" as a genre within their respective media. "Radio drama" has been used in both senses—originally transmitted in a live performance, it has also been used to describe the more high-brow and serious end of the dramatic output of radio.

Drama is often combined with music and dance: the drama in opera is sung throughout; musicals include spoken dialogue and songs; and some forms of drama have regular musical accompaniment (melodrama and Japanese Nô, for example). In certain periods of history (the ancient Roman and modern Romantic) dramas have been written to be read rather than performed. In improvisation, the drama does not pre-exist the moment of performance; performers devise a dramatic script spontaneously before an audience.

Puppetry

Puppetry is a form of theatre or performance which involves the manipulation of puppets. It is very ancient, and is believed to have originated 30,000 years BC. Puppetry takes many forms but they all share the process of animating inanimate performing objects. Puppetry is used in almost all human societies both as an entertainment – in performance – and ceremonially in rituals and celebrations such as carnival.

Most puppetry involves storytelling. The impact of puppetry depends on the process of transformation of puppets, which has much in common with magic and with play. Thus puppetry can create complex and magical theatre with relatively small resources.

Puppeteers on Puppetry

"Through puppetry we accept the outrageous, the absurd or even the impossible, and will permit puppets to say and do things no human could. We allow a puppet to talk to us when no one else can get us to speak. We allow a puppet to smile at us even when we have not been introduced. We also allow a puppet to touch us when a person would lose an arm for the same offence" (Anita Sinclair).

"Puppetry is a highly effective and dynamically creative means of exploring the richness of interpersonal communication. By its very nature, puppetry concentrates on the puppet rather than the puppeteer. This provides a safety zone for the puppeteer and allows for exploration of unlimited themes through a safe and non-threatening environment for communication". He adds, "Designing a puppet involves the same processes that a performer uses in building a character. A puppet must always have a valid reason for being. The marvellous thrill of puppetry is that puppets by their very nature do things that are not humanly possible. This allows for the imagination to explore countless different possibilities" (David Logan).

History of Puppetry

Puppetry is a very ancient art form, probably first originating about 30,000 years ago. Puppets have been used since the earliest times to animate and communicate the ideas and needs of human societies. Some historians claim that they pre-date actors in theatre. There is evidence that they were used in Egypt as early as 2000 BC when string-operated figures of wood were manipulated to perform the action of kneading bread. Wire controlled, articulated puppets made of clay and ivory have also been found in Egyptian tombs. Hieroglyphs also describe 'walking statues' being used in Ancient Egyptian religious dramas. The oldest written record of puppetry can be found in the written records of Xenophon dating from around 422 B.C.

Asia

Evidence of earliest puppetry comes from the excavations at the Indus Valley Civilization. Archaeologists have unearthed terracotta dolls with detachable heads capable of manipulation by a string dating to 2500 BC. Other excavations include terracotta animals which could be manipulated up and down a stick—archiving minimum animation in both cases. The epic Mahabharata; Tamil literature from the Sangam Era, and various literary works dating from the late centuries BCE to the early centuries of the Common Era—including Ashokan edicts—describe puppets. Works like the Natya Shastra and the Kamasutra elaborate on puppetry in some detail. The Javanese Wayang theater was influenced by Indian traditions. Europeans developed puppetry as a result of extensive contact with the Eastern World.

Some scholars trace the origin of puppets to India 4000 years ago, where the main character in Sanskrit plays was known as sutradhara 'the holder of strings'. China has had a flourishing history of puppetry for 2000 years, originally in pi-ying xi, the "theatre of the lantern shadows", or, as it is more commonly known today, Chinese shadow theatre. By the Song Dynasty (960-1279 AD), puppets played to all social classes including the courts, yet puppeteers (as in Europe) were considered from a lower social strata. In Taiwan, budaixi puppet shows, somewhat similar to the Japanese Bunraku, occur with puppeteers manipulating in the background or underground.

Some very experienced puppeteers can manipulate their puppets to perform various stunts (*e.g.* somersaults in the air).

Japan has many forms of puppetry. Perhaps the most famous is the bunraku. This developed out of Shinto temple rites, gradually becoming a highly sophisticated form of puppetry. Bunraku owes much to the two great puppeteers, Gidayu Takemoto and Monzaemon Chikamatsu. By 1730 it required three puppeteers to operate each puppet in full view of the audience. Originally, the puppeteers (dressed all in black) would become invisible when standing against a black background, while the torches illuminated only the carved wooden, beautifully painted and costumed puppets.

Dance

Dance is a sport and art form that generally refers to movement of the body, usually rhythmic and to music, used as a form of expression, social interaction or presented in a spiritual or performance setting. *Dance* is also used to describe methods of non-verbal communication (see body language) between humans or animals (bee dance, patterns of behaviour such as a mating dance), motion in inanimate objects (*the leaves danced in the wind*), and certain musical forms or genres. In sports, gymnastics, figure skating and synchronized swimming are *dance* disciplines while martial arts *kata* are often compared to dances.

Definitions of what constitutes dance are dependent on social, cultural, aesthetic, artistic and moral constraints and range from functional movement (such as folk dance) to virtuoso techniques such as ballet. Dance can be participatory, social or performed for an audience. It can also be ceremonial, competitive or erotic. Dance movements may be without significance in themselves, such as in ballet or European folk dance, or have a gestural vocabulary/symbolic system as in many Asian dances. Dance can embody or express ideas, emotions or tell a story.

Dancing has evolved many styles. Breakdancing and Krumping are related to the hip hop culture. African dance is interpretive. Ballet, Ballroom, Waltz, and Tango are classical styles of dance while Square and the Electric Slide are forms of step dances.

Every dance, no matter what style, has something in common. It not only involves flexibility and body movement, but also physics. If the proper physics is not taken into consideration, injuries *can* and are *likely* to occur.

Choreography is the art of creating dances. The person who creates (*i.e.*, choreographs) a dance is known as the choreographer.

Exhibition

Exhibitions are traditionally the space in which art objects (in the most general sense) meet an audience. The exhibit is universally understood to be for some temporary period unless, as is rarely true, it is stated to be a "permanent exhibition". In American English, they may be called "exhibit", "exposition" (the French word) or "show". In UK English, they are always called "exhibitions" or "shows", and an individual item in the show is an "exhibit".

Such expositions may present pictures, drawings, video, sound, installation, performance, interactive art or sculptures by individual artists, groups of artists or collections of a specific form of art. The art works may be presented in museums, art halls, art clubs or private art galleries, or at some place the principal business of which is not the display or sale of art, such as a coffeehouse. An important distinction is noted between those exhibits where some or all of the works are for sale, normally in private art galleries, and those where they are not. Sometimes the event is organized on a specific occasion, like a birthday, anniversary or commemoration.

Postal Display

1. *Rationale for Proposed Strategy:* Leprosy is a disease, which still strikes fear in the societies as a mutilating, disfiguring, contagious and incurable disease. Because of the horrifying nature of the enigmatic physical disfigurement and since no cure was discovered until

the 20th century, leprosy has, for centuries, been a highly stigmatizing disease. Though leprosy is not a disease of the poor, yet it affects poor to a much greater extent because of their social and economic vulnerability. The stigma attached to leprosy leads to loss of employment even before manual labour becomes more difficult due to disability, which often results from late or no treatment. It also leads to exclusion from society, causing physical and emotional distress. Even to this day, when leprosy is completely curable with MDT (multi drug therapy), some parts of India uphold the belief that leprosy is a divine curse, a punishment of the past sins, and a result of immoral sexual behavior. These beliefs reinforce the image of the *'leper'* as being physically and morally unclean, to be blamed for contracting the disease and therefore to be ostracized. The repulsive physical image, the fear of infection and the belief that it is incurable are the root causes of the inhuman treatment that is often meted out to those who have leprosy.

At all levels of society, leprosy often makes women more vulnerable, socially and economically, than men. Hence gender equity needs equal focus besides reducing stigma and discrimination. Mere information and education, to the sundry about the signs and symptoms of leprosy and its curability, shall not work. It is imperative to break the barrier between persons affected by leprosy and the rest of the society, by appealing to peoples' emotions and their ability to empathies with those they feared and shunned. NLEP workers also had to face such barriers and this is what led to a paradigm shift, of looking at this problem with a new perspective. Discrimination, and specially discrimination against a particular category of people, is the worst kind of human rights violation. Such categorizations are a creation of human mind. Disease is a condition of being human. It could happen to anyone. Simply, because some people have suffered from leprosy, they are put in a certain category and treated miserably.

This is thoroughly against the concept of human rights that should be enjoyed by all human beings, whatever their situation is and wherever they are. There has been no comprehensive attempt to reduce stigma based on scientific interventions addressing the total community with specific reference to leprosy. It is therefore high time a culturally acceptable stigma reduction programme is developed and executed.

As of now, with the elimination of leprosy having been achieved, it has to be sustained and initiatives for *"Leprosy Free India"* to be taken. To accomplish this mission the following challenges need to be addressed:

The Urban Challenge: Special IEC strategies and campaigns to reach urban audiences, comprises a key feature of the strategy that should soon be implemented in identified urban areas.

Other Special Groups: The high rates of leprosy in some districts in low prevalence states and the extremely high rates in some districts in endemic states indicate the need for area specific and target group specific focus in the years to come. Special efforts will have to continue to reach the poor and marginalized–women, tribal communities and hard to reach groups through customized IEC in focused areas. An integral aspect of program's IEC strategy is to reduce stigma towards women affected by leprosy, by empowering them to seek treatment and motivate them for self-reporting. Equally vital is to enhance the access of tribal groups to services and information, in order to counter the myths and misconceptions.

Focus on Providers: The program's IEC strategy has addressed the need to motivate providers; nevertheless they have received less attention than other target groups. In the post integration period, the focus will have to include improving quality of service delivery by motivating providers especially the new entrants in the system and counseling patients. Appropriate strategies and tools such as non-monetary recognition in local events- needs to be developed and implemented to recognize the contribution of the providers.

Advocacy: With the goal of the programme having been achieved the task ahead is even more daunting. This success will have to be sustained at all levels. This will help strengthen the image of the programme that influencers have, and motivate people associated with the programme at all levels. A significant advocacy task remains at the district level: the continued involvement of state/district/block and village level administrators and influencers remains a crucial and significant achievement of the programme goals.

Sustainability: The IEC experience in the leprosy programme holds valuable lessons for other programmes. In many ways, the leprosy programme has been part of the collective experience that has shown the way for other health programmes, namely polio, RCH, HIV/AIDS, TB, in which communication is a key component. IEC has become an integral part of service delivery, is an achievement the leprosy programme justifiably can be proud of. At the same time, the way ahead hold some challenges. These include addressing hard-to-reach groups and finding more cost effective and sustainable methods to implement IEC, focus on public awareness, devising a complain mechanism, remedial and redressal measures and last but not the least generate awareness within the leprosy affected persons. These steps would help to retain the momentum of IEC efforts so as to achieve and sustain the programme goal

2. *Objectives:* To develop—effective communication vis-à-vis the target audiences and take on the task of effectively delivering the same, specifically cover clients, health providers, influencers and the masses.

   To compliment—and support the detection and treatment services being provided through the General Health Care System, making it more acceptable to the population so that delay in reporting for diagnosis and treatment is reduced and better patient compliance in taking MDT course is achieved

   To strive to—remove stigma surrounding leprosy and prevent discrimination against leprosy affected persons.

Active—participation of communities & clients is developed through various means of communication.

3. *Targets and priorities:* The following persons / groups are main target to receive IEC/BCC services-

   Community- at—large and selected communities where stigma is more deep rooted.

   Leprosy—Affected Persons

   General Health—Care Staff

   Local NGOs and—Community Based Organizations (CBO)

   Disabled—Peoples Organizations (DPOs)

As per objectives of this strategy the priorities are as follow–

Leprosy—Affected Persons are to be empowered to fight against discriminations and for improved health seeking behavior. They are to be informed about all provisions for them and counseled for better compliance.

Communities in—endemic pockets and inaccessible areas are informed & encouraged for self reporting at early stage and participate in NLEP. Level of prevailing awareness and stigma varies from place to place, needing various need based IEC strategy.

Partners,—policy makers and administrator are encouraged to develop 'self care groups' and 'Community Based Rehabilitation' through advocacy meetings.

GHC-staff,—general practitioners and other service providers are oriented to scientific facts and means to improve quality of services and non discriminatory behavior thus preventing iatrogenic stigma. ASHA, AWW and volunteers should also be included in service provider group for IEC purpose.

4. *Plans for IEC / IPC / BCC Activities:* Activities for communication to change behaviors can be designed on principles of social marketing. Social marketing is a distinct marketing discipline that has evolved since the 1970s. Its focus is on influencing behaviors that will

improve social outcomes such as improving health or preventing injuries. Unlike marketing theories that aim to promote a certain brand of commercial product, its general intent is to improve people's quality of life. As such, it is a useful approach for public servants tasked with achieving behavioral change.

Social marketing is a practical approach that integrates the insights from individual, interpersonal and community theories and evidence. Typically, the approach aims to change both the individual and the environment around the individual. The changed behavior of individuals and the changed environment interact, gradually establishing new social norms.

Inter Personal Communication : The effective way to deal with difficult challenge of stigma removal is to embark on intensive inter-personal communication (IPC) with the target groups.

- Women mobilization we should take the confidence of females as well as head of the family in community. Women health workers/volunteers should be employed for awareness campaign in villages to reduce stigma. Group discussion especially with the women folk should be organized to motivate them for self reporting and provide correct knowledge about leprosy
- Old Leprosy Peoples' association usually old age people face more stigmas due to economic dependence than others. These individuals can be groomed as Peer Educators and used to disseminate the information on leprosy among other members, and also reporting the cases to Primary Health Centres. For this they could be given some kind of recognition, which would act as an incentive for more such people to come forward and support the community.
- Complain mechanism will help the leprosy affected persons or others to register or lodge a complain through a *toll free* number in case of discrimination at the workplace, family or society level. Besides the use of IVRS (interactive voice recognition system) will help

people to acquire information on leprosy on this toll free information.

- Remedial & redressal measures should be built in IEC campaigns so that the credibility of IEC massages remains high.
- Awareness within the affected persons: some healing therapies for leprosy affected persons shall aid these persons to build positive vibes and regain their lost confidence. These classes could be organized by the NGOs, CBOs in collaboration with other local level functionaries and govt. departments.
- Village level meetings village leaders should allow patients in different meetings, they should co-operate with patients and help them in their needs. Gram-Sabha can be organized where patients and villagers will participate together.
- Health camps in the village where leprosy affected persons as well as others are treated together and the villagers could observe the normal behavior of doctor with the patient.
- Cultural programme for leprosy awareness through regional folk arts. Street theatres, folk music, puppet show, dance theatre, rallies and house visits are to be organized for 'difficult to reach populations' and highly stigmatized population groups.
- Community feast organized during any local fare where leprosy affected persons also can serve food
- Advocacy meetings can be organized to reduce stigma & discrimination. Non discriminatory behavior of service providers is to be demonstrated.
- Sensitization of the media persons during above mentioned programme activities so that they write positive about leprosy affected persons, service providers
- Motivate the youth to come forward and educate the community about leprosy. Scouts and Guide, NYK volunteers, NCC cadets can take the lead role. Inviting

budding writers to write positive and motivational stories on leprosy

- Door to door contact and counseling- training volunteers within the community and educating them on various issues of leprosy, who in turn will educate the entire community. Advocacy of old age persons, religious leaders and motivating them to carry forward the message to other members of the community, as these people have more stigma. Organize group counseling and group meetings in the village.

Information spread through mass media remains important component as out -reach of electronic media is increasing and large number of people are informed in short time. The content of the information should be changed from frightening images of people disabled with leprosy to positive images of healthy cured persons sharing their experiences about the curability of leprosy. Such messages if came through the various programmes shown by Regional television will have to be the acceptance. Mass Media Activities being carried out by Central Leprosy Division directly are:

Kalyani and Non-Kalyani (TV Spots & Radio Spots) and News paper advertisement on Leprosy day. Kalyani programme has already been merged with other health programmes similarly Non-Kalyani programme can also be merged with these programmes.

- Awareness Generation- Certain level of awareness has developed in the communities due to the persistent efforts in communication during last decade. However continuous efforts are needed to cover the till now uncovered areas. Coverage will have to move from high risk centric to general community at large and high stigmatized population groups in particular.
- Advertisement through local newspapers, posters, wall writing
- Community Newspaper if available should be utilized for spreading such messages. This would give them a sense of oneness and ownership of the programme.

Through—community radio listening followed by discussions shall help to dispel myths and misconceptions

- Health Melas organized under NRHM are good platform for leprosy awareness stalls.s

GHC staff is to be equipped with IPC & counseling skills. Needy cases are counseled and target persons / groups are addressed properly by GHC staff so that the objectives are achieved at the earliest.

Other activities include -

- Hoarding
- Posters and exhibitions.
- Wall painting
- Rallies (including banners etc.)
- Quiz
- Folk Shows

IPC / advocacy meetings for Influencers/ opinion leaders

Implementation of IEC

Central Level: The Centre will provide leadership and develop core messages, mass media and advocacy events. Detailed planning, choice of communication channels and monitoring should be decentralized to ensure local relevance and wide reach of information.

State Level Activities: The states and districts will base their specific strategies on the core framework and messages, and will encourage local adaptation and innovation to reach all possible groups with the most appropriate communication tools. NRHM infrastructure on IEC will be utilized for maximum benefit. Inter-sectoral coordination at the State level would be needed for the effective implementation of the IEC strategy, through NRHM mechanism At the State level, various departments *e.g.* Health, Education, Panchayati Raj, ICDS Department would contacted for providing effective linkages.

The state have to get IEC action plan prepared by the districts as per local needs. And develop the state plan on IEC.

District Level Activities: At the District level a 'Advisory-cum-Monitoring Committee' or district coordinating Agency (DCA) need to be formed to prepare implementation plan in association with other health departments under NRHM and to carry out the activities jointly. Necessary instructions and leadership from the district collector to all the concerned departmental heads in the district for their active and effective involvement in favor of the leprosy awareness and stigma reduction will be very useful. Support should also be taken from the local MLAs and MP who will provide necessary backup for generation of people's movement in favour of leprosy.

The DCA will also coordinate with various other agencies in respect of development of location specific media, develop functional linkages with other key stake holders like the Self help groups, community based organizations etc, develop feedback and provide necessary modifications.

The DCA members can be identified from among the local NGOs., teachers training institute, community polytechnic or the local degree college.

Block Level Activities

— The Medical officer, block PHC will be the coordinator of IEC activities in the block.

— He may draw support from the Block Development Officer, Block Extension Educator, local NGOs, Panchayat leaders, teachers etc.

Banners, posters and hoardings could be placed at the venue of the Community Group Meetings.

Leaflets, broachers, posters could be used to disseminate information on leprosy, myths and misconceptions during the Focused Group Discussions.

Cultural Sensitivity: It has been characteristic of the development of IEC activities for NLEP that communities should be involved in a bottom-up approach this will help to reduce the distance between service providers, patients and communities. For example, special initiatives should be taken to decrease social distance between tribal communities and non-tribal service provides, targeting the latter to increase their understanding and tolerance of cultural variation.

Folk Art

Folk art describes a wide range of objects that reflect the craft traditions and traditional social values of various social groups. These art works from 'common folk' are generally produced by people who have little or no academic artistic training, nor a desire to emulate "fine art". In the collectibles and antique industry, these items are categorized by established techniques and styles of a particular region or culture. Along with painting, sculpture, and other decorative art forms, some also consider utilitarian objects such as tools and costume as folk art.

Decorative value

Antique folk art is distinguished from traditional art in that while it is collected today based mostly on its artistic merit; it was never intended as a category to be art for art's sake. Examples include: weathervanes, old store signs and carved figures, itinerant portraits, carousel horses, fire buckets, painted game boards, cast iron doorstops and many other similar lines of highly collectible "whimsical" antiques.

Characteristics

Characteristically folk art is not influenced by movements in academic or fine art circles, and, in many cases, folk art excludes works executed by professional artists and sold as "high art" or "fine art" to the society's art patrons. On the other hand, many 18th and 19th century American folk art painters made their living by their work, including itinerant portrait painters, some of whom produced large bodies of work.

Other terms that overlap with folk art are naïve art, Pop art, outsider art, traditional art, "self-taught" art and even "working class" art. As one might expect, all these terms have different connotations; but they are all at times used interchangeably with the term folk art, for which a satisfactory definition has proven hard to come by.

Psychology of Awareness

The Psychology Awareness Initiative was designed to give each teacher maximum flexibility in helping promote awareness of psychology in their schools and in their communities. Below is a list of suggestions put together by the TOPSS Board that may be used as a guide for implementing your own Psychology Awareness programmes. If you have any questions about any of these suggestions, please contact a board member for more information. Also, if you have a suggested activity that has worked for you, let us know so that we can include it on this list.

Find funding resources for conducting teaching workshops and conferences:

- Psychology Awareness on your Campus
  - o Use the school TV channel to promote psychology awareness or focus on specific psychology related issues.
  - o Make up t-shirts highlighting psychological information or people.
  - o Take out special advertisements or write an article for your school paper on psychology related issues.
  - o Perform a parody of a psychologist at school talent shows.
  - o Promote or create a school Psychology Club.
  - o Put psychological information on your class or school website.
  - o Have poster campaigns illustrating psychological issues.
  - o Sponsor psychological trivia contests and award prizes through school announcements or website.
  - o Invite professional speakers to your class and invite other classes to listen in.

  - o Hold a Psychology Fair.
  - o Showcase student work in psychology in a public area at school.
  - o Team teach with another teacher on coordinated lessons.
- Psychology Awareness in the Community
  - o Put on a display at the community/public library/ local museum.
  - o Put on a display or have an informational booth at a school Open House or PTSA meeting.
  - o Create a reach out programme with middle and elementary school aged students.
  - o Promote Mental Health Awareness in your community—help identify supportive resources.
  - o Create psychology trunks that illustrate different psychological principles and take them to community outlets.
  - o Create a service learning programme at your school for psychology students.
  - o Create a video highlighting the school's psychology programme or the field of psychology in general.
  - o Create a public website that includes information on psychology.
  - o Design or offer Continuing Education programmes in Psychology for the community.
  - o Invite College or Health Professionals to speak on psychological topics to the public.
  - o Create a Psychology Newsletter providing information to the community on psychological issues.
  - o Create bookmarks highlighting psychology information and make them available in your public library.

Psychology Awareness Through Student Research

- For the School Population:

  - o Create posters indicating how psychological research affects and improves our daily lives.
  - o Highlight student research projects in the school paper or poster displays in the library.
  - o Recognize past winners of psychology contests and fairs at your school and in the community newspaper.
  - o Use classrooms to gather data on relevant issues that can be shared with the school population.
  - o Communicate about the efficacies of different psychological treatments.
- For Parents
  - o Create a lesson or an activity that students can take back home to share with their parents or family.
- For other Teachers
  - o Research important issues relevant to education, teaching methodology, discipline or other teacher relevant topics and share this information.

Reporting

In writing, a report is a document characterised by information or other content reflective of inquiry or investigation, which is tailored to the context of a given situation and audience. The purpose of reports is usually to inform. However, reports may include persuasive elements, such as recommendations, suggestions, or other motivating conclusions that indicate possible future actions the report reader might take. Reports can be public or private, and often address questions posed by individuals in government, business, education, and science. Reports often take the structure of scientific investigation: Introduction, Methods, Results and Discussion (IMRAD). They may sometimes follow a problem-solution structure based on the audience's questions or concerns. As for format, reports range from a simpler format with headings to indicate topics, to more complex formats including charts, tables, figures, pictures, tables of contents, abstracts, summaries, appendices, footnotes, hyperlinks, and references.

UNIT-X

Policies and Legislation

Policies and Legislative Measures Pertaining to the Disabled

Disability and The Policy Agenda

The last two decades have seen disability issues occupy an increasingly prominent place on the policy agenda. This includes particular policy arenas- education, health, housing, transport- as well as discussions around anti-discrimination and human rights legislation that embrace disability on a number of fronts.

A contributory factor to the intensification of debate has been the disabled people movement, which by challenging discrimination and promoting individual rights, have politicised disability issues across all countries. The movement has highlighted notions of disadvantage and exclusion and has been contributory factor to the 'soup' of policy change. We now use a completely different vocabulary and way of thinking when discussing disability issues. There has been a parallel challenge to professionals, policy-makers and academics to ensure they work in partnership with disabled people.

No Enabling Measures for India's Disabled

They still struggle to live with dignity due to state apathy. Observing December 3 as the World Disability Day, a peaceful demonstration was staged in the Indian capital to protest against government's failure to provide education, health and employment to people with disability.

The jubilation has been short-lived. The excitement and enthusiasm that greeted the news that India had ratified the United Nations Convention on Rights of Persons with Disabilities and the 11th Five-Year Plan which endorsed the ratification with important mandates, have given way to anger.

More than a year has passed, and with World Disability Day on December 3, there is still no sign of the government fulfilling any of its promises.

In India barely 50% of disabled children reach adulthood; no more than 20% survive to middle age.

To protest this inaction, people with disability and their relatives, friends, teachers and activists staged a peaceful dharna (demonstration) at India Gate, Delhi, on December 3 and continued the vigil throughout the winter night to shame a government that has failed to provide education, health and employment to people with disability.

"These are basic but crucial issues," said Javed Abidi, convenor of Disabled Rights Group. "These are achievable goals and the government must take responsibility."

Among the demands are those policies enshrined in the 11th Five-Year Plan -- implementation of a clear plan of action on disability issues by the ministry and allocation of 3% of its resources to the disabled.

"How long does it take for the system to wake up and understand that the Convention and the 11th Plan are not mere documents but policies that need to be actually carried out? Is a year not long enough to wait, watch and hope?" asks Abidi.

The Plan's four-pronged approach includes the suggestion that the concerned departments not only formulate detailed rules and guidelines but also set up monitoring mechanisms at various levels and develop a review system.

Unfulfilled Promises

For disability rights activists, this day is a grim reminder that empty promises offer little reason to celebrate. According to Census 2001, persons with disability constitute over 2% of the country's total population, which, activists say, is clearly an underestimate in a huge country like India.

They point out that in South Asia itself, Bangladesh reported 5.6% and Sri Lanka reported 7.0% of disabled people among their respective total populations, while 6.3% of China's population has a disability of some kind.

Worse for India is the fact that, according to a 2007 World Bank Report, barely 50% of disabled children reach adulthood; no more than 20% survive to middle age.

"It is very humiliating to have to carry my daughter in our public transport, eyed by curious onlookers"

A serious deficiency in the census data is the adoption of a definition that varies from the definition in the Persons with Disabilities Act, 1995. "There is an urgent need to draw up proper definitions and a system of data collection relating to persons with disability," says Shampa Sengupta, director of Sruti Disability Rights Centre. Activists assume that even at a conservative level, persons with disability constitute anywhere between five to six percent of India's total population.

Every year, on World Disability Day, to show that it is working on the problem, the government felicitates a few disabled students who fare well in their exams, or a few employers who have given employment to people with disabilities.

"What is the significance of felicitating 20 such students when only one percent of the disabled population has access to education? Disability is not an issue of charity- disabled people have equal rights as non-disabled people," says Sengupta.

The insensitivity of the administration to the problem is evident everywhere. In response to several public interest litigations, the Supreme Court has directed that people with disability must be able to access public transport.

But for a few exceptions like the Delhi Metro, which has made provision for people in wheelchairs and for the blind, bus, train and aeroplane services across the country remain indifferent to the special needs of disabled people. There are no ambu-lifts to assist the disabled in boarding aeroplanes, nor are trains equipped to allow wheelchairs through the narrow passages between seats and berths.

Legislative Measures

Critical Elements: There are a number of critical elements that are needed in implementing legislation, whether it takes the form of one or more separate laws. The legislation should:

* Refer explicitly to the Convention and to the Convention's acknowledgement that the concept of disability is still evolving, and to the notions of "discrimination on the ground of disability," "reasonable accommodation" and other important terms defined in the Convention;
* Prohibit discrimination on the ground of disability in all areas covered by the Convention;
* Identify duty-bearers, including different levels of government and non-State actors;
* Confer rights on individuals and groups to:
    - Raise allegations of discrimination on the ground of disability;
    - Have those claims investigated; and
    - Have access to appropriate remedies;
* Provide for independent agencies to:
    - Hear allegations of systematic discrimination and individual cases;
    - Investigate and report on those allegations; and
    - Seek systematic remedies and change through appropriate legal and other channels.

Linking Implementing Legislation to the Convention

Implementing legislation should include the terms of the Convention or a specific reference to them, in order to indicate clearly that the laws should be interpreted in accordance with the letter and spirit of the Convention.

The Convention is based on an understanding that disability results from the interaction between a person and his/her environment, and that disability is not something that resides in the individual as the result of some impairment. This understanding has important implications for legislation to implement the Convention, particularly in identifying the obstacles that hinder the full realization of the rights of persons with disabilities and in determining appropriate remedies. Parliamentarians might wish to consult with experts on disability issues, including persons with disabilities and their representative organizations, to update their understanding of the nature and forms of disability and the ways in which social barriers to participation can be removed.

Types of Disability to be Addressed in Legislation

The Convention provides a non-exhaustive list of disabilities to be addressed by legislation, in other words, it sets a minimum. The Convention describes persons with disabilities as including "those who have long-term physical, mental, intellectual or sensory impairments which in interaction with various barriers may hinder their full and effective participation in society on an equal basis with others."

This definition does not exhaust the categories of disabilities that fall under the protection of the Convention; other types of disability, such as short-term disabilities, could be covered by the Convention and thus could be covered by the laws of individual States parties, especially given the social context of disability. Since article 4 (4) underlines the fact that the Convention is not intended to undermine or replace higher standards of protection of the rights of persons with disabilities under national law, it is open to a State to adopt a wider definition. A State is not required to limit its own definition to the categories mentioned under article 2 of the Convention.

PWD Act, 1995 The Persons with Disabilities (Equal Opportunities, Protection of Rights and Full Participation) Act, 1995

The following Act of Parliament received the assent of the President on the 1st January, 1996, and is hereby published for general information:- No.1 OF 1996 [1st January 1996]. An Act to give effect to the Proclamation on the Full Participation and Equality of the People with Disabilities in the Asian and Pacific Region.

WHEREAS the Meeting to Launch the Asian and Pacific Decade of Disabled Persons 1993-2002 convened by the Economic and Social Commission for Asia and Pacific held at Beijing on 1st to 5th December,1992, adopted the Proclamation on the Full Participation and Equality of People with Disabilities in the Asian and Pacific Region;

AND WHEREAS India is a signatory to the said Proclamation; AND WHEREAS it is considered necessary to implement the Proclamation aforesaid.

Be it enacted by Parliament in the Forty-sixth Year of the Republic of India as follows:-

Preliminary

1. (1) This Act may be called the Persons With Disabilities (Equal Opportunities, Protection of Rights and Full Participation) Act, 1995.

   (2) It extends to the whole of India except the State of Jammu and Kashmir.

   (3) It shall come into force on such date as the Central Government may. by notification, appoint.

2. In this Act, unless the context otherwise requires,-

   (a) "Appropriate Government" means,-

      (i) In relation to the Central Government or any establishment wholly or substantially financed by that Government, or a Cantonment Board constituted under the Cantonment Act, 1924, the Central Government ;

      (ii) In relation to a State Government or any establishment wholly or substantially financed by that Government, or any local authority., other than a Cantonment Board, the State Government;

(iii) In respect of the Central Co-ordination Committee and the Central Executive Committee, the Central Government;

(iv) In respect of the State Co-ordination Committee and the State Executive Committee, the State Government;

(b) "Blindness" refers to a condition where a person suffers from any of the following conditions, namely:-

(i) Total absence of sight. or

(ii) Visual acuity not exceeding 6160 or 201200 (snellen) in the better eye with correcting lenses; or

(iii) Limitation of the field of vision subtending an angle of 20 degree or worse;

(c) "Central Co-ordination Committee" means the Central Co-ordination Committee constituted under sub-section (1) of section 3;

(d) "Central Executive Committee" means the Central Executive Committee constituted under sub-section (1) of section 9;

(e) "Cerebral palsy" means a group of non-progressive conditions of a person characterized by abnormal motor control posture resulting from brain insult or injuries occurring in the pre-natal, peri-natal or infant period of development;

(f) "Chief Commissioner" means the Chief Commissioner appointed under subsection (1) of section 57;

(g) "Commissioner" means the Commissioner appointed under sub-section (1) of section 60;

(h) "Competent authority" means the authority appointed under section 50;

(i) "Disability" means-

(i) Blindness;

(ii) Low vision;

(iii) Leprosy-cured;

(iv) Hearing impairment;

(v) Loco motor disability;

(vi) Mental retardation;

(vii) Mental illness;

(j) "Employer" means,-

(i) In relation to a Government, the authority notified by the Head of the Department in this behalf or where no such authority is notified, the Head of the Department; and

(ii) In relation to an establishment, the chief executive officer of that the establishment;

(k) "Establishment" means a corporation established by or under a Central, Provincial or State Act, or an authority or a body owned or controlled or aided by the Government or a local authority or a Government company as defined in section 617 of 'the Companies Act, 1956 and includes Departments of a Government;

(l) "Hearing impairment" means loss of sixty decibels or more in the better year in the conversational range of' frequencies;

(m) "Institution for persons with disabilities" means an institution for the reception. Care, protection, education, training, rehabilitation or any other service of persons with disabilities;

(n) "Leprosy cured person" means any person who has been cured of leprosy but is suffering from-

(i) Loss of sensation in hands or feet as well as loss of sensation and paresis in the eye and eye-lid but with no manifest deformity;

(ii) Manifest deformity and paresis; but having sufficient mobility in their hands and feet to enable them to engage in normal economic activity;

(iii) Extreme physical deformity as well as advanced age which prevents him from undertaking any gainful occupation, and the expression "leprosy cured" shall be construed accordingly;

(o) "Loco motor disability" means disability of the bones, joints muscles leading to substantial restriction of the movement of the limbs or any form of cerebral palsy,

(p) "Medical authority" means any hospital or institution specified for the purposes of this Act by notification by the appropriate Government;

(q) "Mental illness" means any mental disorder other than mental retardation;

(r) "Mental retardation" means a condition of arrested or incomplete development of mind of a person which is specially characterized by sub normality of intelligence;

(s) "Notification" means a notification published in the, Official Gazette;

(t) "Person with disability" means a person suffering from not less than forty per cent. of any disability as certified by a medical authority;

(u) "Person with low vision" means a person with impairment of visual functioning even after treatment or standard refractive correction but who uses or is potentially capable of using vision for the planning or execution of a task with appropriate assistive device;

(v) "Prescribed" means prescribed by rules made under this Act;

(w) "Rehabilitation" refers to a process aimed at enabling persons with disabilities to reach and maintain their optimal physical, sensory, intellectual, psychiatric or social functional levels;

(x) "Special Employment Exchange" means any office or place established and maintained by the Government for the collection and furnishing of information, either by keeping of registers or otherwise, respecting-

(i) Persons who seek to engage employees from amongst the persons suffering from disabilities;

(ii) Persons with disability who seek employment;

(iii) Vacancies to which person with disability seeking employment may be appointed;

(y) "State Co-ordination Committee" means the State Co-ordination Committee constituted under sub-section (1) of section 19;

(z) "State Executive Committee" means the State Executive Committee constituted under sub-section (l) of section 19

The Coordination Committee

3. (1) The Central Government shall by notification constitute a body to be known as the Central Co-ordination Committee to exercise the powers conferred on, and to perform the functions assigned to it, under this Act.

(2) The Central Co-ordination Committee shall consist of-

(a) The Minister in charge of the Department of Welfare in the Central Government, Chairperson, ex officio;

(b) The Minister of State in-charge of the Department of Welfare in the Central Government, Vice-Chairperson, ex officio;

(c) Secretaries to the Government of India in-charge of the Departments of Welfare, Education, Woman and Child Development, Expenditure, Personnel, Training and Public Grievances, Health, Rural Development, Industrial Development, Urban Affairs and Employment, Science and Technology. Legal Affairs, Public Enterprises, Members, ex officio;

(d) Chief Commissioner, Member, ex officio;

(e) Chairman Railway Board, Member, ex officio;

(f) Director-General of Lab our, Employment and Training, Member, ex officio;

(g) Director, National Council for Educational Research and Training, Member, ex officio;

(h) Three Members of Parliament. of whom two shall be elected by the House of the People and one by the Council of States, Members;

(i) Three persons to be nominated by the Central Government to represent the interests, which in the opinion of that Government ought to be represented, Members;

(j) Directors of the-

(i) National Institute for the Visually Handicapped, Dehradun;

(ii) National Institute for the Mentally Handicapped, Secundrabad;

(iii) National Institute for the Orthopaedically Handicapped, Calcutta;

(iv) Ali Yavar Jung National Institute for the Hearing Handicapped, Bombay, Members, ex officio;

(k) Four Members to be nominated by the Central Government by rotation to represent the States and the Union territories in such manner as may be prescribed by the Central Government:

Provided that no appointment under this clause shall be made except on the recommendation of the State Government or, as the case may be, the Union territory;

(l) Five persons as far as practicable, being persons with disabilities. to represent non-governmental Organizations or associations which are concerned with disabilities, to he nominated by the Central Government, one from each area of disability, Members:

Provided that while nominating persons under this clause, the Central Government shall nominate at least one woman and one person belonging to Scheduled Castes or Scheduled Tribes;

(m) Joint Secretary to the Government of India in the Ministry of Welfare dealing with the welfare of the handicapped, Member-Secretary, ex officio.

(3) The office of the Member of the Central Co-ordination Committee shall not disqualify its holder for being chosen as or for being a Member of either House of Parliament.

4. (1) Save as otherwise provided by or under this Act a Member of Central Co-ordination Committee nominated under clause (i) or clause (l) of sub-section (2) of section 3 shall hold office for a term of three years from the date of his nomination:

Provided that such a Member shall, notwithstanding the expiration of his term, continue to hold office until his successor enters upon his office.

(2) The term of office of an ex officio Member shall come to an end as soon as he ceases to hold the office by virtue of which he was so nominated.

(3) The Central Government may if it thinks fit remove any Member nominated under clause (i) or clause (1) of subsection (2) of section 3, before the expiry of his term of office after giving him a reasonable opportunity of showing cause against the same.

(4) A Member nominated under clause (i) or clause (1) of subsection (2) of section 3 may at any time resign his office by writing under his hand addressed to the Central Government and the seat of the said Member shall thereupon become vacant.

(5) A casual vacancy in the Central Co-ordination Committee shall be filled by a fresh nomination and the person nominated to fill the vacancy shall hold office only for the remainder of the term for

which the Member in whose place he was so Dominated.

(6) A Member nominated under clause (i) or clause (l) of subsection (2) of section 3 shall be eligible for

(7) Members nominated under clause (i) and clause (1) of sub-section (2) of section 3 shall receive such allowances as may, be prescribed by the Central Government.

5. (1) No person shall be a Member of the Central Coordination Committee, who-

(a) Is, or at any time has been, adjudged insolvent or has suspended payment of his debts or has compounded with his creditors, or

(b) Is of unsound mind and stands so declared by a competent court, or

(c) Is or has been convicted of an offence which, in the opinion of the Central Government, involves moral turpitude, or

(d) Is or at any time has been convicted of an offence under this Act. or

(e) Has so abused in the opinion of the Central Government his position as a Member as to render his continuance in the Central Coordination Committee detrimental to the interests of the general public.

(2) No order of removal shall be made by the Central Government under this section unless the Member concerned has been given a reasonable opportunity of showing cause against the same.

(3) Notwithstanding anything contained in sub-section (1) or sub-section (6) of section 4, a Member who has been removed under this section shall not be eligible for renomination as a Member.

6. If a Member of the Central Coordination Committee becomes subject to any of the disqualifications specified in section 5, his scat shall become vacant.

7. Lie Central Coordination Committee shall meet at least once in every six months and shall observe such rules of procedure in regard to the transaction of business at its meetings as may be prescribed by the Central Government.

8. (1) Subject to the provisions of this Act, the function of the Central Coordination Committee shall be to serve as the national focal point on disability matters and facilitate the continuous evolution of a comprehensive policy towards solving the problems faced by persons with disabilities.

(2) In particular and without prejudice to the generality of the foregoing, the Central Coordination Committee may perform all or any, of the following functions, namely:-

(a) Review and coordinate the activities of all the Departments of Government and other Governmental and non-Govemmental Organizations which are dealing with matters relating to persons with disabilities;

(b) Develop a national policy to address issues faced by, persons with disabilities;

(c) Advise the Central Government on the formulation oil policies, programmes, legislation and projects with respect to disability,

(d) Take up the cause of persons with disabilities with the concerned authorities and the international organizations with a view, to provide for schemes and projects for the disabled in the national plans and other programmes and policies evolved by the international agencies;

(e) Review in consultation with the donor agencies their funding policies from the perspective of their impact on persons with disabilities;

(f) Take such other steps to ensure barrier free environment in public places, work places, public utilities, schools and other institutions;

(g) Monitor and evaluate the impact of policies and programmes designed for achieving equality and full participation of persons with disabilities;

(h) To perform such other functions as may be prescribed by the Central Government.

9. (1) The Central Government shall constitute a Committee to be known as the Central Executive Committee to perform the functions assigned to it under this Act.

(2) The Central Executive Committee shall consist of-

(a) The Secretary to the Government of India in the Ministry of Welfare, Chairperson, ex officio;

(b) The Chief Commissioner, Member, ex officio;

(c) The Director-General for Health Services, Member, ex officio;

(d) The Director-General, Employment and Training, Member, ex officio;

(e) Six persons not below the rank of a Joint Secretary to the Government of India, to represent the Ministries or Departments of Rural Development, Education. Welfare, Personnel Public Grievances and Pension and Urban Affairs and Employment, Science and Technology, Members, ex officio;

(f) The Financial Advisor, Ministry of Welfare in the Central Government, Member, ex officio;

(g) Advisor (Tariff) Railway Board, Member, ex officio;

(h) Four members to be nominated by the Central Government, by rotation, to represent the State Governments and the Union territories

in such manner as may be prescribed by the Central Government;

(i) One person to be nominated by the Central Government to represent the interest, which in the opinion of the Central Government ought to be represented, Member;

(j) Five persons, as far as practicable, being persons with disabilities, to represent non-governmental organizations or associations which are concerned with disabilities, to he nominated by the Central Government, one from each area of disability, Members:

Provided that while nominating persons under this clause, the Central Government shall nominate at least one woman and one person belonging to Scheduled Castes or Scheduled Tribes;

(k) Joint Secretary to the Government of India in the Ministry of Welfare dealing with the welfare of the handicapped, Member-Secretary, ex officio.

(3) Members nominated under clause (i) and clause (j) of sub-section (2) shall receive such allowances as may be prescribed by the Central Government.

(4) A Member nominated under clause (i) or clause (i) of sub-section (2) may at any time resign his office by writing under his hand addressed to the Central Government and the scat of the said Member shall thereupon become vacant.

10. (1) The Central Executive Committee shall be the executive body of the Central Coordination Committee and shall be responsible for carrying out the decisions of the Central Coordination Committee.

(2) Without prejudice to the provisions of sub-section (1), the Central Executive Committee shall also perform such other functions as may be delegated to it by the Central Coordination Committee.

11. The Central Executive Committee shall meet at least once in three months and shall observe such rules of procedure in regard to the transaction of business at its meetings as may be prescribed by the Central Government.

12. (1) The Central Executive Committee may associate with itself in such manner and for such purposes as may be prescribed by the Central Government any person whose assistance or advice it may desire to obtain in performing any of its functions under this Act.

(2) A person associated with the Central Executive Committee under sub-section (1) for any purpose shall have the right to take part in the discussions of the Central Executive Committee relevant to that purpose, but shall not have a right to vote at a meeting of the said Committee, and shall not be a member for any other purpose.

(3) A person associated with the said Committee under sub-section (1) for any purpose shall be paid such fees and allowances, for attending its meetings and for attending to any other work of the said Committee, as may be prescribed by the Central Government.

The State Coordination Committee

13. (1) Every State Government shall, by notification, constitute a body to be known as the State Coordination Committee to exercise the powers conferred on, and to perform the function assigned to it, under this Act.

(2) the State Coordination Committee shall consist of-

(a) The Minister in-charge of the Department of Social Welfare in the State Government, Chairperson, ex officio;

(b) the Minister of State in-charge of the Department of Social Welfare, if any, Vice-Chairperson, ex officio;

(c) Secretaries to the State Government in-charge of the Departments of Welfare, Education, Woman and Child Development, Expenditure, Personnel Training and Public Grievances, Health, Rural Development, Industrial Development, Urban Affairs and Employment, Science and Technology, Public Enterprises, by whatever name called, Members, ex officio;

(d) Secretary of any other Department, which the State Government considers necessary, Member, ex officio;

(e) Chairman Bureau of Public Enterprises (by whatever name called) Member, ex officio;

(f) Five persons, as far as practicable, being persons with disabilities, to represent non-governmental organizations or associations which are concerned with disabilities, to be nominated by the State Government, one from each area of disability, Members:

Provided that while nominating persons under this clause, the State Government shall nominate at least one woman and one person belonging to Scheduled Castes or Scheduled Tribes;

(g) Three Members of State Legislature, of whom two shall be elected by the Legislative Assembly and one by the Legislative Council, if any;

(h) Three persons to be nominated by that State Government to represent agriculture, industry or trade or any other interest, which in the opinion of State Government ought to be represented, Members, ex officio;

(i) The Commissioner, Member, ex officio;

(j) Secretary to the State Government dealing with the welfare of the handicapped, Member-Secretary, ex officio.

(3) Notwithstanding anything contained in this section, no State Coordination Committee shall be constituted for a Union territory and in relation to a Union territory; the Central Coordination Committee shall exercise the functions and perform the functions of a State Coordination Committee for the Union territory:

Provided that in relation to a Union territory. The Central Coordination Committee may delegate all or any of its powers and functions under this sub-section to such person or body of persons as the Central Government may specify.

14. (1) Save as otherwise provided by or under this Act, a Member of a State Coordination Committee nominated under clause (f) or clause (h) of subsection (2) of section 13 shall hold office for a term of three years from the date of his nomination:

Provided that such a Member shall, notwithstanding the expiration of his term, continue to hold office until his successor enters upon his office.

(2) The term of office of an ex officio Member shall come to an end as soon as he ceases to hold the office by virtue of which he was so nominated.

(3) The State Government may, if it thinks fit, remove any7 Member nominated under clause (f) or clause (h) of sub-section (2) of section 13, before the expiry of his term of office after giving him a reasonable opportunity of showing cause against the same.

(4) A Member nominated under clause (f) or clause (h) of sub-section (2) of section 13 may. At any time, resign his office by writing under his hand addressed to the State Government and the seat of the said Member shall thereupon become vacant.

(5) A casual vacancy in the State Coordination Committee shall be filled by a fresh nomination and the person nominated to fill the vacancy shall hold office only for the remainder of the term for

which the Member in whose place he was so nominated.

(6) A Member nominated under clause (f) and clause (h) of sub-section (2) of section 13 shall be eligible for renomination.

(7) Members nominated under clause (f) and clause (h) of sub-section (2) of section13 shall receive such allowances as may he prescribed by the State Government.

15. (1) No pet-son shall he a Member of the State Coordination Committee, who—

(a) Is, or at any time, has been adjudged insolvent or has suspended payment of his debts or has compounded with his creditors, or

(b) Is of unsound mind and stands so declared by a competent court, or

(c) Is or has been convicted of an offence which in the opinion of the State Government involves moral turpitude, or

(d) Is or at any time has been convicted of an offence under this Act or

(e) Has so abused, in the opinion of the State Government, his position as a member as to render his continuance in the State Coordination Committee detrimental to the interests of the general public.

(2) No order of removal shall be made by the State Government under this section unless the Member concerned has been given a reasonable opportunity of showing cause against the same.

(3) Notwithstanding anything contained in sub-section (1) or sub-section (6) of section 14, a Member who has been removed under this section shall net be eligible for renomination as a Member.

16. If a Member of the State Coordination Committee becomes subject to any of the disqualifications specified in section 15, his seat shall become vacant.

17. The State Coordination Committee shall meet at least once in every six months and shall observe such rules of procedure in regard to the transaction of business at its meetings as may be prescribed.

18. (1) Subject to the provisions of this Act, the function of the State Coordination Committee shall be to serve as the state focal point on disability matters and facilitate the continuous evolution of a comprehensive policy towards solving the problems faced by persons with disabilities.

(2) In particular and without prejudice to the generality of the foregoing function the State Coordination Committee may, within the State perform all or any of the following functions, namely.-

(a) Review and coordinate the activities of all the Departments of Government and other Governmental and non-Govemmental Organizations which are dealing with matters relating to persons with disabilities.,

(b) Develop a State policy to address issues faced by persons with disabilities;

(c) Advise the State Government on the formulation of policies. Programmes, legislation and projects with respect to disability;

(d) Review, in consultation with the donor agencies, their funding from the perspective of their impact on persons with disabilities;

(e) Take such other steps to ensure barrier free environment in pupil's places. Work places, public utilities, schools and other institutions;

(f) Monitor and evaluate the impact of policies and programmes designed for achieving equality and full participation of persons with disabilities;

(g) To perform such other functions as may be prescribed by the State Government

19. (1) The State Government shall constitute a committee to be known as the State Executive Committee to perform the functions assigned to it under this Act.

(2) The State Executive Committee shall consist of-

(a) The Secretary, Department of Social Welfare, Chairperson, ex officio;

(b) The Commissioner, Member, ex officio;

(c) Nine persons not below the rank of a Joint Secretary to the State Government, to represent the Departments of Health, Finance, Rural Development, Education, Welfare, Personnel Public Grievances, Urban Affairs Labour and Employment, Science and Technology, Members, ex officio;

(d) One person to be nominated by the State Government to represent the interest, which in the opinion of the State Government ought to be represented. Member;

(e) Five persons, as far as practicable being persons with disabilities. to represent non-governmental organizations or associations which arc concerned with disabilities, to be nominated by the State Government, one from each area of disability, Members:

Provided that while nominating persons under this clause, the State Government shall nominate at least one woman and one person belonging to Scheduled Castes or Scheduled Tribes;

(f) Joint Secretary dealing with the disability division in the Department of Welfare, Member-Secretary, ex officio.

(3) Members nominated under clause (d) and clause (e) of sub-section (2) shall receive such allowances as may be prescribed by the State Government.

(4) A Member nominated under clause (d) or clause (e) may at any time resign his office by writing under

his hand addressed to the State Government and the scat of the said Member shall thereupon become vacant.

20. (1) The State Executive Committee shall be the executive body of the State Coordination Committee and shall be responsible for carrying out the decisions of the State Coordination Committee.

(2) Without prejudice to the provisions of sub-section (1), the State Executive Committee shall also perform such other functions as may be delegated to it by the State Coordination Committee.

21. The State Executive Committee shall meet at least once in three months and shall observe such rules of procedure in regard to the transaction of business at its meetings as may be prescribed by, the State Government.

22. (1) The State Executive Committee may associate with itself in such manner and for such purposes as may he prescribed by the State Government any person whose assistance or advice it may desire to obtain in performing any of its functions under this Act.

(2) A person associated with the State Executive Committee under sub-section (1) for any purpose shall have the right to take part in the discussions of the State Executive Committee relevant to that purpose, but shall not have a right to vote at a meeting of the said Committee, and shall not he a member for any other purpose.

(3) A person associated wills the said Committee under sub-section (1) for any purpose shall be paid such fees and allowances, for attending its meetings and for attending to any other work of the said Committee, as may be prescribed by the State Government.

23. In the performance of its functions under this Act,-

(a) The Central Coordination Committee shall be bound by such directions in writing, as the Central Government may give to it; and

(b) The State Coordination Committee shall be bound by such directions in writing, as the Central Coordination Committee or the State, Government may give to it:

Provided that where a direction given by the State Government is inconsistent with any direction given by the Central Coordination Committee, the matter shall be referred to the Central Government for its decision.

24. No act or proceeding of the Central Coordination Committee, the Central Executive Committee, a State Coordination Committee or a State Executive Committee shall be called in question on the ground merely on the existence of any vacancy in or any defect in the constitution of such Committees.

Preventation and Early Detection of Disabilities

25. Within the limits of their economic capacity and development, the appropriate Governments and the local authorities, with a view to preventing the occurrence of disabilities, shall-

(a) Undertake or cause to be undertaken surveys, investigations and research concerning the cause of occurrence of disabilities;

(b) Promote various methods of preventing disabilities;

(c) Screen all the children at least once in a year for the purpose of identifying "at-risk" cases;

(d) Provide facilities for training to the staff at the primary health centers;

(e) Sponsor or cause to be sponsored awareness campaigns and is disseminated or cause to be disseminated information for general hygiene. Health and sanitation,

(f) Take measures for pre-natal, parental and post-natal care of mother and child;

(g) Educate the public through the pre-schools, schools, primary health Centers, village level workers and anganwadi workers;

(h) Create awareness amongst the masses through television, radio and other mass media on the causes of disabilities and the preventive measures to be adopted;

Education

26. The appropriate Governments and the local authorities shall-

(a) Ensure that every child with a disability has access to free education in an appropriate environment till he attains the age of eighteen years;

(b) Endeavor to promote the integration of students with disabilities in the normal schools;

(c) Promote setting up of special schools in Government and private sector for those in need of special education, in such a manner that children with disabilities living in any part of the country have access to such schools;

(d) Endeavor to equip the special schools for children with disabilities with vocational training facilities.

27. The appropriate Governments and the local authorities shall by notification make schemes for-

(a) Conducting part-time classes in respect of children with disabilities who having completed education up to class fifth and could not continue their studies on a whole-time basis;

(b) Conducting special part-time classes for providing functional literacy for children in the age group of sixteen and above;

(c) Imparting non-formal education by utilizing the available manpower in rural areas after giving them appropriate orientation;

(d) Imparting education through open schools or open universities;

(e) Conducting class and discussions through interactive electronic or other media;.

(f) Providing every child with disability free of cost special books and equipments needed for his education.

28. The appropriate Governments shall initiate or cause to be initiated research by official and non-governmental agencies for the purpose of designing and developing new assistive devices, teaching aids, special teaching materials or such other items as are necessary to give a child with disability equal opportunities in education.

29. The appropriate Governments shall set up adequate number of teachers' training institutions and assist the national institutes and other voluntary organizations to develop teachers' training programmes specializing in disabilities so that requisite trained manpower is available for special schools and integrated schools for children with disabilities.

30. Without prejudice to the foregoing provisions, (be appropriate Governments shall by notification prepare a comprehensive education scheme which shall make Provision for-

(a) Transport facilities to the children with disabilities or in the alternative financial incentives to parents or guardians to enable their children with disabilities to attend schools.

(b) The removal of architectural barriers from schools. colleges or other institution, imparting vocational and professional training;

(c) The supply of books, uniforms and other materials to children with disabilities attending school.

(d) The grant of scholarship to students with disabilities..

(e) Setting up of appropriate fora for the redressal of grievances of parent, regarding the placement of their children with disabilities;

(f) Suitable modification in the examination system to eliminate purely mathematical questions for the benefit of blind students and students with low vision;

(g) Restructuring of curriculum for the benefit of children with disabilities;

(h) restructuring the curriculum for benefit of students with hearing impairment to facilitate them to take only one language as part of their curriculum.

31. All educational institutions shall provide or cause to be provided amanuensis to blind students and students with or low vision.

Employment

32. Appropriate Governments shall—

(a) Identify posts, in the establishments, which can be reserved for the persons with disability;

(b) At periodical intervals not exceeding three years, review the list of posts identified and up-date the list taking into consideration the developments in technology.

33. Every appropriate Government shall appoint in every establishment such percentage of vacancies not less than three per cent. for persons or class of persons with disability of which one per cent. each shall be reserved for persons suffering from-

(i) Blindness or low vision;

(ii) Bearing impairment;

(iii) Loco motor disability or cerebral palsy, in the posts identified for each disability:

Provided that the appropriate Government may, having regard to the type of work carried on in any department or establishment, by notification subject to such conditions, if any, as may be specified in such notification, exempt any establishment from the provisions of this section.

34. (1) The appropriate Government may, by notification. Require that from such date as May he specified. By notification. The employer in every establishment

shall furnish such information or return as may be prescribed in relation to vacancies appointed for person, with disability that have occurred or are about to occur in that establishment to such Special Employment Exchange as may be prescribed and the establishment shall thereupon comply with such requisition.

(2) The form in which and the intervals of time for which information or returns shall be furnished and the particulars, they shall contain shall be such as may be prescribed.

35. Any person authorized by the Special Employment Exchange in writing, shall have access to any relevant record or document in the possession of any establishment, and may enter at any reasonable time and premises where he believes such record or document to be, and inspect or take copies of relevant records or documents or ask any question necessary for obtaining any information.

36. Where in any recruitment year any vacancy under section 33, cannot be filled up due to non-availability of a suitable person with disability or, for any other sufficient reason, such vacancy shall be carried forward in the succeeding recruitment year and if ;r the succeeding recruitment year also suitable person with disability is not available, it may first be filled by interchange among the three categories and only when there is no parson with disability available for the post in that Year, the employer shall fill up the vacancy by appointment of a person, other than a person with disability:

Provided that if the nature of vacancies in an establishment is such that a given category of person can not be employed, the vacancies may be interchanged among the three categories with the prior approval of the appropriate Government.

37. (1) Every employer shall maintain such record in relation to the person. With disability employed in

his establishment in such form and in such manner as may be prescribed by the appropriate Government.

(2) The records maintained under sub-section (1) shall be open to inspection at all reasonable hours by such persons as may be authorized in this behalf by general or special order by the appropriate Government.

38. (1) The appropriate Governments and local authorities shall by notification formulate schemes for ensuring employment of persons with disabilities, and such schemes may provide for-

(a) The training and welfare of persons with disabilities;

(b) The relaxation of upper age limit;

(c) Regulating the employment;

(d) Health and safety measures and creation of a non-handicapping environment in places where persons with disabilities are employed;

(e) The manner in which and the person by whom the cost of operating the schemes is to be defrayed; and

(f) Constituting the authority responsible for the administration of the scheme.

39. All Government educational institutions and other educational institutions receiving aid from the Government, shall reserve not less than three per cent seat for persons with disabilities.

40. The appropriate Governments and local authorities shall reserve not less than three per cent. in all poverty alleviation schemes for the benefit of persons with disabilities.

41. The appropriate Governments and the local authorities shall, within the limits of their economic capacity and development, provide incentives to employers both in public and private sectors to ensure that at least five

per cent. of their work force is composed of persons with disabilities.

Affirmative Action

42. The appropriate Governments shall by notification make schemes to provide aids and appliances to persons with disabilities.

43. The appropriate Governments and local authorities shall by notification frame schemes in favor of persons with disabilities, for the preferential allotment of land at concession] rates for-

(a) House;

(b) Setting up business;

(c) Setting up of special recreation centers;

(d) Establishment of special schools;

(e) Establishment of research centers;

(f) Establishment of factories by entrepreneurs with disabilities

Non-discrimination

44. Establishments in the transport sector shall, within the limits of their economic capacity and development for the benefit of persons with disabilities, take special measures to-

(a) Adapt rail compartments, buses. Vessels and aircrafts in such a way as to permit easy access to such persons;

(b) Adapt toilets in rail compartments, vessels, aircrafts and waiting rooms in such a way as to permit the wheel chair users to use them conveniently.

45. The appropriate Governments and the local authorities shall, within the limits of their economic capacity and development. Provide for-

(a) Installation of auditory signals at red lights in the public roads for the benefit of persons with visually handicap;

(b) Causing curb cuts and slopes to be made in pavements for the easy access of wheel chair users;

(c) Engraving on the surface of the zebra crossing for the blind or for persons with low vision;

(d) Engraving on the edges of railway platforms for the blind or for persons with low vision;

(e) Devising appropriate symbols of disability;

(f) Warning signals at appropriate places.

46. The appropriate Governments and the local authorities shall, within the limits of their economic capacity and development, provide for-

(a) Ramps in public buildings;

(b) Braille symbols and auditory signals in elevators or lifts;

(c) Braille symbols and auditory signals in elevators or lifts;

(d) Ramps in hospitals, primary health centers and other medical care and rehabilitation institutions.

47. (1) No establishment shall dispense with or reduce in rank, an employee who acquires a disability during his service.

Provided that, if an employee, after acquiring disability is not suitable for the post he was holding, could be shifted to some other post with the same pay scale and service benefits.

Provided further that if it is not possible to adjust the employee against any post, he may be kept on a supernumerary post until a suitable post is available or he attains the age of superannuation, whichever is earlier.

(2) No promotion shall be denied to a person merely on the ground of his disability:

Provided that the appropriate Government may, having regard to the type of work carried on in any establishment, by notification and subject to such conditions, if any, as may be specified in such notification, exempt any establishment from the provisions of this section.

Research and Manpower Development

48. The appropriate Governments and local authorities shall promote and sponsor research, inter alia,, in the following areas-
    (a) Prevention of disability;
    (b) Rehabilitation including community based rehabilitation;
    (c) Development of assistive devices including their psychosocial aspects;
    (d) Job identification;
    (e) On site modifications in offices and factories.

49. The appropriate Governments shall provide financial assistance to universities, other institutions of higher learning, professional bodies and non-governmental research-. units or institutions, for undertaking research for special education. rehabilitation and manpower development.

Recognition of Institutions for Persons with Disabilities

50. The State Government shall appoint any authority, as it deems fit to be a competent authority for the purposes of this Act.

51. Save as otherwise provided under this Act, no person shall establish or maintain any institution for persons with disabilities except under and in accordance with a certificate of registration issued in this behalf by the competent authority:

    Provided that a person maintaining an institution for persons with disabilities immediately before the commencement of this Act may continue to maintain such institution for a period of six months from such commencement and if he has made an application for such certificate under this section within the said period of six months, till the disposal of such application.

52. (1) Every application for a certificate of registration shall be made to the competent authority in such form and in such manner as may be prescribed by the State Government.

(2) On receipt of an application under sub-section (1), the competent authority shall make such enquiries as it may deem fit and where it is satisfied that the applicant has cornplied with the requirements of this Act and the rules made thereunder it shall grant a certificate of registration to the applicant and where it is not so satisfied the competent authority shall. by order. refuse to grant the certificate applied for:

Provided that before making any order refusing to grant a certificate the competent authority shall give to the applicant a reasonable opportunity of being heard and every order of refusal to grant a certificate shall he communicated to the applicant in such manner as may be prescribed by the State Government.

(3) No certificate of registration shall be granted under sub-section (2) unless the institution with respect to which an application has been made is in a position to provide such facilities and maintain such standards as may be prescribed by the State Government.

(4) A certificate of registration granted under this section,-

(a) Shall, unless revoked under section 53, remain in force for such period as may, be prescribed by, the State Government.

(b) May be renewed from time to time for a like period; and

(c) Shall be in such form and shall be subject to such conditions as may be Prescribed by the State Government

(5) An application for renewal of a certificate of registration shall be made not less than sixty days before the period of validity.

(6) The certificate of registration shall he displayed by the institution in a conspicuous place.

53. (1) the competent authority may, if it has reasonable cause to believe that the Holder of the certificate of registration granted under sub-section (2) of section 52 has-

(a) Made a statement in relation to any application for the issue of renewal of the certificate which is incorrect or false in material particulars; or

(b) Committed or has caused to be committed any breach of rules or any conditions subject to which the certificate was granted, it may after making such inquiry, as it deems fit, by order, revoke the certificate:

Provided that no such order shall he made until an opportunity is given to the holder of the certificate to show cause as to why the certificate should not be revoked.

(2) Where a certificate in respect of an institution has been revoked under sub-section (1), such institution shall cease to function from the date of such revocation.

Provided that where an appeal lies under section 54 against the order of revocation, such institution shall cease to function—

(a) Where no appeal has been preferred immediately on the expiry of the period prescribed for the filing of such appeal, or

(b) Where such appeal has been preferred, but the order of revocation has been upheld, from the date of the order of appeal.

(3) On the revocation of a certificate in respect of an institution, the competent authority may direct that

any person with disability who is an inmate of such institution on the date of such revocation, shall be-

(a) Restored to the custody of her or his parent, spouse or lawful guardian, as the case may be, or

(b) Transferred to any other institution specified by the competent authority.

(4) Every institution, which holds a certificate of registration, which is revoked, under this section shall, immediately after such revocation. Surrender such certificate to the Competent authority.

54. (1) Any person aggrieved by the order of the competent authority, refusing to grant a certificate or revoking a certificate may, within such period as may he prescribed by the State Government, prefer an appeal to that Government against such refusal or revocation.

(2) The order of the State Government on such appeal shall he final.

55. Nothing contained in this Chapter shall apply, to an institution for persons with disabilities established or maintained by the Central Government or State Government.

Institution for Persons With Severe Disabilities

56. The appropriate Government may establish and maintain institutions for persons with severe disabilities at such places as it thinks fit.

(2) Where, the appropriate Government is of opinion that any institution other than an institution. Established under sub-section (1), is fit for the rehabilitation of the persons with severe disabilities, the Government may recognize such institution as an institution for persons with severe disabilities for the purposes of this Act:

Provided that no institution shall be recognized under this section unless such institution has complied with

the requirements of this Act and the rules made there under.

(3) Every institution established under sub-section (1) shall be maintained in such manner and satisfy such conditions as may be prescribed b), the appropriate Government.

(4) For the purposes of this section "person with severe disability" means a person with eighty per cent. or more of one or more disabilities.

The Chief Commissioner and Commissioners for Persons with Disabilities

57. (1) The Central Government may, by notification appoint a Chief Commissioner for persons with disabilities for the purposes of this Act.

(2) A person shall not be qualified for appointment as the Chief Commissioner unless he has special knowledge or practical experience in respect of matters relating to rehabilitation.

(3) The salary and allowances payable to and other terms and conditions of service (including pension, gratuity and other retirement benefits of the Chief Commissioner shall be such as may be prescribed by the Central Government.

(4) The Central Government shall determine the nature and categories of officers and other employees required to assist the Chief Commissioner in the discharge of his functions and provide the Chief Commissioner with such officers and other employees as it thinks fit.

(6) The salaries and allowances and other conditions of service of officers and employees provided to the Chief Commissioner shall be such as may be prescribed by the Central Government.

58. The Chief commissioner shall —

(a) Coordinate the work of the Commissioners;

(b) Monitor the utilization of' funds disbursed by the Central Government;

(c) Take steps to safeguard the rights and facilities made available to Persons with disabilities;

(d) Submit reports to the Central Government on the implementation of the Act at such intervals as that Government may prescribe.

59. Without prejudice to the provisions of section 58 the Chief Commissioner may of his own motion or on the application of any aggrieved person or otherwise look into complaints with respect to matters relating to —

(a) Deprivation of rights of persons with Disabilities.

(b) Non-implementation of laws, rules, byelaws, regulations. Executive orders, guidelines or instructions made or issued by the appropriate Governments and the local authorities for the welfare and protection of rights or persons with disabilities. And take up the matter with the appropriate authorities.

60. (1) Every State Government may, by notification appoint a Commissioner for persons with disabilities for the purpose of this Act.

(2) A person shall not be qualified for appointment as a Commissioner unless he has special knowledge or practical experience in respect of matters relating to rehabilitation.

(3) The salary and allowances payable to and other terms and conditions of service (including pension gratuity and other retirement benefits) of the Commissioner shall be such as may he prescribed by the State Government.

(4) The State Government shall determine the nature and categories of officers and other employees required to assist the Commissioner in the discharge of his functions and provide the Commissioner with such officers and other employees as it thinks fit.

(5) The officers and employees provided to the Commissioner shall discharge their functions under the general superintendence of the Commissioner.

(6) The salaries and allowances and other conditions of service of officers and employees provided to the Commissioner shall be such as may he prescribed by the State Government.

61. The Commissioner within the State shall-

(a) Coordinate with the departments of the State Government for the programmes and schemes, for the benefit of persons with disabilities;

(b) Monitor the utilization of funds disbursed by the State Government;

(c) Take steps to safeguard the rights and facilities made available to persons with disabilities.

(d) Submit reports to the State Government on the implementation of the Act at such intervals as that Government may prescribe and forward a copy thereof to the Chief Commissioner.

62. Without prejudice to the provisions of section 61 the Commissioner may of his own motion or on the application of any aggrieved person or otherwise look into complaints with respect to matters relating to—

(a) Deprivation of rights of persons with disabilities;

(b) Non-implementation of laws, rules, bye-laws, regulations, executive orders, guidelines or instructions made or issued by the appropriate Governments and the local authorities for the welfare and protection of rights of persons with disabilities, And take up the matter with the appropriate authorities.

63. The Chief Commissioner and the Commissioners shall, for the purpose of discharging their functions under this Act, have the same powers as are vested in a court under the Code of Civil Procedure, 1908 while trying a suit, in respect of the following matters, namely:-

(a) Summoning and enforcing the attendance of witnesses;

(b) Requiring the discovery and production of any documents;

(c) Requisitioning any public record or copy thereof from any court or office;

(d) Receiving evidence on affidavits; and

(e) Issuing commissions for the examination of witnesses or documents.

(2) Every proceeding before the Chief Commissioner and Commissioners shall be a judicial proceeding within the meaning directions 193 and 228 of the Indian Penal Code and the Chief Commissioner, the Commissioner, the competent authority, shall be deemed to he a civil court for the purposes of section 195 and Chapter XXVI of the Code of Criminal Procedure, 1973.

64. (1) The Chief Commissioner shall prepare in such form and at such time for each financial year as may be prescribed by the Central Government an annual report giving a full account of his activities during the previous financial year and forward a copy thereof to the Central Government.

(2) The Central Government shall cause the annual report to be laid before each House of Parliament along with the recommendations explaining the action taken or proposed to be taken on the recommendation made therein in so far as they relate to the Central Government and the reasons for non-acceptance, if any, of any such rccommendation or part.

65. (1) The Commissioner shall prepare in such form and at such time for each financial year as may be prescribed by the State Government an annual report giving a full account of his activities during the previous financial year and forward a copy thereof to the State Government.

The State Government shall cause the annual report to be laid before each State Legislature along with the recommendations explaining the action taken or proposed to be taken on the recommendation made therein in so far as they relate to the State

Government and the reasons for non-acceptance, if any, of any such recommendation or part.

Social security

66. (1) The appropriate Governments and the local authorities shall within the limits of their economic capacity and development undertake or cause to be undertaken rehabilitation of all persons with disabilities.

(2) For purposes of sub-section (1), the appropriate Governments and local authorities shall grant financial assistance to non-governmental organizations.

(3) The appropriate Governments and local authorities while formulating rehabilitation policies shall consult the non-governmental organizations working for the cause of persons with disabilities.

67. (1) The appropriate Government shall by notification frame an insurance scheme for the benefit of its employees with disabilities.

(2) Notwithstanding anything contained in this section, the appropriate Government may instead of framing an insurance scheme frame an alternative security scheme for its employees with disabilities.

68. The appropriate Governments shall within the limits of their economic capacity and development shall by notification frame a scheme for payment of an unemployment allowance to persons with disabilities registered with the Special Employment Exchange for more than two years and who could not he placed in any gainful occupation.

Miscellaneous

69. Whoever fraudulently avails or attempts to avail, any benefit meant for persons with disabilities, shall be punishable with imprisonment for a term which may extend to two years or with fine which may extend to twenty thousand rupees or with both.

70. The Chief Commissioner, the Commissioners and other officers and staff provided to them shall be deemed to be public servants within the meaning of section 21 of the Indian Penal Code.

71. No suit, prosecution or other legal proceeding shall lie against the Central Government, the State Governments or the local authority or any officer of the Government in respect of anything which is done in good faith or intended to be done in pursuance of this Act and any rules or orders made there under.

72. The provisions of this Act, or the rules made there under shall be in addition to, and not in derogation of any other law for the time being in force or any rules, order or any instructions issued there under, enacted or issued for the benefit of persons with disabilities.

73. (1) The appropriate Government may, by notification, make rules for carrying out the provisions of this Act.

(2) In particular, and without prejudice to the generality of the foregoing powers, such rules may provide for all or any of the following matters, namely:-

(a) The manner in which a State Government or a Union territory shall be chosen under clause (k) of sub-section (2) of section 3;

(b) Allowances, which members shall receive under subsection (7) of section 4;

(c) Rules of procedure, which the Central Coordination Committee shall observe in regard to the transaction of business in its meetings under section 7;

(d) Such other functions, which the Central Coordination Committee may perform under clause (h) of sub-section (2) of section 8;

(e) The manner in which a State Government or a Union Territory shall be chosen under clause (h) of sub-section (2) of section 9;

(f) The allowances, which the Members shall receive under sub-section (3) of section 9;

(g) Rules of procedure, which the Central Executive Committee shall observe in regard to transaction of business at its meetings under section 11;

(h) The manner and purposes for which a person may be associated under sub-section (I) of section 12;

(i) Fees and allowances which a person associated with the Central Executive Committee shall received under sub-section (3) of section 12;

(j) Allowances which members shall received under sub-section (7) of section 14;

(k) Rules of procedure, which a State Coordination Committee shall observe in regard to transaction of business in its meetings under section 17;

(l) Such other functions, which a State Coordination Committee may perform under clause (g) of sub-section (2) of section 18;

(m) The allowances, which Members shall receive under sub-section (3) of section 19;

(n) Rules of procedure, which a State Executive Committee shall observe in regard to transaction of business at its meetings under section 21;

(o) The manner and purposes for which a person may be associated under sub-section (1) of section 22;

(p) Fees and allowances which a person associated with the State Executive Committee may receive under sub-section (3) of Section 22;

(q) Information or return which the employer in every establishment should furnish and the

Special Employment Exchange to which such information or return shall be furnished under sub-section (1) of section 34;

(r) The form and the manner in which record shall be maintained by an employer under sub-section (1) of section 37;

(s) The form and manner in which an application shall be made under sub-section (1) of section 52;

(t) The manner in which an order of refusal shall be communicated under sub-section (2) of section 52;

(u) Facilities or standards required to be provided or maintained under sub-section (3) of section 52;

(v) The period for which a certificate of registration shall be valid under clause (a) of sub-section (4) of section 52;

(w) The form in which and conditions subject to which a certificate of registration shall be granted under clause (c) of sub-section (4) of section 52;

(x) Period within which an appeal shall lie under sub-section (1) of section 54;

(y) The manner in which an institution for persons with severe disabilities shall be maintained and conditions which have to be satisfied under sub-section (3) of section 56;

(z) The salary, allowances and other terms and conditions of service of the Chief Commissioner under sub-section (6) of section 57;

(za) the salary, allowances and other conditions of service of officers and employees under sub-section (6) of section 57;

(zb) intervals at which the Chief Commissioner shall report to the Central Government under clause (d) of section 58;

(zc) the salary, allowances and other terms and conditions of service of the Commissioner under sub-section (3) of section 60;

(zd) the salary, allowances and other conditions of service of officers and employees under sub-section (6) of section 60;

(ze) intervals within which the Commissioner shall report to the State Government under clause (d) of section 61;

(zf) the form and time in which annual report shall be prepared under sub-section (1) of section 64;

(zg) the form and time in which annual report shall be prepared under sub-section (1) of section 65;

(zh) any other matter which is required to be or may be prescribed.

(3) Every notification made by the Central Government under die proviso to section 33, proviso to sub-section (2) of section 47, every scheme framed by it under section 27, section 30, sub-section (1) of section 38. section 42, section 43, section 67, section 68 and every rule made by it under sub-section (1). shall be laid. as soon as may be after it is made, before each House of Parliament, while it is in session for a tow period of thirty days which may be comprised in one session or in two or more successive sessions, and if. before the expiry of the session immediately following the session or the successive sessions aforesaid, berth Houses agree in making any modification in the rule, notification or scheme, both Houses agree that the rule, notification or scheme should not be Made, the rule, notification or scheme shall thereafter have effect only in such modified form or be of no effect, as the case may be; so, however, that any such modification or annulment shall be without prejudice to the validity of anything previously done under that rule. Notification or scheme, as the case may be.

(4) Every notification made by the State Government under the provison to section 33 proviso to sub-section (2) of section 47, every scheme made by it under section 27, section 30, sub-section (1) of section 38, section 42. section 43, section 67. section 68 and every rule made by it under sub-section (1), shall be laid. as soon as may be after it is made, before each House of State Legislature, where it consists of two Houses or where such legislature consists of one House before that House.

74. In section 12 of the Legal Services Authorities Act. 1987, for clause (d), the following clause shall he substituted, namely:-

"(d) a person with disability as defined in clause (i) of section 2 of the Persons With Disabilities (Equal Opportunities, Protection of Rights and Full Participation) Act. 1995."

Rehabilitation Council Act of India Act 1992

Arrangement of Sections

The Schedule

The Rehabilitation Council of India Act 1992

An Act to provide for the constitution of Rehabilitation Council of India for regulating thc training of rehabilitation professionals and the maintenance of a Central Rehabilitation Register and for Matters connected therewith or incidental thereto.

Be it enacted by Parliament in the Forty-third Year of the Republic of India as follows:-

Parliamentary

Short title and Commencement: This Act may be called the Rehabilitation Council of India Act,1992 It shall come into force on such date as the Central Government may, by notification in the Official Gazette, appoint.

Definition

In this Act, unless the context otherwise requires,-

1. "Chairperson" means the Chairperson of the Council appointed under sub-section (3) section 3;
2. "Council" means the Rehabilitation Council of India constituted under section 3;
3. "handicapped" means a person-
   - o visually handicapped;
   - o hearing handicapped ;
   - o suffering from locomotor disability; or
   - o suffering from mental retardation;
4. "hearing handicapped" means with hearing impairment of 70 decibels and above, in better ear or total loss of hearing in both ears;
5. "locomotor disability" means a person's inability to execute distinctive activities associated with moving, both himself and objects from place to place and such inability resulting from affliction of either bones joints muscles or nerves;
6. "member" means a member appointed under sub-section (3) of section 3 and includes the Chairperson;
7. "Member-Secretary" means the Member-Secretary appointed under sub-section (1) of section 8;
8. "mental retardation" means a condition of arrested or incomplete development of mind of person which is specially characterized by sub-normality of intelligence;
9. "notification means" a notification published in the Official Gazette;
10. "prescribed" means prescribed by regulation;
11. "recognized rehabilitation qualifications" means any of the qualifications included in the Schedule;
12. "Register" means the Central Rehabilitation Register maintained under sub-section (1) of section 23;
13. "regulation" means regulation made under the Act;

"rehabilitation professional" means-

1. audiologists and speech therapists; clinical psychologists;
2. hearing aid and ear mould technicians;
3. rehabilitation engineers and technicians;
4. special teachers for educating and training the handicapped;
5. vocational counselors, employment officers and placement officers dealing with handicapped;
6. multi-purpose rehabilitation therapists, technicians; or
7. such other category of professionals as the Central Government may, in consultation with the Council, notify from time to time;

14. "visually handicapped" means a persons who suffers from any of the following conditions namely-
    1. total absence of sight;
    2. visual acquity not exceeding 6/60 or 20/200(snellen) in the better eye with the correcting lenses; or
    3. limitation of the field of vision subtending and angle of degree or worse.

Any reference in this Act to any enactment or any provision thereof shall, in relation to an area in which such enactment or such provision is not in force, be construed as a reference to the corresponding law or the relevant provision of the corresponding law is any in force is that area.

The Rehabilitation Council of India

Constitution and incorporation of Rehabilitation Council of India.

With effect from such date as the Central Government may, by notification, appoint in this behalf, there shall be constituted for the purposes of this Act a Council to be called the Rehabilitation Council of India.

The Council shall be a body corporate by the name aforesaid, having perpetual succession and a common seal, with power, subject to the provisions of this Act, to acquire, hold and dispose of property both movable and immovable and to contact and shall by the said name sue and be sued.

The Council shall consist of the following members, namely:-

1. a Chairperson, from amongst the persons having experience in social work or rehabilitation, to be appointed by the Central Govt.;
2. three members to be appointed by the Central Government to represent respectively the Ministers of the Central Government dealing with-
   - o Welfare
   - o Health and
   - o Finance
3. one member to be appointed by the Central Government to represent the University Grants Commission;
4. one member to be appointed by the Central Government to represent the Directors General of Indian Council of Medical Research;
5. two members to be appointed by the Central Government to represent the Ministry or department of the States or the Union territories dealing with Social Welfare by rotation in alphabetical order.
6. such number of members not exceeding six as many be appointed by the Central Government from amongst the rehabilitation professionals representatives working in voluntary organization;
7. such number of members not exceeding six as many be appointed by the Central Government from amongst the medical practitioners enrolled under the Indian Medical Council Act 1956 and engaged in rehabilitation of the handicapped;
8. Three members of Parliament of whom two shall be elected by the house of the People and one by the Council of States;
   1. such number of members not exceeding three as may be nominated by the Central Government from

amongst the social workers who are actively engaged in assisting the disabled;

2. The Members-Secretary ex-officio

9. The office of member of the board all not disqualify its holder for being chosen as, or for being a Member of either House of Parliament.

Term of Office of Chairperson and Members

The Chairperson or a member shall hold a office for a term of two years from the date of his appointment or until his successor shall have been duly appointed whichever is longer. A casual vacancy in the Council shall be filled in accordance with the provisions of sections 3 and the person so appointed shall hold office only for the remainder of the term for which the member in whose place he was appointed would have held that office.

The Council shall meet at least once in each year at such time and place as may be appointed by the Council and shall observe such rules of procedure in the transaction of business at a meeting as may be presented. The Chairperson or, if for any reason, he is unable to attend the meeting of the council, any member elected by the members present from amongst themselves at the meeting shall preside at the meeting.

Disqualification

All questions which come up before any meeting of the Council shall be decided by a majority of votes of the members present and voting and in the event of an equality of votes, the Chairperson, or in his absence, the person presiding shall have a second or casting vote:

No. Person shall be a member if he-

1. is, or become of unsound mind or is so declared by a competent court; or
2. is, or has been, convicted of any offence which, in the opinion of the Central Government, involves moral turpitude; or
3. is, or at any time has been adjudicated as insolvent

Vacation of office by members

If a member-

1. becomes subject to any of the disqualification mentioned in by members section 5; or
2. is absent without excuse, sufficient in the opinion of the council from three consecutive meeting of the Council; or
3. ceases to be enrolled on the Indian Medical Register in the case of a member referred to in clause (g) of sub-section (3) of section 3.

Executive Committee and Other Committees

The Council shall constitute from amongst its members an Executive Committee and such other committee for general or special purposes as the Council deems necessary to carry out the purposes of this Act. The Executive Committee shall consist of the Chairperson who shall be member who shall be nominated by the Council from amongst its members.

The Chairperson shall be the Chairperson of the Executive Committee:

In addition to the powers and duties conferred and imposed upon it by this Act, the Executive Committee or any other Committee shall exercise and discharge such powers and duties as the Council may confer or impose upon it by any regulations which may be made in this behalf.

Member Secretary and Employees of Council

The Central Government shall appoint the Member-Secretary of the Member Council to exercise such powers and perform such duties under the direction of the Council as may be prescribed or as may be delegated to him by the Chairperson.

The Council shall, with the previous sanction of the Central Government employ such officers and other employees as it deems necessary to carry out the purpose of this Act.

The Council shall, with the previous sanction of the Central Government fix the allowances to be paid to the Chairperson and other members and determine the conditions of services of the Member-Secretary, officers and other employees of the Council.

Vacancies in the Council not to invalidate date acts, etc.

No act or proceeding of the Council or any committee thereof shall Vacancies in the be called in question on the ground merely of the existence of any council or a committee thereof as the case may be.

Dissolution of Rehabilitation Council and Transfer of Right

On and from the date of the constitution of the Council, the Rehabilitation Council shall stand dissolved and on such dissolution:

1. all properties and assets, movable and immovable, of or belonging Council and to, the Rehabilitation Council shall vest in the Council
2. all the rights and liabilities of the Rehabilitation Council shall be transferred to, and be the rights and liabilities of, the Council;
3. without prejudice to the provision of clause (b) all liabilities incurred all contracts entered into and all matters and things engaged to be done by, with or for the Rehabilitation Council immediately before the date, for or in connection with the purposes of the said rehabilitation Council shall be deemed to have been incurred, entered into, or engaged to be done by, with or for, the Council;
4. all sums of money due to the Rehabilitation Council immediately before that date shall be deemed to be due to the Council;
5. all suits and other legal proceedings instituted or which could have been instiuted by or against the Rehabilitation Council immediately before that date may be continued or may be instituted by or against the Council; and

6. every employee holding any office under the rehabilitation Council immediately before that date shall hold his office in the Council by the same tenure and upon the same terms and conditions of service as respects remuneration, leave provident fund retirement and other terminal benefits as he would have held such office as if the Council had not been constituted and shall continue to do so as an employee of the Council or until the expiry of a period of six months from the date of such employee opts not to be the employee of the Council within such period.

Notwithstanding anything contained in the Industrial Disputes Act, 1947 or any other law for the time being in force, absorption of any employee by the Council in its regular service under this section shall not entitle such employee to any compensation under that Act or other law and no such claim shall be entertained by any court, tribunal or other authority.

Explanation:-In this section "Rehabilitation Council" means the Rehabilitation Council a society and registered under the Societies Act, 1860 and functioning as such immediately before the constitution of the Council.

Functions of The Council

Recognition of Qualifications Granted by University etc., in India for Rehabilitation Professionals: The qualification granted by any University or other institution in India which are included in the Schedule shall be recognized qualifications for rehabilitation professional.

Any University or other institution which grants qualification for the rehabilitation professional not included in the schedule may apply to the Central Government to have any such qualification recognized and the Central Government after consulting the Council may by notification, amend the Schedule so as to include such qualification therein and any such notification may also direct that an entry shall be made in the last column of the schedule against such qualifications only when granted after a specified date.

Recognition of Qualification by Institutions Outside India

12 The Council may enter into negotiation with the authority in any country outside India for settling of a scheme or reciprocity for the recognition of qualifications, and the pursuance of any such Scheme, the Central Government may, by notification amend the schedule so as to include therein any qualification which the Council has decided should be recognized and by such notification may also direct that an entry shall be made in the last column of the schedule declaring that it shall be the recognized qualification only when granted after a specified date.

Rights of persons possessing qualifications included in the schedule to be enrolled.

Subject to the other provisions contained in this Act, any qualification included in the Schedule shall be sufficient qualifications for enrolment on the Register.

No person, other than the rehabilitation professional who process a recognized rehabilitation qualification and is enrolled in the Register-

1. shall hold office as rehabilitation professional or any such office(by whatever designation called) in Government or in any institution maintained by a local or other authority;
2. shall practice as rehabilitation professional anywhere in India;
3. shall be entitled to sign or authenticate any certificate required by any law to be signed or authenticated by a rehabilitation professional.
4. shall be entitled to give any evidence in any court as an expert under section 45 of the Indian Evidence Act, 1872 in any matter relating to the handicapped.

Provided that if a person possesses the recognized rehabilitation professional qualification on the date of commencement of this Act, he shall be deemed to be an enrolled rehabilitation professional for a period of six months from such commencement, and if he has made an application for enrolment on the Register within said period for six months, till such application is disposed of.

Any person who acts in contravention of any provision of subsection (2) shall be punished with imprisonment for a term which may extend to one year or with fine which may extend to one thousand rupees or with both.

Power to require information as to courses of study and examination.

Every university or institution in India which grants a recognized qualification shall furnish such information as the Council may from time to time, require as to the courses of study and examinations to be undergone in order to obtain such qualification, as to the ages at which such courses of study and examinations are required to be undergone and such qualification is conferred and generally as to the requisites for obtaining such qualification.

Inspectors at Examinations

The Council shall appoint such member of Inspector as it may deem requisite to inspect any University or Institution where education for practicing as rehabilitation professional is given or to attend any examination held by any University or Institution for the purpose of recommending to the Central Government recognition of qualifications granted by that University or Institution as recognized rehabilitation qualifications.

The Inspectors appointed under sub-section (1) shall not interfere with the conduct of any training or examination but shall report to the Council on the adequacy of the standards of education including staff, equipment, accommodation, training and other facilities prescribed for giving such education or of the sufficiency of every examination which they attend.

The Council shall forward a copy of the report of the Inspector under sub-section (2) to the University or Institution concerned and shall also forward a copy, with the remarks of the University or the Institution thereon, to the Central Government.

Visitors Examination

The Council may appoint such number Visitors as it may deem requisite to inspect any University or institution wherein education for rehabilitation professional is given or attend any examination for the purpose of granting recognized rehabilitation qualifications. Any persons whether he is a member of the Council or not,may be appointed as a visitor under sub-section (1) but a person who is appointed as an Inspector under sub-section (1) of section 15 for any inspection or examination shall not be appointed as a Visitor for the same inspection or examination.

The Visitor shall not interfere with the conduct of any training or examination but shall report to the Chairperson on the adequacy of the standards of education including staff, equipment, accommodation, training and other facilities prescribed for giving education to the rehabilitation professionals or on sufficiency of every examination which they attend.

The report of a Visitor shall be treated as confidential unless in any particular case the Chairperson otherwise, directs.

Provided that if the Central Government requires a copy of the report of a Visitor the Council shall furnish the Same.

Withdrawal of Recognition

When upon report by the Inspector or the Visitor it appears to the Council:-

1. that the courses of study and examination to be undergone in or the proficiency required from candidates at any examination held by any University or institution, or
2. that the staff, equipment, accommodation training and other facilities for instruction and training provided in such University or institution do not conform to the standard prescribed by the Council, the Council shall make representation to that effect to the Central Government.

After considering such representation the Central Government may send it to the University or institution with an intimation of the period within which the University or institution may submit its explanation to that Government.

On the receipt of the explanation or where no explanation is submitted within the period fixed then, on the expiry of that period, the Central Government after making such further inquiry if any, as it may think fit, may, by notification, direct that an entry shall be made in the schedule against the said recognized rehabilitation qualification declaring that it shall be the recognized rehabilitation qualification only when granted before a specified date or that the said recognized rehabilitation qualification if granted to students of a specified University or institution shall be recognized rehabilitation qualification only when granted before a specified date, or as the case may be that the said recognized rehabilitation qualification shall be recognized rehabilitation qualification in relation to a specified University or institution only when granted after a specified date.

Minimum Standards of Education

The Council may prescribed the minimum standards of education required for granting recognized rehabilitation qualification by Universities or institutions in India.

Registration in Register

The Member-Secretary of the Council may, on report of an application made by any person in the prescribed manner enter his name in the in Register provided that the Member-Secretary is satisfied that such person possess recognized rehabilitation qualification.

Privileges of Persons Who are Registered on Register

Subject to the condition and restriction laid down in this Act regarding engagement in the area of rehabilitation of the handicapped by person possessing the recognized rehabilitation qualifications, every person whose name is for the time being borne on the Register shall be entitled to practice as a rehabilitation professional in any part of India and to recover in due course of law in respect of such practice any expenses, charges is respect of medicaments or other appliances or any fees to which he may be entitled.

Professional Conduct and Removal of Names from Register

The Council may prescribe standards of professional conduct and etiquette and a code of ethics for rehabilitation professionals. Regulations made by the Council under sub-section (1) may specify which violation thereof shall constitute infamous conduct in any professional respect, that is to say, professional misconduct, and such provision shall have effect notwithstanding anything contained in any other law for the time being in force. The Council may order that the name of any person shall be removed from the Register where it is satisfied, after giving that person a reasonable opportunity of being heard and after such further inquiry, if any as it may deem fit to make:

1. that his name has been entered in the Register by error or on account of misrepresentation or suppression of a material fact;
2. that he has convicted of any offence or has been guilty of any infamous conduct in any professional respect, or has violated the standard of professional conduct and etiquette or the code of ethics prescribed under sub-section (1) which, in the opinion of the Council, renders him unfit to be kept in the Register.

An order under sub-section (3) may direct that any person whose name is ordered to be removed from the Register shall be ineligible for registration under this Act either permanently or for such period of years as may be specified.

Appeal against Order of removal from Register

Where the name of any person has been removed from the Register on any ground other than that he is not possessed of the requisite rehabilitation qualifications, he may appeal, in the prescribed manner and subject to such conditions, including conditions as to payment of a fee, as may be prescribed to the Central Government whose decision thereon shall be final.

No appeal under sub-section (1) shall be admitted if it is preferred after the expiry of a period of thirty days from the date of the order under sub-section (3) of section 21:

Provided that an appeal may be admitted after the expiry of the said period of thirty days if the appellant satisfies the Central Government that he had sufficient cause for not preferring the appeal within the said period.

Register

It shall be the duty of the Member-Secretary to keep and maintain the Register in accordance with the provision of this Act and any order made by the Council and from time to time to revise the Register and publish it in the Official Gazette.

The Register shall be deemed to be a public document within the meaning of the Indian Evidence Act 1872 and may be proved by a copy thereof.

Information to be Furnished by Council and Publication Thereof

The Council shall furnish such reports copies of its minutes abstracts of its accounts and other information to the Central Government as that Government may require. The Central Government may publish in such manner as it may think fit, any report, copy abstract or other information furnished to it by the Council under this section or under section 16.

Cognizance of Offenses

Notwithstanding anything contained in the code of Criminal procedure 1973, no court shall take cognizance of an offence punishable under this Act expect upon a complaint, in writing, made by any person authorised in this behalf by the Council.

Protection of Action Taken in Good Faith

No suit, prosecution or other legal proceeding shall lie against the Central Government, Council Chairperson, members, Member-Secretary or any officer or other employee of the Council for anything which is in good faith done or intended to be done under this Act.

Employees of Council to be Public Servants

The Chairperson members, Member-Secretary, officers and other employees of the Council shall, while acting or purporting to act in pursuance of the provisions of this Act or of any rule and regulation made thereunder be deemed to be public servants within the meaning of section 21 of the Indian Penal Code.

Power to Make Rules

The Central Government may, by notification, make rules to carry out the purposes of this Act.

Power to Make Regulations

The Council may, with the previous sanction of the Central Government, make, by notification, regulation generally to carry out the purpose of this Act, and without prejudice to the generality of the foregoing power, such regulations may provide for-

1. the management of the property of the council;
2. the maintenance and audit of the account of the council;
3. the resignation of members of the council;
4. the powers and duties of the Chairperson;
5. the rules of procedure in the transaction business under sub-section (3) of section 4;
6. the function of the Executive Committee and other committee constituted under section 7;
7. the powers and duties of the Member-Secretary under sub-section (1) of the section 8;
8. the qualification, appointment powers and duties of, and procedure to be followed by Inspectors and Visitors;
9. the courses and period of study or of training to be undertaken the subject of examination and standards of proficiency therein to be obtained in any university or any institution for grant of recognized rehabilitation qualification;
10. the standards of staff, equipment, accommodation, training and other facilities for study or training of the rehabilitation professionals;

11. the conduct of examination, qualification of examiners, and the condition of the admission to such examinations;
12. the standards of professional conduct and etiquette and code of ethics to be observed by rehabilitation professional under sub-section (1) of section 21;
13. the particulars to be stated, and proof of qualification to be given, in application for registration under this Act;
14. the manner in which and the condition subject to which an appeal may be preferred under sub-section (1) of section 22;
15. the fees to be paid on application and appeals under this Act;
16. any other matter which is to be, or may be, prescribed.

Laying of Rules and Regulations before Parliament

Every rule and every regulation made under this Act shall be laid as soon as may be after it is made, before each House of Parliament, while it is in session for a total period of thirty days which may be comprised in one session or in two or more successive sessions and if, before the expiry of the session immediately following the session or the successive session aforesaid, both Houses agree in making any modification in the rule or regulation or both Houses agree that the rule or regulation should not be made, the rule or regulation shall thereafter have effect only in such modified from or be of no effect, as the case may be; so, however that any such modification or annulment shall be without prejudice to the validity of anything previously done under that rule or regulation.

The National Trust for Welfare of Persons with Autism, Cerebral Palsy, Mental Retardation and Multiple Disabilities Act, 1999

No. 44 of 1999 (30th December 1999)

An Act to provide for the constitution of a body at the national level for the Welfare of Persons with Autism, Cerebral Palsy, Mental Retardation and Multiple Disabilities and for matters connected therewith or incidental thereto.

Be it enacted by Parliament in the Fiftieth Year of the Republic of India as follows:

Preliminary

1. This Act may be called the National Trust for Welfare of Persons with Autism, Cerebral Palsy, Mental Retardation and Multiple Disabilities Act, 1999
2. It extends to the whole of India expect the State of Jammu and Kashmir.

   a. "autism" means a condition of uneven skill development primarily affecting the communication and social abilities of a person, marked by repetitive and ritualistic behavior;

   b. "Board" means Board of trustees constituted under section 3;

   c. "cerebral palsy" means a group of non-progressive condition of a person characterized by abnormal motor control posture resulting from brain insult or injuries occurring in the pre-natal, perinatal or infant period of development;

   d. "Chairperson" means the Chairperson of the Board appointed under clause (a) sub-section (4) of section 3;

   e. "Chief Executive" Officer" means the Chief Executive Officer appointed under sub-section (1) of section 8;

   f. "Member" means a Member of the Board and includes the Chairperson;

   g. "Mental retardation" means a condition of arrested or incomplete development of mind of person, which is specially characterized by sub-normality of intelligence;

   h. "Multiple disabilities" means a combination of two or more disabilities as defined in clause (i) of section 2 of the Persons with Disabilities (Equal Opportunities, Protection of Rights and Full Participation) Act, 1995;

i. "Notification" means notification published in the Official Gazette;

j. "Persons" with disability" means a person suffering from any of the conditions relating to autism, cerebral palsy, mental retardation or a combination of any two or more of such conditions and includes a person suffering from severe multiple disability;

k. "Prescribed" means prescribed by rules made under this Act;

l. "Professional" means a person who is having special expertise in a field, which would promote the welfare of persons with disability;

m. "Registered organization" means an association of persons with disability or an association of parents of persons with disability or a voluntary, as the case may be, registered under section 12;

n. "Regulation" means the regulations made by the Board under this Act;

o. "Severe disability" means disability with eighty percent or more of one or more of multiple disabilities;

p. "Trust" means the National Trust for Welfare of Persons with Autism, Cerebral Palsy Mental Retardation and Multiple Disability constituted under sub section (1) of section 3.

The National Trust For Welfare of Persons with Autism, Cerebral Palsy, Mental Retardation and Multiple Disability

— With effect from such date as the Central Government may, by notification, appointment, there shall be constituted, for the purpose of this Act, a body by the name of the National Trust for Welfare of persons with Autism, Cerebral Palsy, Mental Retardation and Multiple Disabilities which shall be a body corporate by the name aforesaid, having perpetual succession and a common seal, with power, subject to the provision of this Act, to acquire, hold and dispose of property, both movable and immovable, and both movable and immovable, and contact, and shall, by the said name, sure or be sued.

1. The general superintendence, direction and management of the affairs and business of the Trust shall vest in a Board which may exercise all powers and do all acts and things which may be exercised or done by the Trust.
2. The head office of the Trust shall be at New Delhi and the Board may, with the previous approval of the Central Government, establish offices at other places in India.
3. The Board shall consist of-
    a. a chaïrperson to be appointed by the Central Government from amongst, the persons having expertise and experience in the field of autism, cerebral palsy, mental retardation and multiple disability;
    b. nine persons to be appointed in accordance with such procedure as may be prescribed from amongst the registered organization out of which three members each shall be from voluntary organization, association of persons with autism, cerebral palsy, mental retardation and multiple disability and from associations of persons with disability, members:

        Provided that initial appointment under this clause shall be made by the Central Government by nomination;
    c. eight persons not be below the rank of joint Secretary to the Government of India nominated by the Govt. represent the Ministries or Departments of Social Justice and Empowerment, Women and Child Development, Health and Family Welfare, Finance, Labour, Education, Urban Affairs and Employment and Rural Employment and Poverty Alleviation, Members, ex-offico;
    d. three persons to be nominated by the Board representing the associations of traďe, commerce

and industry engaged in philanthropic activities, members;

e. the Chief Executive Officer, who shall be of the rank of Joint Secretary to the Government of India, Member Secretary, ex-officio;

4. The Board may associate with itself, in such manner and for such purpose as may be determined by regulation, any person whose assistance or advice it may desire for carrying for any other out the objects of the Trust:

Provided that such person shall have a right to take part in the discussion relevant to that purpose but shall not have right to vote at a meeting of the Board and shall not be a member for any other purpose:

Provide further that the maximum number of persons so associated shall not exceed eight and so far as possible the person so associated shall belong to the registered organization or from the professional.

0. The Chairperson or a Member shall hold office for a term of three years from the date of his appointment or until his successor shall have been duly appointed, whichever is longer:

Provide that no person shall hold office as the Chairperson or other Member after he has attained the age of sixty-five years.

1. The conditions of service of the Chairperson and other Members shall be such as may be prescribed.
2. A casual vacancy in the Board shall be filled in accordance with the provisions of section 3 and a person appointed shall hold office only for the remainder of the term for which the member, in whose place he was appointed, would have held that office.
3. Before appointing any person as the Chairperson or a Member, the Central Government shall satisfy itself that the person does not and will not, have

any such financial or other interest as is likely to affect prejudicially his function as such member.

4. No Member of the Board shall be a beneficiary of the Trust during the period such Member holds office.
5. The Board shall meet at least once in three months at such time and place as may be determined by the Board by regulations and shall observe such rules of procedure in the transaction of business at a meeting as may be prescribed.
6. The Chairperson, if for any reason is unable to attend the meeting of the Board, b any Member elected by the Members present from amongst themselves at the meeting, shall preside at the meeting.
7. All question which come up before any meeting of the Board shall be decided by a majority of votes of the Members present and voting, and in the event of an equality of votes, the Chairperson, or in his absence, the person presenting shall have a second or casting vote.

— The Chairperson may resign his office by writing under his hand addressed to the Central Government:

Provide that the Chairperson shall continue in office until the appointment of his successor is made by the Central Government.

1. A Member may resign from office by writing under his hand addressed to the Chairperson.
   - No person shall be a member if he-
   - is, or become, of unsound mind or is so declared by a competent court; or

a. is, or has been, convicted of an offence, which in the opinion of the Central Government, involves moral turpitude; or

b. is, or at any time has been, adjudicated as an insolvent.

- If a member -

- becomes subject to any of the disqualification mentioned in section 6; or

a. is, without obtaining leave of absence, absent from three consecutive meeting of the Board; or

b. tenders his resignation under section 5, his seat shall thereupon become vacant.

— The Central Government shall appoint the Chief Executive Officer to exercise such powers and performs such duties under the direction of the Board as may be prescribed or as may be delegated to him by the Chairperson.

1. The Board shall, with the previous approval of the Central Government, appoint such other officers and employees as it considers necessary to carry out the objectives of the Trust.
2. The salary and allowances payable to, and the other terms and conditions of service of, the Chief Executive Officer, other officers and employees of the Trust shall be such as may be determined by regulations.

   - No act or proceeding of the Board shall be called in question on the ground merely of the existence of any vacancy, in or any defect in the constitution of, the Board.

Objects of the Trusts

- The objects of the trust shall be:
- to enable and empower persons with disability to live as independently and as fully as possible within and as close to the community to which they belong;

  a. to strengthen facilities to provide support to persons with disability to live within their own families;

  b. to extend support to registered organization to provide need based services during the period of crises in the family of persons with disability ;

  c. to deal with problems of persons with disability who do not have family support;

d. to promote measures for the care and protraction of persons with disability in the event of death of their parent or guardian;

e. to evolve procedure for the appointment of guardians and trustees for persons with disability requiring such protection;

f. to facilitate the realization of equal opportunities, protection of right and full participation of persons with disability; and

g. to do any other act which is incidental to the aforesaid object.

Powers and Duties of the Board

- The Board shall:
- receive from the Central Government a one-time contribution of rupees one hundred crores for a corpus, the income where of shall be utilized to provide for adequate standard of living for persons with disability;

a. receive bequest of movable property any person for the benefit of the person with disability in general and for furtherance of the objectives of the Trust in particular:

Provide that it shall be obligatory on the part of the Board to make arrangement for adequate standard of living for the beneficiary named in the bequest, if any and to utilize the property bequeathed for any other purpose for which the bequest has been made: Provide further that the Board shall not be under any obligation to utilize the entire amount mentioned in the bequest for the exclusive benefit of the persons with disability named as beneficiary in the bequest;

b. receive from the Central Government such sums as may be considered necessary in each financial year for providing financial assistance to registered organization for carrying out any approved Programme.

For the purpose of sub-section (1), the expression "approved Programme" means

c. any Programme which promote independent living in the community for persons with disability by-
   i. creating a conducive environment in the community;
   ii. counseling and training of family members of persons with disability;
   iii. setting up of adult training units, individual and group homes;

d. any programme which promotes respite care, foster family care or day care service for persons with disability;

e. Setting up residential hostels and residential homes for persons with disability;

f. Development of self-help group persons with disability to pursue the realization of their rights;

g. setting up of local committee to grant approval fir guardianship and

h. such other programmes which promote the objective of the Trust.

- While earmarking funds for the purpose of clause:(c) of sub-section (2), preference shall be given to woman with disability or to persons with severe disability and to senior citizen with disability.

Explanation: For the purpose of this sub-section, the expression;

- "Persons with severe disability" shall have the same meaning as is assigned to it under sub-section (4) of section 56 of the persons with Disabilities (Equal Opportunities, Protection of Right and Full Participation) Act, 1995;

   a. "Senior citizen' means a person who is above the age of sixty-five years or more.

Procedure for Registration

— Any association of person with disability, or any association of parents of persons with disability or a voluntary organization whose main object is promotion of welfare of persons with disability may make an application for registration to the Board.

1. An application for registration shall be made in such form and manner and at such place as the Board may by regulation provide and shall contain such particulars and accompanied with such documents and such fees may be provided in the regulation.
2. On receipt of application for registration, the Board may make such inquires as it thinks fit in respect of genuineness of the application and correctness of any particulars thereon.
3. Upon receipt of such application the Board shall either grant registration to the applicant or reject such application for reasons to be recorded in writing:

Provided that where registration has been refused to the application, the said applicant may again make an application for registration after removing defects, if any in its previous application.

Local level Committees

— The Board shall constitute a local level committee for such area as may be specified by it from time to time.

1. A local committee shall consist of:-
   - an officer of the civil service of the Union or of the State, not below the rank of a District Magistrate or a District Commissioner of a district;
     a. a representative of a registered organization; and
     b. a person with disability as defined in clause (t) of section 2 of the persons with disabilities (Equal Opportunities, Protection of rights and Full Participation) Act, 1995
2. A local level committee shall continue to work for a period of three years from the date of its constitution or till such time it is reconstituted by the Board

3. A local level committee shall meet at least once in every three months or at such interval as may be necessary.

— A parent of a person with disability or his relative may make as application to the local level committee for appointment of any person of his choice to act as a guardian of the persons with disability.

1. Any registered organization may make an application in the prescribed form to the local level committee for appointment of a guardian for a person with disability:

   Provide that no such application shall be entertained by the local level committee, unless the consent of the guardian of the disabled person is also obtained.

   2. While considering the application for appointment of a guardian, the local level committee shall consider:-

   - whether the person with disability needs a guardian;

   a. the purpose for which the guardianship is required for person with disability.

3. The local level committee shall receive, process and decide applications received under sub-section (1) and (2), in such manner as may be determined by regulation: Provide that while making recommendation for the appointment of a guardian, the local level committee shall provide for the obligation which are to be fulfilled by the guardian.

4. The local committee shall send to the Board the particulars received by it and orders passed thereon at such interval as may be determined by regulations.

   - Every person appointed as a guardian of a person with disability under this chapter shall, wherever required, either have the care of such person of disability and his property or be responsible for the maintenance of the person with disability.

— Every person appointed as a guardian under section 14 shall, within a period of six months from the date of his appointment, deliver to the authority which appointed him, an inventory of immovable property belonging to the person with disability and all assets and other movable property received on behalf of the person with disability, together with a statement of all claims due to and all debts and liabilities due by such person with disability.

1. Every guardian shall also furnish to the said appointing authority within a period of three moths at the close of every financial year, an account of the property and assets in his charge, the sums received and disbursed on account of the person with disability and the balance remaining with him

— Whenever a parent or a relative of a person with disability or a registered organization find that the guardian is:-

- abusing or neglecting a person with disability; or
    a. misappropriating or neglecting the property, it may in accordance with the prescribed procedure apply to the committee for the removal of such guardian.

1. Upon receiving such application the committee may, if it is satisfied that there is a ground for removal and for reasons to be recorded in writing, remove such guardian and appoint a new guardian in his place or if such a guardian is not available make such other arrangement as may necessary for the care and protection of person with disability.
2. Any person removed under sub-section (2) shall be bound to deliver the charge of all property of the person with disability to the new guardian, and to account for all moneys received or disbursed by him.

Explanation,- For the Purpose of this chapter, the expression "relative" includes any person related to the person with disability by blood, marriage or adoption.

Accountability and Monitoring

— The books and documents in the procession of the Board shall be open to inspection by any registered organization

1. Any registered organization can submit a written requisition to the Board the access of any book or document maintained by the Board.
2. The Board shall frame such regulations as it think necessary for allowing the access of any books or document to a registered organization.
    - The Board shall determine by regulations the procedure for evaluating the prefunding status of registered organization seeking financial assistance from it and such regulations may also provide for the guidelines for monitoring and evaluating the activities of the registered organizations who are receiving financial assistance from the Trust.

— The Board shall in each year hold an annual general meeting of registered organizations, and not, more than six months shall elapse between the date of one annual general meeting and that of the next.

1. A notice of the annual general meeting along with a statement of accounts and records of its activities during the preceding year be sent by the Board to every registered organization at such time as may be determined by regulations.
2. The quorum for such meeting shall be such number of persons of the registered organization as may be determined by regulation.

Finance, Accounts and Audit

- The Central Government may, after due appropriation made by parliament by law in this behalf, make to the Trust a one-time contribution of rupees one hundred crores for a corpus, the income whereof may be utilized the objects of the Trust under this Act.

— There shall be constitute a fund to be called the National Trust for Welfare of persons with Autism, Cerebral Palsy, Mental Retardation and Multiple disabilities Fund and there shall be credited thereto-

- all money received from the Central government;
  a. all moneys received by the trust by way of grants, gifts, donation, benefaction, bequests or transfers;
  b. all moneys received by the Trust in any other manner or from any other source.

1. All moneys belonging to the fund shall be deposited in such banks or invested in such manner as the Board may, subjects to approval of the Central Government, decide.
2. The funds shall be applied towards meeting the administrative and other expenses of the Trust including expenses incurred in the exercise of its powers and performance of duties by the Board in relation to any of its activities under section 10 or for anything relatable thereto.

- The Board shall prepare, in such form and at such time in each financial year as may be prescribed, the budget for the next financial year showing the estimated receipt and expenditure of the Trust and shall forward the same to the Central Government,

— The Board shall maintain proper accounts and other relevant records and prepare an annual statement of accounts of the Trust including the income and expenditure accounts in such form as the Central Government may prescribe and in accordance with such general direction as may be issued by that Government in constitution with the Comptroller and Auditor-General of India.

1. The accounts of the Trust shall be audited by the Comptroller and Auditor General of India at such intervals as may be specified by him and any expenditure incurred by him in connection with such

audit shall be payable by the Board of the Comptroller and Auditor-General of India.

2. The Comptroller and Auditor-General of India and by other person appointed by him in connection with the audit of the accounts of the Trust shall have the same rights, privileges and authority in connection with such audit as the Comptroller and Auditor-General of India generally has in connection with the audit of the Government accounts, and in particular, shall have the right to demand and production of books of accounts, connected vouchers and other documents and papers and to inspect any of the officcs of the Trust.
3. The accounts of the Trust as certified by the Comptroller, and Auditor-General of India or any other person appointed by him in this behalf, together with the audit report thereon, shall be forwarded annually to the Central Government, and that Government shall cause the same to be laid before each House of Parliament.
   - The Board shall prepare every year, in such form within such time as may be prescribed an annual report giving a true and full accounts of its activities during the previous year and copies thereof shall be forward to the Central Government and that Government shall cause the same to be laid before each House of Parliament.
   - All orders and decisions of the Board and instrument issued in the name of the Trust shall be authenticated by the signature of the Chairperson, the Chief Executive Officer or any other officer authorized by the Chairperson, in this behalf.
   - The Board shall furnish to the Central Government such reports, returns and other information as that Government may require time to time.

Miscellaneous

— Without prejudice to the foregoing provisions of this Act, the Board shall, in exercise of its power or the performance of its duties under this Act, be bound by such direction on questions of policy as the Central Government may give in writing it from time to time:

Provided that the Board shall, as far as practicable, be given an opportunity to express its views before any direction is given under this sub-section.

1. The decision of the Central Government whether a question is one if policy or not shall be final.

— If the Central Government on the complaint of a registered organization or otherwise has reason to believe that the Board in unable to perform or has persistently made default in the performance of the duties imposed on it, the Central Government may issue notice to the Board asking why it should not be superseded: Provide that no order superseding the Board shall be made by the Central Government, unless a notice affording reasonable opportunity to the Board has been given in writing that why it should not be superseded.

1. The Central Government after recording reasons in writing and by issuing a notification in the Official Gazette supersede the Board for a period of not more than six months: provided that on the expiration of the period of super session Central Government may reconstitute the Board, in accordance with section 3.
2. Upon the publication of the notification under sub-section (2),-
   - all the members of the Board shall, not withstanding that their term of office had not expired as on the date of super session, vacate their office as such members;
     a. all the powers and duties which may, buy or under the provision of this Act, be exercised or performed by or on behalf of the trust shall, during the period of supersession, be exercised and performed by such person as the Central Government may direct.

3. On the expiration of the period of super session specified in the notification issued under sub-section (2), the Central Government may:-
   - extend the period of super session for such further period as it may consider necessary so that the total period of supersession does not exceed more than six months; or

a. reconstitute the Board in the manner provided in section 3.
   - Notwithstanding anything contained in the Income-tax Act, 1961, or any other law for the time being in force relating to tax on income. profit or gains, the Trust shall not be liable to pay income-tax or any other tax in respect of its income, profits or gains derived.
   - No suit, prosecution or other legal proceeding shall lie against the Central Government or the Trust or any member of the Board or Chief Executive officer or any officer or other employee of the Trust or any other person authorized by the Board to perform duties under this Act for any loss or damage caused or likely to be caused by anything which is done in good faith. Explanation:- For the purpose of this section, the expression "good faith" shall have the same meaning as is assigned to it in the Indian Penal Code.
   - All Members, Chief Executive Officer, other officers and employees of the Trust shall be deemed, when acting or purporting to act in pursuance of any of the provisions of this Act, to be public servant within the meaning of section 21 of the Indian Penal Code.
   - The Board may, by general pr special order in writing, delegate to the Chairperson or any members or any officer of the Trust or any other person subject to such conditions

and limitations, if any, as may be specified in the order such of its powers under this Act, (except the power to make regulations under section 35) as it may deem necessary.

— The Central Government may, by notification in the Official Gazette, make rules for carrying out the provisions of this Act.

1. In particular, and without prejudice to the generality of the foregoing powers, such rules may provide for all or any of the following matters, namely:-

- the procedure in accordance with which the person representing registered organization shall be elected under clause (b) of sub-section (4) of section 3;

a. the condition of service of the Chairperson and Members under sub-section (2) of section 4;

b. the rules procedure in the transaction of business at meeting of the Board under sub-section (2) of section 14;

c. the powers and duties of Chief Executive Officer under sub-section (1) of section 8;

d. the form in which an application for guardianship may be made by a registered organization under sub-section (2) of section 23;

e. the procedure in accordance with which a guardian may be removed under section 17;

f. the form in which, and the time within which, the budget of the trust shall be forwarded to the Central Government under section 23;

g. the form in which the annual statement of accounts shall be maintained under sub-section (1) of section 24;

h. the form in which, and the time within which, the annual reports shall be prepared and forwarded under section 25;

i. any other matter which is required to be, or may be, prescribed.

- The Board may, with the previous approval of the Central Government, by notification in the Official Gazette, make regulations consistent with this Act and rules generally to carry out the purpose of this Act.
- In particular, and without prejudice to the generality of the foregoing power, such regulation may provide for all or any of the following matters, namely:-
- the manner and purpose for which a person may be associated under sub-section (5) of section 3;

a. the time and place at which the Board shall meet under sub-section (6) of section 4;

b. the terms and conditions of service of, Chief Executive Officer, other officer and employees of the Trust under sub-section (3) of section 8;

c. the form manner in which the application shall be made for registration under sub-section (2) of section 12 and the particulars which such application shall contain under that sub-section;

d. the manner in which application for guardianship shall be received, proceed and decided by the local level committee under sub-section (4) of section 114;

e. the particulars of application and orders passed thereon by the local level committee under sub-section (5) of section 14;

f. the procedure for evaluating the pre-funding status of the registered organization and framing of guidelines for monitoring and evaluating the activities of such registered organization under section 19;

g. the time within which notice for annual general meeting shall be sent and quorum for such meeting under sub-section (2) and (3) of section 20; and

h. any other matter which is required to be, or may be provided by regulation.

- Every rule and every regulation made under this Act shall be laid. as soon as may be after it is made, before each House of Parliament, while it is in session, for a total period of thirty days which may be comprised in one session or in two or more successive session, and if, before the expiry of the session immediately following the session or successive session aforesaid, both House agree in making any modification, in the rule or regulation or both House agree that the rule pr regulation should not be made, the rule or regulation shall thereafter have effect only in such modified form or be no effect, as the case may be, so, however, that any such modification or annulment shall be without prejudice to the validity of anything previously done under that rule or regulation.

Services and Programmes for the Disabled

Okay, my social worker self is kicking in here. I used to help people fill out Medicaid applications for a living. I have also helped people with SSI and other programmes. I may have a few details wrong below. Please let me know about any inaccuracies.

Here are the services available in the United States (with a focus on programmes people on immune might use; I am skipping many useful programmes such as WIC or state programmes for pregnant women, as well as information for immigrants—you can ask me privately if you wish):

Federal Programmes administered by Federal Agencies

Social Security (SS). Retirement programme for people over a certain age (65?) and their dependents (spouses and children up to age 18 or 21 if in school). Payments are based on the amount you have put into the system through deductions in your pay. If you qualify more than once, you get the highest amount.

Social Security Disability (SSD aka SSDI). Social Security for people whose work life has been cut short by disability or illness. Otherwise same as SS (except your age is factored in so fewer payments into the system because of age don't hurt you).

Supplemental Security Income (SSI). SS for people with no work history or too little for SSD or SS who can not work due to disability or illness (or over 65). Anyone earning less than the SSI amount via SS or SSD can get the difference via SSI. States set the payment amount.

Medicare. Limited health coverage. Different versions available, some for a cost. Available to the elderly or to those on SSI 2 years into the benefits. Not sure about availibility to those on SSD.

Worker's Compensation. I believe this is federal but I am not sure. Your benefits are based on the income you earned on which worker's compensation insurance was paid at the job at which you were injured. You must have an on-the-job injury that prevents or limits you from working for at least 3 days. Any medical expenses are covered. I do not believe that income or assets lower your benefits but your benefits would end if you were able to take a job earning you a similar amount. I know very little about this programme except that most details get worked out by attorneys and not by regulations.

Federal Programmes Administered by State Government (usually Welfare)

Medicaid (health coverage). I believe the feds pay for half and the state pays for the other half. There are federal guidelines and all who qualify must get it (this is called an entitlement programme, *i.e.*, there are no waiting lists. Most of these programmes are like that). The states may set some of their own requirements and standards and benefits and have their own applications. You get Medicaid automatically with SSI and AFDC (there is legislation to change the later). You must be poor and one of the following: elderly, disabled, a minor, pregnant, or AFDC eligible (*i.e.*, a parent). All foster children get Medicaid and parents who adopt disabled children can negotiate for Medicaid for the children.

Food Stamps (FS). Money or coupons to be used to buy food. States set benefit amounts and may set some requirements. I think this is completely federally funded. Based on income, not ability to work, and single adults with no children are eligible.

Aid to Families with Dependent Children (AFDC). What is usually meant when one says "welfare" but that term means Medicaid, Food Stamps, General Relief, and other programmes too. Monthly income to children with one parent in the home whose income is below a certain level or two parents if at least one parent is disabled or unemployed and looking for work. Some (all?) states give benefits to pregnant women with no children. Emancipated minors are eligible. Funds from this programme can be used for families with unofficial foster children (including relatives). This programme is partially federally funded and there are wide variations in eligibility and benefits from state to state.

Unemployment. You must be able and willing to work and you must be seeking work according to their schedule and requirements. Part-time is okay. Your benefits are based on the income you earned on which unemployment tax was paid within a 12 month period prior to your application (not the 12 months directly prior). Benefits are of a fixed amount. States have differing eligibility (slight) but I think benefits are set and paid for at the federal level.

State Programmes

State Disability. Some (all?) states have a programme that is similar to SSD. It may take people with more temporary disabilities than does SS. It is based on your work history.

General Relief (GR). Small monthly cash benefits to adults who do not qualify for other forms of cash assistance or who are in the application process for SSI (you pay back any GR or FS received during the retroactive SS payment period).

Aid for the disabled. Varies from state to state and in many states it is the same thing as GR.

Qualifying for These Programmes

Each programme has a set of qualifications you must pass in order to be found eligible. You must pass each one separately.

1) *Citizenship:* American citizens and permanent residents are eligible for all programmes. Documented and undocumented immigrants are eligible for a few (varies from state to state).

2) *Residency:* U.S. residencey for federal programmes (usually) and state residency for state programmes. Residency means, where do you get your mail. Agencies are not allowed to discriminate against you for being homeless but you do need a mailing address for most programmes.

3) *Work History:* For SS and SSD, you must have a certain number of credits (age-based) to qualify and number of credits determines total payment. You earn credits by reaching a certain income threshold each quarter (3 calender months). Only income on which you or your employer paid SS tax counts.

4) *Disability:* There is some range here, depending on the programme. Medicaid is supposed to use the same standards as SS but I am finding Medicaid in Mass. to be more stringent. If you have a disability from a certain list, you automatically qualify. This is for terminal illness and other major things, and sometimes blindness. There are several levels to pass (this is my paraphrasing, not the official list):

   A) You must have one or more medically documented disabilities/conditions. Both physiological and psychological conditions count. Caveat: it helps if they've heard of it and have a diagnosis for it (SS does not for CFS).

   B) Your disability must be severe enough to substantially affect your life.

C) Your disability must last for at least 12 months.

D) Your disability must make it impossible for you to maintain substantial employment (generally defined as earning $500 or more a month).

E) Your inability to work must last for at least 12 months.

5) *Income:* For some programmes you must be below a certain income level (spouse's income counts) to get benefits (Medicaid, but a system exists for people making slightly too much). For some programmes your benefits are prorated depending on your income (SSI, AFDC, FS, GR). For some programmes, the fee you pay for the benefits depends on your income (Medicare, I think). Generally, you can subtract expenses from income for such things as business or rental income. Income includes alimony and child support (some states let you keep some extra of the latter). You can deduct from your income any child support or alimony you pay as well as medical expenses.

6) *Assets:* Some programmes will cut you off if your assets are over a certain level. The level and what counts towards assets vary substantially. Your home rarely counts (you must live in it). Some programmes will not count one car, others will exclude the first $1500 or so of the car's value. SS counted my computer but decided it was worth very little. Household items do not count. Cash on hand, stamps, coins, bank accounts, stocks and bonds, etc always count. The level for most programmes is about $2000 (for a single person) but some programmes, especially GR and FS, can be as low as $150. (FS, GR, SSI, Medicaid, AFDC). Some programmes have a waiting period if you transfer assets before applying.

7) Willingness to work, or participate in rehab, etc. This is not the case for SS, SSD, SSI, or any other programme where you qualified by being too disabled to work. In California, all FS and GR recipeients must work unless

they are disabled (waiting for SSI counts), have (small?) children, or are elderly. Other states have different rules and there are broad changes being implemented everywhere about adult or head of household AFDC recipiants. Work usually includes any of the following: working at least 10 (varies) hours a month at a job of your choosing or one assigned by the agency (volunteer), actively seeking employment (documented like Unemployment requires), going to school or a training programme. This is a requirement to keep benefits, not to obtain them.

8) *Other:* I am leaving out some of the obvious requirements you must prove such as age or parentage. Single parents on AFDC must assist the agency in finding the absent parent if they are supposed to pay child support and are not. You must also meet basic requirements such as completing forms on time, meeting with your worker as scheduled (some can be done by phone or mail), providing documentation, including SS cards and birth certificates and photo identification, etc.

Bibliography

Aggarwal, Santosh : *Three Language Formula: An Educational Problem*, New Delhi, Sian, 1991.

Allen, G. : *New Education: American Opinion*, May issue, 1971.

Allen, V.: *Children as Teachers: Theory and Research on Tutoring*, New York, Academic Press, 1976.

Bentley, T. : *Learning beyond the Classroom: Education for a Changing World*, London, Routledge. 1998.

Boud. D. and Miller, N. : *Working with Experience: Animating Learning*, London, Routledge, 1997.

Brauen, Marsha L.: *Issues and Options in Outcomes-Based Accountability for Students With Disabilities*, Rockville, MD: Westat, 1994.

Bryant, N.D. & McLouglin, J.A.: *Teaching the Learning Disabled Adolescent*, Houghton Mifflin Co, Boston, 1972.

Carr, W. & Kemmis, S. : *Becoming Critical: Education, Knowledge and Action Research*, London, Falmer, 1986.

Cenkner, William : *A Tradition of Teachers: Sankara and the Jagadgurus Today*, Delhi, Motilal Banarsidass, 1983.

Chumbow, B.S. : *The Place of Mother Tongue in the National Policy of Education,* Port Harcourt, Nigeria, 1990.

Clay, M.: *Reading: the Patterning of Complex Behavior*, Auckland, Heinemann Educational Books, 1979.

Cramer, S. & Ellis, W: *Learning disabilities*, Paul H. Brokes, Baltimore, 1996.

Cremins, James J.: *Legal and Political Issues in Special Education*, Springfield, IL: C.C. Thomas, 1983.

Dillon, S.: *Schools Slow in Closing Gaps between Races*, New York Times, 2006.

Donaldson, Gordon A. : *Cultivating Leadership in Schools*, New York, College Press, 2001.

Elliott, J. : *Action Research for Educational Change*, Milton Keynes, Open University, 1991.

Evers, C. & Lakomski, G. : *Knowing Educational Administration*, Oxford, Pergamon, 1991.

Fisher, K.: *Leading Self-Directed Work Teams*, NY: McGraw-Hill, 1993.

Fitz-Gibbon, C.: *Peer and Cross-age Tutoring*, New York, Macmillan, 1992.

Foot, H.: *Children Helping Children*, New York: John Wiley & Sons, 1990.

Fordham, P., Holland, D. and Millican, J. : *Adult Literacy, A Handbook for Development Workers*, Oxford, Oxfam, 1995.

Galbraith, M.W. : *Education Through Community Organizations*, San Francisco, Jossey-Bass, 1990.

Giddens, A. : *A Contemporary Critique of Historical Materialism*, London, Macmillan, 1981.

Goodlad, John I. : *Educational Renewal: Better Teachers, Better Schools*, San Francisco, Jossey-Bass, 1994.

Hare, P.: *Groups, Teams, and Social Interaction: Theories and Applications*, NY: Praeger Publishers, 1992.

Haroutinian-Gordon, S. : *Turning the Soul, Teaching through Conversation in the High School*, Chicago, University of Chicago Press, 1991.

Jeffs, T. and Smith, M. : *Using Informal Education*, Milton Keynes, Open University Press, 1990.

Kinlaw, D.: *Developing Superior Work Teams*, Lexington, MA: Lexington Books, 1991.

Kirkwood, G. and Kirkwood, C. : *Living Adult Education, Freire in Scotland*, Milton Keynes, Open University Press, 1989.

Lerner, J.W.: *Children with Learning Disabilities, Houghton* Mifflin, Boston, 1971.

Lovett, T. : *Adult Education, Community Development and the Working Class*, London, Ward Lock, 1975.

Luecking, R. & Hathaway, S.: *School to Work Transition for Youth with Severe Disabilities: A Planning and Procedures Manual*, Rockville, MD: TransCen, 1992.

Marsick, V.J. and Wa tkins, K.E. : *Informal and Incidental Learning in the Workplace*, London, Routledge, 1991.

McGinn, Noel F. : *Education and Development in Korea*, Cambridge, Harvard University Press, 1980.

Nias, J. : *Seeing anew: Teachers' Theories of Action*, Australia, Deakin University, 1987.

Nuna, S.C. : *Education and Development*, NIEPA, New Delhi, 1987.

Petty, W. T., & Jensen, J. M.: *Developing Children's Language*, Boston, Allyn & Bacon, 1980.

Piaget, J.: *The Psychology of Intelligence*, London, Routledge & Kegan Paul, 1950.

Premi, M.K. : *Educational Planning in India*, New Delhi, Sterling, 1972.

Roderick, R. : *Habermas and the Foundations of Critical Theory*, Basingstoke, Macmillan, 1986.

Rosen, N.: *Teamwork and the Bottom Line: Groups Make a Difference*, Hillsdale, NJ: Lawrence Erlbaum, 1989.

Simkins, T. : *Non-formal Education and Development*, Manchester, Manchester University, 1977.

Swezey, R., & Salas, E.: *Teams: Their Training and Performance*, Norwood, NJ: Ablex Publishing Corp., 1992.

Thomas, A. : *Educating Children at Home*, London, Cassell, 1998.

Turnbull, H. Rutherford: *Free Appropriate Public Education: The Law and Children With Disabilities*, Denver, CO: Love Publishing Co., 1998.

Washbrook, David A. : *The Emergence of Provincial Politics: The Madras Presidency, 1870-1920*. Cambridge, Cambridge University Press, 1976.

Yeaxlee, B. : *Lifelong Education, A Sketch of the Range and Significance of the Adult Education Movement*, London, Cassell and Company, 1929.

Index

A

Associated Disorder, 176.
Austism, 176.

B

Barrier Free Environment, 171, 174, 310, 316.
Behavior Disorders, 191, 205.
Blindness, 3, 17, 18, 22, 37, 38, 39, 40, 41, 42, 43, 44, 45, 47, 55, 56, 57, 58, 59, 60, 61, 62, 149, 163, 164, 166, 168, 203, 226, 227, 255, 302, 322, 377.

C

Cerebral Palsy, 4, 15, 148, 149, 150, 151, 155, 156, 159, 161, 162, 167, 171, 172, 173, 200, 245, 302, 304, 322, 355, 356, 357, 358, 368.
Classification of Disabilities, 1.
Community Based Rehabilitation, 141, 249, 269, 327.
Crisis Management, 127, 239.

D

Disability Management, 238, 244, 245, 248.

E

Educational Programmes, 20, 23, 56, 63, 91, 96, 129, 130, 168, 233.
Emotional Disorders, 115, 192.
Epilepsy, 150, 157, 172, 186, 190, 191.
Evaluation, 16, 23, 49, 66, 70, 83, 97, 98, 103, 104, 127, 128, 132, 134, 135, 136, 137, 144, 200, 203, 212, 234, 235, 236, 237, 239, 243, 244, 249, 250, 272.

F

Folk Art, 292, 293.

H

Hearing Impairment, 3, 73, 75, 80, 82, 83, 85, 86, 90, 91, 138, 151, 167, 216, 303, 322, 341.
Hearing Loss, 16, 73, 75, 76, 77, 78, 79, 80, 83, 84, 85, 86, 87, 88, 89, 94, 101, 102.

L

Learning Disabilities, 16, 17, 22, 27, 63, 64, 65, 66, 109, 146, 150, 171, 176, 177, 202, 203, 206, 208,

209, 210, 211, 212, 213, 214, 215, 216, 217, 218, 219, 220, 221, 222, 223, 224, 225, 230, 231, 232, 233, 234, 237.
Legislation, 6, 13, 17, 22, 36, 69, 178, 252, 256, 257, 296, 299, 300, 309, 316, 375.
Locomotor Disabilities, 131, 147, 153, 170.

M

Management, 39, 44, 127, 128, 168, 195, 197, 238, 239, 244, 245, 246, 248, 270, 277, 354, 358.
Media Selection, 273, 276.
Mental Illness, 1, 18, 19, 97, 113, 114, 115, 118, 122, 124, 125, 147, 148, 167, 303, 304.
Moderate, 2, 5, 59, 61, 98, 102, 107, 108, 109, 111, 121, 166, 187, 188, 203, 237.
Multiple Disabilities, 15, 199, 355, 356, 357.
Multiple Disabilities, 15, 17, 70, 109, 199, 200, 355, 356, 357, 368.

N

National Trust, 15, 355, 356, 357, 368.

O

Opportunity, 69, 71, 158, 180, 195, 212, 242, 307, 308, 314, 315, 328, 329, 352, 370.
Organisation, 59, 147.

P

Plus Curriculum, 67, 72.
Policy, 9, 31, 34, 117, 127, 129, 178, 286, 296, 309, 316, 370.
Postal Display, 282.
Protection, 5, 12, 13, 15, 19, 79, 163, 166, 241, 254, 255, 258, 259, 260, 262, 300, 301, 303, 332, 333, 340, 353, 356, 362, 363, 364, 366.
Puppetry, 279, 280, 281.

R

Relationship, 27, 33, 34, 68, 165, 186, 200, 206, 219, 229, 234, 256, 266, 294, 310.
Reporting, 52, 54, 69, 127, 165, 166, 209, 218, 269, 284, 285, 286, 287, 295.

S

Sheltered Workshop, 249, 250, 252, 254.
Students Awareness, 271.

T

Taylor, 217.

V

Vocational Training, 15, 141, 170, 171, 249, 320.

W

Welfare, 10, 11, 15, 19, 208, 305, 307, 310, 311, 312, 313, 317, 324, 332, 333, 343, 355, 356, 357, 358, 364, 368, 375, 376.

□□□